IN THEIR OWN WORDS

The Front-Line Sales Manager – Field General

A PARADIGM SHIFT FOR SALESFORCE MANAGEMENT

Also by Noel Capon*

Corporate Strategic Planning
with John U. Farley and James M. Hulbert

Planning the Development of Builders, Leaders, and Managers of 21st Century Business

Toward an Integrative Explanation of Corporate Financial Performance
with John U. Farley and Scott Hoenig

The Marketing of Financial Services: A Book of Cases

The Asian Marketing Case Book
with Wilfried Van Honacker

Key Account Management and Planning

Managing Global Accounts
with Dave Potter and Fred Schindler

Managing Global Accounts Video Book

Strategic Account Strategy

Sales Eats First
with Gary Tubridy

Total Integrated Marketing
with James M. Hulbert and Nigel E. Piercy

The Marketing Mavens

Managing Marketing in the 21st Century (4th ed.)

Capon's Marketing Framework (4th ed.)

Capon's Marketing Essentials

Capon 's Marketing Video Book

The Virgin Marketer (4th ed.)

Versions of Capon's marketing textbooks, with local coauthors/publishers, are available in Asia-Pacific, Brazil (Portuguese), China (Mandarin), Europe, India, Middle East, Spanish Latin America, Russia (Russian).

Also by Gary S. Tubridy**

Growth in 2011: A Tale of Two Cities

How Companies Use Their Sales Force to Outmaneuver the Competition in a Slow Growth Economy

Advancing the Art of Customer Motivated Selling

Sales Leadership Imperatives in a Tough Economy

Making the Most out of an Indifferent Economy

Sales Force Renewal

Tough Times Call For Creative Action

Sales Leadership in Challenging Times

Imperatives of Breakthrough Sales Leadership

Sales and Marketing: Collaborating To Grow

Sales Force Multipliers – Approaches to Extending Sales Reach and Impact

Mobilizing for Sales Growth: Sales Operations to the Rescue

From Transaction to Solution Selling
with Noel Capon

Increase Sales Yield by Optimizing Investment in Sales Resource
with Marc Metzner

The Changing Customer Contract: A New Role for Sales

The Value Selling Anthology

*mostly available at www.wessexlearning.com
**mostly available at www.alexandergroup.com

IN THEIR OWN WORDS

The Front-Line Sales Manager – Field General

A PARADIGM SHIFT FOR SALESFORCE MANAGEMENT

Noel Capon

R.C. Kopf Professor of International Marketing
Columbia Business School, New York, NY

Gary Tubridy

Senior Vice President, The Alexander Group, Stamford, CT

Florin Mihoc

Fulbright Fellow; Visiting Scholar, Columbia Business School, New York, NY

Wessex Press, Inc.
www.wessexlearning.com

Noel Capon, R.C. Kopf Professor of International Marketing, Columbia Business School, founded Wessex Press, Inc. in 2007. Wessex is a small publisher with global reach focusing predominantly on marketing, management, and other higher-education textbooks. Wessex's goal is to provide top-quality learning materials at affordable prices. Publishing under the Wessex Press and AxcessCapon brands, Wessex Press, Inc. offers titles in multiple print and digital formats. Wessex also offers video books.

Library of Congress Cataloging-in-Publication Data

Noel Capon, Gary Tubridy, Florin Mihoc / In Their Own Words: The Front-Line Sales Manager – Field General

    p. cm.

  ISBN 978-1-7325469-3-6 (hardcover)
           978-1-7325469-4-3 (softcover)

Developmental Editor: Lyn Maize

Copyeditor: Christy Goldfinch

Proofreader: Sharon Stewart

Design/Production: Anna Botelho

Cover Image: iStock by Getty Images / Credit: Palto

Brief Table of Contents

Detailed Table of Contents

Preface

The best way to secure an overview of key elements in any field is probably to read some leading textbooks (digital and/or traditional printed versions). After all, academically authored textbooks are still foundational for instructors offering courses for young people entering their preferred fields. Hence, if you want to understand the core elements of sales management, just go to sales management textbooks. In the table of contents, you will find those topics the author(s) believes sales managers need to know. Your sales management textbook will probably have, among others, chapters on the selling process; recruiting, selecting, training, coaching, deploying, measuring, and compensating salespeople; leadership and motivation; sales forecasting; salesforce organization; salesforce size; sales strategy; and sales-territory design—the usual suspects.

What you will typically *not* find is any discussion (certainly not a deep discussion) of the various roles at different levels within the sales management hierarchy. We believe this omission is regrettable, and represents a yawning gap for today's readers. Most domestic salesforces comprise some variation of the following structure: sales vice president (SVP)/national sales manager (NSM); regional sales managers (RSMs); front-line sales managers (FLSMs), also called district sales managers (DSMs); and sellers, including strategic/key account managers (SAMs/KAMs). Large salesforces may squeeze in some zone managers; smaller sales organizations typically omit a level (or levels) in their hierarchies. Global firms have various arrangements regarding global and multinational sales efforts, often including global account managers (GAMs).

The unaddressed questions are the following: How do various managerial jobs in the sales management hierarchy differ from one other? How do they work together in today's complex organizations? The simple answer concerns authority/responsibility. In many firms, a typical SVP/NSM has three to six geographically organized, directly reporting RSMs; each RSM has three to six, geographically organized, directly reporting FLSMs; each FLSM has responsibility for six to ten sellers. Clearly, the degree of authority/responsibility is greater the higher up the hierarchy. But other than authority/responsibility differences, how do these managerial jobs differ from level to level?

In *The Front-Line Sales Manager – Field General*, our perspective is very straightforward. We believe *the firm succeeds or fails based on the performance of its sellers*. If sellers succeed in making their sales goals, all things equal, the firm makes profits, survives, and grows, and shareholder value increases. Conversely, if sellers fail, the firm fails, and no one gets a paycheck! Just ask former employees at Blockbuster, Kodak, Lotus, Sun, Toys 'R' Us, or any of the other tens of thousands of business organizations that fail annually.

The key influence on seller success in today's complex and ever-changing business environment is the sellers' direct supervisor—*the front-line sales manager*. The FLSM hires and fires sellers, travels and visits customers with sellers, and closes sales with sellers. The FLSM leads, directs, and manages sellers; secures firm resources to assist the selling process; and is, by far, the dominant influence in sellers' work lives. Regrettably, the sales management literature has not given FLSMs the level of attention this role deserves. *The Front-Line Sales Manager – Field General* aims to redress this unfortunate reality.

To inform the book's structure and content, we have sourced a variety of related strategic material and frameworks from our own research. To bring the book to life, we have provided extensive commentary from successful sales leaders and FLSMs from many well-known corporations, drawn from our new clinical research study.[1] We believe that knowing what sales leaders and successful FLSMs actually say about specific topics provides valuable *color* to the book. Further, these real-life reports make the messages more applicable for today's sales management challenges.

The new approach we advocate—spotlighting the FLSM—represents a paradigm shift for sales management.[2] By adopting an FLSM focus, and arguing for its high significance within the salesforce, we do not mean to diminish the roles of sales leaders and senior sales managers. Rather, we frame these roles in a somewhat different manner from the status quo. We believe the key to a successful salesforce is high performance by FLSMs and their sellers. From this perspective, each and every more senior sales manager and sales leader is non-revenue-generating overhead! The key purpose of these jobs is to make that overhead count. There should be just one objective for these roles: Make sellers and FLSMs successful—nothing more, nothing less. In the final analysis, nothing else matters.

For the salesforce to be successful, FLSMs must be successful. Hence, the most extensive part of this book concerns the FLSM. The FLSM is the core focus of seven chapters in Part I. But the ability of FLSMs to be successful rests on the internal environment in which they do their jobs. This environment is created and sustained via decisions made by senior managers and sales leaders. For this reason, the chapters in Part II identify key decision areas for supporting FLSMs and their sellers.

As noted above, the material in *The Front-Line Sales Manager – Field General* draws heavily from a clinical research study conducted by the authors. The study comprised one-hour telephone interviews with sales leaders and successful FLSMs at a diverse group of 23 participating firms—manufacturing, business services, financial services, healthcare, high-tech. We spoke first with sales leaders, then asked them to identify their most successful FLSMs. Appendices 1 and 2 show participating firms and interviewees, respectively. Appendices 3 and 4 show interview guides for sales leaders and FLSMs. Additionally, our findings are informed by less formal conversations with other sales leaders and FLSMs.

We are grateful for the access, time commitment, and candor these sales leaders and FLSMs provided. We trust that the new perspectives we offer will bring valuable ideas and insights to those readers who do, or will, serve in the trenches, with their sellers, as FLSMs. Also, we aim to provide value to sales leaders and senior sales managers who support those *field generals*.

Noel Capon

Gary Tubridy

Florin Mihoc

---

1. Because some participant comments address multiple issues, they do double duty in more than one chapter.
2. The concept of *paradigm shift* was identified by U.S. physicist/philosopher Thomas Kuhn in 1962 to describe a fundamental change in the basic concepts and experimental practices of a scientific discipline—Wikipedia, retrieved August 24, 2018, from *https://en.wikipedia.org/wiki/Paradigm_shift*.

Who Should Read This Book

The Front-Line Sales Manager – Field General focuses on one critical element of firm functioning—the field salesforce. We zero in on one role in particular—the front-line sales manager (FLSM). That person is directly responsible for leading, directing, and managing a group of sellers. If FLSMs are successful, the firm achieves its sales-revenue goals; assuming costs are under control, it earns profits. Profits allow the firm to survive, grow, and enhance shareholder value. Conversely, if FLSMs fail, nobody gets a paycheck!

FLSM success or failure is critical for the firm. So, who should be concerned? Who should read this book? Broadly speaking, we identify three separate audiences:

- **The salesforce.** This book has value for the entire salesforce, from sales leaders to individual sellers. In particular, three groups should read the book, but for different reasons:
  - *Front-line sales managers (FLSMs).* You will learn how to do your jobs better.
  - *Sales leaders/senior sales managers.* You will gain deep understanding of how excellent FLSMs behave and learn critical steps for building such a cadre. You will also be able to clarify key decisions you must make, and learn how to construct a supportive environment to optimize FLSM performance.
  - *Sellers.* You will understand how the best FLSMs lead, direct, and manage their sellers, and learn what to ask for in your managers. Some of you may prepare yourselves for future FLSM positions.

- **Senior firm managers.** This book reinforces the important salesforce role in achieving firm objectives. The book emphasizes the critical FLSM job; it identifies the powerful support that you—senior firm managers up to and including the CEO—can provide the salesforce to optimize FLSM and firm success.

- **Functional leaders and firm employees at large.** The salesforce in general, and FLSMs in particular, are critical in achieving firm success. Functional leaders—customer service, finance, human resources, marketing, operations, R&D—must work with FLSMs to optimize firm performance. By more fully understanding the FLSM job, readers from firm functions will be better able to provide support for salesforce efforts to enhance customer relationships and secure sales revenues.

The Front-Line Sales Manager – Field General celebrates the importance of FLSMs to the firm's current and future health. More importantly, the book offers a roadmap for firms and their sales leaders to provide FLSMs with *the will and the skill* to get behind a customer-centric strategy, and embrace the multitude of organizational changes to make that happen.

Furthermore, this book plows new ground in demonstrating and exploring one of the most under-researched, yet overly important, roles in business—not only in the salesforce but in the entire firm. We believe our work offers value to many constituencies. Enjoy!

Prologue

It's no secret that the past few years have seen major changes in the business environment. The ground rules for achieving business success by satisfying customer needs and securing competitive advantage have been upended. Globalization, political developments, economic dislocations, social changes, new/emerging technologies, legal/regulatory rulings, global warming/other evolutions in the physical environment have each played critical roles. Few organizations and organizational functions have escaped the onslaught—not least the field salesforce.

Well-run sales organizations enable their firms to deliver business value to customers, and financial value to shareholders. Indeed, in these firms, the sales function leads the way in achieving meaningful competitive advantage. To put it bluntly, sales has shifted from *tactically important to strategically critical*. Authors Capon and Tubridy first addressed this issue in their 2011 book, *Sales Eats First*. In a very real sense, *The Front-Line Sales Manager – Field General* is a follow-up volume that digs more deeply into one specific salesforce role. Indeed, as the title subhead indicates, we believe the focus of this book represents a paradigm shift for salesforce management.

Five tectonic shifts have greatly influenced how successful sales organizations function. The sales leaders we interviewed testified to their importance:

- **Greater access to information.** Largely driven by Internet searches and social media, buyers have access to far more information about products/services, the firm, and its competitors than ever before. Sellers increasingly face more sophisticated, highly informed buyers.

    "What keeps me awake at night is: Are my customers going to know more than I know? Because of this tremendous access to information, there is now an element of strategic sourcing. Customers are smarter and better trained. They have a much better understanding of value—value to them, and to us."[1]

- **Increased competitive intensity.** In addition to ever-more-aggressive traditional competitors, firms face a host of new competitors—from adjacent industries, foreign countries, entrepreneurial start-ups, and other (sometimes unlikely) sources. Competitive offers are frequently tantalizing and alarmingly low-priced.

    "For most of my career, I always knew a good deal about my competitors. In several cases, I had even worked for one or more of them earlier in my career. Now they seem to be coming from everywhere. In some cases, China is very aggressive (with its huge population, potential economies of scale are enormous), but in others, very focused entrepreneurial start-ups are changing how we have to compete."

---

1. This and the following quotations are from sales leaders.

■ *Cloud technology.* Customers demand value, rather than the products/services that deliver value. They don't want to buy software, they just want the value software provides. Cloud technology also enables linking stand-alone products into powerful and increasingly complex systems that enable innovative solutions on a grand scale.

> "We used to sell products; those products delivered the benefits and values our customers wanted. Nowadays, customers don't want the products, they just want to receive that value directly. In a couple of years' time, our firm will be scarcely recognizable as the firm we were a couple of years ago."

■ *New buyers.* Environmental pressures on customers are shifting organizational buying decisions. Traditional decision makers/influencers are giving way to user and executive communities. And these new decision makers/influencers expect new and different values than their predecessors.

> "For years, we sold products to information technology [IT] executives; procurement was always involved, but IT called the shots. Now, those decisions are shifting into the business units. We have to demonstrate outcomes, so marketing could be the major decision maker, or some supply-chain executive. It's not that our old relationships don't matter—they still do. Rather, we have to find (and convince) new decision makers and influencers that we can deliver the outcomes they require."

■ *Greater procurement professionalism.* In many firms, procurement (purchasing) was traditionally a low-level administrative function. Recent years have seen vast improvements in procurement expertise, along with price-reducing methodologies like strategic sourcing and online reverse auctions.

> "Today, the guys on the other side of the table are just smarter and better trained than they used to be. They have serious cost-reduction objectives set by their top management; they push us very hard. They do their homework; they develop deep knowledge in some product areas. We hold our own in negotiations, but it's getting increasingly difficult."

Implications for sales organizations are profound. For firms that continue to operate traditionally, such turmoil is incredibly challenging. But the flip side is opportunity: Great sales leaders can (and do) stand out by embracing and exploiting change to benefit their firms. They know that two truths prevail:

■ *Sales organizations can be the secret sauce to meet customer requirements and defeat competitors.* Sales organizations are the *pivot point* between deep understanding of customer needs, and innovative firm solutions to satisfy those needs. Sales organizations are the *glue* binding the firm to its customers. The best sales organizations adapt quickly to changing environments. They combine efficiency and effectiveness, and considerable agility, to delight newly empowered customers.

■ *Sales organizations cannot adapt without the hands-on engagement of front-line sales managers (FLSMs).* Most sales organizations fall short in being that *secret sauce.* They require transformation in how they serve customers; they also need transformation in how they partner with internal functions to enhance the customer experience. This transformational vision must emanate from sales leaders; but the field—specifically FLSMs—must drive transformative actions. Without active FLSM engagement, attempts at sales transformations always fail.

That's correct! Without active FLSM engagement, necessary salesforce transformations will not occur. Many firms spend significant time, money, managerial, and other resources to develop products/services that, by all accounts, should delight customers. Yet top managers too often forget a fundamental truth: Success depends on *both* product/service performance *and* sales execution. Truth be told, most firms would be better off with mediocre products/services and *great* sales execution. To successfully address today's challenging times, most sales organizations must undergo significant transformation. But such transformations can only occur with full engagement of highly competent FLSMs.

Unfortunately, too many FLSMs are no more skilled than their sellers at surviving, let alone thriving, in today's customer-centric world. They are simply unable to embrace the tectonic shifts we just described; neither can they support (let alone execute) the required new strategic approaches. But, given the right transformational vision, a clearly articulated roadmap, and the necessary tools for participation, FLSMs can take the lead and make great things happen.

For those firms serious about capturing new opportunities, increasing market share, and generally growing revenues, change is in the wind. Sales leaders must step up to the plate, assess environmental imperatives, build new strategies, and set the sales transformation in process. Crucially, sales leaders must also equip FLSMs to do their job, as they are perhaps the most important change agents of all.

Before embarking on this book, we have three questions for readers. Do you believe:

■ a high-performing sales organization is critical to your firm's success?

■ your firm's salesforce requires transformation to meet corporate and business unit objectives?

■ FLSMs must play a critical role in driving success in your sales organization?

If you answered *Yes* to these three questions, read on. We know you are busier today than ever before. But we firmly believe the time and effort you spend reading this book will be worth it.

Acknowledgments

The authors acknowledge the contributions of Shirley Shi and Ashutosh Singh for research assistance. They also thank Matt Greenstein, Mike Meisenheimer, and Kyle Uebelhor, principals at The Alexander Group, for their insightful comments regarding FLSMs. Author FM thanks the Fulbright program for funding his year of study in the U.S. to participate on this project.

Part I

The Front-Line Sales Manager

Successful firms earn profits today and promise profits tomorrow. Their profit trajectories enable them to survive and grow as intact organizations, and enhance financial value for shareholders. The core of these firms' success is their ability to attract, retain, and grow customers. How do firms achieve this result? The simple answer: They not only deliver value to customers; they secure differential advantage by providing greater customer value than their competitors.

In many of these successful firms, the sales function is the critical interface between the firm and its current and potential customers. Salespeople lead the way, making the link between customer needs and the firm's ability to offer value to satisfy those needs. How well sellers can accomplish this task depends directly on the quality of the firm's sales organization.

Most importantly, the ability of sellers to be successful is a function of how well they are led, directed, and managed. That task centers on the role of the front-line sales manager (FLSM). Indeed, in Part I of this book, we show that the FLSM position may be the most important in the entire salesforce. Well-run sales organizations expend great time and effort to secure differential advantage in their marketplaces. But they fail if their FLSMs are ineffective. In this book, you will hear directly from sales leaders and their FLSMs at top corporations. We further support discussions with examples, personal stories, strategic frameworks, and commonsense suggestions based on many years of research and practice. You will learn how FLSMs must transition from being *tactically important* to being *strategically critical*.

As one perceptive sales leader shared with us:

> "In our firm, corporate *gets it*. Our leaders know revenue growth is crucial to our future, and that the salesforce must perform. So we continue to get investment to improve the sales organization, while some of our competitors suffer. That's great for us, but we are also channeling more resources into the front-line sales manager. These guys are critical to our future, because of the roles they play, and the enormous leverage they have on our selling efforts."

Across the corporate landscape, salesforces differ on many dimensions. Yet, one truth remains self-evident: When the salesforce is successful, good things happen. Unfortunately, too many FLSMs lack the skills to ensure their sellers *thrive* in today's customer-centric world. FLSMs frequently come to the job unprepared to embrace the tectonic shifts described in the Prologue. How can they support, let alone execute, new strategic approaches required for success?

As you will see throughout this book, given the right transformational vision, a clearly articulated roadmap, and the necessary tools, competencies, and knowledge for participation, FLSMs can—and do—take the lead and make great things happen.

We show our approach for building and maintaining a high-performing salesforce in two parts. In Part I, we present a sixfold *acumen* framework—*strategic, organizational, business, team building, resource, personal*—that identifies the core requirements for FLSMs (and their sales teams) to perform at a high level.

- ■ **Chapter 1** discusses the critical importance of the FLSM to firm success. The chapter identifies the FLSM's unique role as a boundary spanner. We examine the intricacies of buying and selling processes, and success requirements for *six acumen dimensions*. High-performing FLSMs score well on each dimension.

- ■ **Chapter 2** introduces the competencies and insights FLSMs must acquire to develop high levels of *strategic acumen*—the ability to think and act strategically.

- ■ **Chapter 3** examines *organizational acumen*—the ability to identify, and interface with, members of customer decision-making units (DMUs), and understand their decision-making processes (DMPs).

- ■ **Chapter 4** focuses on *business acumen*, the ability to make deals and drive sales revenues.

- ■ **Chapter 5** explores *team-building acumen*, the ability to successfully build, lead, and manage a high-performing team of sellers.

- ■ **Chapter 6** focuses on working with, and securing additional resources to support, the selling effort—permanent, temporary, and customer resources—*resource acumen*.

- ■ **Chapter 7** outlines the attributes of *personal acumen* for successful FLSMs. Critical elements include leadership, personal drive, passion, and engagement.

In Part II, we take the strong position that the job of sales leaders and senior sales managers is to set the conditions for FLSMs and their sales teams to be successful. In the three chapters in Part II, we highlight these requirements for higher managerial levels.

Chapter 1

Scoping Out the Front-Line Sales Manager

"I'm so glad it's Friday; only two more days in the business week."

—Front-line sales manager

In many firms, the salesforce is critical for earning revenues and driving growth. When the salesforce is successful, good things happen: Revenues and profits increase, the firm survives and grows, and shareholder value increases. Conversely, if the salesforce fails in its core task, the firm does not earn sufficient revenues to survive, and *no one gets a paycheck.* These simple relationships crystalize the importance of the sales function for firms large and small, in all industries, offering products and/or services, in all countries around the world. Of course, many different things must occur for a firm to be successful, but the revenue-generating task sets the salesforce apart from other organizational functions.

Across the corporate landscape, salesforces differ on many dimensions—size, geographic scope, product/service breadth and complexity, organization structure, number of managerial levels, field sales versus tele/Internet sales, support structures, seller/managerial tenure. Regardless, there are core commonalities: Sellers conduct day-to-day selling activities; sellers report to, and are directed/led/managed by, sales managers. Depending on the type and size of the sales organization, these managers have various titles—district sales manager, regional sales manager, national sales manager, sales vice president, key/strategic/global account manager. Throughout this book, for managers leading, directing, and managing individual sellers, we use the term **front-line sales manager** (FLSM).

In this introductory chapter, we address four key topics. First, we make the case for the critical importance of the FLSM role. Second, we examine the challenge of the FLSM job by discussing its nature as a boundary-spanning position. Third, we lay out a model of the selling process; after all, the heart of the FLSM job is to lead firm resources successfully through the process that drives customers to purchase firm products/services. Finally, we identify key competencies for executing the FLSM job successfully, using a sixfold acumen framework.

The Front-Line Sales Manager's Importance

Salesforce success is critically dependent on the actions of individual sellers. But day-to-day seller activities and performance are highly dependent on the FLSM. Essentially, the firm grants the FLSM a franchise to sell its products/services in some space, typically, but not always, defined by geography—

frequently (but not always) called a sales district. The FLSM is responsible for fully staffing seller slots (FTEs—full-time equivalents) granted by sales leaders, and ensuring those sellers perform at a high level. The FLSM is the focal point for implementing sales-leader requirements, and forwarding customer and market information into the firm's decision-making processes. In short, we believe the FLSM role is one of the most organizationally important, both for the salesforce and for the firm overall. Notwithstanding our assertion that the FLSM acts as a field general, in a very real sense the FLSM is also a staff sergeant, making sure the firm's sales strategy is well executed.

Unfortunately, the FLSM role has not been a topic of much interest to researchers in the sales arena, nor even to many sales organizations.[1] As one sales leader put it:

> "The FLSM is an unattended area. The sales community has kind of skipped over this category. But in our firm, we believe the FLSM role is absolutely critical."

Our belief in the importance of the FLSM role is the motivation for this book, and for the research study that provides much of the material from which we draw our conclusions. The basic premise is very clear: *The FLSM position is critical for firm success.* We tested this assertion with sales leaders and received an overwhelmingly positive endorsement.

Perhaps the most important support from these sales leaders was unstated. This support was reflected in the time commitment we received from those we interviewed, and in their willingness to provide successful FLSMs for us to interview. Twenty-three sales leaders, and even more FLSMs, from a broad swath of companies gave up an hour or more of their valuable time to talk to us. The sales leader from a global information technology firm was quite explicit:

> "I think this work you are doing to study the power of the FLSM is really important. The FLSM is the most important role in just about any company. Now, I say that because you can take all the senior sales leadership away, but if you've got great FLSMs and their teams on the street, you can keep the lights on. I just think the focus you've got here is the right one."

As we shall see in future chapters, FLSMs do many things. But what really matters is *leading, directing, managing, and encouraging* their sales teams to enhance sales and profit performance. Our respondents understood the critical nature of the FLSM role in achieving the firm's performance goals. The sales leader continued:

> "Any time you're in management, you are overhead. But I look at FLSMs and I say: 'Yeah, that's right, but they do three or four things that really *move the needle* more than anything else for the company.'"

This sort of statement from sales-leader interviewees was not unusual. We heard similar comments from various sales leaders:

> "FLSMs are, in my opinion, the most important group of people if we are going to be successful."

> "At our company, we reached an alignment in perspective that the FLSM is the most important role in the sales organization."

"[FLSMs] are fantastically important. They are some of our most talented people. When we talk about different managerial layers, I think they're more valuable than the layer directly above them. The best ones have this unique combination of understanding where the business is going, and deep client knowledge—from spending multiple hours daily with sellers and customers. They have their fingers on the pulse of what is going on. It's an incredibly valuable combination; we don't see it elsewhere within the sales organization."

"They are the *quarterback*, managing all the project managers internally, and their salespeople."

"FLSMs are the most talented people on your team. Successful battles aren't won without field generals that are empowered. The FLSM is the field general…. This person has the moral authority of connectedness."

"From my perspective, the FLSM is one of the most important *cogs in the wheel*. The FLSM takes our product portfolio and guides the sales team to maximize opportunities. They also provide feedback, because we continue to innovate, looking for the next big *turn of the crank*, the next set of innovative solutions. FLSMs are constantly looking for unsolved customer needs and requirements, and bringing them back to the business. They go through an opportunity assessment process, so we aren't always doing one-offs."

As these remarks demonstrate, sales leaders confirm the importance of FLSMs in the normal course of business. But when things change dramatically (Prologue), the FLSM role becomes even more vital. The sales leader at a healthcare firm reflected on the situation when his firm combined two somewhat specialized salesforces into a single generalized salesforce:

"When we made the change, our FLSMs had the hardest transition. They had to learn about new marketplaces, a totally new (for them) product portfolio, and how the new organization worked. They had to know these areas so well that they could support their teams. If not, they would lose credibility."

So, why do so many sales leaders believe their FLSMs are so important? There seems to be one underlying core issue—the FLSM is a **boundary-role** position:

■ *The FLSM receives messages from sales leaders and senior sales managers.* The FLSM interprets and reframes these communications, then passes them on to the sales team for action with customers. Conversely, the FLSM reflects sales-team perspectives about the market, customers, and competitors *up the line* to sales leaders and senior sales managers.

■ *The FLSM must secure sales revenue performance from the sales team.* Simultaneously, the FLSM *must address issues emanating from sales-team interactions with customers.* The FLSM must resolve these issues by interfacing with sales leaders, senior sales managers, and/or firm personnel in other functions.

So, the FLSM role is critically important for salesforce success, largely because it is a boundary-role position. Let's now examine FLSM **boundary spanning**.

The Boundary-Spanning Front-Line Sales Manager

Within business organizations, FLSMs have a special place: they are boundary spanners. *Boundary spanners live and work on the boundaries between two (or more) organizational units.*[2] The boundary spanner's task involves moving information to-and-fro across the boundary, from one organizational unit to another. Boundary spanners also deal with the disparate objectives of different organizational units (or organizations), and attempt to resolve conflicts between them. Sometimes, boundaries are *external*—between firm organizational units and entities like customers, regulatory agencies, shareholders. Sometimes, boundaries are *internal*—between different firm functions—like R&D and manufacturing, or marketing and sales. Sometimes, boundaries are *hierarchical*—between one organizational level and another. Most importantly, the FLSM role spans *multiple boundaries.*

External Boundaries

FLSMs and their sellers span the external, interorganizational boundary between the firm and its customers. The FLSM leads/directs/manages sellers so as to persuade customers to purchase firm products/services; the customer seeks assurances these purchases will satisfy its needs. To effect such transactions, sellers/FLSMs must learn about customer objectives, strategies, needs, priorities, problems, pain points, organization structures, systems, processes. Sellers/FLSMs must also learn about individuals and groups at the customer: roles and responsibilities, decision makers/influencers, and specifically decision-making units (DMUs) and decision-making processes (DMPs) for purchasing products/services the firm offers.[3] Only by securing good customer insight can sellers/FLSMs hope to match customer requirements with firm offers, and persuade customers to buy. Sellers/FLSMs must also be well aware of the various environmental and competitive pressures that influence (or have the potential to influence) customer purchase decisions.

Simultaneously, the FLSM must deal with firm pressure for results—sales revenues overall, but also finer-grained performance like sales of specific products/services or sales to specific markets/market segments. Other performance metrics like achieving target price levels, securing new customers, and retaining current customers may also be important.

What makes the FLSM role so important for the firm's current and future health is the *crucial nature of this external boundary.* Sales/purchases take place across the firm-customer boundary. If FLSMs/sellers do a good job, products/services flow from firm to customer; simultaneously, purchase dollars/sales revenues flow from customer to the firm.

Sales leaders are very clear about the importance of the FLSM's role in spanning this external boundary. The sales leader for a software firm told us:

> "The way we look at it, marketing designs the offer our firm makes to customers, but the salesforce executes. No matter how good a job we do in training salespeople, they must be managed on a day-to-day basis, so we offer great value to our customers. That's the FLSM's job."

Other sales leaders told us:

> "We rely on our FLSMs to be the authoritative company voice on addressing customers. Our sellers deal with customers day-to-day, but the FLSMs back them up and step in whenever they are needed."

> "The FLSM has one of the most difficult jobs in the company—new initiatives, new messages, new KPIs [key performance indicators]—all being driven down to that person. And every customer issue bubbling up from the other end. Above and below, everything converges on the FLSM."

One FLSM, whose firm sold to the banking industry, discussed his role in the negotiating process:

> "When we are negotiating deals, my sellers have a little room to shave prices; that works for about 10 percent of the cases. I have a little more flexibility; that takes care of about 20 percent. But for the vast majority of cases, I am the negotiating channel between the customer and our top management."

Internal Boundaries

The FLSM also spans the internal boundary between sellers and the firm's entire management structure. The FLSM must transmit senior management information and requirements to sellers, but must also represent sellers and their perspectives to senior management. Information flowing from senior levels ranges from positive/want to hear—new products/price reductions—to negative/don't want to hear—fewer resources/higher quotas. The same is true in the reverse direction from sellers to senior levels: positive—sales increases/joint initiatives with customers; negative—sales contracts canceled/competitor's breakthrough product securing customer adoption.[4]

Several respondents identified the FLSM's internal-boundary-spanning role as a critical characteristic of the FLSM job. The sales leader at a medical-technology firm put it this way:

> "The FLSM *makes the wheels turn*. [The problem] is that he's pulled in two directions—down to the reps and up to senior management. It's a push-and-pull job. The FLSM's challenge is to stay close to the sales team and their customers, but also have the right focus internally."

Sales leaders were especially fond of using metaphors to illustrate the internal-boundary-spanning nature of the FLSM's job:

> "The FLSM is the *glue* between the corporation and the salespeople. Their role is getting the big picture—the macros; effectively managing their teams; and keeping people motivated and engaged. It's vital for the FLSM to lead the team through the changes we are facing."

> "FLSMs are the *bridge—boots on ground*. It's very easy for non-customer-interaction positions to lose perspective on the needs/trends in customers. Only top-talented people fill this position—with both strategic understanding and daily-tasks competence."

"FLSMs are the *meniscus* between how things *rub* together, or don't. The overall link between the corporation and the salesforce is so crucial. It's imperative that FLSMs are the most talented people in the management team."

"The FLSM operates where the *rubber meets the road*. The judgment of these guys is so key and critical. FLSMs must make sure they absorb communications from top-level sales management and the executive team, and send them on to salespeople. But they must also discern what doesn't need to be communicated down the line."

Finally, one FLSM employed an *hourglass* metaphor:

"The FLSM is in charge of the section where sand passes through. If this section doesn't work, sales don't exist. It's like someone trying to stop that little funnel and the hourglass doesn't work. The FLSM must minimize the friction so the sand passes through."

The boundary between sales leaders/senior sales managers and sellers is arguably the most important internal boundary FLSMs must negotiate, but it is by no means the only one. Other functions—customer service, technical service, marketing—often interface with customers on a regular basis. FLSMs frequently negotiate these interactions too. Furthermore, FLSMs may interact with other parts of the firm on an irregular basis—accounting, contracting, legal, R&D. As one FLSM told us:

"Of course, I spend a lot of time in the field working with my sellers, but some of my most important efforts are internal. I interface with many other firm functions; it's a whole grab bag of interactions. They range from solving jurisdictional disputes to securing resources to solve customer problems."

Multiple Boundaries

What we learned from sales leaders pretty much confirmed our starting beliefs. First, the FLSM role is critically important for firm success, as only FLSMs and their sellers earn sales revenues. Second, the FLSM role is challenging and difficult, largely because of its boundary-spanning nature. Of course, the FLSM is only one of several organizational positions that function as boundary spanners. What makes the FLSM job different from most other boundary-spanning roles? The FLSM spans multiple boundaries: *external*—with customers; *internal-hierarchical*—with sales leaders and senior sales managers; *internal-nonhierarchical*—with other firm functions. Being positioned on a single boundary is difficult, and can be very uncomfortable and stressful. For FLSMs, sitting on two or more boundaries (of very different types) magnifies stress, and heightens both challenges and responsibilities.

The Selling Process

Of all the boundaries the FLSM spans, perhaps most critical is the external boundary between the firm and its customers. FLSMs and their sellers traverse this boundary on a day-to-day basis as they attempt to persuade customers to purchase the firm's products/services. But all customers are not alike; they may engage in very different purchasing activities. Correspondingly, the selling process in which sellers/FLSMs engage must also differ. Furthermore, it's one thing for a seller to make a sale. It's quite another for the firm to deliver on sellers' promises, and hence raise the probability of future sales. For this reason, we consider the selling process as comprising two parts—*making the sale* and *after the sale*.

Making the Sale

We can usefully conceptualize three types of customer buying processes and three corresponding selling processes—Figure 1.1.

Figure 1.1 Making the Sale

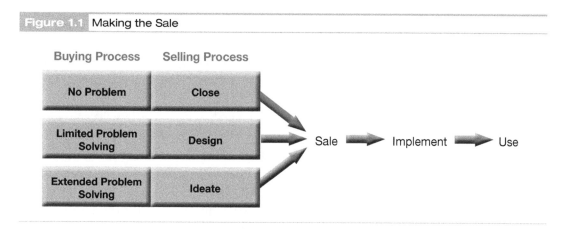

Buying Process—*No Problem* (NP); Selling Process—*Close*. The customer has well-defined purchase criteria, frequently makes this type of purchase, and selects among several familiar suppliers. The various offers are well known, and very similar across suppliers. Choices are made rapidly, with little effort, often based on price, terms, delivery, personal relationships, brand loyalty. NP purchase decisions are often made by a single individual, typically a purchasing executive.

The buyer's job is relatively straightforward: Get the best deal. For NP purchases, frequently, *the devil is in the details*, as the seller seeks to *close* the sale. When the *details* are comparable among potential suppliers, firm brand image and the seller's personal brand equity, earned during myriad interactions with customer executives, may be decisive.[5]

One FLSM built on this reasoning:

> "I have very experienced guys in my team. They've been calling on the same customers for many years, so they're really well known by customer executives. They've built reputations for open, frank discussion, and delivering on their promises. We're never the lowest-price supplier, but the trust customers have in my sellers is worth two or three percentage points in price."

Buying Process—*Limited Problem Solving* (LPS); Selling Process—*Design*. The customer has well-defined purchase criteria, but one (or more) alternatives is novel. Performance is uncertain for the new alternative; the customer must test and/or gather more data. Examples: potential new supplier; replacing the traditional purchase with a new option. Typically, LPS purchase decisions involve several influencers/decision makers.

The customer must decide among several noncomparable options. The seller's job is to persuade the customer that the firm's offer is superior to all others. The core task is to secure deep understanding of customer needs, then demonstrate, via offer *design*, that the firm provides net differential advantage.

As one FLSM told us:

> "I make sure my guys dig deep at the customer, always trying to find ways to add a little bit of extra value. We don't have to be that much better than the competition, so every little extra-value item helps. If we can't find it in product then we look at service—front and back, and up and down."

Buying Process—*Extended Problem Solving* (EPS); Selling Process—*Ideate*. The customer makes a novel purchase; the alternative(s) and/or potential supplier(s) are new. Purchase criteria are poorly developed; the customer expends considerable time/effort resolving uncertainty/reducing risk. EPS purchase decisions often affect several departments and/or management systems—many people are typically involved.

The appropriate seller role is to help the buyer make the purchase decision. The seller and customer *ideate* together—develop approaches to satisfy customer needs, address priorities, solve problems, mitigate pain points. Correspondingly, sellers identify what firm resources/products/services may help address customer issues. The core selling task is to link customer needs and firm capabilities—*solution selling.*

Compared to NP and LPS, the selling process for customers making EPS purchase decisions is the most complex, but frequently has the highest revenue potential. The initial selling task is to engage the customer in *joint* ideation. Two possibilities:

- **Identify.** The seller learns about the customer's struggles as it works on the problem—alone or with a competitive supplier(s). Adhering to the principle of *creeping commitment*—early entry raises eventual success probabilities—the seller engages the customer, most likely with additional firm resources.

- **Generate.** The seller approaches the customer with a *point of view*—about the customer, industry, served markets—implying significant change should be considered. The customer decides to address these issues and commences joint ideation with the seller.

Generally, the seller seeks to win a purchase agreement directly, avoiding an RFP (request for proposal) process. Regardless, the seller may, nonetheless, *assist* in RFP drafting, hence advantaging the firm. The critical seller issue: Be involved early. One FLSM reflected on the dangers of failing to adhere to this prescription:

> "Sometimes an RFP comes across my desk that smells ridiculously like a competitor helped write it. When that happens, we are set up to fail. We realize very quickly that we are just a data point, to ensure the solution's economic cost is not exploiting the customer. So, our role is just to keep the competitor honest. I am like: 'Guys, we got beat to the punch—big time.' It's not just that we're going to lose the business; responding to these RFPs takes a lot of effort we could better spend elsewhere."

Seller tasks in *ideation* take significant time and effort. An experienced strategic account manager put it this way:

> "In my experience, customers are generally open to those *ideation* discussions. They have to find a supplier that can fulfill some need or set of needs [and] solve problems at a pain point. So, working back and forth with suppliers, with both sides making adjustments here and there, was almost second nature to me. Sure, it's a time-consuming process, in part because of the complexity of the interactions. On the one hand, the account team has to work with customer executives in several different roles and locations; on the other hand, the account team has to identify and work with our product specialists, and bring both sides together."

We have presented the three buying processes as independent. In reality, any individual customer may be engaged with the seller in all three types of purchase decision—*no problem, limited problem solving, extended problem solving*—at the same time. In such cases, the selling process—*close, design, ideate*—for one opportunity may influence the selling process at another.

After the Sale

As the firm earns revenues, the selling process moves to *implement* and *use* simultaneously. Success (and especially failure) during these processes should initiate an after-action review. Such reviews allow sellers/FLSMs to identify cause(s) of success (failure), so the firm will be better prepared—win or lose—for the next opportunity.

But, notwithstanding the involvement of other firm functions, the selling process is far from over— two more stages—*implement*, *use*—remain to fulfill one single purpose[6]: The firm *must* deliver on the seller's promises. Customers *must* receive the benefits/values they expect from the firm's products/ services.

Implement. The *implement* process ranges in scope from trivial to highly complex:

- **Trivial.** In many cases, *implement* concerns relatively straightforward issues like delivery arrangements, invoicing, and related tasks. We used to call many of these activities *paperwork.*

- **Complex.** Alternatively, suppose the customer purchased a new turnkey factory—land, factory buildings, production equipment, utilities. Supplier and customer engaged jointly to *ideate*, then worked together on factory layout, machine requirements, and many other decisions. Buyer and seller signed a contract for factory delivery at a specified future date. The seller made the sale; now the firm must complete significant work to deliver on the value proposition specified in the contract.

Most likely, a complex process like factory construction will be the responsibility of a general contractor (internal or external), no doubt aided by various functional specialists (also internal or external). What is the seller's role? In many salesforces, there is a great tendency for sellers to walk away—toss the responsibility *over the wall* to the general contractor: "I made the sale, now it's your job. I have other sales to make." We have seen this tendency throughout our careers; it is a huge error.

The seller was successful for one very important reason: The customer accepted the value proposition the seller offered. The value proposition is a *promise*. The seller made that promise on the firm's behalf; hence, the seller has a responsibility to ensure the firm delivers on that promise. Of course, there is a second reason to stay involved. If *implement* is successful, the seller enhances personal brand equity, and sets the stage for future sales. The reverse is also true: If the firm fails to deliver on the seller's promises, and/or the implementation process is painful for the customer—when it comes to future sales, *forget it*!

In most cases, *implement* falls between these extremes. Some firm function other than sales has direct responsibility. But the seller must stay involved; ultimately, the seller is responsible for the firm-customer relationship. To repeat: The seller made a promise on the firm's behalf; the seller must ensure the firm keeps that promise. Regarding potential additional revenues, one FLSM in higher-education software explained:

> "We have a professional services [PS] team that implements our software. But these new big deals have a long tail for additional consulting and training. We work with the PS organization to unearth these opportunities."

Use. The customer is off and running with the firm's product/service. *Implement* has been completed successfully. Now the seller must look to the future.[7] Three issues are important:

■ *Murphy's Law.* Stuff happens! No matter how good an overall job the seller and firm have done in *implement*, there will inevitably be problems—some small, some large. In either case, the seller must learn about any problem right away, then get it fixed as soon as possible. Effective sellers develop early warning processes so the issue (of whatever type) is not allowed to fester, and work hard to ensure the problem does not negatively affect the firm-customer relationship. As one sales leader said:

> "The best predictor of customer loyalty is the ability to respond swiftly and effectively to problems if and when they arise."

One FLSM told us how he approached the issue of potential problems:

> "I insist on knowing about any product/service failure/outage as soon as possible. I emphasize to my team the standard procedure whenever a failure/outage occurs anywhere in my region: I should be informed immediately. If the failure/outage happens during the night, I want an email/text message waiting for me when I wake up: What has gone wrong? What is being done (and/or needs to be done) to repair the situation? What is the plan for following through? [I require] phone numbers so I can reach the team member closest to the problem. This is a top priority for me. Maintaining credibility with the customer is critical. Any problem must be fixed. I view that as my personal responsibility."

Indeed, since customer executives also know about Murphy's Law, an effective seller can turn a seemingly difficult situation into a brand-building success. The FLSM went on:

> "We had a serious overnight problem with a major customer. I learned about it at around 6 a.m. I made a bunch of phone calls, got things moving, and by

midmorning everything was back on track. As it turned out, I had an important late-morning meeting with senior customer executives and my boss. Soon after we started the meeting, one customer executive raised the overnight problem, assuming I did not know about it. He was clearly very concerned and said to me point blank: 'What are you going to do about it?' I said quite simply: 'The problem's fixed, don't worry about it.' The executive was astonished that I both knew about the problem, and had got it fixed. That incident did wonders for my personal brand equity at the customer. And it didn't hurt that my boss was there to hear this conversation."

In some services businesses, the firm-customer relationship is ongoing by the very nature of the benefits/value delivered—like consulting. But the imperative for continued closeness with product sales is also likely to increase in the *use* stage as revenue models shift from one-time payments to subscription models.

■ **Ideate.** The seller should view customer *use* of the firm's product/service over a period of time as a *no-cost laboratory*. A laboratory stimulates idea generation. By understanding the customer's experience with firm products/services, the seller may be able to return the selling process to the beginning—*ideate*—to prepare for a future sale. One healthcare FLSM reported on his sales team's success:

> "What we find very often is, we make a sale and the customer is off and running with our product. Then, the customer gets the idea of standardizing on a common product platform. They say: 'Who should we standardize to?' We say: 'Funny you should ask, you can standardize to our product.' They say: 'Great. Since you helped design this thing, let us do it.'"

■ **Recover from failure to win the sale.** The foregoing *implement* and *use* discussions assume the seller was successful in making the sale. But the seller may have failed, and a competitor won the business. What then? Presumably, the winning competitor went through *implement*, then to *use* stages. We just noted potential *implement* problems the winning seller could face, along with *Murphy's Law*, and the potential to *ideate* in the *use* stage.

The seller should be on top of these issues, even though the customer's focus is on the competitor's product/service. By staying closely attuned to competitor performance, the seller may secure insight, and open doors that otherwise would remain closed. Indeed, the seller may be able to initiate a new selling process by restarting at *ideate*.

The importance of the FLSM's role lies in its impact on sales performance by sales-team members. Quite simply, the selling process must be second nature to FLSMs and their sellers. FLSMs must coach sellers to place appropriate time and effort on selling-process elements both *before* and *after* the sale.

Success Requirements for Front-Line Sales Managers

We just described the selling process and the job of individual sellers. If sellers are successful, the firm should thrive. But sellers typically do not act as independent agents. They must be led, directed, managed. That's the job for FLSMs. For this reason, sales leaders we interviewed believed the FLSM role is critical.

The key question we address in Part I of *The Front-Line Sales Manager – Field General* is straightforward: What are the characteristics of an effective FLSM?[8] We answer this question using an **acumen framework**:

> *Acumen*—keenness and depth of perception, discernment, or discrimination, especially in practical matters. Synonyms: acuity, astuteness, expertise, insight, intelligence, judgment, sagacity, sharpness, shrewdness, wisdom.[9]

We believe *acumen* forms the basis of a valuable framework for FLSMs. Drawing on previous discussion in this chapter, we propose a sixfold framework for describing successful FLSMs—Figure 1.2. At some level, each of the six acumen dimensions has relevance for the selling-process elements just discussed—*close, design, ideate*—along with *implement, use.*

Figure 1.2 The FLSM Acumen Framework

Strategic Acumen

The FLSM must possess the ability to think strategically, to understand the various environmental pressures on business organizations—firm and customers. The FLSM must be able to articulate the broad direction of firm efforts and to prioritize resource allocations. In the context of the boundary-role perspective, the FLSM must develop and exercise **strategic acumen** in two areas: *internal*—at the firm—and *external*—at customers.

The Firm. The firm operates in an increasingly challenging, complex, and fast-changing environment (Prologue). Top management has the responsibility to develop a vision and mission for the firm overall, and for individual businesses. In the context of these broad directions, business and marketing leaders decide which markets and market segments the firm should address. Marketers develop value propositions the firm offers to secure customer purchases and earn revenues. Generally, the firm develops a single value proposition for each product/market segment it decides to address. Depending on sales-organization design, individual FLSMs are typically responsible for executing one or more value propositions with their sales teams.

FLSMs are not normally involved in making strategic marketing decisions, but they must be very clear about overall firm/business direction, resource-allocation priorities, and their evolution. FLSMs must make the transition from firm strategic direction to an operating philosophy for their seller teams. They must also ensure that sales-team members are competent to articulate these issues.

Relatedly, in many cases, the firm develops product/market-segment strategies that are relatively independent. Yet, two or more strategies may interact if segment definitions from separate product groups overlap. Resolving such interactions may not occur within marketing organizations; rather, resolution takes place within the salesforce. Someone must sort through the various interactions among different product/market-segment strategies, and develop a coherent sales strategy. If sales leaders/senior sales managers have performed this integration, the FLSM/seller team must execute; if this has not occurred, the FLSM must do this job.

The challenges facing FLSMs are simple in concept, but difficult in execution. Business/marketing leaders typically develop value propositions for target market segments, *not* for individual customers within those segments. Sellers/FLSMs must make the transition from broadscale market segment-level value propositions to benefits/values specific to individual customers. The FLSM has the critical role of ensuring that all sales-team members can make these translations—from *general* to *specific*.

All sellers must understand how firm products/services offer benefits/values to meet individual customer needs, address priorities, solve problems, mitigate pain points, and address critical issues. Sellers must also understand, and communicate, how firm messaging and pricing apply to individual customers. Environmental evolution causes firm value propositions, and market offers, to evolve also. Hence, this general-to-specific translation is an ongoing challenge for FLSMs and their sellers.

Dealing with these translations is a core element of the FLSM job. *Strategic acumen* embraces the ability to shift from the *general* to the *specific*, to understand deeply the thinking at the top of the firm, and to translate those directions and strategies into action by individual sellers. This translation is particularly important in the LPS/design and EPS/ideate buying/selling processes. This task is not simple; only FLSMs commanding a high degree of strategic acumen do this well.

By applying strategic acumen within the firm, the FLSM learns about resources the firm may make available for customers. The FLSM continually updates this knowledge as firm strategy evolves, new products/services are launched, new resources become available, and the firm makes acquisitions. Correspondingly, of course, the FLSM must also deal with product/service withdrawal, fewer resources, and business-unit divestitures.

Customers. FLSMs should employ strategic acumen to translate firm strategies/products/services/ resources into actions that deliver benefits/values to customers. Deep customer understanding allows FLSMs/sellers to generate ideas for helping customers satisfy their needs, solve problems, address priorities, and mitigate pain points. In many cases, such understanding is insufficient; sellers/FLSMs must also learn about customers' customers.

Of course, there is just a single firm on the customer side of each interorganizational boundary, but many individual customers. Furthermore, information about visions, missions, strategies of customer firms is generally more difficult to secure than similar information about the supplier. Whereas the FLSM should be able to directly secure and communicate firm-level issues, securing information on customers is typically a seller responsibility. The FLSM's job is to *coach* sellers on how to obtain this information.

Regardless, understanding customer strategy is the baseline condition for identifying unserved customer needs; such understanding is crucial in EPS/ideate for solution selling.

Organizational Acumen

Firm-based *strategic acumen* focuses on translating firm direction/strategies/value propositions into benefits/values for individual customers. Customer-based *strategic acumen* focuses on securing deep understanding of customer needs, priorities, problems, pain points. **Organizational acumen** is concerned with understanding customer organizations, so the seller communicates the *right* benefits/values to the *right* members of the customer organization, at the *right* time; and builds strong positive relationships with them. *Organizational acumen* represents the heart of the *external*-boundary-spanning role, and represents a significant component of the FLSM job.

Organizational acumen is not a simple skill to acquire and practice. Customer organizations do not possess one single decision-making unit (DMU) or decision-making process (DMP) for procurement decisions. Many organizations have well-developed, formalized DMUs and DMPs for different types of procurement decision. Indeed, customers frequently publish this information to improve seller efficiency and reduce unnecessary customer-supplier interactions. Regardless, notwithstanding formal customer procedures, most organizations possess a host of *unpublished* informal procedures that may trump formal purchasing systems and processes. Furthermore, for sharing ideas that may lead to joint development projects, there may be no established DMU or DMP, formal or informal.

Identifying key players for customer purchases is a critical first step in exercising organizational acumen, but it is only the beginning. The seller must be able to interface with, address, and then influence DMU members to support firm offers, and secure sales. The seller earns this support by building good business and personal relationships with members of the customer organization, and generally improving *personal brand equity*.

FLSMs with good organizational acumen play two important roles. First, they communicate the essence of understanding the customer organization to their sellers, then help them interface with, address, and influence customer personnel in the firm's favor.

The second FLSM role involves more direct action. Customers often implement internal processes designed to *protect* executives from sellers. Purchasing may play this *gatekeeper* role, but many individuals can frustrate seller attempts to secure the access they seek. FLSMs with good organizational acumen break through these barriers. Driven by a desire to truly serve customers, these FLSMs find innovative ways to skirt formal organizational processes that customers use to deny sellers access.

Organizational acumen is especially important in the LPS/design and EPS/ideate buying/selling processes. *Design*—ensure the *right* customer businesses/departments/individuals play the *right* roles in the design process; *ideate*—identify customer locations that offer attractive potential for developing new ideas.

Business Acumen

Strategic acumen concerns translating broadscale value propositions into actual benefits/values for customers. **Business acumen** is concerned with effectively communicating these benefits/values, and making them *real* for customer decision makers/influencers. When sellers/FLSMs effectively employ *business acumen*, they make deals. For effective action, FLSMs must also possess good *organizational acumen* so as to identify the DMUs and DMP for each particular opportunity.

In communicating firm benefits/values, sellers must work at two levels. At one level, sellers offer benefits/values to the customer organization as a whole. Mostly these benefits/values are either *functional* or *economic*. *Functional:* Firm products/services enable the customer organization to do something it couldn't previously do, or do it better—satisfy a need, address a priority, solve a problem, mitigate a pain point. Many sellers do a good job communicating these types of benefits/values. What sellers are generally less able to communicate effectively are *economic* benefits/values—the dollars-and-cents benefits that result from delivering functional benefits/values. To make this functional-economic translation may require in-depth understanding of customer operations, and great facility with financial analysis. Effective FLSMs know how to secure the necessary customer information, and possess the financial skills, to make the appropriate calculations.

The second level of communicating benefits/values is to individual customer personnel. After all, *organizations* do not make purchase decisions; *individuals* in organizations make purchase decisions. Furthermore, DMU members make/influence purchase decisions for both business and personal reasons. From a business perspective, classically, *purchasing* executives are concerned about price; *manufacturing* executives focus on production efficiency; *engineers* are concerned with product/service design. Frequently, senior managers take more holistic perspectives, focusing on economic issues like total cost of ownership and long-run firm profits. Over and above these role-related preferences, individuals occupying such roles likely have idiosyncratic benefit/value preferences. Finally, many personal issues—direct financial reward, gifts, promotion opportunities—may also affect individual decision making/influence.

The successful seller must understand customer DMUs and DMPs, the benefits/values that customer firms require, and specific individual benefit/value concerns related to potential purchase of the firm's products/services.

Making firm benefits/values *come alive* to customers so the seller makes a sale is rarely simple. The FLSM must coach sellers so they understand customer issues inside and out. Sellers must be able to act on these issues as second nature, day-to-day. Successful FLSMs must possess great *business acumen*.

Business acumen is particularly important in the LPS/design and EPS/ideate buying/selling processes. Good business acumen allows sellers to develop and evaluate opportunities, and make persuasive arguments in favor of firm products/services, and win deals.[10]

Team-Building Acumen

Organizational acumen focuses on customer organizations; **team-building acumen** focuses on the firm, and specifically on the FLSM's team of sellers. *Team-building acumen* is concerned with building and sustaining a high-performing sales team. The FLSM's sales team comprises several sellers the FLSM believes will be successful in the future, based on past performance and/or future potential. *Team-building acumen* requires continually assessing sellers, moving out poor performers, and making appropriate replacement decisions.

The effective FLSM helps team members develop the knowledge, skills, abilities (KSAs) necessary to succeed. The FLSM uses a variety of approaches—assessing, coaching, modeling behavior. The FLSM requires team members to take advantage of firm systems and processes designed to enhance sales performance via intellectual capital development, including training programs. The FLSM also encourages and promotes individual development initiatives. Notwithstanding the drive for individual excellence, *team building* means what it says: *The FLSM must blend a set of high-performing/high-potential individuals into a mutually supportive team.* Team performance should become greater than the sum of its parts. This team-building component of the FLSM job is important for all buying processes.

Resource Acumen

Resource acumen focuses mostly on resources *within* the firm, but *outside* the FLSM's direct sphere of authority/responsibility. We take the strong view that the sales organization *owns* the firm-customer relationship. But other functions interface with customers on a regular basis—customer service, logistics, marketing, technical service. The first component is the ability to work with these functions on a continuous basis, in meeting the challenge of serving customers. The FLSM must ensure these firm-customer relationships mesh seamlessly with seller/FLSM actions. Quite simply, the FLSM must exercise *resource acumen* so all these resources are pulling in the same direction, most often in the *implement* and *use* selling-process stages. This *resource acumen* component is a critical element in the FLSM's *internal*-boundary-spanning role, and a significant component of the FLSM job.

Secondly, the FLSM must identify and locate critical firm resources required in the selling process, typically on a temporary basis. The FLSM must secure agreement from key internal stakeholders to make these resources available, as necessary, to satisfy customer needs, address priorities, solve problems, mitigate pain points. Required resources embrace various types of specialist expertise, along with sales leader/senior management involvement. It may be difficult for individual sellers to reach the desired levers of resource-allocation power. FLSMs with high levels of resource acumen work with sellers to identify critical internal capabilities, then do what it takes to gain alignment with customer opportunities. This component of resource acumen is critical in the LPS/design and EPS/ideate buying/selling processes. (Of course, firm resources are also required for *implement*, where they are generally pretty well defined and do not require significant involvement from sellers/FLSMs to secure.)

A special aspect of securing resources to serve customers on a temporary basis concerns placing supplier personnel on customer teams/task forces.

Finally, astute planning may allow the FLSM to secure customer personnel to act as credible resources to advance the firm's agenda. FLSMs may use various approaches to place satisfied customer personnel in the role of advocating for the firm and its products/services.

Personal Acumen

Over and above the five acumen dimensions just discussed—*strategic, organizational, business, team building, resource*—the successful FLSM must possess a series of personal qualities—**personal acumen**. Most particularly, the FLSM must be a leader. *Leadership* encompasses all acumen dimensions, but takes these abilities to a higher level. At root, the FLSM *leads* firm efforts to make sales at individual customers. In most cases, the FLSM is not the *tip of the spear*; team members— sellers, the FLSM's direct reports—play that role.

But the FLSM is right next to sellers when they address customers. The FLSM directs sellers—individuals the FLSM has selected, coached, and trained—to execute firm value propositions. The FLSM makes sure the sales team has the *right* resources to do the job, and is fearless in breaking down internal and other barriers to support the sales team.

What the successful FLSM does not do is *micromanage*. Rather, this FLSM supports sellers in implementing firm strategy, and taking sensible risks. In executing the *leadership* role, the FLSM must be the *go-to* person for critical issues individual sellers cannot resolve alone. Furthermore, the FLSM must possess a variety of positive attributes that build personal brand equity, trust, and credibility. The FLSM works hard and smart, and is always available to team members. *Personal acumen* is always important for FLSMs.

To become a successful FLSM, the path is very clear: Get up to speed on the six acumen dimensions— *strategic, organizational, business, team building, resource, personal.* Chapters 2 through 7 provide key elements of each of these dimensions.

A Word about Front-Line Sales Manager Evolution

For the most part, FLSMs have authority/responsibility for a five-to-ten-person team of directly reporting sellers. Typically, these sellers work in geographically designed sales territories; these territories aggregate to the FLSM's district.

In some firms, a growing focus on key/strategic/global accounts has ushered in a new type of FLSM, acting alongside the traditional model. Using the shorthand of the 80:20 rule—80 percent of sales derive from 20 percent of customers—the traditional FLSM role continues for the 80 percent of customers responsible for 20 percent of sales.

But for the 20 percent of customers responsible for 80 percent of sales, the firm implements a different FLSM model. Indeed, here the FLSM has a quite different title—key/strategic/global account manager (KAM/SAM/GAM). As with the traditional model, these new-model FLSMs have several personnel (sales and support) reporting to them. But rather than having responsibility for a specific geographic territory, these individuals serve the key/strategic/global account wherever it is appropriate to do so.

A second important distinction from the traditional model concerns reporting relationships. In the traditional model, typically, sellers report solid-line to the FLSM; all other personnel involved with the FLSM/sellers have, at most, dotted-line relationships. In the new model, these relationships may be quite different: Some sellers may be dotted-line to the FLSM-KAM/SAM/GAM; some support personnel may have solid-line relationships.

Example 1: The KAM/SAM/GAM manages sellers, dedicated to the customer, from individual businesses/product groups. These sellers report solid-line to their businesses/product groups, but dotted-line to the KAM/SAM/GAM.

Example 2: The GAM has global customer responsibility; sellers in various countries focus efforts exclusively on the GAM's customer. These sellers report solid-line to their country/geographic-region heads, but dotted-line to the GAM.

Example 3: The KAM/SAM/GAM has dedicated technical experts working with the customer. These personnel report solid-line to the KAM/SAM/GAM, but dotted-line to their functional specialties.

One healthcare sales leader explained the FLSM evolution at his firm:

> "The FLSM role is taking on a totally different orientation. We give our traditional FLSMs a geographic area with five to eight sales professionals. Those sellers call on hospitals in their geographic territories. But today, the FLSM role is giving way to account leaders [ALs]. ALs may have just a single (or very few) customer(s), and no direct reports. But they have access to several business/product-specific subject-matter experts. These FLSMs are less tied to geography, so I have a strategic account vice president [SAVP] who visits his customer up and down the entire West Coast. We even give these SAVPs P&L responsibility. We tell them: 'You need to grow the top line by X percent; reduce cost-to-serve by Y percent; and improve profitability by Z percent.' But we also tell them: 'You are empowered to make investments in your account.'
>
> "We also have enterprise-support managers. These people are responsible for two things: First: *Ease of doing business,* because crap happens on a daily basis—administrative snafus, pricing gets loaded incorrectly, clinicians need additional training, whatever. Second: They are responsible for the back-end—*use* stage—value realization. They make sure the customer uses our technology as designed, to maximize value. They also provide recommendations on how customers should change their practices to enhance value capture."

Summary

In this introductory Chapter 1, we assert that the FLSM job is the most important position in the salesforce, and one of the most important in the firm. Our reasoning is very straightforward: The firm requires sales revenues to make profits, survive and grow, enhance shareholder value. Securing revenues is the responsibility of sellers who are led, directed, and managed by FLSMs. This perspective is a paradigm shift in addressing sales management issues, and is clearly endorsed by the many sales leaders we interviewed.

The fundamental basis for FLSM importance is the boundary-spanning roles they occupy: *external*—between the firm and customers; *internal*—between the sales team and sales leaders/senior sales managers, corporate leaders, and many firm functions. Occupying these multiple boundary roles is critical for making sales—*close, design, ideate*—and for post-sales activities—*implement, use.* For the most part, FLSMs only periodically engage deeply in these activities. The FLSM's major job is to ensure sellers continually improve their abilities, and reach their performance targets.

We base our framework for becoming a successful FLSM on the *acumen* notion—acuity, astuteness, expertise, insight, intelligence, judgment, sagacity, sharpness, shrewdness, wisdom. The successful FLSM must possess six acumen types—*strategic, organizational, business, team building, resource, personal*. We spend the next six chapters exploring these acumen dimensions. They are the six core pillars of successful FLSM performance.

Though they may use different terms, sales leaders support our position. From two sales leaders:

> "What makes you a high-performing FLSM? Really, it is just based on the core values, being organized, being here, being vocal, and [being] positive."

> "The FLSM role is to *model, express*, and *reinforce* behavior. FLSMs are expected to role-model what they ask from their teams. They should reinforce that by seeing all the good happenings in their teams, and calling it out when they see it. Indeed, recognition and rewards are crucial."

Notwithstanding our development of six fundamental pillars—acumen dimensions—for the FLSM job, we must dispel any notion that these requirements are somehow fixed and immutable. The environment evolves; customers evolve; competitors evolve; firm strategy evolves; sales organizations evolve; success requirements evolve. FLSMs who are very successful today may be less successful tomorrow if they do not continually improve their skill sets and up their games. A biotech sales leader shared his perspective:

> "FLSMs must be flexible and open to change. What makes a successful FLSM in our firm is not so much what they bring to the job. It's more about what they learn when they are in the job. How they are able to grow and develop from the feedback they receive. Not only should FLSMs be open to feedback, they must seek feedback, and be good and willing learners."

We believe the following chapters lay out, for the first time, a comprehensive framework for FLSM success. We did not develop this framework out of whole cloth. Rather, we took what sales leaders and successful FLSMs told us, and built upon their perspectives. Indeed, their comments and observations are dotted throughout the pages. Though there may seem to be nothing particularly revolutionary in the coming chapters, we believe *The Front-Line Sales Manager—Field General* offers a different and novel perspective to most common practice. We hope readers agree, and find useful information to improve FLSM, sales-team, and overall sales-organization performance in their firms.

Endnotes

1. Compared to the literature on individual salespeople, published work on front-line sales managers is sparse and, for the most part, rather dated. Recent papers about sales managers, each bemoaning the paucity of published research but including extensive literature reviews, are: D.R. Deete-Schmelz, D.J. Goebel, K.N. Kennedy, "What Are the Characteristics of an Effective Sales Manager? An Exploratory Study Comparing Salesperson and Sales Manager Perspectives," *Journal of Personal Selling & Sales Management*, 28 (Winter 2008), pp. 7–20; R. Mehta, R. Anderson, K. Dubas, A.J. Dubinsky, S.S. Liu, "How Do Sales Managers Perceive Their Roles?" *Journal of Managerial Issues*, XI (Winter 1999), pp. 406–426.

2. Literature on boundary roles includes: D.W. Organ, "Linking Pins between Organizations and Environment," *Business Horizons*, 14 (December 1971), pp. 73–80; J.S. Adams, "The Structure and Dynamics of Behavior in Organizational Boundary Roles," in M. Dunnette (Ed.), *Handbook of Industrial and Organizational Psychology*, Chicago: Rand McNally, 1976, pp. 1175–1199; R.E. Speakman, "Influence and Information: An Exploratory Investigation of the Boundary Role Person's Basis of Power," *Academy of Management Journal*, 22 (1979), pp. 104–117; S.J. Lysonski and E.M. Johnson, "The Sales Manager as a Boundary Spanner: A Role Theory Analysis," *Journal of Personal Selling & Sales Management*, 3 (November 1983), pp. 8–21; J. Singh and G.K. Rhoads, "Boundary Role Ambiguity in Marketing-Oriented Positions: A Multidimensional, Multifaceted Operationalization," *Journal of Marketing Research*, 28 (August 1991), pp. 328–338; J. Singh, "Boundary Role Ambiguity: Facets, Determinants, and Impacts," *Journal of Marketing*, 57 (April 1993), pp. 11–31.

3. Throughout the book, we use the terms decision-making unit (DMU) and decision-making process (DMP). In all cases, we refer to purchasing decisions.

4. Regarding the internal-boundary-spanning nature of the FLSM's job: In a very real sense, the FLSM role is similar to that of the front-line supervisor (FLS) in a manufacturing plant. The FLS sits between factory management and factory workers. The FLS secures productivity performance by ensuring shop-floor workers implement actions required by manufacturing bosses. Although the FLS (typically a promoted shop-floor worker) has line authority, it may take considerable skill to secure *worker compliance*. F.J. Roethlisberger, "The Foreman: Master and Victim of Double Talk," *Harvard Business Review*, 23 (September 1945), pp. 283–298.

5. Regarding *no problem* (NP) opportunities, the core question suppliers must address is the following: What is the appropriate way to interface with customers and close sales? As price becomes increasingly important, winning suppliers will be low-cost leaders. Yet, field salesforces are expensive. Telesales is less expensive, but suppliers are increasingly making NP sales on the Internet, sometimes with personal interaction via *live-chat* systems. Outsourcing sales to third parties is another option. Correspondingly, many firms are transferring selling resources to LPS and EPS buying processes.

6. Theodore Levitt addressed this topic in T. Levitt, "After the Sales Is Over," *Harvard Business Review*, 61 (September–October 1983), pp. 87–93.

7. In many situations, especially for services, supplier and customer employees are in continuous contact.

8. Deete-Schmelz, Goebel, Kennedy *op. cit.* For an early study, A.J. Dubinsky and T.N. Ingram, "Important Front-Line Sales Management Qualifications: What Sales Executives Think," *Journal of Personal Selling & Sales Management*, 3 (May 1983), pp. 18–25. Also, H. Spencer, "Salesmen and Sales Managers," *California Management Review*, XV (Fall 1972), pp. 98–105.

9. *Merriam-Webster Collegiate Dictionary* (11th ed.).

10. This section focuses on *business acumen* as it concerns working with customers. Some elements of the FLSM job, like justification for allocating resources, concern the firm. We wrap such issues into *resource acumen*.

Chapter 2

Strategic Acumen

The essence of **strategic acumen** is the ability to think and act strategically. Front-line sales managers (FLSMs) must understand the various competitive and environmental pressures that business organizations—firm, customers, competitors—face. FLSMs must develop and exercise *strategic acumen* so they can enhance relationships with customers, and address the five customer-related tectonic shifts we identified in the Prologue—*greater access to information, increased competitive intensity, cloud technology, new buyers, greater procurement professionalism.*

In many cases, the firm approaches these challenges by evolving the nature of customer relationships from simply being a *vendor* (although that may be quite appropriate in many cases) to becoming a *valued supplier*, or even a *partner*—by forming a strategic relationship. As one sales leader told us:

> "We are really trying to work on having a strategic relationship with our customers, and be seen more as consultants than opportunists. Our clients range from very large and complex, to smaller and straightforward, so engaging with them strategically really depends on the type of customer they are."

There are two broad arenas where FLSMs should exercise strategic acumen—*internal* at the firm, *external* at customers. Specifically, strategic acumen comprises five dimensions—*company resonance, customer resonance, individual value propositions, integrating multiple value propositions, district leadership*—Figure 2.1. All these strategic acumen dimensions come together as FLSMs and their sellers strive to deliver the value customers desire, and set the stage for earning revenues.

Figure 2.1 Strategic Acumen Dimensions

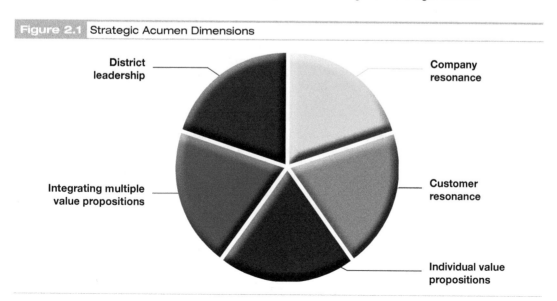

District leadership

Company resonance

Integrating multiple value propositions

Customer resonance

Individual value propositions

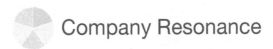 Company Resonance

Mike Smith was a seller for Wongyang Inc., a midsize Asia-based company in the household-textiles industry. Mike was responsible for sales of a new line of furniture-covering fabrics—*Repel*—in the Eastern U.S. Mike reported to Jack Dempsey, sales vice president for the *Repel* line. In addition to Mike, Jack had four other direct reports, each responsible for a geographically defined sales territory. The *Repel* business unit was one of several in Wongyang's corporate portfolio.

At 9:30 a.m. one spring morning, Mike arrived at Furnzen, a successful fast-growing furniture manufacturer with a broad product line, for a previously scheduled appointment. While waiting at Furnzen's offices, he noticed a well-dressed woman who seemed to know her way around. Mike, who was often complimented on his interpersonal skills, introduced himself:

"Good morning, my name is Mike Smith, I'm a sales representative for Wongyang. I'm responsible for *Repel*, our new line of household fabrics."

The woman responded:

"Good to meet you. I'm Hillary Stein, Furnzen's CEO. Wongyang's name has been coming up quite a lot at some recent industry meetings, but I don't know much about your firm, except they're in household textiles. I'd like to know Wongyang's overall strategy to see if they're a firm with which we could do business. I only have a couple of minutes, so can you give me the elevator speech on Wongyang?"

Mike hesitated:

"Well, I've only been with the firm a little over one year, and haven't really been exposed to the breadth of Wongyang's product line, or the firm's future directions. But I can tell you all about *Repel*. It has many positive characteristics, and I think it can be a great product for Furnzen. First of all—"

Hillary Stein cut Mike off:

"That's okay, you can talk to design and procurement about that. I have to be going; I'm already late for a meeting."

Mike sensed that Ms. Stein was disappointed by the interaction.

What do you think? Quite clearly, Mike's proposed message about the great features/benefits of *Repel* was mismatched to his audience—CEO Hillary Stein. Mike was totally unable to answer Stein's question about Wongyang's overall strategy. Who knows what could have followed from a competent answer—favored entrée for Mike into Furnzen's management structure, opportunities for other Wongyang businesses....

Indeed, how often does a salesperson get to present to the CEO of a customer, current or potential? And isn't it reasonable that a CEO would be interested in long-term supplier potential by getting a sense of its overall strategy?

■ **Question for FLSM readers: How well would your salespeople have responded in Mike's situation?**
■ **Question for salesperson readers: How well would you have responded? Has your management prepared you to respond to the sort of question Hillary Stein posed to Mike?**

So, what went wrong in Mike Smith's case? Who is to blame for Mike's lack of knowledge about Wongyang? What deficiency should be corrected? How?

Company resonance—the ability to articulate firm direction and strategy, and make them resonate with customers—is the baseline for strategic acumen—*table stakes*. The heart of strategic acumen is to take the fruits of such firm-wide decisions—typically made at high organizational levels, and/or in different organizational functions—and make them resonate with customers. Success in this task leads customers to purchase, both now and in the future.

Notwithstanding the importance of this aspect of the job, FLSMs must be discerning about strategic direction reaching them from the top of the organization. Hopefully, these approaches are well-thought-through. But FLSMs must be on the lookout for the *strategy du jour*, and protect sellers from wasting time on improperly thought-through and short-lived initiatives.

One FLSM related the practice of her current and potential customers:

> **"They very closely investigate their vendors. They want to see what we have in our product development pipeline, what we're investing in for the future. They want to know if we're a solid company going forward that they want to do business with."**

For FLSMs to be able to think and act strategically and coach sellers to behave appropriately—not like Mike Smith—requires good understanding of pressures on firms, and the strategies firms use to create, and take advantage of, opportunities. *The Front-Line Sales Manager – Field General* is not meant to function as a boot camp on corporate strategy, so we do not delve too deeply into these issues. Rather, we present simple, yet powerful, frameworks on competitive and environmental pressures, and firm strategy making. These frameworks have long pedigrees, and can prove very useful to FLSMs and their sellers.

Competitive pressures embrace a *competitive structure framework* comprising *current direct competitors, new direct entrants, indirect competitors, supply-chain competitors (suppliers, buyers)*. **Environmental pressures** are well captured by the *PESTLE framework*:

P — *political*
E — *economic*
S — *sociocultural*
T — *technological*
L — *legal/regulatory*
E — *environmental (physical)*

We diagram both sets of pressures in Figure 2.2, and describe them in more detail in Appendix 5.

But knowing about competitive and environmental pressures is only one part of *company resonance*; understanding how firms chart direction through such increasingly turbulent waters is quite another. For this purpose, we offer a fivefold *growth-strategy framework* for FLSMs to organize their thoughts about the future. FLSMs can also use this framework to question sales leaders about where the firm is headed, and help sellers construct their *elevator speeches*. Framework components are *vision, mission, growth path, timing of entry, market/market-segment strategy*—detailed in Appendix 6.

Let us be very clear. The Mike Smith vignette opening this section illustrates strategic acumen *failure* at a very basic level. Quite simply, Mike knew nothing about his firm, Wongyang, beyond his direct sales responsibilities for *Repel*. What sorts of things did Hillary Stein want to know? Stein is CEO of a successful fast-growing potential customer. She specifically asked about Wongyang's strategy. She wanted some idea of what Wongyang is doing now, and its future direction. Will Wongyang be around for the long run? What sorts of products can Furnzen expect to see going forward? What is Wongyang's perspective on quality? Would it be worthwhile for Furnzen to invest in bringing Wongyang on board as a new supplier? Stein would have been satisfied with an elevator

Figure 2.2 Competitive Structure and PESTLE Frameworks

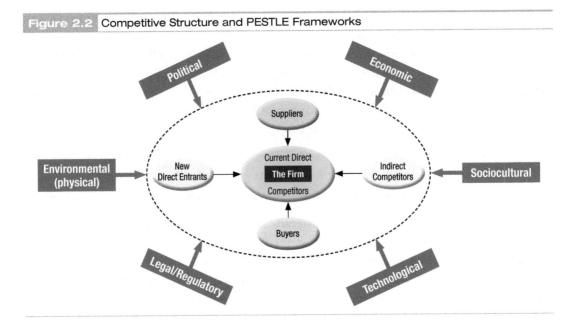

speech crafted from the growth-strategy framework in Appendix 6. Is this company resonance failure Mike's fault? Hardly. Certainly, FLSM Jack Dempsey was not doing his job, but perhaps the problem is even more systemic—senior management failure to clearly articulate firm direction and/or failure to educate and train FLSMs. But more on that in Chapter 8.

Note that the growth-strategy framework's starting point is *vision*, a statement of higher purpose for the corporation and individual businesses. Senior management has the responsibility to articulate vision. Sales leaders are responsible for ensuring that vision statements are well understood by the entire salesforce. FLSMs have the specific responsibility for seller competence. One sales leader at a healthcare firm reported on his firm's perspective:

> "We are a purpose-driven organization. Our CEO tells us: 'At the heart of it, we are people caring for people.' I think that is very resonant. The organization's mantra is good medicine is good business. We instill a sense of care/responsibility: Is this solution good for both, the patient and the hospital? The salesforce in the rare disease space is an excellent place for sales reps who genuinely want to serve others and make their living out of it. We rely on our FLSMs to make this happen."

Firms often pair vision with a corporate *values* statement—customer focus, environmental friendliness, integrity, respect for individuals. Taken together, *vision and values* provide a solid sense of what the firm is all about. But just stating vision and values is insufficient. Senior management must also ensure that organization members live by, and can articulate, them. The following response we heard from several sales managers and other executives over the years is unacceptable:

> "Vision and values? Yes, our top management developed these a couple years ago. I think they're on our website. Somewhere I have a card where they're printed out. Here it is; I don't actually remember them myself."

Corporations are realizing that many employees have insufficient knowledge about what their firms stand for. Eli Lilly, Verizon, and others have instituted internal branding programs designed to educate employees about their organizations. These programs incorporate mass communications techniques as well as face-to-face communications in small group sessions. The salesforce is a critical audience for these initiatives.

Several sales leaders strongly supported the requirement that FLSMs and sellers be able to clearly articulate firm strategy. One asserted:

> "We insist that our sellers can articulate the firm's future direction. For the most part, customers want to know where we are headed. Shall we be around for the long run? What can they expect from us? We invest in our customers, but they also invest time and effort in us, their suppliers. They want to make sure that investment is not wasted."

The sales leader at a global information technology (IT) firm, responsible for the Americas, focused on the critical role of FLSMs in driving this message to their sellers:

> "The CEO, and the board, and the executive-leadership team, and even guys in my role have the glossy laminates. When we're standing up in front of 500 people presenting these slides, it all sounds glorious. But the FLSMs are the ones who have to take that information and make it real. They are the ones who say: 'This is what we are about. This is why it matters. This is why it helps us win.' They become the cultural-ministry officers for the company."

This sales leader's language is telling—*cultural-ministry officers*. Essentially, he is saying FLSMs have the core responsibility to understand the direction senior leaders are setting for the firm, then ensure each and every seller can articulate that direction to customers.

In this regard, another sales leader focused on the FLSM's coaching role:

> "The best FLSMs focus on connecting daily tasks with corporate goals and strategy. They communicate the big picture, and show how that makes a difference. These FLSMs make their sellers feel more connected to the company and its mission. They recognize when an individual sales rep makes a particular contribution, or aligns activities with corporate strategy."

The sales leader continued:

> "For example, one of our corporate strategies is placing instruments to gain a foothold at diagnostic labs where we don't have a presence. One of Jack X's reps made such a placement. Rather than just congratulate the rep on the phone, Jack made it into a big deal. He waited for a team meeting, then congratulated the rep. He emphasized the detailed work to earn customer trust, and how the placement would lead to future business. He told the team how the rep's efforts directly implemented the corporate strategy, and furthered the firm's ambitions. Correspondingly, he told the team that, although making sales of our cash-cow products was still important, that was not the firm's future direction—seller efforts should link directly to the corporate strategy."

The FLSM must take the firm's various strategic thrusts and ensure they become second nature to sellers. Hillary Stein asked Mike Smith for his Wongyang elevator speech. Certainly, each FLSM should make sure all sellers can deliver that speech, as and when appropriate. The FLSM should also make sure their sellers possess significant depth of firm understanding overall. The company resonance dimension of strategic acumen is a core FLSM responsibility.

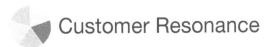 ## Customer Resonance

FLSMs and their sellers must know where their firms are headed—company resonance. Sellers, coached by FLSMs, must also know where their customers are headed—**customer resonance**. Deep understanding of both firm and customers is increasingly important for linking firm and customers in selling/buying agreements.

In the previous section, we discussed the competitive structure and PESTLE frameworks for understanding competitive and environmental pressures the firm faces—Figure 2.2 and Appendix 5. But for FLSMs, a focus on their own firms is insufficient. FLSMs must also ensure their sellers are competent to figure out the implications of competitive and environmental pressures *on their customers*. Indeed, the ability to assess these implications is an important element of strategic acumen. FLSMs can use the competitive structure and PESTLE frameworks to coach sellers to develop a comparable level of insight about the pressures their customers face, as they have about their own firms.

In addition to focusing on the present-day situation for current and potential customers, sellers/FLSMs should also gain insight into these customers' future directions. As one sales leader emphasized:

> "I want my FLSMs to look at the broad environment, not just their own industry
> environment. I don't want them focused on buggy whips and transatlantic liners, when
> the entire industry may be headed for extinction. I want them to look through their
> customers to their customers' customers. I want them to show customers what their
> futures are going to be."

Previously, we presented a fivefold growth-strategy framework—Appendix 6—*vision, mission, growth path, timing of entry, market/market-segment strategy*. FLSMs should coach sellers to use this (or a comparable) framework to gain insight into their customers' directions for growth.

More specifically, customers address various markets. They segment those markets, then make decisions about which market segments to target. They develop *positioning* statements for target segments—*customer targets, competitor targets, value proposition, reasons to believe*—Appendix 6—then formulate both *market-facing* and *firm-facing* implementation plans. Sellers may use this *positioning framework* to gain insight into how customers approach their markets/market segments.

Customer resonance focuses on making the firm's value propositions, typically developed for multiple customers in various market segments, *come alive* for individual customers. Of course, FLSMs/sellers can be successful only if they possess deep insight into individual customers, and the competitors they face at those customers. But customers (and competitors) are moving targets. Each current/potential customer has its own specific needs, priorities, problems, pain points that firm value propositions may address. These matters evolve over time, so the customer-insight journey never ends. Competitors also evolve their capabilities, resources, value propositions.

One FLSM whose firm sold into the banking industry was very clear about the evolutionary impact of how he and his sellers had to approach customers:

> **"The entire industry has definitely changed. When I started in this business it was all about educating the customer or the prospect on what he could get. Now they are all educated; they know what is out there. Today, when you go to sell them something, you have to have a strategic reason for them to do business with you, and spend their money."**

To serve individual customers well, FLSMs/sellers should be very familiar with both competitive and environmental pressures each customer faces, their growth strategies, and how they address their markets. Only sufficiently deep knowledge will enable sellers to operate effectively when customers face *extended problem solving* (EPS) and *limited problem solving* (LPS) buying processes; and *ideate* and *design*, respectively, are the appropriate selling processes.

The goal for FLSMs should be to ensure their sellers are competent to have the following sort of experience:

Lily King, one of your sellers, was at LaGuardia airport (New York), sitting on the Boston Shuttle, waiting to take off. Just before the aircraft doors closed, a woman boarded the plane and took the adjacent seat. Lily quickly learned the woman was CEO of one of her major customers. Lily had never previously met the CEO, and took the opportunity to strike up a conversation with her.

One hour or so later, the aircraft landed at Boston's Logan airport; Lily bid farewell to the CEO and went on her way. A senior customer executive met the CEO and asked about her flight. The CEO replied: "I just had a most interesting conversation with Lily King; she's a salesperson at supplier XYZ with responsibility for our firm. Lily seems to have a good relationship with some of our people, and has a great handle on our options for the sorts of products she is selling. I was amazed at her degree of customer resonance—how much she knew about us, our customers, our competitors, and the issues we and the rest of the industry are facing. Lily raised some topics I had not even thought about; the conversation gave me a couple of directions for things we should take a look at. Can you get hold of Lily and set up a meeting with her and an appropriate senior executive from XYZ? I want to pursue some of these topics."

- ■ **Question for FLSM readers: Could your sellers generate this sort of positive response by employing customer resonance in a similar situation? It's a simple question, but a very powerful one. Clearly, Lily King's FLSM is far ahead of Jack Dempsey (Mike Smith's FLSM—opening vignette) on coaching what their sellers need to know for high-level conversations with customer executives.**
- ■ **Question for salesperson readers: Would you secure the same sort of reaction Lily earned if you had been in a similar situation? How good a job is your FLSM doing in preparing you for the sort of conversation Lily had with her customer's CEO?**

One sales leader we interviewed confirmed the importance of the abilities Lily King brought to the conversation with the customer's CEO:

> **"Our best FLSMs constantly make it their business, and the business of their sellers, to know more than the customer knows. We want them to bring some deep industry perspective to the table, so they're really creating value for customers."**

This sort of deep insight can lead to developing creative value propositions.

CASE STUDY | Konica Minolta

Konica Minolta (KM) provides copiers to corporations globally. Traditionally, KM's benefits/values focused on product attributes—*speeds and feeds*. Then, a KM account manager made an insightful observation. At current/potential customers, wastebaskets adjacent to copy machines were full of uncollected copies. At individual customers, KM audits revealed the actual amounts of wasted paper and ink; they were substantial. KM introduced a proprietary system that reduced copy waste by up to 60 percent.

Displaying great customer resonance, KM learned that in certain U.S. industries using high quantities of water in production processes—apparel, footwear—factories operated under capacity. The reason: These factories reached federally mandated ceilings on water use at less than full capacity. By introducing KM's copy-waste-reduction system, these customers convinced regulators they saved immense water quantities; they saved paper, and hence water used in paper production.

The result: Regulators allowed these firms to increase production. In addition to purchase savings on paper/toner, KM was able to calculate the precise economic benefit customers received from increased production/sales by installing KM copiers and the copy-waste-reduction system.

In some firms, top management takes the lead in identifying and evaluating environmental imperatives. Senior executives develop a *point of view* on industry evolution. Such points of view are valuable input into the FLSM's strategic acumen. The sales leader at a major Internet retailer told us:

> "We get very good information about industry direction from top management. Our CEO makes a practice of articulating a point of view about where the industry is headed. So, our FLSMs and their sellers don't go into customers saying: 'I'm here to help, tell me about your needs, problems/pain points.' Frankly, customers don't always know what they want. Of course, we always take what they say very seriously, but we lead with: 'This is our perspective on the industry, how it's evolving, how we think it affects you, and what we may be able to bring to the table.' This approach generates a very different sort of conversation, and one our sellers are very comfortable having. Customers are very responsive, and we have very deep discussions. Sometimes customers have a different perspective; in those cases, the give-and-take is great for building the relationship."

Relatedly, an important element of securing customer insight is the ability to read customer financial statements, and to make inferences about financial health and potential pain points. FLSMs should have sufficient financial acumen to examine line items on customer income statements and balance sheets, be able to understand how customers compare to their close competitors, and make hypotheses about problem areas.[1]

Although sellers naturally focus efforts on direct customers, at the end of the day, the firm is only successful if its customers are also successful. Hence, in many cases, FLSMs must push beyond the firm's strategy to understand and influence customer strategy. As one FLSM recounted:

> "I am also accountable for our customers' successes. This is a different customer engagement and discussion versus winning a deal. We want them to address their customer prospects without us in the room—doing the selling for both of us."

Strategic acumen has many facets. Certainly, the FLSM must have deep understanding of the firm's future direction—*company resonance*. But to do a first-rate job in the marketplace, securing customers and defeating competitors, FLSMs must also possess, and coach their sellers to possess, good *customer resonance* also.

One FLSM's approach to leading, directing, and managing his district combined strong elements of both company and customer resonance.

> "I have a five-year plan for my district. I know everything in my company's business portfolio, and what is coming down the road. I tell my sellers: 'In those off-times, you should be doing the Johnny Appleseed thing—plan for future purchases.' They should develop future opportunities for two or even three years out. They should not just show up for deals that are about to happen.
>
> "Customers like someone who has a great plan, who is looking out for them down the road versus only focused on real-time opportunities. I really stress to my team: 'If you're going to really be a partner for your customers, you have to be part of their strategic planning process. You have to know what they are looking at in the next four to five years.'"

We have just discussed two types of resonance—*company* and *customer*. Both resonances are extremely important, but FLSMs earn real payoff when they integrate the two. Integration occurs when the firm can influence the customer's strategy, and vice versa. Most likely this sort of interaction occurs in situations where the customer is a major account. As an Oracle sales leader commented:

> "[Product development plans are] the sort of conversation the customer wants to have. Can they influence where Oracle is taking its software? If the answer is yes, and there's a good feeling about managing the risk, and they're going to get return on investment in value, that's actually a pretty easy sell."[2]

 ## Individual Value Propositions

The marketing department is typically responsible for developing market/market-segment strategies and implementation plans—Appendix 6. The *positioning statement*—with *customer targets, competitor targets, value proposition, reasons to believe*—is the heart of the market-segment strategy; the **value proposition** is the heart of positioning. Marketers must not only construct positioning statements and value propositions, they must also communicate them to the salesforce. Sellers and FLSMs employ value propositions to secure customer agreements to purchase/influence purchase of firm products/services. FLSMs must address several issues concerning value propositions, discussed next.

From General to Specific Value Propositions

Each market segment comprises many individual customers. Hence, marketing-developed value propositions are, of necessity, broad and general. FLSMs/sellers must make the translation from *general* to *specific*, so these value propositions come alive at individual customers.

One sales leader strongly emphasized the importance of this translation:

> "FLSMs are the bridge between what is happening in the C-Suite, and customer needs. It's very easy for those of us who don't interact with customers every day to lose perspective about their concerns, problems, requirements. Things that make all kinds of sense at a general aggregated level do not always make sense for an individual customer!"

Bottom line: General-to-specific translation of value propositions is a critical element of strategic acumen.

Evolving Value Propositions

The translation of *general* to *specific* value propositions becomes more challenging when, for whatever reason, value propositions arriving from marketing evolve and change. FLSMs must adjust to these new value propositions, then make the necessary *general* to *specific* translations. The FLSM's difficulty is compounded when sellers must position these new value propositions to different customer decision-making units (DMUs), operating with different decision-making processes (DMPs). (Of course, some sellers may not be able to make the transition to new value propositions; we defer this topic to Chapter 5.)

The sales leader for a high-tech firm described the challenge:

> "For many years, we have sold our products/services to corporate information technology [IT] departments. We developed good competitive advantage, with a strong value proposition that has evolved consistently over time. But now our customer target is shifting from IT into the business units. These new customers require quite different value propositions, but IT is still in the picture. So, we have to satisfy both the business units and IT. What makes things even more difficult is that satisfying the business units can put significant extra work on corporate IT, so that really challenges our FLSMs and their sellers."

So, evolving value propositions are a challenge but, on the other hand, FLSMs/sellers may be able to offer a second-order value proposition: the expectation of a continuous stream of innovations, each providing specific (and different) values. A successful FLSM explained:

> "In our industry, many customers seek competitive advantage by being first-to-market with new products. We are an important supplier and our R&D department does a great job of putting out product improvements on a fairly regular basis. Of course, there are always copycats that follow us with similar products at lower prices. But I have a couple of major customers that stick with me, even when competitor prices are lower and the products have become comparable. The reason is very simple: They get the first look at our new products. That gives them a head start in their markets. And that's great additional value for them."

We illustrate FLSM challenges of evolving value propositions via a deep dive into social networking service LinkedIn.

CASE STUDY LinkedIn

LinkedIn is a *disruptive innovator*, a game-changer in human resource management. Essentially, LinkedIn offers firms the ability to search for talent (like executive search firms do), rather than simply post job opportunities and wait for potential candidates to find them. LinkedIn's challenge was to monetize its free-for-members platform, now comprising more than 500 million members. In its search for revenues, LinkedIn developed increasingly complex value propositions, initially based on selling advertising space on its platform. LinkedIn earns revenues in three ways—hire, market, sell:

- Hire—*Talent Solutions*. LinkedIn helps with recruiting by offering corporations tools to access its platform to advertise job openings.
- Market—*Marketing Solutions*. LinkedIn provides brand-building opportunities for firms. LinkedIn earns revenues via advertising.
- Sell—*Sales Solutions*. LinkedIn helps customers better interact with their customers. LinkedIn earns revenues via subscriptions.

LinkedIn earns Talent Solutions revenues on a per-use basis. The more strategic Marketing Solutions and Sales Solutions revenues derive from annual contracts. Although LinkedIn also secures revenues from individual members who upgrade to premium status, its FLSMs and sellers mostly drive company revenues from customer firms. LinkedIn also offers various tools for specific hiring challenges, like securing 500 nurses for a medical facility in Texas.

In the initial stages of LinkedIn's search for revenues, sellers focused on *Talent Solutions*, essentially helping solve short-term tactical recruiting-and-hiring problems. After a couple of years, LinkedIn shifted to a broader strategic focus—*Marketing Solutions*, *Sales Solutions*. This evolution placed significant stress on its FLSMs' strategic acumen to absorb the evolutionary thinking developed at LinkedIn corporate, and to implement the new customer value propositions with their sellers. Said one LinkedIn FLSM:

> "Our conversation used to be about selling advertising space—tactical buys to solve hiring issues. We morphed into strategic conversation, where we are not merely solving narrow human resource [HR] challenges, but a business issue where decision makers are in marketing and branding organizations."

More recently, LinkedIn's selling effort has become more consultative, as FLSMs work with their sellers to act more as customer partners. The conversation has changed, from posting *help-wanted* advertisements, to offering advice to HR departments on how to identify and persuade top people to join their organizations. Essentially, LinkedIn has taken the executive search model and massively increased the scale of operations. Simultaneously, LinkedIn sellers face diverse competition from firms like CareerBuilder, Glassdoor, Dice. Dealing with several transitions in the corporate value proposition, while simultaneously fending off competitors, requires FLSMs to possess significant strategic acumen. One LinkedIn sales leader provided an example of the sort of problem FLSMs and their sellers now solve for customers:

> "Suppose a grocery chain wanted to hire a top high-tech person to develop and implement an online grocery operation. Why would a top-tech person choose to work for a grocery? Because it would be interesting to work for that grocery, and building that online platform. But they wouldn't think to work for a grocer in the first place, without LinkedIn. Moreover, how do you, as a grocer, attract that top talent? Talent acquisition and HR is a brand recognition thing, moving the whole discussion to marketing as well. How do they know you as a brand of a great company to work for? So, it is really helping bridge those two gaps: Get all recruiters on the platform, and get all the jobs on the platform, and change that discussion, and helping those customers with their business challenges versus just recruiting. It is not only a hiring discussion, but a strategic-level discussion."

LinkedIn's corporate evolution from recruiting/hiring to strategic discussions with customers has placed a heavy burden on FLSMs/sellers—they do things today they were not doing just a few years previously. The way LinkedIn works with customers is changing because of this mind-shift. LinkedIn helped define how industries can recruit. This immense shift in value propositions required significant strategic acumen by FLSMs.

Evolving Value Proposition Types

Value propositions offered to customer organizations fall into two general categories:

- **Functional**—enables the customer organization to do something it couldn't previously do, or do it better—satisfy a need, address a priority, solve a problem, mitigate a pain point.

- **Economic**—delivers some form of economic benefit—reduce costs and/or investment, secure more favorable credit terms, earn higher prices.

As noted previously, a central FLSM role is to make the translation from marketing-developed, broadscale, general value propositions into specific customer-based value propositions. Functional value propositions continue to be important for customers but, increasingly, customers today are seeking economic value. Hence, suppliers must transition functional value propositions to deliver economic value.

Marty Homlish—former CEO, SAP Global Marketing—succinctly explained the transformation SAP made from *functional* value to *economic* value:

> "We used to talk about successful implementation like this: 'Customer XYZ implemented SAP Supply-Chain Management. They had to do it in 100 days, but they went live in 99 days and only had one critical crisis [i.e., *functional* value].' But that was not the issue. The real story was: 'Customer XYZ implemented SAP Supply-Chain Management. As a result, it reduced its on-hand inventory from 2.8 months' supply to 2.1 months', and its on-the-water inventory from one month to two weeks. And customer XYZ saved $500 million [i.e., *economic* value].'"[3]

Cost/investment savings may represent an important element of economic value, but a singular focus on costs and investment is too narrow. The core value FLSMs and sellers offer customers should be increased return on investment (ROI). As one sales leader put it:

> "In today's market, you have to have deep knowledge about customer needs. The FLSM must inject true value into the message. It's not just about reducing customer costs. We have to be able to talk about increasing customer ROI, so increased revenues are also part of the story. The FLSM has to augment our sellers' capabilities so they can be very effective doing that."

This shift in *economic* value propositions from a focus on *cost/investment savings* to *revenue generation* has important implications for FLSMs/sellers. When the firm focuses on *economic* value via cost/investment savings, the core focus of customer-insight efforts is on customer operations—Figure 2.3. But when *economic* value delivery concerns customer revenue enhancement, the focus shifts to the firm's customer's customers—Figure 2.4.

Figure 2.3 Cost and Investment Savings: Focus of Customer-Insight Efforts

Firm ⟶ Customer

Figure 2.4 Revenue Enhancement: Focus of Customer-Insight Efforts

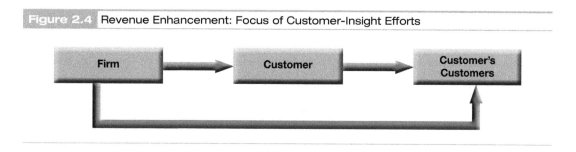

To clarify this important point:

$$ROI = Profit/Investment = (Revenues - Costs)/Investment$$

This equation demonstrates that FLSMs and their sellers have essentially three ways to enhance customer ROI:

- Increase customer revenues
- Reduce customer costs
- Reduce customer investment

One sales leader shared the approach his FLSMs use:

"We add value by smoking out quality issues and by providing better quality products. For the hospital, this means better patient outcomes, leading to higher reimbursement rates [increased revenues]."

In our interviews, we identified several cases of suppliers developing value propositions focused on increasing customer revenues. Each case had significant implications for FLSM and seller strategic acumen. We pursue revenue enhancement efforts with two case studies: SAP and Cisco. As these examples illustrate, this customer-revenue-focused evolution has ushered in entirely new DMUs and DMPs for customer procurement.

CASE STUDY SAP

SAP's traditional value proposition concerns making customer operations more efficient. But SAP has realized the power of the ROI formula. Rather than focusing only on increasing customer efficiency by reducing customer costs and/or investments, SAP has enhanced its value proposition by turning its attention to its customers' marketing activities, thus helping its customers enhance their revenues by improving their service to their own customers.

One important SAP customer operates a major sports arena in a U.S. urban center. This customer developed new objectives for increasing revenues by enhancing its customer service. As SAP evolved its generalized value proposition, the SAP FLSM employed strategic acumen to work with the local seller to translate that value proposition into benefits/values that resonated with the customer. Working with the seller, the FLSM identified three areas of attack—before, during, and after games:

- Before the game. **After sports fans purchase tickets, they receive email offers for merchandise that can be delivered before the game or picked up at the arena on game day; information on the best driving routes, parking tips, and public transportation options/schedules from their homes; and promotions for an arena tour and discount offers for refreshments at the game.**
- During the game. **Sport fans receive text message updates on queue length, wait time, and travel time from their seats to various refreshment locations.**
- After the game. **The fans receive real-time guidance for a safe, fast exit from the arena and discount offers for future games and related events.**

The FLSM translated SAP's generalized new value proposition for addressing customer marketing issues into specific, significant value for enhancing the sports-arena customer's marketing efforts.

The customer target was also very different from those in SAP's traditional model. When SAP's *economic* value proposition focused on efficiency and cost savings related to customer operations—*functional* values—key decision makers/influencers were IT personnel. But when the value proposition shifted to a focus on increasing customer revenues, key players in the customer's DMU became marketing, customer service, finance.

The high-tech industry is facing similar DMU and DMP evolution as in the medical-diagnostics industry and the SAP sports-arena illustration: Previously, corporate IT held the budgets and decision-making authority/responsibility for corporate-wide procurement decisions; today, that authority/responsibility is shifting to business units. As a leading IT corporation, Cisco must ensure its field resources are fluent in helping customers use its technology to achieve business goals.

CASE STUDY | Cisco

Cisco is best known for products that power the Internet; Cisco sellers have done a good job of building relationships with customer IT personnel, and providing technology solutions that drive business outcomes. One such solution is Cisco's video-conferencing technology *Telepresence*, which helps organizations be more cost- and time-efficient: Rather than have employees fly to meetings and amass large travel, hotel, and entertainment expenses, they simply sign into *Telepresence* for conducting/joining meetings. Cisco practices what it preaches: Famously, then CEO John Chambers made over 200 CEO calls in a single month using *Telepresence*. But a Cisco FLSM and his local seller used strategic acumen not only to improve customer efficiency, but also to enhance customer revenue generation.

The customer was a major retail bank that provided specialist services to retail customers. Traditionally, various specialists—subject-matter experts (SMEs)—traveled from branch to branch, meeting customers for prearranged appointments. The bank faced several problems with this approach: Customers would not show up for appointments made several days earlier: Missed appointments added to travel time created significant inefficiencies in SMEs' schedules. Also, as a rule, SMEs did not visit remote branch locations.

Cisco introduced the *Telepresence* solution. All SMEs would be housed in a central location (no travel); each branch would have at least one video-conferencing room where customers could interface with the desired SME. No need to make an appointment—minimal wait time. The number of SME-customer interactions would increase; hence, revenues would increase also.

The purchasing DMU was totally different from the traditional Cisco sale. Included were senior business leaders, marketing/customer service executives, SMEs, branch management, bank architects.

In this new model, not only does Cisco address different customer needs as it enters customer-business units, it faces different competitors. Suppose a specific business unit is addressing an HR coaching/training challenge; Cisco may believe it can add value and secure efficiencies via *Telepresence*, but will face new competitors that traditionally compete in the HR coaching/training space. Cisco's FLSMs/sellers must learn the required business outcomes/key imperatives for success in this new arena (for Cisco), so Cisco can secure differential advantage. In short: Cisco FLSMs/sellers must take core value propositions and make them real at target customers—the key is strategic acumen.

As a Cisco executive noted:

> **"The FLSM looms large in making sure we reach the right buyers and influencers. Buying decisions for tech are moving out of IT and into the functions. We must be fluent in helping customers *use* technology to achieve their own business goals."**

Value for Individuals

Listen up. Customer organizations do not make purchase decisions. *Individuals* within customer organizations make purchase decisions! Furthermore, we would be naïve to assume the only values involved in procurement decisions were those concerning the supplier and customer organizations. Certainly (in addition to salary) individual sellers benefit personally from sales success—bonuses, commissions. Similarly, procurement personnel may earn bonuses for securing products/services at prices below criterion levels.

A comparable straightforward calculus does not generally apply when personal benefits/values cross the interorganizational boundary between supplier and customer. It is generally permissible for buyers (and sellers) to receive **psychological value**—*affiliation, reassurance, recognition, security, status*—but many functional and economic benefits are strictly prohibited (and often illegal). At most, a buyer may accept small holiday gifts, meals, trips. Indeed, some firms (Walmart) strictly prohibit any form of gift whatsoever.

Regardless, customer executives do have personal organizational goals they must reach, over and above a general requirement to make the best procurement decisions for their organizations. One FLSM was quite specific about this issue:

> "I insist that my sellers work hard to identify specific goals that customer executives are striving to meet—specifically their MBOs [management by objectives]. Of course, MBOs tend to change from year to year, but knowing them gives us the ability to modify our value propositions to make them more beneficial for these decision makers/influencers."

Equally important, lack of understanding of, or concern for, psychological value can get in the way of making a sale. Consider what we heard from an FLSM at a major technology firm:

> "We knew that our products were just what the customer wanted, but my seller couldn't discern why we weren't making any progress. My seller made presentations to senior customer executives; they were all on board, so it was baffling. It took us a while to figure out that the final decision had been delegated to a low-level manager. This guy was adamantly against our solution; he kept finding ways to delay. We couldn't figure it out since the senior guys had more or less given him the go-ahead. Ultimately, we realized this decision maker was worried about his job; he thought our product would make him obsolete. So, my seller and I just kept visiting—every single week for several months—and educating him. Eventually, our efforts paid off and he signed the contract. It was a long slog and took lots of patience."

In this situation, neither the seller nor the FLSM initially understood the importance of reassurance and security to the ultimate decision maker.

The bottom line: In addition to providing value to customer organizations, FLSMs/sellers must make value propositions resonate with individual decision makers/influencers.

Integrating Multiple Value Propositions

FLSMs must make the translation from marketing-developed *general* value propositions to finer-grained value propositions directed at *specific* customers. Marketing's value propositions are central elements in market-segment strategies; developing value propositions for specific customers is a central element of strategic acumen that successful FLSMs possess. In many cases, the firm develops different market-segment strategies relatively independently, often in separate organizational units— product groups/ business units.

Yet, two or more product/market-segment strategies may interact if segment definitions from separate product groups/business units overlap. Resolving such interactions and figuring out implications for value propositions frequently do not occur within marketing organizations. Rather, resolution takes place within the salesforce. Someone must sort through the various interactions/ overlaps among different market-segment strategies, and develop an **integrated value proposition** to take to customers. If sales leaders/senior sales managers have performed this integration, the FLSM and seller team have the execution job. If this integration has not occurred, the FLSM must perform it.

Developing value propositions for individual customers is one thing; integrating disparate value propositions from multiple product groups/business units into a coherent offer is quite another. Essentially, FLSMs must make the transition from several individual value propositions developed by marketers—*marketing-developed*—to an integrated *sales-driven* value proposition.

One FLSM at a global healthcare firm described his failed effort to integrate a series of product-based value propositions into a sales-driven value proposition:

> "Our firm is very well positioned in the hospital market. We have a highly respected corporate brand and some great product brands. Many of our products are used in hospital operating rooms. I worked with several senior executives to develop an integrated value proposition. We would place several individual products together in a bundled offer for these operating rooms. Over and above our great product quality, hospitals would receive considerable value from one-stop shopping, including better inventory management. I tested this idea with several hospital customers; they were quite enthusiastic. Unfortunately, this initiative did not get off the ground; I couldn't get the product organizations to shave their prices, so we could make an offer that customers would accept."

In a second healthcare example, the firm sold both *razors and razor blades*—actually, infusion pumps and disposable tubing. The sales leader described the problem, and how one of his FLSMs addressed it:

> "The firm's core business is selling infusion pumps—capital hardware. We also sell two types of disposable tubing: medicated—almost part of pump acquisition; nonmedicated—generic tubing that is available from several suppliers.
>
> "The firm tries to lump pump and tubing sales together. A complication is that we have separate organizational units for capital equipment and disposables. We have cases

where both *capital* and *disposables* teams want to get their deals done, but they are not brought together. Then we make the pump sale, but it's really tough to sell generic tubing on its own.

"So, we developed a value statement that integrates pump and tubing. But, we have to *slow down* the capital team to let the disposable guys get in front of the customer. To make this occur, I tell the capital guys what happened with another account, and give them concrete examples of why they should slow down, and why we should bring these two pieces together. If that works, we secure both one-time revenues from pump sales, and recurring revenues from tubing."

Another FLSM was more successful at integrating multiple, seemingly disparate, value propositions. He explained his approach for dealing with pressure from customers for lower prices:

"Although we had great products, from time to time customers pressed me hard on price for a particular product. Typically, these requests came at the end of the month, or the end of the quarter. I suspect this pattern is much the same for many salespeople. I had pricing authority, but I would never go along with straight price reductions. I told customers the following: 'I cannot reduce price, but I will trade price for market share. If you increase your order for product X, I can give you a price reduction on product Y.' Sometimes customers accepted this sort of deal; sometimes they did not. But I don't believe I lost many sales by holding firm on price."

These examples concern bundling products to develop more attractive customer offers. Valuable though such efforts are, FLSMs can go far beyond these value-added approaches to develop totally new seller-driven value propositions that bring immense value to the firm and customers. We illustrate this approach at Philips Medical Systems.

CASE STUDY | Philips Medical Systems

Prior to passage of the Affordable Care Act, hospitals/hospital systems focused procurement efforts on reducing prices for capital goods and on myriad cost efficiencies. Philips Medical Systems (PMS) and other suppliers were caught in a downward price spiral. One PMS sales leader explained the background and PMS's shift in focus:

"In the last several years, customers wanted low-hanging fruit—pricing and getting cost out of their organizations—via materials management. Vendors just beat up on each other. We don't have a lot left to provide, so we are looking at customer efficiency and improving effectiveness of customers' healthcare delivery models—improving their Affordable Care Act scorecards that affect the global payments they receive. We may look at some systemic hospital problems like hospital-acquired infections (HAIs). Everyone knows hospitals can reduce HAI rates with better compliance to handwashing protocols. If we can help with something like that, it's a huge customer value.

"When we address a specific macro-problem for a hospital system, we often focus on a solution set, not typically a single product. Rather, we offer a suite of products, or products wrapped in services, like consulting, or a new financial model involving shared risk. We may bring in noncompetitor partners to round out the solution to solve the customer's problem."

Diagnostics—hardware/machines, software/reagents—are a significant cost center for hospital organizations. Historically, in most cases, different areas within the hospital were responsible for purchasing hardware that best fit their specific area needs. Departments often did not talk to each other regarding their procurement activities. As a result, a typical hospital system might possess many different diagnostic machines from many different vendors, making it difficult to keep track of hardware investments. Lack of transparency on such significant capital outlays was a serious problem. Relatedly, opportunities for technological innovation are extremely fertile; the risk of acquiring a new diagnostic machine that would shortly become obsolete is nontrivial.

Enter a PMS FLSM. Recognizing how this ubiquitous hospital-industry problem affected a specific hospital system in his district, the FLSM identified an opportunity. He worked with the local account manager and his own boss (regional sales manager) to scope out the situation. The FLSM built an extended PMS team to take a series of product-based, generalized value propositions developed in marketing, and formulated a specific value proposition for Georgia Regents Medical Center (GRMC). Specifically, the PMS team defined a model to improve patient outcomes and reduce hospital costs via new technologies, operations planning, and support and consulting services—making the sale via the ideate selling process, corresponding with GRMC's buying process of extended problem solving (EPS).

The starting point for the entire set of activities that concluded with the PMS/GRMC multimillion-dollar deal was a conversation between the local PMS account manager and GRMC's CEO. Essentially, the CEO said:

> **"My vision is for a different relationship between hospitals and their suppliers. I believe there must be changes in how these two sets of organizations work together. Your firm has great technology, but we have to go beyond that to ultimately deliver better healthcare at lower costs."**

The challenge for PMS was figuring out how to leverage its technological competence in a way that could meet the CEO's goal. PMS addressed this challenge by forming a long-term partnership that provided multiple GRMC sites (including a 632-bed medical center, cancer center, children's hospital) with a comprehensive range of consulting and maintenance services, advanced medical technologies, and operational performance planning—at a predetermined monthly price. As part of the deal, PMS agreed to give GRMC rapid access to new equipment and new technologies, educational resources, imaging systems, patient monitoring, clinical informatics solutions, lighting, and consumer products.

One of PMS's core technologies is patient monitoring. Patient monitoring and linkages to IT are growing ever more complex. Specific concerns include interfacing of monitoring devices with the hospital's electronic medical records systems, easier patient monitoring, diagnosing, reducing hospital risks and costs, better treatment—as well as managing the entire system. At the same time, PMS seeks safer ways to manage patients, to reduce costs by standardizing customer solutions, and building expertise in IT.

The PMS FLSM drove the process that led to the contract. He demonstrated superb strategic acumen—*customer resonance* in understanding GRMC's strategic situation, and *company resonance* in knowing his firm's ability to address GRMC's issues. (The FLSM also demonstrated great *business acumen*—Chapter 4—in driving the project to a successful conclusion.) But we should not forget how this process was initiated: The *local PMS account manager* had a conversation with GRMC's CEO.

The message from this case study is very clear: It is insufficient for the FLSM to possess great strategic acumen. The FLSM must ensure that sellers on the team *also* possess good strategic acumen, so they, at the very least, can spot an opportunity to develop integrated value propositions for their customers.

As customers evolve, the FLSM functions as a universal joint, linking the two domains—firm and customer—across the interorganizational boundary. Critical to the linking equation is the FLSM's ability to integrate multiple value propositions to create deals for the firm and its customers. Let us make no mistake: PMS has an enviable product line driven by technological prowess. But the PMS/GRMC deal would never have happened without the FLSM and his seller. The PMS case study demonstrates the immense value an FLSM can bring to the firm and its customers by exercising great strategic acumen.

District Leadership[4]

Arguably, the most important arena for FLSMs to exercise strategic acumen is **district leadership**. This dimension focuses on the FLSM's direct area of responsibility/authority—the sales district. (For KAMs/SAMs/GAMs, the *district* may comprise a single customer.) The FLSM's job is to meet district quota by allocating resources against opportunities.

Typically, firms assign FLSMs authority/responsibility for securing revenues from some set of current/potential customers, mostly (but not necessarily) defined by geography—frequently called sales districts. The firm provides each FLSM with one major resource—seller FTEs (full-time equivalents). The FLSM's job is to meld chosen sellers, each assigned to a sales territory, into an effective sales team by exercising *team-building acumen*—Chapter 5. Successful FLSMs meet sales-district quotas; their sellers meet sales-territory quotas. District performance contributes to achieving firm objectives.

Sales-territory design is directly related to the sales revenue opportunity available for each seller. The extent to which sellers are successful in their territories depends on how hard and smart they work. An important element in seller motivation is the sales quota. From discussion with interviewees, we learned that sales-territory design and sales-quota setting were intimately related in many firms. Hence, in this section, we focus on both territory design and quota setting. These elements relate directly to resource-allocation decisions at the district level. (We defer discussion of individual seller issues to Chapter 5, Team-Building Acumen.)

Given a set of sales territories, a team of sellers, and district and individual seller quotas, the FLSM must direct seller efforts to identify and execute on revenue opportunities. Success in these efforts drives district- and territory-quota attainment. This leadership role requires significant strategic acumen.

But this assertion raises two important questions:

- Who designs sales territories?
- Who sets sales-territory quotas?

Territory Design and Quota Setting

Within the sales district, key variables for affecting district performance are sales-territory design and quota setting. We found considerable variation across firms in their approaches to these decisions—*centralization* versus *decentralization*. Generally, firms employing centralized processes—the majority in our sample—made both territory-design and FLSM/seller quota-setting decisions at high organizational levels—no questions asked. (The starting point for quota setting was often a corporate finance group.) The few more-decentralized firms also made some of these decisions at high organizational levels, but allowed some local autonomy.

Centralized Decision Making. A strong *centralized* norm seemed to apply for both territory-design and quota-setting decisions—*corporate knows best!* Most firms designed sales territories at the top of the sales organization—FLSMs had no role whatsoever. Furthermore, these firms mostly assigned sales quotas by territory—FLSM quotas were frequently the sum of individual territory quotas.[5]

The centralization perspective was best captured by one FLSM at a national software firm:

"Corporate designs sales territories and sets quotas. The quotas just come down from on high—sometimes I think there's a little man behind the curtain who comes up with them. I have no influence whatsoever; I assume there's a team at corporate that knows what it's doing—running algorithms, designing territories, setting quotas. I don't even get to pass out the quotas."

This particular FLSM was very content with centralized territory design and quota setting:

"I think this quota system is great. At my previous software firm, the FLSMs sliced and diced their district quotas as they saw fit. I always thought this was too subjective. Of course, neither my guys nor I are necessarily happy with our quotas, but I have a good deal of trust in the anonymity of our system."

Decentralized Decision Making. In a minority of firms in our sample, we found equally strong decentralized cultures for both territory-design and quota-setting decisions. Two FLSMs told us their situations:

"In my group, I am accountable for my results; I have absolute authority to do what it takes to hit that number. Of course, I run these decisions by senior management, but I make the final calls. If I had the goals but not the authority, it would make for a very unfriendly environment."

"I absolutely have a significant role in territory design. Opportunities come and go, so I am free, with my boss's approval, to make adjustments to territory boundaries—modify a territory boundary here and there, shift one or more current/potential customers from one sales territory to another."

Other FLSMs had the ability to allocate territory quotas:

"As far as quotas are concerned, I have a district quota; I divide this quota up for my sellers/territories."

"I own the overall number for my team; that doesn't change. But I can spread out that number how I feel is appropriate, based on opportunities, based on growth, based on penetration, based on number of available customers, users versus nonusers. Essentially, my sellers and I look at three things—size of the prize, degree of difficulty, and time to close."

Centralized/Decentralized Decision Making. In other firms, the FLSMs we interviewed had the ability to make marginal territory-design changes and/or marginal quota adjustments. Such changes may escape the corporate radar in strongly centralized organizations, following the *frog-in-hot-water* axiom.[6] Conditions for making local changes include a sympathetic manager and a successful track record of meeting district quota by the FLSM.

We found a marginal impact of FLSMs in setting their sales quotas. Mostly, FLSM district quotas were set in stone, but one FLSM discussed his quota:

> "This year, there's not much tweaking. But in other years, I've secured a greater change. We're not talking 10 percent, more like 3, 4, or 5 percent."

Although most territory quotas were also set at the top of the organization, some FLSMs had the ability to modify individual seller quotas. Some FLSMs worked with sympathetic bosses to make minor changes in territory quotas. One FLSM told us:

> "My quota and quotas for all my guys come from the sales VP. I assume he is parceling out his number to the various districts and sales territories. There is no discussion about my number, and sales-territory quotas are pretty firm. But if I see something that is off, I discuss this with my RSM [regional sales manager]. If I can convince him, we make the change—a little higher quota here, a little lower quota there. But my district quota doesn't change."

Decentralized versus Centralized Decision Making. Believers in decentralization allow FLSMs considerable autonomy to run their districts. Based on territory performance and other feedback, managerial experience, and opportunity distribution, the FLSM modifies territory design by shifting boundaries. The FLSM also sets territory quotas—by dividing up the district quota.

The general arguments in favor of decentralization are twofold:

- FLSMs have the responsibility for achieving district sales results; they should also have the authority to make resource-allocation decisions—territory design, quota setting—as they see fit.

- FLSMs are closer to the action than managers at more senior levels; hence, territory-design and quota-setting decisions are best made at the local level.

The major argument for centralization is also twofold:

- *Corporate knows best.* Sales leaders have access to far more data, analytic power, and consulting advice than any FLSM can possibly have.

- Leading, directing, and managing a sales district is a really tough job—removing the territory-design and quota-setting decisions allows FLSMs more time to do their jobs.

Notwithstanding the various arguments in favor of/against decentralized/centralized decision making for territory design and quota setting, most interviewees revealed that their firms employed centralized systems. Hence, we can view the FLSM's task in leading the district (most cases) as *constrained strategy making*.

Constrained Strategy Making

As noted above, FLSMs may have little ability to influence either sales-territory design or sales quotas. Nonetheless, FLSMs make many other resource-allocation decisions in their sales districts—which products/services should receive selling effort (overall and at individual customers) and which market segments to target. FLSMs must also assess whether to pursue current versus potential customers; likely short-term revenues versus more long-run customer investments; small versus medium versus large customers. FLSMs must also decide what additional resources to request from the firm—customer service, marketing, subject-matter experts, sales leaders/senior sales managers, even top management for involvement with specific customers. Certainly, FLSMs make these judgments based on what is best for customers, and what is best for the firm in driving quota attainment. One FLSM in educational software described his approach:

> "You have to break up customers into the *buyers* and the *liars*, or A, B, C segments, and prioritize them; you have to focus. Each territory in my region is quite different from the others, so the issues that concern customers are quite different also. To make our efforts effective, we have strategic plans for each of our account executives, for their territories. Then, they have account plans; within those account plans they have opportunity plans that we track on a regular basis."

In their boundary-role positions, FLSMs face many pressures from within their own firms—product managers, marketing executives, sales leaders/senior sales managers. Sometimes these pressures are reflected in FLSM and seller objectives/quotas. As one FLSM told us:

> "I have to balance customer requirements with imperatives that come down from corporate. And I have to guide my team, so we achieve the *right* balance between old and new business."

One global high-tech FLSM described the pressure he faced from a senior executive in one of his firm's businesses:

> "Historically, the firm implemented a policy that required extensive testing of all new products, to be as sure as we possibly could that all bugs had been eliminated. This process was very time consuming, but we had earned a great reputation for delivering fail-safe new products.
>
> "Our new CEO had a different view. As a way of securing faster sales growth, he believed we should launch new products faster. Then we would receive customer feedback if product modifications were required. Of course, we still did very extensive testing, but we no longer went that extra mile to be totally sure.
>
> "In one of our businesses, R&D developed a new product that promised significant advantages for many customers. Senior executives wanted the salesforce to place this new product at a marquee customer to provide credibility for a broader selling effort. They selected one of my customers.
>
> "Frankly, I was very nervous. If I made the sale, the customer would use the product in a critical part of its operations. A failure would have severe consequences. So, I pushed back and refused. I was not at all popular in that business, but I had the authority to make that decision. As it turned out, senior business executives were successful in persuading another FLSM to sell the product to his customer. Installation went fine, but a few months later the product failed. The customer was furious, and the FLSM was fired!"

The bottom line: In a perfect world (as many would view the situation), FLSMs would have authority over important strategic issues like territory design and sales-quota setting. But, for many FLSMs, the world is not perfect. Regardless, there are many other areas in *leading the district* where strategic decision making is critical. To be successful in these areas, FLSMs must possess good strategic acumen.

Strategic Change: Exploring Strategic Acumen

So far in this chapter, we have presented the five core dimensions of strategic acumen—*company resonance, customer resonance, individual value propositions, integrating multiple value propositions, district leadership*. Now we turn our attention to specific situations where change is a major driver of firm and/or customer behavior.

For FLSMs, strategic acumen is always important, but it's most important when things change. Earlier in this chapter, we discussed competitive and environmental pressures. These pressures are important drivers of firm and customer evolution, and strategic change for business organizations large and small. In this section, we illustrate FLSM's exercise of strategic acumen in three different scenarios—Figure 2.5—major firm change, minor customer change (B); minor firm change, major customer change (C); major change for both firm and customer (D).[7]

Figure 2.5 Strategic Change Framework

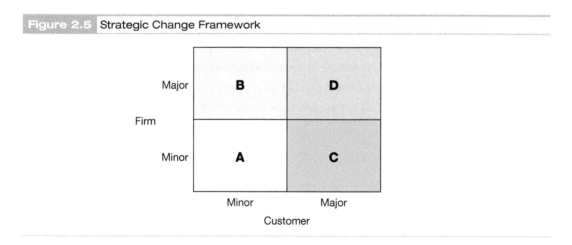

Major Firm Change, Minor Customer Change (B)

In this scenario, regardless of competitor and/or environmental pressures, customer needs are relatively stable. But the firm makes a major strategic change, so as to provide enhanced customer value and gain differential advantage. Indeed, customers, operating in a traditional manner, may not even realize they have unsatisfied needs, problems, pain points that require addressing. Nonetheless, the firm's newly developed value proposition aims to improve customer performance.

In such situations, new value propositions frequently require sales approaches to different customer decision makers/influencers. Indeed, sometimes, traditional decision-making unit (DMU) members reject (and/or try to sabotage) supplier innovations. We saw this earlier in the chapter when the low-level buyer was concerned about his job.

Not only may DMU membership change, so also may the purchasing decision-making process (DMP). Necessarily, FLSM and seller actions must be quite different from traditional approaches. Such shifts require significant strategic acumen. One firm we interviewed went through such a strategic evolution. The sales leader told us:

> "We've operated in the retail display space for many years; traditionally, display design was the core competence. We answered RFPs, gave good service performance, and had great customer relationships. At fast-moving-consumer-goods [FMCG] firms, marketing and branding held the budgets—they didn't focus much on cost; we did just fine. But when these firms realized display costs were rather high, procurement got involved and our margins shrank.
>
> "So, we have developed a multiproduct/multimanufacturer display solution for retailers; we get deeply involved in the supply chain. We may go to, say, a General Mills and propose a *baking-center* display for Publix or Safeway, for various General Mills products; or a single display for products from several different manufacturers. We don't just focus on the display, we purchase products and deliver fully loaded pallets [displays] direct to stores. We take care of the entire fulfillment process with a turnkey operation. From the retailer's perspective, our approach is a great resource saver—a one-invoice solution. And for FMCG firms, we manage the entire process, and free up working capital.
>
> "But to make this new system work can be pretty complex, because sometimes there are nine different vendors per display. We have one value proposition for retailers, and a quite different value proposition for FMCG firms. We rely on our FLSMs to make these new value propositions resonate with our customers. We are addressing new buyers and new influencers; at FMCG firms, it could be product and brand managers, logistics, finance. The salesforce is taking the initiative—the seller role is now a *complex solution provider*. FLSMs are leading the charge. Our broader end-to-end solution gets us deep into the supply chain, and helps fight procurement's attempt to break our offer apart and commoditize it. We have made a major strategic shift; FLSMs are modeling the new behaviors for our sellers. We have been very successful."

We note several key points from this example:

- The multiproduct/multimanufacturer display is a significant innovation in the retail display industry, and a major strategic change for this supplier. The display offers both FMCG firms and retailers significantly enhanced value versus the traditional system.

- Although macro-customers—FMCG firms—are the same, micro-customers—decision makers/ influencers—are quite different.

- The firm's innovation lives and dies on the backs of FLSMs. FLSMs must truly understand the new system, and articulate its value to their sellers.

- FLSMs/sellers must explain the new system to customers, and convince them the innovation will deliver promised value.

- If FLSMs do not possess sufficient strategic acumen, the innovation fails.

A second illustration relates to Philips Medical Systems (PMS), discussed earlier in the chapter. The FLSM picks up the story:

> "In patient monitoring, we've been through several years of fierce price competition. Each major supplier has cut prices to win business, but we're essentially at the end of the road on that strategy; we can't go down any further. So, with one big hospital system, we decided to innovate to make this customer more efficient and effective, and to reduce their costs. They were in deep trouble, and had no idea how to move forward.
>
> "All hospitals buy lots of patient-monitoring devices [PMDs], but procurement has been fragmented and uncoordinated. Essentially, hospitals do not know where their PMDs are. Some are in use, some are on shelves in storage closets, some are with discharged patients. Of course, this problem is exacerbated when hospitals are brought together in new hospital combinations.
>
> "We have good internal systems for inventory management and control, so we innovated by adapting these systems for one major-hospital-system customer. We worked with them to audit their PMD inventory, tracking down all their PMDs—different models, different technologies, demo products—by serial number. This hospital system can now make more efficient use of current inventory, and avoid unnecessary capital investment for new PMDs. Going forward, the hospital system can be more efficient in procurement, now that it has a much better handle on its inventory.
>
> "For PMS, this effort was a major service innovation—taking our internal processes and reworking them. For the hospital system, it was a relatively minor change in how it handled inventory, but brought high efficiencies. At some level, PMS may sell more PMDs when hospitals are inefficient buyers, so this innovation was a long-term investment in customer stability/effectiveness."

A key factor for the retail display firm was a new value proposition. The supplier shifted from offering individual displays to the multiproduct/multimanufacturer display. The ability to articulate the value associated with this strategic change was critical for FLSMs and their sellers. Regardless, as the PMS illustration shows, a major strategic change in value proposition may *not* require a newly developed product/service but, rather, the reframing of an existing product/service in a form that provides a compelling value proposition.

Recall our earlier discussion of SAP's evolution from value propositions based on *functional* value to value propositions based on *economic* value. The requirement for FLSMs and their sellers was not to introduce new products/services to customers, but to reframe what SAP already did. The challenge was to restate SAP's offer in terms of *economic* value—saving $500 million, in that example—rather than *functional* value—implementing a service.

When the firm makes a major change, but change at the customer is relatively minor, the firm will be successful only if FLSMs possess good strategic acumen so they and their sellers can effectively communicate the new value proposition.

Minor Firm Change, Major Customer Change (C)

In the previous section, the retail display firm developed a new value proposition to address needs of which customers were essentially unaware. The firm successfully innovated the multiproduct/multimanufacturer display solution to secure differential advantage. FLSMs used their strategic acumen to execute the new strategy. But what happens if customer needs change, but the firm does not evolve its product/service offerings to satisfy those evolving needs? We can predict significant problems.

FLSMs and their sellers have the responsibility to secure sales revenues. But, to be effective over time, they must also understand the various competitive and environmental pressures facing their customers. They must be clear about customers' evolving strategies and, consequently, their needs, priorities, problems, pain points. Of course, responsibility for developing new products/services typically lies elsewhere in the firm, most likely with some combination of top management, marketing, R&D.

Managers occupying these positions should take note of their FLSM's strategic acumen. If they fail to do so, disaster may occur. The following example supplied by an FLSM at a U.S. technology firm is a cautionary tale:

> "Last year our firm's results were not good, and this year isn't looking any better. The basic problem is that we've been slow to transform. We have not sufficiently listened to what customers say. We have not absorbed their feedback and incorporated it into our product development cycle. So, we have not created products that really fit their needs. Right now, we do not have enough to sell, so we're trying to piece together everything and anything. It's a very difficult position.
>
> "We have a situation where two or three large customers provide the firm with 60 percent of revenues. We built products based on what these guys asked us to build. We did not build products based on a vision of where we thought the industry was going. We did not lead the market, but some of our competitors did.
>
> "Some of our smaller customers are more innovative than the big guys. The smaller firms have fewer decision makers/influencers, have simpler decision processes, and are generally far less bureaucratic. Field sales passed their requirements up the ladder. But because of our focus on the large customers, we do not have products for our smaller, more innovative customers. What's even worse, the big guys are now trying to innovate and follow their smaller competitors, so we don't have good products for them either. Essentially, we're trying to force square pegs into round holes.
>
> "My biggest problem right now is with my guys. It's very frustrating for them. They work their accounts; they figure out what their customers are asking for, and literally, we almost do not have anything to sell to them—not good products, nor good solutions. My job has become very difficult."

In this firm, FLSMs did their jobs. They passed customer requirements into their organization, but nothing happened. Perhaps FLSMs didn't push hard enough. Regardless, what seems quite clear is that senior managers had tunnel vision. They were so focused on the firm's major customers, they did not comprehend the disruptive innovations caused by smaller customers.[8] Indeed, this sort of situation is the one time when listening to customers and satisfying their expressed needs is *not* the right way to go.

Stating this position sounds like heresy. Of course, the firm should not ignore its major customers, but it should, as noted earlier in the chapter, take a broader perspective by developing a *point of view* about the industry's future, so it can avoid the sort of situation we just described. Obviously, this sort of direction did not occur at the U.S. technology firm. But let's be clear about this failure: The problem was not with the FLSMs. They knew, and reported, what their smaller innovative customers were doing, but the firm did not respond. Senior management either didn't hear the message, or did hear, but decided, erroneously, to focus only on what the major current revenue drivers were requesting. Senior management has the responsibility to set FLSMs up for success, for translating firm-level value propositions into individual customer-focused value propositions that have a reasonable chance of success. Quite clearly, this did not occur. Rather, FLSMs were set up for failure.

This example raises many serious questions for corporations: How can FLSMs be set up for success? Not set up for failure? And particularly for this firm: How did this situation occur? Who was responsible? What should have occurred? How can the firm fix the problem? We address these issues in Part II.

Major Change for Both Firm and Customer (D)

Competitive and environmental pressures are so significant in many industries that strategic change is occurring at both customers and suppliers. Not only must FLSMs and sellers learn about, and integrate, the firm's new strategy and generalized value propositions, they must also contend with significant strategic change at customers.

Many of our interview firms faced situations where competitive and environmental pressures were driving significant evolution in customer needs. Fundamental to providing value for such customers is a requirement for deep knowledge of those evolving needs, priorities, problems, pain points, and the factors causing them. The FLSM must play a major role in ensuring individual sellers understand these external factors, and can address the impact on their customers. Speaking at a general level, one sales leader, whose firm supplies diagnostic products to the hospital industry, told us about the problems his customers were facing:

> "Hospital labs are in a jam: They are losing testing expertise as senior laboratory technicians retire, just as prevention becomes increasingly important and testing grows. A big pain point for our customers is downtime, whether that's for scheduled maintenance or for a broken instrument part. If test results are late, lab people get screamed at by the doctors—they don't like that! And it's bad for morale in the lab.
>
> "What we have to do is make sure we can satisfy customers' evolving needs. We must secure in-depth customer knowledge, then structure deals that make key influencers and decision makers happy, and secure internal approvals. Our general approach is to make the customer's process more streamlined—better workflow, integrated systems, multiple tests at the same time, and putting two technologies together to improve efficiency and save hospital labor costs. Customer needs have evolved drastically, and we have had to evolve our value proposition to keep pace. Our guys used to focus their selling effort on building relationships with laboratory personnel, and showing how our products

outperformed the competition. Relationships are still important, but today it's a whole different ballgame."

In such situations, where customer needs are evolving so significantly, the firm's value proposition must also evolve. The diagnostic supplier's sales leader is essentially saying that, historically, two types of value were important for making sales: *functional value*—how their products outperformed the competition; and *psychological value*—relationships with laboratory personnel, trust, comfort in doing business with a particular seller/supplier.

For this diagnostic supplier, these functional and psychological values are still important, but, as discussed earlier, successful value propositions now also concern *economic value*—more streamlined, better workflow, integrated systems, multiple tests at the same time, putting two technologies together to improve efficiency and save hospital labor costs. For many firms, this new focus on economic value is a major change for FLSMs and their sellers. FLSMs require deep strategic acumen to make this transition.

In medical diagnostics, laboratory directors no longer rule the roost. Hospital administrators are now central to many procurement processes. Even the physician role has shifted from decision maker to influencer. Hospitals have created *evaluation committees* that require potential vendors to complete an evaluation process before any contracts are signed. Consider what one sales leader told us:

> "The buying process has totally changed. In the past, we just had to convince the lab director and take the order over to purchasing—once in a while there'd be an RFP. Today, the lab director's influence continues to decline; there's more likely to be a full-scale, in-depth analysis, involving many more people, before the customer produces the RFP. Along with that evolution, the products are more complex. We used to sell products like a bench analyzer—a big laboratory might order 30 at a time—but now we could be dealing with an automated line; different automated modules; uncapping, recapping, sealing, and resealing samples; robotic arms for analyzing then replacing; and storage capabilities. We make it easy for the laboratory to locate a sample tube, rather than have a person spending their time looking for it. There's so much more instrument complexity than ever before. It's much more complex to write the RFP, and much more complex to respond to one."

The underlying driver in this industry is enormous cost pressures hospitals face. Procurement is a major place to seek cost savings. As a result, capital expenditures come under increased scrutiny; more people get involved, and these decisions are made at more senior levels in the hospital organization.

Change is also endemic in the financial services industry. The sales leader for a major bank talked about the problems his firm faced:

> "As a way of improving our position with major customers, we have developed a new approach to integrating our various product offerings, so we provide a new and quite different value proposition. This development is a major strategic change for us. But our customers are also facing tremendous environmental turbulence, so they are embarking on new directions, and also evolving their value propositions. These two value proposition changes place enormous pressure on our front-line managers to make our

new direction fit with our customers' new directions. This *fit* is different customer-by-customer, as each makes quite different decisions about their futures."

It's very clear that many firms are facing enormous changes. How to respond to those changes is a difficult supplier challenge. A core role for FLSMs is to help customers navigate the changes they face. As one sales leader put it:

"A key job for our FLSMs is to help customers craft a vision for them to steer by."

To be able to successfully execute this job requires FLSMs to possess great strategic acumen.

The Bosses Are Not Always Right

As illustrations in the previous section make clear, a key component of FLSM strategic acumen is the ability to make the translation from firm direction, set at the top of the corporation, into action by sellers when they interface with customers. But guess what? As we showed with the U.S. technology firm, top management does not always get it right.

If we step back a little, that's really not too surprising. FLSMs/sellers deal with specific customer needs on a day-to-day basis. Senior management necessarily makes general/broad-scope decisions that have implications for a whole set of customers, as well as for FLSMs/sellers. If senior managers have done a good job, their decisions make sense for most customers, most FLSMs, and most sellers, most of the time. But not all the time!

There will be situations when an FLSM, possessing good strategic acumen, knows it's time to push back against the corporate direction. Of course, FLSMs do not take such action lightly; indeed, they must be prepared to face the consequences if their *superior* insight proves to have been *inferior*. Consider the situation faced by an IBM FLSM in the early 2000s.

CASE STUDY | **IBM**

In the 1960s and 1970s, IBM became the world's dominant computer manufacturer by innovating and continually improving its mainframe products. As the 20th century concluded, in addition to its many other hardware and software products, IBM had a small (but growing) services business. Top IBM managers decided that services represented IBM's future; they believed sale of service contracts would drive hardware and software sales. Essentially, IBM was shifting its core value proposition, previously based on hardware and software, to services. The word went out from corporate to the salesforce: "Place your major selling efforts on securing revenues from services."

From the perspective of one FLSM working in the financial services industry, this corporate edict made no sense as a blanket requirement for all IBM customers. Together with his sales team, this FLSM had been working with a local account manager for more than a year to replace a bank customer's out-of-date servers with IBM mainframes. The FLSM believed a few months' more work could lead to significant mainframe revenues for IBM.

In this situation, the account manager reported dotted-line to the FLSM; her solid-line relationship was through a different organizational unit. The direct-report manager was so laser-focused on implementing the new corporate directive—services—he wanted to fire the account manager. She was not securing sufficient services revenue.

The FLSM pushed back hard. He successfully escalated the firing decision, retained the account manager, and kept the focus on mainframe sales. Within one year, IBM earned significant mainframe revenues from the bank, thoroughly justifying the FLSM's judgment.

Let us be very clear. We are not advocating that FLSMs ignore corporate edicts. Generally, such action is career-terminating behavior. What we are saying is that, no matter how valid and well-thought-through a particular corporate initiative may be, situations may occur where it does not make sense for a specific customer. Then is the time for strategic acumen to kick in, and for FLSMs to push back strongly.

Notwithstanding IBM senior management's ultimate reversal of the decision to fire the account manager, sometimes senior managers really do get it wrong! The resource-allocation decisions senior managers make, and the broadscale value propositions they develop for translation to specific customer firms, may not always be on target. To further the firm's interest, FLSMs must possess good strategic acumen.

Summary

Chapter 2 focuses on the first of six acumen dimensions effective FLSMs must possess—*strategic acumen*. The core of strategic acumen is the ability to think and act strategically. We present the *competitive structure* and *PESTLE* frameworks for competitive and environmental pressures to help FLSMs understand external factors. We also offer a vision, mission, growth path, timing of entry, market/market-segment *growth-strategy framework*, including the critical *positioning* model, that FLSMs can use to sharpen their strategic thinking. Using these frameworks, FLSMs can gain deep understanding of their own firm's future direction and those of the various customers FLSMs and their sellers address.

The chapter's core contribution is identification of five dimensions of strategic acumen—*company resonance, customer resonance, individual value propositions, integrating multiple value propositions, district leadership*. These dimensions demonstrate the depth and complexity of strategic acumen. Mastering each of these elements, then ensuring sellers are up to speed, is not a simple matter.

The chapter then explores strategic acumen in several quite different strategic situations concerning the firm and customers: major firm change, minor customer change; minor firm change, major customer change; major change for both firm and customer. In each scenario, we illustrate the focal FLSM's actions. As competitive and environmental pressures grow and external turbulence increases, both firm and customers will continue to evolve their strategies. Leading the district will continue to be highly challenging for FLSMs; good strategic acumen will become ever more essential.

Endnotes

1. For a tutorial on fundamental financial issues for marketing and sales management decisions—*Financial Analysis for Marketing Decisions* (video book), Bronxville, NY: Wessex Learning, 2014; *http://videobooks.wessexlearning.com/p/financial-analysis-for-marketing-decisions* (free preface, thereafter $9).

2. From N. Capon and G. Tubridy, *Sales Eats First*, Bronxville, NY: Wessex, 2011, p. 20.

3. Personal communication. Mr. Homlish is currently CEO AMP, Omnicom Group. Previously, Homlish was marketing chief at Sony (responsible for U.S. *PlayStation* launch), SAP, and Hewlett-Packard.

4. Throughout the book, we use the term *district* to specify the area of authority/responsibility for the FLSM. In many organizations, the FLSM has the title district sales manager (DSM). In other organizations, the title may be regional sales manager (RSM) or strategic/key/global account manager (SAM/KAM/GAM).

5. The once favored bottom-up/top-down approach to quota setting seems to have largely disappeared (at least among our interviewees) in favor of a more strictly top-down process.

6. Place a frog in a pan of boiling water; the frog jumps out. Place a frog in a pan of cold water and heat slowly; the frog is boiled alive.

7. We ignore the case of little strategic change for both firm and customer (A).

8. For background on disruptive innovations, C.M. Christensen, *The Innovator's Dilemma: When New Technologies Cause Great Firms to Fail*, Boston, MA: Harvard Business School Press, 1997.

Chapter 3

Organizational Acumen

New York City, March 15. Jake Jackson, investment banker, takes a telephone call from Russell Simpson, his representative in the Rocky Mountain states:

> Russell: "I just got out of a meeting in Denver with Bill Parks, CFO [chief financial officer] at Classic Beverages [CB]. I presented your ideas about CB's upcoming IPO [initial public offering] to Bill and his direct reports. They are all very excited. We really seem to have addressed all the questions they had when we visited together a few weeks ago."

> Jake: "Great work, Russell; sounds like we're in good shape to win the lead underwriter position on this IPO. When you visited CB, did you get to talk to CEO Norman Welch?"

> Russell: "Not this visit, but we exchanged waves across the dining room. Recall, we had a great meeting with Norman when you and I last visited CB together."

> Jake: "Right! But with the IPO coming up, I want to make absolutely sure we've got the top guy on board. Tell you what: Why don't you invite Norman to New York. I'll host him; have him meet some of our senior leaders to show we are dedicated to supporting CB. Why don't you suggest he comes for a Friday meeting, and invite his spouse as well? They can spend the weekend seeing the sights and taking in a Broadway show or two. Manhattan is great place to visit in the spring."

April 25. Jake Jackson takes a telephone call from Russell Simpson:

> Russell: "Jake, you really did a great job on the New York visit. I just met with Norman and Bill. Norman couldn't stop talking about his New York trip. He was really impressed by meeting the big bosses. He and his wife had a great time. Norman and Bill are totally committed to us."

June 15. Jake Jackson takes a telephone call from Russell Simpson:

> Russell: "Jake, I just got out of a meeting with Norman Welch. I'm afraid it's bad news. We're not going to get the IPO; they decided to go with Goldman."

> Jake: "What? How could that be? I thought we had this one in the bag. And that we'd sealed the deal with Norman's New York trip."

> Russell: "So did I. But it turns out there was a majority owner who didn't agree. Norman reported that he told her CB was all set to go with us, but she would not budge. Apparently, she'd had several meetings with Goldman people that Norman and Bill didn't know about; and they were, it seems, very persuasive. Of course, had we also met with her, we might have been able to convince her, but that didn't happen. Seems like we made a big mistake...."

In Chapter 2 we focused on *strategic acumen*. Strategic acumen concerns the ability of the front-line sales manager (FLSM) to think and act strategically, and to coach sellers to think strategically also.

We noted that some combination of competitive and environmental pressures, and evolving customer and firm strategies, is driving change in customer purchasing—decision-making units (DMUs) and decision-making processes (DMPs). Specifically, in two case studies—SAP's sports arena and Cisco's retail bank customers—we showed that purchase decision making moved out of information technology (IT) departments to involve retail distribution: SAP—marketing, customer service; Cisco—branch management. From these and other examples, it is evident that more and different executives are now taking part in the procurement decision-making process—adding complexity to the roles of FLSMs and their sellers.

Making sales to traditional customer decision makers/influencers is one thing. To identify and engage with new and evolving DMUs is quite another. The ability to accomplish this task competently is at the heart of **organizational acumen**—*developing understanding of customer organizations, so sellers communicate the right benefits/values to the right members of customer organizations, at the right time*. FLSMs must possess significant customer-mapping skills, so they and their sellers can scope out appropriate customer contacts and avoid two key errors:

- Type 1—Spending time with customer contacts who turn out to be unimportant—*time waster*.

- Type 2—Failing to identify potential important customer contacts—*missed opportunities*.

Both errors raise problems, but Type 2 errors are ultimately more serious. This is the core error that Russell Simpson and Jake Jackson made in the opening vignette; their investment banking firm lost the deal to be lead underwriter for an IPO. Misdiagnosis is a critical issue, and both errors are easy to make. But they can be avoided if FLSMs possess good organizational acumen. Two examples:

> *The contact lens seller waited to see an eye doctor. The receptionist asked how his products compared with the doctor's current purchases. The seller patiently answered all her questions and left with an order. What he did not know initially: The receptionist was the doctor's wife; she made most purchasing decisions.*

> *A man entered the largest Chevrolet dealership in West Texas, dirty and disheveled, looking like he'd just left an oil rig. The experienced salespeople passed him on to the rookie, who treated the customer well. It turned out the man was president of the region's largest oil-drilling firm; he purchased two pickups and three Corvettes—several thousand dollars in sales commissions for the rookie.*

Specifically, organizational acumen comprises six dimensions—*identify the right customer contacts; avoid irrelevant customer contacts; address the right customer contacts; plan interventions carefully; discover opportunities; build personal brand equity*—Figure 3.1.

Identifying the right customer contacts is the FLSM's first challenge in scoping out customer DMUs. That is where we commence.

Figure 3.1 Organizational Acumen Dimensions

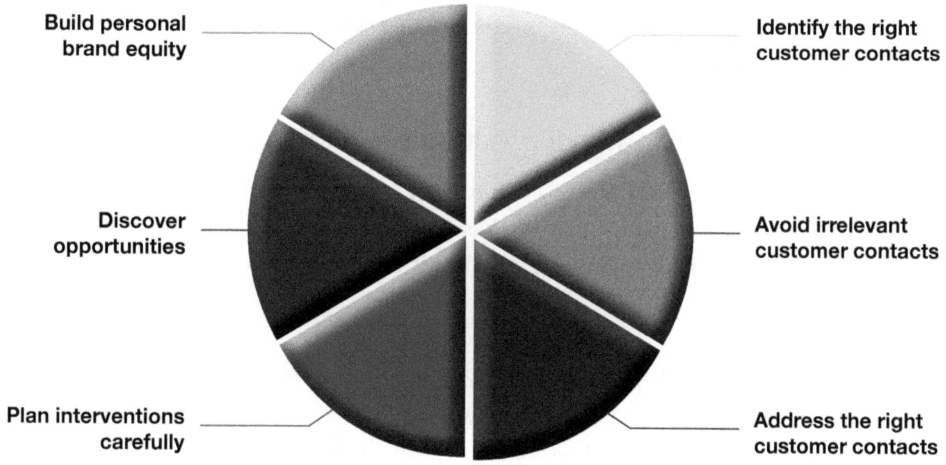

Build personal
brand equity

Identify the right
customer contacts

Discover
opportunities

Avoid irrelevant
customer contacts

Plan interventions
carefully

Address the right
customer contacts

 Identify the Right Customer Contacts

A core component of the FLSM job is helping sellers identify individuals who play meaningful roles in customer purchase decision making, regardless of organizational function, level, position, title. Failure to identify such individuals is a Type 2 error. A refrain we heard time and again in our research concerned evolving customer DMUs, and the important role FLSMs play in teasing out the current reality of buying-decision DMUs and DMPs. For a comprehensive set of relevant customer roles—Table 3.1.

Table 3.1 Relevant Customer Roles for Customer Purchase Decisions

Initiator	Recognizes a problem and sets the purchase process in motion.
Gatekeeper	Has the power to impede access to decision makers/influencers. Secretaries, administrative assistants, and purchasing agents often play this role.
Information provider	Provides the seller/FLSM with important information about the customer.
Coach	Helps the seller/FLSM navigate the customer organization; advises on how to address decision makers/influencers.
Specifier	Exercises influence indirectly by providing expertise like setting specifications.
Influencer	Often another business leader or colleague, this person's opinion is valued by the decision maker.
Champion/sponsor	Promotes the firm's interests; may have previous positive experiences and/or personal relationships with supplier personnel.
Spoiler	Tries to prevent purchase of firm products; may have unknown agenda—previous negative experience with the firm, relationship with competitive suppliers.
Decision maker	Has formal power to make the purchase decision; typically the budget holder.
Buyer	Has formal power to execute the purchase, like a purchasing agent.
User	May have little direct role in the purchase decision, but may have veto power. The factory worker/union official who says: "My guys will not work with that red stuff."

A common theme from our interviewees was that DMUs and DMPs are changing. These changes pose significant challenges for sellers; a key FLSM role is to employ *organizational acumen* to help sellers navigate customer organizations so they can identify and address the right contacts. Although we heard about many examples of DMU evolution, there were several broad-based reasons.

Shifting Locus of Decision-Making Authority—Horizontal

Perhaps the most common refrain was a *horizontal shift* in authority/responsibility for purchasing decisions. Customer executives who make purchase decisions were at essentially similar managerial levels as previous decision makers, but were now in different functions/departments, business units. Causes were various.

Evolution in Value Propositions. In Chapter 2, we discussed how firms are evolving their value propositions to address new opportunities as they grapple with competitive and environmental pressures. Recall the case study on Cisco's success with *Telepresence* at a retail bank, in which Cisco's sales leader told us:

> "The FLSM looms large in making sure we reach the right buyers and influencers. Buying decisions for tech are moving out of IT and into the functions. We must be fluent in helping customers use technology to achieve their own business goals."

Indeed, Cisco's bank customer's DMU (and DMP) for *Telepresence* was very different from a conventional Cisco sale. Traditionally, Cisco focused selling efforts on customer technical personnel, often with chief technology officer (CTO) titles, and other senior leaders in IT organizations. For the *Telepresence* sale, senior business leaders and marketing/customer service executives were critical. Bank branch managers also played an important role; after all, they had to agree to structural changes in their branches to accommodate video conferencing. Cisco also had to work with bank architects to install *Telepresence*. Bank specialists were another important constituency; the FLSM/seller had to ensure specialists were comfortable providing advice via videolink versus the traditional face-to-face approach.

Likewise, the DMU (and DMP) at SAP's sports arena customer for its service-based initiative was very different from tradition DMUs (SAP case study—Chapter 2). Historically, the customer's technology organization made purchase decisions on SAP products. The shift in focus to address sports fans put marketing and customer service executives in the driver's seat. The FLSM/seller had to navigate very different parts of the sports-arena organization to craft customer value propositions that would provide enhanced services that sports fans would value.

We heard a similar story from another FLSM in high tech. This FLSM explained his firm's experience:

> "I've been selling successfully for 15 years, and I can tell you, our largest challenge is right in front of us. We were traditionally a hardware firm; we sold (for want of a better word) appliances to customer IT organizations, and we did very, very well for a very long time. But, today, customers have shifted from the traditional hardware/appliance model to a *consumption model*—more service-type procurement. IT is slipping, and the overall IT budget is moving out of the IT organization into the lines of business.

"As an example, forever we sold security appliances into IT. Right now, because of the hacking situation—every day we hear about a breach—that's being moved out of IT. Now the budget's in legal, in compliance, or in HR [human resources]. Educating sellers on how to sell into lines of business is going to be critical for our long-term success."

In the foregoing examples, DMU (and DMP) changes occurred as a by-product of evolution in value propositions. But causality may run in the opposite direction. In Chapter 2, we explored the case of the retail display firm offering multiproduct/multimanufacturer displays. One driving rationale for this innovation was to reduce procurement's influence in selecting displays. Recall, that sales leader told us:

"We are addressing new buyers and new influencers; at FMCG [fast-moving consuming goods] firms it could be product and brand managers, logistics, and finance.... Our broader end-to-end solution gets us deep into the supply chain, and helps fight procurement's attempt to break our offer apart and commoditize it."

Product/Organizational Maturity. In some customer industries, new product introductions are difficult to understand/work with. Effective purchasing decisions can only be made by experts. Later, as the product evolves and becomes more user friendly, ordinary mortals can make competent procurement decisions. Example: When the only serious computer products were mainframes, technical competence was critical for making good purchasing decisions. Nowadays, by contrast, purchasing servers and personal computers is far simpler; technical expertise is far less important, and may even be irrelevant. One FLSM at a higher-education software firm provided a contemporary example:

"Ten years ago, we just worked with IT departments. Now, we spend more time with areas like enrollment management [e.g., recruiting, financial aid], finance, HR, than with IT. Because, that's where decisions are being made—by users or administrators for the business side. It's become easier for clients to adopt new technologies. Soft applications are not so much a burden on IT. Various departments are buying these *point solutions* without any IT involvement."

A companion FLSM expanded on this theme:

"No longer are chief information officers [CIOs] driving purchases. They're the guys who stop the sale! CIOs used to be our partners. Now they say: 'Hey, I don't have enough support staff; I don't want another product on my mantel.' So, we work with end users— admissions, recruiting, HR, CFOs, registrars—we build those relationships. When they put in a budget request, it carries much more weight."

One sales leader commented specifically on customers purchasing innovative products versus those customers buying mature products.

"In targeting individual customers, we make an important distinction about the customer's relationship to our product. If the product is an innovation, one set of people are important. On the other hand, if the product is more mature, decision makers and influencers are typically quite different. We also know that innovators and early adopters are willing to accept some pain to secure the new values we are offering, but the early majority and others are not."[1]

New Players. We noted in the Prologue to this book that one tectonic shift involved the greater skill and professionalism of procurement executives. Quite simply, the folks on the other side of the table are smarter, are better-trained, and have superior information and resources than purchasing executives of previous eras. We secured a good example regarding changes in customer executives involved in the buying process, and changes in the buying process itself, from an FLSM whose firm sold banking software:

> "There have been major personnel changes at leading banks; many of these heavy-hitters now work for middle-market banks where we play. They have brought in new systems and processes, and vendor management. Relationships have shifted from personal to something more sterile. Building relationships is still important, but much more difficult. No more buddying-up with the guy you used to work with. It's all about requests for information and requests for proposal. Figuring out the cast of characters is much more difficult. Our strong suit is great customer service, but it's more difficult to get traction when these new guys only want to talk about features, function, dollars, and not necessarily in that order."

Shifting Locus of Decision-Making Authority—Vertical

As a general rule, when corporations face financial difficulties, the locus of buying decisions often moves upward, especially for capital expenditures. Quite simply, top management wants a closer look. This practice was widespread in the 2008/2009 financial crisis and still continues at corporations in many industries.

One industry where this practice is currently occurring is hospitals—they face enormous cost pressures. The shift in procurement decisions has been exacerbated by the consolidation of individual hospitals into hospital systems, hence raising the ante on procurement inefficiencies. A medical-supply sales leader confirmed this assertion:

> "Ten to 15 years ago, most hospitals were stand-alone entities, responsible for delivering healthcare in their communities. But in the recent massive *industrialization*, many of these hospitals have been gobbled up into large, integrated delivery networks. The old days of selling to individual hospitals have disappeared. The customer is now the network. Procurement decisions are bigger, and are made at the network level. Two factors are driving this change—economy and risk. Economy: The networks believe they will get better deals by procuring for the entire system rather than hospital by hospital. (They're probably correct.) Risk: The networks want to standardize purchases to drive out variability: the less product/process variability, the less healthcare outcome variability. This industry evolution has totally changed our go-to-market strategy."

It's not so long ago that physicians made many hospital procurement decisions; now they are far less important in that role. Hospital administrators are central to the purchase process, as physicians have shifted from decision makers to influencers. Indeed, as we noted earlier, hospitals are creating *evaluation committees* that require potential vendors to complete an evaluation process before any contracts are signed.

We revisit what the sales leader from a hospital-diagnostics supplier told us:

> "The buying process has totally changed. In the past, we just had to convince the laboratory director and take the order over to purchasing—once in a while, there'd be an RFP. Today, the lab director's influence continues to decline; there's more likely to be a full-scale, in-depth analysis, involving many more people, before the customer produces the RFP."

Regarding the upward movement of purchasing decisions in the hospital space, we heard a similar story from the sales leader at a medical technology firm:

> "Today, there's a lot of technological parity; high-quality technology is still *a ticket to the dance*, but that's all it is. There's still some product conversation, about meeting a minimum threshold, but very quickly the conversation shifts to a challenge or set of challenges a healthcare system is facing. There's a particular macro-problem like a quality metric—length of hospital stay, hospital-acquired infections, safety, patient satisfaction—there are many more. This conversation typically happens at the high C-Suite [level]. We are trying to help them solve one of these problems."

Purchasing-Decision Influence Outside the Customer

In the foregoing parts of this section, we have made the implicit assumption that the buying process is located within the customer organization. Such an assumption may be valid for most customers, for most purchase decisions, but not in all cases. Consider what we heard from the banking industry software FLSM:

> "Product complexity is so great today that many banks have turned to consultants to help them decide on systems and vendors. Furthermore, because of pressure on bank margins, these consultants are acting as procurement agents, pushing down prices. So, we have to work with consultants as well as with our ultimate bank customers."

In some industries, the purchase process is so complex that FLSMs and sellers must navigate an entire ecosystem comprising several different business entities. One challenge hospitals face in reducing costs is conducting fewer surgical procedures in hospitals. But there are many built-in systemic factors that prevent some procedures from moving to outpatient surgery centers. One such factor is insufficient reliability in pain management. Surgeons often use narcotics for pain relief, but several potential post-operative side effects may occur. Hence, patients stay in the hospital longer, driving up costs. One healthcare industry sales leader shared his expectations for FLSMs:

> "We sell a product that infuses local anesthetic that solves the problem. With our product, the transition to the surgery center can happen. Of course, we expect our sellers and FLSMs to be able to explain the technical issues, how the drug works, and where to place the catheter—the functional stuff. But we also expect them to talk to Blue Cross/ Blue Shield. 'Why don't you reimburse this differently? Surgeons will treat these patients

in a surgery center. And you'll save a lot of money as reimbursement rates are much lower.'

"FLSMs must highlight such opportunities; the insurers just don't have good clarity, or they have clarity but not the wherewithal to go down that path. The FLSMs should make this seamless and connect all the *economic dots*. The FLSM goes to the payer, but the FLSM also talks to the surgery center's contact with the payer, so they go to the payer also. And many of these centers are owned and run by physicians, so there's an economic incentive for them. Our sellers and FLSMs work that angle also."

More generally, another sales leader in the medical industry stated:

"We have several different customer types—the government [reimbursement rules for Medicaid and Medicare], payers, physicians, and patients. In the salesforce, we focus on payers and physicians. Our corporate affairs and marketing departments are responsible for government and patients, respectively."

For many firms, identifying and interacting with key customer contacts is not easy. Members of a purchasing department may seem an obvious place to start, but for many revenue opportunities, purchasing may only be one party in a much broader DMU. The DMU may embrace other functions and higher organizational levels. Indeed, purchasing may play a *gatekeeping* role, making it difficult for less experienced sellers to identify and interact with decision makers/influencers. The FLSM has a key role to play in helping sellers navigate the customer organization beyond purchasing.

For firms whose sellers focus on a single product or narrow product line, the customer DMU may be fairly constant for all purchases of a specific type. But for sellers offering multiple products/services, especially if the product/service range is broad and satisfies multiple customer needs, the seller may have to identify and address members of multiple DMUs. Furthermore, for any individual opportunity the DMU evolves as customer and firms work together, especially in *ideate* and *design* selling processes. Various customer (and firm) personnel may be involved in the process of identifying and agreeing on customer needs, and surfacing alternative products/services to satisfy them.

Relatedly, as customer organizations develop and evolve, reporting relationships evolve also; individuals change positions, or leave the customer organization. The seller may have to address a changing cast of characters, occupying multiple roles, in various customer DMUs. And when mergers and acquisitions occur, procurement departments also merge. In such situations, it may take many months before clarity emerges about DMU membership (and DMPs). Uncertainty rules as the merged organization strives to realize economies from the organizational consolidation, and customer personnel jockey for position and decision-making authority.

One FLSM at the higher-education software firm noted earlier told us:

"We work with both the central administration and the individual campuses. They tend to work in a very collaborative manner. We try to work with both ends of the system, but in the end, the campuses hold the purse strings. They are going to make the decision in that particular campus."

The FLSM's key role in identifying the *right* customer contacts is to *coach* sellers so they can identify people occupying various roles in customer purchase decision making. FLSMs should also work with sellers on a day-to-day basis to aid such identification, and ensure sellers are thorough in following through.

 ## Avoid Irrelevant Customer Contacts

Spending time with irrelevant customer contacts who have no meaningful role in the purchase decision is a Type 1 error. Such persons may occupy positions in different functions at a variety of levels in the customer organization. We frequently find the following pattern up and down managerial hierarchies: Customer employees present themselves to sellers as having far more influence on purchase decisions than is actually the case.

Certainly, these customer executives may genuinely misunderstand their roles. Perhaps (more likely), they express their importance in the DMU as a means of enhancing their own self-worth. One FLSM told us:

> "The customer was a large organization; it was difficult to get a really good handle on individuals involved in the purchase decision, or how exactly the decision would be made. So, my seller and I were chasing down lots of leads. I was directed to this midlevel customer executive and set up a meeting. Let's call him Jack Pucci.
>
> "As we started the meeting, Jack proceeded to tell me that all purchase decisions regarding our products flowed through his office. In effect, he told me his office was the *nerve center* for the technologies we offered. Jack made the choices between our products and competitor products. Clearly, Jack was a really important guy.
>
> "Then I noticed a couple of things: For someone that important, Jack had a pretty small office. I was also put off by [his lack of grooming and too-casual body language]— did not seem *senior managerish*. And, Jack seemed clueless on some fundamental technical issues concerning our product line and those of our competitors. It didn't take me long to decide that Jack was a fraud. Certainly, he did some paper pushing regarding purchases, but he had no meaningful role in purchase decision making. I ended the meeting pretty quickly.
>
> "A few weeks later, I received a phone call from Bill, a former colleague who had left my firm to work for a competitor. Bill told me he was having trouble cracking into this customer (same as us), and could I help. Frankly, I didn't think Bill should be calling me with this sort of request. So, I told him that since we were now competitors I couldn't really help very much. Nonetheless, I suggested that if he wanted the real scoop, he should talk to Jack Pucci; I gave him Jack's telephone number. I also told Bill that an expensive steak dinner and a glass or two of a good Merlot would probably loosen Jack's tongue.
>
> "A couple of weeks after that conversation, Bill left a message on my answering machine. [Message deleted for improper language.]"

Most FLSMs and their sellers come across their own Jack Puccis. They can be enormous time sinks. An important element of organizational acumen is to be able to sniff out these time wasters and move on.

Perhaps more generally, serious situations occur when the DMU evolves, but the seller continues to focus efforts on the historically important decision makers/influencers. Working with these customer individuals may be very comfortable; indeed, this relationship may continue to earn revenues. But the clock is ticking; focusing on the historically important people may lead to disaster. What may be required is an escalation and broadening of the set of customer contacts. The FLSM at a technology parts and solutions firm explained the situation at one of his firm's long-term customers when escalation and contact broadening did not occur:

> "At this Canadian cable customer, we had almost a sole-source arrangement based on the great relationship between our seller and one customer individual. The situation was great for us; we worked out deals in a bar on the back of a napkin. [But then] the customer's sourcing organization got involved. From the CTO down, people had strategic initiatives to achieve, and many individual organizational units got involved. We were caught short; we didn't have any of the right relationships. And we lost an RFP, even though most of the embedded base was our products.
>
> "We lost because we did not transform and expand our relationships within the customer, and take more of a solutions-based approach to understand the problem and initiative it was pursuing. We were just myopically focused on our guy, and the stuff he was buying from us, so we lost. That lost RFP kept us out of the customer for several years; it was really devastating."

In this situation, the traditional customer contact became irrelevant. This contact was great for existing business, but focusing on one individual blinded the firm's sellers to changes occurring within the customer. These changes gave rise to different requirements, different DMUs, and different DMPs. There is a salutary warning here for many FLSMs and their sellers. We have noted that major changes are occurring in DMUs and DMPs. When such changes occur, the relationships sellers and FLSMs have built with historically great customer contacts may not only become less important, they may become *irrelevant*.

Sometimes the firm makes a strategic decision as to where seller time is best spent—with one type of customer versus another. Sales leaders decide to reduce/eliminate/transfer selling efforts from one customer type to another. The FLSM's job is to ensure that sellers implement the corporate decision. The sales leader at a healthcare firm that focused on rare diseases explained her situation:

> "Historically, my salesforce was responsible for three types of customer—physicians, payers, patients. We spent a lot of time with all three. For patients, we helped with getting the right treatment, getting payers to pay, and helping with all the difficult administrative processes involved. A while ago, we made a strategic decision to place all of our efforts on physicians and payers, and pass patients over to an inside salesforce. Some sellers really bond with patients and find it difficult to give up patient contact, but this was something we had to do. My FLSMs enforced the new strategy."

The message from this section should be very clear. The FLSM should not allow a seller's relationship with a specific individual(s) at a customer, or a customer type, to get in the way of understanding the evolving nature of the DMU, or implementing a sales-leader-driven strategic change. FLSMs must ensure that sellers place their efforts where they earn the greatest returns.

 # Address the Right Customer Contacts

Once the *right* customer contacts are identified, FLSMs should work with sellers to isolate situations where the seller requires additional resources to address those individuals. Important areas for FLSM intervention:

Ensure Sellers Understand the Customer's Buying Process

It's one thing to be clear about the cast of characters (DMU) involved in any particular purchase decision; it's quite another to understand the purchase-decision process (DMP). All we know for certain is there is a start and an end (assuming a purchase/sale actually occurs). Furthermore, the buying-process framework—*no problem* (NP), *limited problem solving* (LPS), *extended problem solving* (EPS)—Chapter 1—is a useful way to link purchase-decision processes with the three selling processes—*close, design, ideate.*

Those frameworks help somewhat, but there may be little commonality among different purchase processes. One FLSM was very clear on this point. He observed:

> "If you have seen *one* buying process, you have seen *one* buying process. It's really something that I have to understand. Because it's ever evolving with our customers regarding how they make decisions."

One FLSM in wholesaling put it this way:

> "If you have two dealers in the same small town on opposite corners and they have been there for 50 years, it is amazing when you walk through their front doors how completely different they are."

The FLSM has responsibility for making sure sellers know the specific buying process for a particular purchase. One FLSM dealing with a complex purchase involving several different businesses observed:

> "My role is to make sure all our individual businesses really understand the buying process, and the best path to success. Essentially, I am a sort of orchestra conductor. Each business has its own salesperson responsible for sales of its products/service. I direct their activities at the customer.
>
> "Sometimes there is a particularly aggressive seller for one business who acts as a catalyst for sellers in other businesses. If one of them goes outside the guardrails of what needs to happen, and how it should happen—then it will blow up.

> "So, I have to pull them back. I tell them: 'I'm looking out for your interests.' I tell fellow FLSMs I mentor: 'This role is two-faced: one face to the customer, one face to the sellers.'"

Not only are purchase decisions moving across functions and to higher organizational levels, in some organizations, involved executives may be less willing to actually make buying decisions. One FLSM lamented:

> "As more people get involved in the buying decision, you really have to navigate through the many different departments and organizational levels. We find more and more that nobody wants to put their single stamp of approval. They want to make sure this is a matrix decision across the organization to move forward on any particular purchase decision. That means we really have to up our game."

Anticipate the Changing Cast of Characters. As human resource markets become more efficient, people move from company to company. As one sales leader told us (noted earlier):

> "From the time we make the first customer contact, it takes around three months to make the sale and get the customer up and running on our services. But when we go back a year later for contract renewal, we often find our original contacts have moved on."

FLSMs and sellers must anticipate these sorts of changes at their customers. FLSMs must ensure they and their sellers develop and use systems and processes to learn about these changes. FLSMs must also ensure they and their sellers take necessary actions to develop new relationships. Once identified, seller and FLSM together decide how they should address these new customer contacts. One FLSM told us:

> "There have been many changes in our industry. Across the board, the cast of characters involved in purchase decisions has evolved considerably. There's no consistent pattern so that makes life difficult for sellers, especially new hires. I spend quite a lot of time focusing on specific customers, working with sellers to scope out decision makers and influencers. Sometimes I get personally involved at customers to help figure this out but, for the most part, I give my sellers advice and counsel—mostly, that does the trick."

On some occasions, the newly appointed customer executive has difficulty learning the new role requirements. FLSMs/sellers may be able to offer significant personal value in helping these appointees settle into their roles. On the other hand, it is not unusual for newly appointed customer executives to want to make their marks; hence, FLSMs/sellers should anticipate changes in traditional ways of doing business. The more elevated in the customer organization these personnel changes occur, the more likely the supplier will face previously unforeseen actions. These changes are especially likely if the customer has appointed a new CEO/CFO or head of procurement.

Help Sellers Manage Their Customers

Directly assisting sellers with customers is more common with junior sellers—with more experienced sellers, required FLSM assistance may be relatively rare. We demonstrate such assistance by revisiting an example from Chapter 2 in which an FLSM worked with her seller to manage a customer where the senior customer executives were on board with the supplier's proposed technology solution but, bafflingly, the low-level decision maker was adamantly against it:

> "Ultimately, we realized this decision maker was worried about his job; he thought our product would make him obsolete. So, my seller and I just kept visiting—every single week for several months—and educating him. Eventually, our efforts paid off and he signed the contract. It was a long slog and took lots of patience."

The extent to which FLSMs should be directly involved with sellers in actually making sales can be controversial. We address this topic in the following section—*Plan Interventions Carefully*.

Secure Customer Access at Higher Organizational Levels

Suppose the seller cannot gain access to the customer's high organizational levels. Or, the seller believes a more senior firm executive should interface with the customer—for example, discussing long-term firm-customer relationships. The FLSM may play this role; alternatively, the FLSM persuades a more senior executive to get involved.

One FLSM recounted his experience concerning a seller who had developed many solid relationships with customer personnel. These individuals would each be influential in the buying decision, but the actual decision maker was more senior—the CFO. The problem: All of the account manager's key contacts had asked her not to go over their heads to the CFO. The account manager believed it was important that her firm develop a direct CFO relationship, but did not want to jeopardize her own relationships with the less-senior employees by acting against their wishes. The account manager's FLSM takes up the story:

> "The account manager had done a fantastic job. We wanted to build on her relationships, but we also knew we had to work with the CFO. So, we decided we would preserve her relationships and I would go to the CFO. My secretary made the appointment and I had a great meeting. My account manager kept faith with her contacts and the entire interorganizational relationship moved forward."

Some purchase decisions demand high-level customer access and high-level involvement from supplier executives. The FLSM plays a major role ensuring these interactions occur. The sales leader at a large high-tech firm elaborated on a current project—supporting a large telephone carrier in modernizing its network:

> "We have modeling tools that look at power requirements, maintenance costs, operating costs; we develop justifications for modernizing. We tell you what your payback is going to be, and we're also going to help you introduce new services. That's a services engagement that takes several months, but it's recurring business because these networks are enormous.
>
> "The carriers just don't have the resources or staff to do this work. In most cases, they've been outsourcing, or reducing staff and making fewer people do more work. They don't have the time, or they have political boundaries that must be crossed—these carriers are organized into silos. We are able to kind of look at the big picture for them. We can cut across those silo boundaries because we have no *political affiliations*.

"That's why sales becomes most important at a higher level. We're going in and *killing somebody's dog*, so to speak. Taking the work from them, or work they can't do—they say they can do it, but it isn't getting done. So, you've got to sell that at a much higher level—director or VP—versus the traditional *box sale* to the network engineer/front-line manager. Our FLSMs engineer those interactions."

Provide Customers with Subject-Matter Experts

The FLSM identifies and secures this resource to work with sellers and customers. The FLSM uses *organizational acumen* to figure out what is needed, then employs *resource acumen* (Chapter 6) to secure what is required.

Many firms provide such backup for sellers in the form of sales/product specialists and/or other **subject-matter experts (SMEs)**. The purpose of these SMEs is to provide support to sellers when they get out of their depth in product, solutions, or technology knowledge at customers. As the firm's product line and/or selling process becomes more complex, SMEs tend to be a more common support service.

But SMEs are an expensive resource, and can be used as a crutch by lazy sellers who do not expend the time and effort to learn the full details of the products they are selling. For this reason, many firms deliberately plan for SME supply to be less than anticipated demand. One FLSM highlighted the supply/demand imbalance and her role in supporting her sellers:

"As our product line has expanded, it has become increasingly difficult for sellers to get their heads around the full intricacies of our offers. We expect sellers to manage both the first and second customer conversations, but often they need help beyond that. That's when they call in our SMEs. The problem is that we don't have enough of these support people, so I have to get involved to spring these resources to help my guys."

Circumvent Gatekeepers

Finding a way to reach the *right* customer contacts is a critical element of organizational acumen. Earlier in the chapter, we discussed gatekeepers. It is not unusual for customer organizations to insert barriers, designed to stop sellers from meeting, and developing relationships with, critical customer executives. On other occasions, individual executives implement barriers to protect their organizational positions, to heighten their importance, or for other personal reasons.

The best FLSMs identify such roadblocks, then figure out ways to get around them. One FLSM at a high-tech firm described how a senior customer executive attempted to block his access to key decision makers/influencers, and how he dealt with the problem:

"When I first called on the SVP [senior vice president] for procurement, he told me there was a company rule that vendors like me could not talk to any executive, except him. I said: 'If that's the way things are, of course I'll abide by the rule. But I need a letter from you to that effect, copied to the executive committee. I've already met several of them, and I have to be able to explain why I can't talk to them anymore.' The SVP never did write the letter—there was no such rule. And later on, we became good friends and worked well together."

FLSMs have a critical role to play in helping sellers address the *right* customer contacts. In addition to requiring high levels of organizational acumen to be effective with customers, FLSMs may also require significant *resource acumen*—Chapter 6—to secure appropriate firm resources.

 ## Plan Interventions Carefully

FLSMs should heed carefully an observation made by one FLSM we interviewed:

> **"Buyers have very little time these days. They are not going to give you a second chance if you don't show them it's worth meeting you and working with you on an ongoing basis."**

It's one thing for FLSMs to work with sellers to identify key contacts in various customer DMUs; it's quite another to decide whether or not to intervene in the selling process. These decisions require good organizational acumen. An FLSM who is doing a good job should be well briefed by sellers on seller-customer relationships, and all potential deals in process. Certainly, the FLSM wants to win business for the firm, but some FLSMs have a greater predisposition to get involved in the actual selling process than others.

Regardless, we can identify three situations concerning seller competence to win a particular deal that FLSMs may have to address:

- *Competent seller.* The FLSM believes the seller is competent to conclude a specific deal at a particular customer. What should the FLSM do? Just get out of the seller's way! There are better things to do, better ways to spend time. The seller does not need *help* from the FLSM. As we note in Chapter 7, *micromanagement* is in no one's interest.

- *Non-competent seller.* The FLSM believes the seller is unlikely to make the sale alone; the FLSM should become involved (subject to time constraints—see below). The sale requires good *strategic, organizational*, and/or *business acumen*—Chapter 4—but the seller does not possess sufficiently high acumen levels. Of course, FLSMs should be coaching sellers to improve, making decisions on additional training, or planning for a replacement. Regardless, if the FLSM believes the seller is insufficiently competent in a specific situation, the firm's chances of success improve when the FLSM becomes personally involved in the selling process.

- *Unclear situation.* The FLSM is genuinely unsure whether intervention is needed. Several elements enter the decision of whether (or not) to intervene:
  - *Probability of winning.* The FLSM must realistically assess the improved chances of moving a sale forward if the FLSM intervenes.
  - *FLSM workload.* Time is a scarce resource for FLSMs. They must trade off possible intervention in any deal, with other time demands. One FLSM told us:

    > **"I work very hard to keep on top of all the opportunities my guys are pursuing. I try to get personally involved when I think my presence can help us move forward. But there are only so many hours in the day, and I have to make choices. I've no doubt that some of the deals we lose could have gone our way**

had I been involved (or more involved). But I like to think I get involved in the most important deals so that, overall, my district comes out ahead."

– *Seller's perspective.* Generally, if the seller requests FLSM involvement, getting involved is probably the correct decision, subject to time constraints. But what if the seller expresses confidence in his/her abilities, but the FLSM is unsure? To become involved may (or may not) raise the chances of success.

If the seller believes s/he is doing fine with a particular customer, FLSM involvement may have negative consequences. For example, such intervention may deprive the seller of personal success that would have built his/her confidence. Intervention may generate resentment against the FLSM. One sales leader reported:

> "Once in a while we identify an FLSM who likes to get *in for the kill*. The seller has brought the sale to virtual completion, then the FLSM shows up at the last minute. This sort of behavior is very disruptive to the sales team. I work hard to discourage this sort of behavior. Sometimes it's a tough call, but I want our sellers to receive both the financial and the *psychological* rewards of making the sale."

In general, FLSMs have a broader perspective on firm-customer relationships than individual sellers. FLSMs also usually (though not always) bring greater experience, and a more powerful organizational position. Hence, they can enhance the firm's selling process. But the decision may not be straightforward. FLSMs should make the intervention decision *very carefully*.

Of course, when it's difficult for sellers to get in front of key DMU members, it may be equally as or more difficult for competitor sellers also. The seller's goal is to provide a reason for target customer personnel to spend time with them (and not with competitor sellers). Sometimes, as noted above, the FLSM (or a more senior manager, functional expert) can provide this reason. The seller may also develop an expectation in the target individual that the time will not be wasted.

 Discover Opportunities

Woody Allen is famously credited with the saying, "80 percent of life is just showing up." Translated to the sales world, FLSMs and sellers should be in the *right* place at the *right* time. For one FLSM, this meant being in a particular men's room at the customer's offices:

> "After a meeting at the customer's offices, I was walking the halls, seeing if I could touch base with any executive who would spare a few minutes to chat, so I could build/sustain relationships. I was in the men's room when Dennis entered. I didn't know Dennis well, but we'd been in a couple of meetings together, and he knew who I was. I asked Dennis how things were going. Dennis said he was dealing with a difficult problem, but it didn't relate to our products. I said, 'Try me anyway.'
>
> "It turned out it was a security problem, so finding a solution was imperative. I didn't know much about this area, but I thought it possible that we had some researchers who might know something, so I told Dennis I would follow up. It turned out we had some

guys working on a related issue. I persuaded Dennis to set up an initial meeting between our experts and his colleagues.

"To cut a long story short, we formed a joint firm-customer taskforce to work on the problem. Six months later, we delivered a beta version of our solution; within one year the customer was buying commercial quantities. During the next few years, we earned substantial revenues from this collaboration."

The core message from this example starts with this FLSM's organizational acumen and intense focus on the customer. The FLSM had become well known at the customer's offices; he could walk the halls and be welcomed when he popped into executive offices. He had made it his business to participate in many customer meetings, so he had a passing acquaintance with Dennis, sufficient for Dennis to share his problem and be prepared to set up the initial meeting with the firm's experts.

Of course, organizational acumen was necessary, but not sufficient, to earn the success that this FLSM achieved. He also displayed significant *resource acumen*—Chapter 6—to identify the appropriate internal experts and persuade them to form a firm-customer taskforce to work on Dennis's problem. What this story also demonstrates is the close relationship between organizational acumen and personal brand equity (below). The FLSM's stature within the customer and within his own firm was a critical element in getting the project off the ground.

This bathroom-meet story is all about pursuing an idiosyncratic opportunity. What is perhaps more important for FLSMs is developing a process to unearth opportunities. The sales leader at a higher-education software firm described his firm's approach:

"We deal with the entire range of higher-education institutions from large universities to much smaller community colleges and private institutions. An account executive [AE] may have a cross-section in their territory. We mandate that each AE completes a territory plan, account plans, and within those plans—*opportunity plans*—that we track.

"We have a tremendous amount of data about the industry so, when we meet with a customer, we try to have a very focused discussion on their challenges and, of course, how we can deliver value to help them, and align with their priorities. We know the registrars' job—what they are trying to do. It's crucial for the FLSM and sellers to identify those needs. And it's very different from talking to a president or a finance VP. You have to really be more than *an inch deep and a mile wide*. You must show your value and your expertise, and bring in the right subject-matter experts, to engage with the client. Then again, these institutions tend to make decisions by committee, so we make sure we maintain close relationships with all major players."

A successful FLSM at a major high-tech firm followed the same basic approach. He averred:

"A key element of the FLSM's coaching job is to help sellers understand *where the opportunity lives*. The FLSM works with a seller and takes a subset of maybe ten accounts. Based on industry knowledge, trends, and what's going on within the account base—maybe it's a vertical like manufacturing—the FLSM educates, and works with, the seller on understanding how to identify opportunities. The key is knowing what concerns a manufacturing client might have around automation or wireless capability. Then, together, the FLSM and seller build a plan for sales calls, and what questions to ask of which people. In some cases, it's important for the FLSM to play a more direct role by engaging with higher-level executives in the C-Suite."

Sellers make sales by discovering opportunities, then persuading customers they can satisfy needs, solve problems, and mitigate pain points by delivering value. Frequently, these opportunities are easy to identify. The seller shows up at the customer; the customer says: "I'm so glad to see you. I have this problem, I think one of your products/services can help. Just explain it to me and I'll give you an order." Of course, that's great—but this happens only if the customer indeed realizes there is a problem.

Perhaps customer executives do not fully understand the various competitive and environmental pressures their firm faces; only an *ideate* process can reveal what they may not realize are problems that could become significant pain points. Initiating and conducting deep customer discussions is not for the faint-hearted, and may require significant skill that the average seller does not possess, even though that seller may be extremely competent in other aspects of the selling job. Here is where the FLSM can be very helpful by initiating the selling process.

Sometimes the FLSM's challenge is less about discovering completely new opportunities, and more about expanding on already identified opportunities. To use a common metaphor, the FLSM has a foot in the door; the task is to find out what is in the house. One FLSM at a medical-diagnostics firm described a recent customer interaction:

"I was on a call with my seller at a north Florida customer; we started at 9 a.m. and ended at 3:30 in the afternoon. It was a strategy meeting and we were completing one of the customer's final requested items—a rather long questionnaire. We were asking ourselves: How do we take advantage of this opportunity? Rather than just say 'yes,' 'no,' 'maybe,' 'five,' 'six,' and quick answers like that, how do we position ourselves and make it bigger? How do we answer so we answer their question, but point out why it would be better for them to select us and not the other guys? We spent the whole day coaching: How do we make this bigger? How do we strategically answer this questionnaire, and not just tactically going, 'OK, we got it done, here it is.'"

Surfacing opportunities is one of the more difficult, yet more important, elements of the selling job. An important part of organizational acumen is the ability of FLSMs both to surface opportunities themselves, and to coach improvement in their sellers.

Build Personal Brand Equity

So far in this chapter, we have focused on the ability of FLSMs and individual sellers to navigate customer organizations to secure access to decision makers/influencers. But it's one thing to identify a decision maker/influencer; it's quite another to secure an appointment. The ability to do so is likely a function of the decision maker's/influencer's belief that a potential meeting will have value. That belief is likely predicated, in part, on the brand image of the firm and its products/services. A second factor influencing success is the FLSM's personal brand equity—the customer's belief that the FLSM can bring value. Like many firm and product/service brands, the FLSM's personal brand typically builds slowly over time.

Not only does the FLSM's personal brand equity open doors for the FLSM and sellers, FLSMs with strong personal brands get the calls when customers encounter problems they must solve, experience pain points they must mitigate. Notwithstanding most firms' attempts to have their operations run smoothly, *stuff happens*. For whatever reason, the customer cannot use the standard RFP system; the key customer executive must call someone.

Question for FLSMs: Will you get the call?

If you, as FLSM, enjoy the most positive brand image in the industry, the answer is *yes*! And your firm will earn the ensuing revenues when you deliver the required customer value.

Perhaps no industry is as prone to *stuff happens* as global package freight—the customer wants the package delivered *yesterday*! In an emerging European market, the FedEx FLSM enjoyed a reputation throughout the continent—with decision makers/influencers at current *and* prospective customers, and other key stakeholders like regulatory authorities, consulting firms, the media—for being the *go-to expert* for addressing difficult logistics challenges. This FLSM secured his reputation over a span of several years through a combination of relationship building, missionary selling, and dedication to securing industry insight. The FLSM's high personal brand equity paid significant dividends. He recalled:

> "I would get a lot of calls and requests during peak shipping times in holiday periods. Shipping instructions could not go through regular channels, in part because many offices were closed. On one occasion, the logistics director for a Canada-based global customer called me late on December 23. Apparently, there had been human errors in his company, and swift action was needed to avoid disrupting the supply chain. Such a disruption would endanger his firm's relationship with its customer. The contact said, 'Hey, this is XXX. I know you're the only person in the industry around here who would pick up the phone at 22:00. Can you help us by rerouting these Canada-APAC pallets within the next few hours?'
>
> "I was able to make this happen. The customer didn't care about the cost to do the work—it was a fraction of the amount for shutting down a production line. We greatly enhanced FedEx's relationship with the account, and started receiving increased business. This success was in the electronics industry, but we had similar experiences in the automotive, aviation, telecom, and military-related industries."

Of course, the ability to help a regular customer in time of need can enhance firm reputation and increase revenues, but the FLSM's brand value can go beyond relationships with current customers. In an automotive industry situation, the company used a freight-forwarding firm to send shipments from its plant in Salt Lake City to Hamburg, Germany. The FLSM recalled:

> "It was literally a few hours before the New Year's Eve stoppage when I got the email, even though I had no direct responsibility in either the U.S. or Germany. The company's German representative wanted super-fast advice on customs regulations and paperwork.

Apparently, the freight forwarder had run into a problem getting products into Germany. I spent a couple of hours phoning and texting with various parties, sorting out this very complicated situation—even the customer's Germany-based peers didn't believe it was possible to solve the problem.

"But we managed to clear the roadblocks, and the shipment got into Germany. In the process, I was able to tell the shipper about new FedEx services and flexible terms. We won all the business from the forwarder."

Building the FLSM's personal brand equity sometimes requires providing advice that may seem to disadvantage the firm but, nonetheless, can lead to significant future revenues. To all readers, just ask yourself this question: Would you send your customer to a competitor if you really believed that was in the customer's best interests?

Let's hear a final anecdote from the FedEx FLSM:

"The logistics head at an Italian telecom equipment maker called me, desperate to know what ocean-freight options were feasible for his shipping needs of bulky semifinished goods and components. I suggested which freight company to use, who to call, and their telephone numbers. [At the time, I was traveling with my boss. He asked], 'Why didn't you try to switch him to our air-freight service?' I told him that I didn't think that suited the customer, and that I believed I had done the right thing. My boss was not pleased.

"The very next day, the Italian logistics head called me with a no-bid ad hoc project to ship products to Sweden. I had told him we were the most efficient and fastest carrier on that route—he just believed me and gave us the business. That turned into a multiyear ongoing deal."

Brand image is important in many domains, but is particularly important in surfacing opportunities (previous section). Consider the initiation of the Philips Medical Systems (PMS)/Georgia Regents Medical Center (GRMC) deal—Chapter 2. Recall the starting point: a conversation between GRMC's CEO and the local PMS account manager. Some combination of Philips's brand value and the local account manager's brand image led the CEO to discuss his vision for a different type of relationship between his hospital system and suppliers.

The CEO would not have wasted his time had he not believed the local PMS sales organization possessed the strategic acumen to leverage PMS's technological expertise into a new supplier-customer relationship. He came to this belief because of the joint brand value offered by PMS and the local sales organization. As PMS's sales leader put it:

"Without those relationships and without the competence and track record we have in Georgia, these types of opportunities rarely manifest themselves. We emphasize to our FLSMs the importance of relationship building. When they do a good job, they *construct something out of nothing*—they identify opportunities where, previously, nothing seemed to exist.

"You have to earn a good reputation with customers. This is vital, especially when competitors are very strong. A long history with customers, through good and tough times, sets a level of trust. You become part of their team, building credibility as a trusted advisor in day-to-day operations, and peering into the future's crystal ball together. Building your *personal brand equity* is key. You do this via specifics, acting as an *honest broker* between our two companies, cutting through the emotions, and communicating up and down the organizations."

So, what is a personal brand worth? We know of no specific study on this topic, but we have some hints from FLSMs:

"My sellers and I had a long history working with one particular customer. I was pretty sure they wanted to select us for an important contract, but the procurement director told me our pricing was out of line with competitors'. He said he couldn't give me the competitive quotes, but told he was going to photocopy the list of competitors and prices in the next-door utility room (copy machine, coffee machine), on his way to the men's room. While he was gone, he said, I was welcome to get a cup of coffee.... We rebid and won the business."

"For several customers, my sellers and I have worked especially hard to build our reputations. I have been personally involved, and believe I am widely accepted and respected by senior executives at these customers. We certainly don't win all the RFPs, but I think we get a 2 to 3 percent price advantage. If we are more than 3 percent above competitors we lose, but at 2 percent above we generally win."

We should note a few of the recurring themes driving development of a strong personal brand equity:

■ Being personally available to customer executives when needed, especially at inconvenient times.

■ Solving customer problems/mitigating pain points quickly and efficiently.

■ Providing vital information.

■ Rapidly responding to issues when they arise.

■ Dealing with third parties on the customer's behalf.

■ Acting outside one's sphere of authority/responsibility to get the job done.

■ Putting customer requirements ahead of short-term firm performance needs.

The opportunities to behave in these ways do not appear at regular intervals, but rather arrive randomly and spontaneously. Nonetheless, by continually acting with integrity, and following the lead FLSMs displayed in this section, FLSMs can enhance their personal brand value.

A Word about Relationships

Thus far in this chapter we have discussed the six core dimensions of organizational acumen: *identify the right customer contacts*; *avoid irrelevant customer contacts*; *address the right customer contacts*;

plan interventions carefully; discover opportunities; build personal brand equity. Lurking around these discussions has been the issue of relationships between seller/FLSM and customer personnel.[2]

Interorganizational relationships often span many years, even decades. The supplier builds its brand image with customers via over-time business transactions, earned through multiple iterations of buying/selling processes. In a very real sense, the seller/FLSM is a temporary custodian of that relationship. A key FLSM task is to maintain and develop those relationships, and enhance the firm's brand value.

In some situations, customer personnel demand to deal directly with the FLSM. Perhaps the customer has a long-time relationship with the firm and knows that the FLSM is key to getting things done. Or the customer may have a personal relationship with the FLSM based on many years of interaction. One FLSM told us:

> "There are some customers that I have known for a long time, that have been with our firm for 20 years or more. They demand to see me; that's probably about 15 percent of my time. These customers would rather deal with me than with our sellers."

Certainly, sellers and FLSMs have a responsibility to earn sales revenues in the short run, but the FLSM must integrate that requirement with being a custodian of the long-run interorganizational relationship. For this reason, the FLSM should broaden the idea of *right* customer contacts to embrace not just current business, but also future business. One FLSM demonstrated the wisdom of this perspective:

> "At one of our customers, most purchasing decisions were effectively made by the purchasing EVP [executive vice president]. He was a long-time employee and was close to the CEO—they had grown up together in the firm. As far as purchasing was concerned, the EVP's word was law; he ran a very tight ship. From our perspective, this was a disaster; he clearly favored our competitor. My seller and I continued working the account, but we only got the crumbs. I made a point of telling my seller to *work the crowd*; spend time with junior procurement folks, and help them out if we could. The competitor was sloppy; their people focused just on the EVP and ignored the juniors.
>
> "Eventually, the EVP retired; the customer reorganized procurement, and several of the junior folks got important positions. They remembered what we had done for them over the years. Now, this firm is one of our best customers."

More generally, FLSMs enhance their personal brand equity by improving relationships with customer decision makers/influencers; the key is adding value. Smart sellers and FLSMs learn a lot about their customers. In discussing strategic acumen, we focused on competitive and environmental pressures, and strategic decision making. But sellers/FLSMs also learn about the inner workings of the customer organization. One FLSM told us:

> "Some of our customers seem to have significant human resource turnover. There always seem to be new people to meet who haven't been with the customer for very long. It typically takes them a few months to learn the ropes. Because we've been around for a while, we can often help them get settled—they appreciate that. In fact, there's one customer that has a somewhat complex budgeting process. Many is the time I've been

able to help someone get their project funded, by telling them how to beat their own firm's system."

It is axiomatic in organizations that information flows much more smoothly vertically—up and down hierarchies—than laterally—across the organization. Hence, it is not unusual for executives in one part of a large corporate organization to know very little about what is going on in other parts of the organization, even though decisions made far away may have important implications for their local organizations, jobs, even careers. By virtue of managing sellers who interface with the entire customer organization, the FLSM may act as a valuable information source for many decision makers/influencers.

A core FLSM task is to work with sellers to burnish the firm's brand, but also to build personal brand equity by enhancing relationships. One FLSM provided his approach:

"I always try to add value. When I meet with my customer contacts, I always ask a lot of open-ended questions. By doing so, issues come up for which the contact would like an answer. After the meeting, I figure out the answer; that gives me a reason to have another visit where I provide the information. Then I repeat the cycle."

Another FLSM reported on his approach to adding personal value to customer employees:

"I think there are many ways to build relationships by providing value to individuals at customers. When we conclude a deal/sign a contract, I make a point of thanking all those involved in making it happen. I want them to know that our firm, and me personally, appreciate their efforts. As a regular practice, I acknowledge individual contributions to projects, especially in the presence of their bosses. I try to help them out with information and contacts, so they can do their jobs better, and I secure resources when I can. I try to understand their specific problems and help out, but I also challenge them to seek the best solution for both our firms.

"I also try to instill this perspective into my team of sellers. I emphasize that taking this strong customer-first perspective does not imply we lose sight of who pays our salaries. We are not being *customers' people*, focused solely on their good fortune. We want to build strong customer relationships but, at root, we do this for a hard-headed business purpose."

One FLSM in telecommunications emphasized the importance of two levels of relationships—the relationships of his sellers with customer individuals, but also the relationships he himself had with customers. Both types of relationships were important, but they had different purposes. The FLSM explained:

"I want my guys to establish relationships with customer contacts, but I also try to establish very strong linkages myself, typically one or more levels higher. So, if I need some customer insight I can't get through normal channels, there's someone I can call [who will be] trustworthy and more open.

"For example, we had a customer situation regarding a fully documented agreement. I noticed the customer was very aggressively trying to return some obsolete products, but not purchasing any new products. This didn't seem right, but we couldn't figure it out. So, I called my high-level contact and asked what was going on. She shared some insight— the customer had a bureaucratic snafu that was delaying certification of our products. We were able to unblock that problem. Of course, I was careful to protect my source."

These efforts by FLSMs mostly concern business relationships, but FLSMs and customer executives may extend these relationships into friendships and personal relationships.[3] Typical approaches are gifts, and invitations to sporting events like the U.S. Open Tennis Championships. More effective approaches may involve attention to issues that concern a particular customer executive, like donating to their favorite charities. One FLSM reported how he and his seller enhanced their relationship with an important buyer:

"From our conversations with this buyer, Jack (my seller) and I knew about his keen interest in his daughter's basketball career. She played for her high school team, and each meeting we had together, he would tell us about her latest exploits—it was a regular topic of conversation. On this one occasion, the buyer told us that her team had reached the state championship finals, and would be playing at a major stadium in New Jersey. So, Jack and I went to the game. The buyer was amazed and delighted to see us."

Notwithstanding efforts by FLSMs, at the end of the day, the conversations that really count are *not* those between the FLSM/sellers and customer personnel. The conversations that really count are those that customer executives have with each other—neither the seller, nor FLSM, nor any participant from the supplier attends. In those meetings firm brand value, personal brand equity, and relationships really matter. Enhancing firm and personal brand equity, and building valued relationships, can shift the odds of success in the firm's favor.

Several years ago, a senior Xerox executive shared his perspective on firm-customer relationships with author NC:

"In *Gulliver's Travels*, Gulliver is shipwrecked and lands unconscious on the beach in Lilliput. In this country, inhabited by little people, Gulliver is a giant; the population is scared. To protect themselves, the Lilliputians tie Gulliver down with many threads. A few threads would not hold Gulliver down, but the many individual threads do the job, even though each individual thread is weak.

"As far as firm-customer relationships are concerned, especially for major customers, Lilliputian threads are relationships. Some threads—with senior executives—are stronger than others. All things equal, more relationships are better than fewer. Building strong relationships is crucial to long-term firm-customer relationships."

Summary

Chapter 3 focuses on the second of six acumen dimensions effective FLSMs must possess—*organizational acumen*. The core of organizational acumen is being able to navigate customer organizations; FLSMs must both possess this skill and develop the skill in their sellers.

Two issues are crucial. First, identify the *right* contacts. The FLSM should make sure that a person of importance to the purchase decision is not ignored. FLSMs should also ensure that neither they nor their sellers are spending time with persons who have no significant role, currently or in the future. Second, the FLSM should make sure the *right* contacts are addressed appropriately with the *right* resources. These resources could be seller, FLSM, functional employees, more senior managers, and/ or subject-matter experts. FLSMs also plan their own interventions carefully.

In addition to developing the right approaches to specific deals, effective FLSMs discover opportunities. Effective FLSMs develop substantial personal brand equity; this is a slow process that takes significant time. Relatedly, superior FLSMs develop and enhance relationships with decision makers/ influencers, both for today's deals and for those in the future.

Endnotes

1. For more on the customer adoption process, N. Capon, *Managing Marketing in the 21st Century* (4th ed.), Bronxville, New York: Wessex, 2017, Chapter 14, pp. 385–386.

2. In a controversial book—M. Dixon and B. Adamson, *The Challenger Sale: Taking Control of the Customer Conversation*, New York: Portfolio, 2011—the authors minimize the importance of relationships. For a rejoinder, N. Capon, "Revisiting the Challenger Sale: Breakthrough Built on a Flimsy Foundation," *Velocity*, Strategic Account Management Association, 17 (3rd Quarter 2015), pp. 42–45.

3. For related material on influence processes, R.B. Cialdini, *Influence: The Psychology of Persuasion*, New York: HarperCollins, 2007; A.R. Cohen and D.L. Bradford, *Influence without Authority*, Hoboken, NJ: Wiley, 2005. Cialdini's persuasion principles: *liking*—people buy from people they like; *reciprocity*—if you give, people give back; *social proof*—people follow the lead of others; *consistency*—people fulfill commitments (especially public and written); *authority*—people defer to experts; *scarcity*—people value what is scarce.

Chapter 4

Business Acumen

The core focus for front-line sales managers (FLSMs) is the ability to *think strategically*. In the context of competitive and environmental pressures, FLSMs must understand the strategic directions of both the firm and its customers, and strive to bring them into alignment. More specifically, working with sellers, FLSMs must translate broadscale value propositions, typically developed by marketing departments, into meaningful benefits/values for specific customers. Finally, FLSMs must develop strategy for their districts.

Compared to strategic acumen—Chapter 2—**business acumen** is more fine-grained, concerned with effectively communicating benefits/values to customers and making them real for DMU members. The core of business acumen *is understanding exactly what it takes to make a sale, and ensuring sellers can do what is necessary to earn revenues*. To accomplish these tasks, FLSMs/sellers must identify, for each customer and potential deal:

- Decision-making unit (DMU) composition—including all customer personnel who can move the firm's interests forward.

- Decision-making process (DMP)—how DMU members interact and make decisions—formal and informal organizational processes, timelines.

- Benefit/value requirements of specific customers overall, and various DMU members.

The first two items speak to organizational acumen—Chapter 3; the third item is the province of business acumen. FLSMs with good *organizational acumen* know how to identify and reach individual DMU members. FLSMs with good *business acumen* know how to bring them value.

Of course, these elements are not cast in stone. Customer needs and required benefits/values, DMUs, and DMPs all evolve. Firm value propositions also evolve. The FLSM/sellers must understand the nature of these evolutions, both at their various customers and at the firm. Building on organizational acumen—evolving DMUs and DMPs—business acumen focuses on understanding the evolution of customer needs and required benefits/values, then behaving effectively to make deals and earn revenues.

Business acumen comprises seven dimensions—*address the evolving customer DMU; secure deep market knowledge—customers, competitors; do the math/make the business case; enhance the firm's face to customers; drive the sale; keep tabs on progress; influence market offers and firm behavior*—Figure 4.1.

Figure 4.1 Business Acumen Dimensions

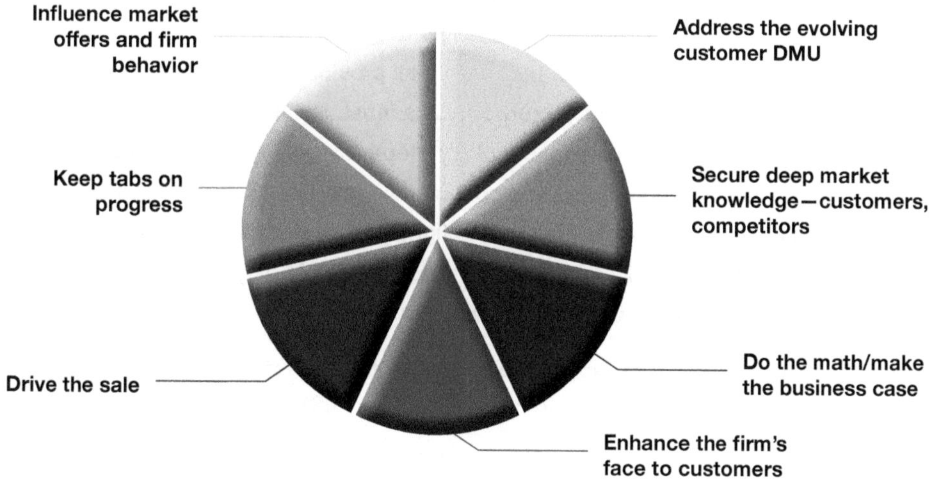

Influence market offers and firm behavior

Keep tabs on progress

Drive the sale

Address the evolving customer DMU

Secure deep market knowledge—customers, competitors

Do the math/make the business case

Enhance the firm's face to customers

 ## Address the Evolving Customer DMU

In Chapter 3, we showed two major dimensions of DMU evolution—horizontal, vertical. Horizontal—decision makers/influencers at roughly similar organizational levels to traditional practice, but in different functions/business units. Vertical—decisions made at higher organizational levels. These evolutions require that FLSMs/sellers possess good business acumen to competently address DMU members.

Shifting Locus of Decision-Making Authority—Horizontal

Chapter 2 showed how the Cisco FLSM's *strategic acumen* allowed him to make the game-changing *Telepresence* value proposition *real* for a retail bank customer. The FLSM also had to manage evolving *organizational* challenges: As compared to traditional Cisco sales, the *Telepresence* offer involved different purchase criteria and different individual decision makers/influencers within the bank. Because the *Telepresence* selling process had many moving parts, it also required considerable *business acumen* from the FLSM and his seller to ensure that the broadscale benefits/values made sense both for the bank overall—in terms of a robust business case—and for individual DMU members.

Cisco's sales leader told us:

> "Cisco's success with this retail bank is a great example of the direction we have to go. Our FLSMs are the front line in identifying new opportunities, and then driving their sellers to identify decision makers and influencers. FLSMs and their teams bring real value to each member of the DMU. The FLSM had to lead DMU members to coalesce around our offer. It's not easy, but we work hard to ensure that our FLSMs have the skills to pull this off."

The sales leader continued:

> "Customers expect relevancy. Cisco knows they want help because they face their own pressures. If Cisco can bring customers something that helps run their business better, they are delighted. But customers don't invite all providers to that discussion, unless they step up and do things differently; credibility is a *must*. In Cisco's case, we have built our brand equity with IT [information technology] departments; the lines of business don't always perceive Cisco with that same consultative mindset. Rather, they may look to traditional consulting partners. We have to fight for a seat at that table *and* be credible—to demonstrate the capability Cisco says it has. The FLSM plays a major role in securing Cisco a seat at that table, and then showing we can do the job better than competitors."

Cisco's FLSMs face an additional challenge, related to its corporate strategy, of working closely with channel partners—90 to 95 percent of Cisco revenues. One FLSM reflected:

> "More horses in the race benefits Cisco, but there has to be trust and value for these partnerships to work. In many cases, the end customer chooses the partner, often based on information we provide. Also, we often match end customers with what we believe is the best partner for that particular set of requirements, based on several criteria. We must be transparent and sensitive to both our partners and end customers. To do that successfully requires significant business sense to keep everybody happy."

In a second Chapter 2 case study, we showed how SAP also moved beyond its traditional value proposition of improving organizational functioning. SAP used business acumen to bring a new and different set of benefits/values to a sports-arena customer. SAP technology allowed the sports arena to provide significant additional value to sports fans in the form of enhanced customer service.

As in the Cisco case study, for SAP's sports-arena customer, revenue generation was critical. Increased revenues derived from additional merchandise sales and refreshment sales at sports events. Also important was SAP's—and its customers'—satisfaction with the new system: Was information about transit schedules and parking accurate? Did customers using the SAP app find shorter lines at the concession stands? And, were these benefits/values sufficiently compelling that sports fans would attend arena events more frequently, hence also enhancing revenues?

In Chapter 2, we also showed that for a medical diagnostics firm, hospital customer requirements had changed sharply and the traditional influence of laboratory directors had declined. Hence, identifying the new DMU and DMP was a critical FLSM responsibility; constructing a compelling business case for the customer required a very different and much higher level of business acumen. As noted in that example, the sales leader explained:

> "Along with that evolution [DMU/DMP], the products are more complex. We used to sell products like a bench analyzer—a big laboratory might order 30 at a time—but now we could be dealing with an automated line; different automated modules; uncapping, recapping, sealing, and resealing samples; robotic arms for analyzing then replacing; and storage capabilities. We make it easy for the laboratory to locate a sample tube, rather

than have a person spending their time looking for it. There's so much more instrument complexity than ever before. It's much more complex to write the RFP, and much more complex to respond to one."

Not only must FLSMs play a major role in persuading customers they will receive promised benefits/values if they make purchases, they must also ensure that customers implement the appropriate measures after the sale—in the *use stage of the selling process*. Reasons:

■ To show the customer that the purchase did indeed deliver promised benefits/values—various functional values and their economic counterparts.

■ If the FLSM can indeed demonstrate delivery of promised value, and secure high customer satisfaction, future sales are more likely. With appropriate concerns for customer confidentiality, a sale at one customer may lead to sales at other customers—for this FLSM and other FLSMs.

■ Careful analysis of use measures may identify problems the firm can address promptly. Unaddressed problems, left to fester, can drive customer dissatisfaction.

■ Such analysis may also identify finer-grained needs that were previously unrecognized, leading to *ideation* and opportunities for future sales.

FLSMs must provide value to the customer organization; they must also lead their teams to gain insight into specific issues that concern each DMU member. Generally, different functional roles have specific requirements, but individuals in those roles may also have idiosyncratic needs the supplier must address.

In Chapter 2, we showed how the Affordable Care Act and growth of value-based reimbursements have placed significant pressure on hospitals/hospital systems. These pressures have led to major shifts in DMUs and DMPs. As the sales leader at a leading supplier of diagnostics health systems told us:

"Our customers are under pressure to do more with less. They are shifting their buying practices from the laboratory to the economic buyer. But beyond that, they want us to be the experts and tell them what to do. They are focused on improving ROI [return on investment]. They want to standardize tests and save hard dollars. They also want to consolidate tests, so they can operate with fewer people. Today, the FLSM role needs extensive customer and competitor knowledge. We have to have the ability to *smoke out* the reality of what's going on with our customers, and figure out what solutions we can bring to the table."

Figuring out detailed customer needs, priorities, and pain points does not stop with addressing patient-diagnostic issues. Hospitals also care about price and payment terms. The FLSM must be front and center of the pricing discussion. In the situation described above, the supplier sold capital equipment and reagents, but made most profit on reagents. Reagent pricing was tiered, based on the hospital system's forecast volume. Every six months, forecasts were checked against actuals; the supplier adjusted prices annually, *if and when* actual volume pushed prices into a different tier. This six-month process gave hospitals a chance to *catch up*, and retain the lower price, when actuals were below forecasts at the six-month mark. One FLSM explained a problem that a specific customer executive faced:

> "There is so much turbulence in hospital systems today—a particular hospital may be in one group today and then in a different group tomorrow. The key executive at our hospital-system customer was concerned that if he agreed to the traditional tiered-pricing arrangement, but then lost a hospital from the system through some sort of divestiture, we would shift him to a higher price tier, even if actuals were on track with forecasts (absent the divestiture). The account manager and I came up with a pricing arrangement that did not penalize the customer for this sort of eventuality. The executive was very happy, and we concluded the deal."

Shifting Locus of Decision-Making Authority—Vertical

The general evolution in DMU membership does not just imply a requirement to interface with different functional/business-unit executives at roughly similar organizational levels to traditional practice. As we noted in Chapter 3, it may also involve moving to higher organizational levels, up to and including the C-Suite. Certainly, the Cisco and SAP case studies demonstrate significant strategic actions for the retail bank and sports arena customers respectively; hence senior leaders in both organizations were also part of the decision-making process. FLSMs drove these interactions, but also had the responsibility to bring in other supplier resources—*resource acumen*—as necessary.

Several interviewees noted FLSM responsibility for addressing senior customer executives. Two sales leaders commented:

> "Our FLSMs have to be able to have an executive-level conversation internally to the company and externally with the customer. You can't bring in our top executives to talk to a customer CIO, CFO, CEO, or CRO [chief revenue officer], as a matter of course. Our FLSMs have to be able to hold those conversations with customer executives, then possibly bring in our top guys if it's really necessary."

> "We have to be much more knowledgeable about holistic customer solutions and their businesses—through greater industry awareness, better training, and on-the-job working. We are transitioning from a transactional salesforce to providing customer solutions. Most of our people have penetrated at the executive level, but now we have to get them comfortable with having business-level discussions. In the past, we haven't had those kinds of discussions in a formalized fashion on a regular basis with top customers. Today, that has become crucial; our FLSMs have a major challenge to help bring their people up to speed."

Senior customer executives are not just senior; most likely they achieved their high positions because they were smarter than their peers. One healthcare FLSM recounted his experience working successfully with senior hospital executives early in the sales process:

> "The people that are doing the *ideation* stage at the hospital level—these are your CMOs [chief marketing officers], CNOs [chief networking officers], VPs of quality. They can smell a sales shtick from a mile away. They bring an entirely different orientation. The minute

they get a whiff that your approach is nothing more than a cleverly designed sales pitch, you get bumped to the back of the line and, at best, you are back into the RFP hamster wheel.

"My approach is very clear: I am not here to sell you a damn thing. I am here to sit down and talk to you about some of the issues and challenges you are facing within your organization, and give you some of our ideas that have helped other organizations in your space."

Regarding senior executive involvement, the FLSM must ensure that such involvement is positive—for the firm, for the customer, for the entire firm-customer relationship—and moves the selling process forward. Of course, some senior supplier managers will not interface with customers! These executives believe that selling should be done by the salesforce, and customer issues are *not my problem*. Without doubt, appropriate senior executive involvement can be extremely positive, but FLSMs should understand that such involvement with customers can have its drawbacks. We address this topic in Chapter 6.

Personal Benefits/Values

In the foregoing discussion, we implicitly assume members of customer organizations were concerned only about organizational benefits/values. But in many cases, certainly with large customers, these individuals are *agents for principals*—shareholders. Hence, these agents' influence and decision making may, of course, be driven in part by personal benefits/values.

We addressed relationship building generally in in Chapter 3; here, we focus specifically on delivering personal benefits/values in the context of a specific purchase decision. Hear what one of the FLSMs we interviewed said about her approach:

"When we work on a deal, we work hard to provide the customer organization with the best value we can. But we know that some group of individuals is going to influence and make the final decision. So, we work hard to figure out these people's MBOs [management by objectives]. Then what we try to do is to orchestrate our proposal, so it helps them achieve their individual MBOs. If we can do that successfully, it can give us a leg up on competition."

This FLSM is talking about providing *functional* value to individual decision makers/influencers. Another FLSM focused on *psychological* value, especially for junior customer employees involved in specific deals. He told us:

"With all the change going on today, we never know who's going to be involved in purchase decisions next year, or the year after. We spend a lot of time working with key influencers/decision makers; they are critical for this year's deal. But we don't forget the less-senior people; some of them are going to be promoted, or they may move to different companies in more senior positions.

"It's often the case that, if we win a piece of business, we meet with a senior management group at the customer to celebrate the start of a new relationship. I work hard to make sure that meeting includes all customer people who played a part in

> bringing the deal to fruition. Then, I recognize the junior folk in the presence of their senior colleagues. 'I want you all to know that Jack/Jane was very helpful in ....' It's my way of thanking them for their contributions, and doing so in front of their bosses certainly doesn't hurt their career prospects!"

Delivery and receipt of the sorts of functional and psychological benefits/values just discussed are typically quite acceptable. The potential problem arises with *economic* value. Many (but certainly not all) customer firms have little problem with their employees receiving small gifts or being taken out to lunch by sellers/FLSMs. But there is a line—between positive relationship building and something negative (like receiving improper payments)—that should not be crossed. These lines are built into the fabric of company cultures, and vary widely. FLSMs should ensure they and their sellers learn about, and do not cross, their customers' lines.

The bottom line: DMUs and DMPs are changing dramatically. FLSMs must be leaders in bringing value to new decision makers/influencers—new functional/business-unit executives and senior customer leaders. The FLSM must bring value to customer organizations, but also recognize that many decision makers/influencers are agents, acting on behalf of shareholders. FLSMs should secure appropriate information and behave accordingly.

Secure Deep Market Knowledge— Customers, Competitors

In this section, we focus on the two key elements of market knowledge—customers and competitors.

Customers

A key aspect of business acumen for FLSMs and their sellers is the ability to secure deep customer knowledge. FLSMs are responsible for guiding sellers to gain customer insight, but may also bring in specialist talent—field marketing, solution specialists, value engineers—to help accomplish this task. Being able to speak the customer's language is critical—including all the acronyms that are second nature to customer employees, but can baffle outsiders. Only in-depth understanding can ultimately identify needs, priorities, problems, pain points, and surface opportunities.

One fundamental area is assessing the customer's financial health. Detailed insight paves the way for deep discussions of potential opportunities. One FLSM told us:

> "I make sure my team has a good grounding in financial analysis, so they can ask customers insightful questions. They must be able to read financial statements, and know all the different ways to deal with revenues and costs. Our training department is big on this topic, but I make sure my sellers really put it to work to isolate paths for us to follow."

Another FLSM responsible for sales of medical hardware to hospitals/hospital systems focused on detailed understanding of customer purchases, not just from the firm, but from all suppliers:

> "We have great products and great corporate support, but it's the FLSM and his account managers that make it happen at the customer. As an FLSM, I make sure my

guys track all equipment and reagent purchases in the hospital system—from us and *all* competitors—so we really understand the size of the business opportunity. We use mathematical models to figure out our pricing strategy and potential profits. I need these data, so I can direct my people and get company resources assigned to work on deals at individual customers."

Purchase-decision timing and firm commitment can be very important. A critical seller/FLSM goal is securing customer agreement to commence discussions early in the purchase process—*ideate* and *design*. By providing advice and counsel, the seller/FLSM can develop *creeping commitment* to the firm's eventual proposal. The medical-hardware FLSM continued:

"We also secure information on when the deal will likely be decided. A big deal could be two to three years in the future; that helps us figure out when we shall need to bring in corporate resources. Sometimes, customers are ready for discussion early on. We like that, so we can get to work and get them comfortable with the solution we develop. Other customers want to wait for the RFP—it's my job to work with my sales executives to get the door open for us to bring in our experts, so they can do their work and put us ahead of competition. Ideally, we lay out a calendar with milestones to guide our intervention at the customer."

Making the transition from broadscale firm value propositions to compelling value propositions from a specific customer's perspective is not a simple matter. One FLSM told us:

"I don't want to undervalue the job my account managers do. They provide a tremendous amount of support to the customer—answering all their questions and providing timely responses. I insist on timeliness. Of course, account managers can't answer all the questions, so one of my key roles is to answer them myself, or figure out who has the answer. Then we get back to the customer ASAP. Sometimes, it's a matter of securing referrals from other customers. There are just so many activities that go into what my team and I do in the field. At the end of the day, we have to come out ahead on the customer's criteria list, and balance that with the right financials."

As we emphasized earlier, the FLSM must ensure sellers make the firm's broadscale value propositions become real at individual customers. One of Philips Medical Systems' (PMS's) core technologies is patient monitoring. Patient monitoring and linkages to IT are growing ever more complex. Specific concerns include how monitoring devices interface with hospital electronic medical records systems, easier patient monitoring, reduced hospital risks/costs, and managing the entire system. Simultaneously, PMS is seeking to offer hospitals ways to manage patients more safely, reduce costs by standardizing solutions, and build expertise in IT.

A small Mississippi hospital was experiencing patient-monitoring issues, but did not have a specific budget to deal with the problems. But the hospital did have a budget for cath labs.[1] One cath lab had several requirements; a second cath lab needed overall quality improvements. To complicate matters, the hospital was also considering acquiring a magnetic resonance imaging (MRI) machine. PMS decided to take a comprehensive approach and provide the hospital with bundling opportunities.

PMS identified and highlighted each issue the hospital perceived as a problem, then formulated an overall approach to address as many problems as possible. The FLSM takes up the story:

> "This was very detailed work. As we addressed one problem after another, a series of IT-related issues emerged. These pretty much all concerned working with patients—effective patient management and making sure hospital equipment was compliant with government regulations. We successfully identified solutions, acting in a consultative capacity. What started life as a small opportunity for which there was no budget, ended up as a complex, longer-run, much more valuable, contract that we won.
>
> "The secret to winning this business was our deep consultative approach to hospital issues—we helped resolve so many. We were able to cope with complex needs, address regulations, and navigate the customer's organization—*organizational acumen*. In today's environment, you win the business when customers feel they are getting the most consultative approach. It's not always about being the lowest price with an acceptable product. It's really about what you can do to help resolve so many of these different customer issues."

One healthcare sales leader reflected on the FLSM's role for a healthcare firm:

> "The FLSM role has become increasingly important. Today's FLSM must get highly involved with their sellers in securing a deep understanding of customers, so we can deliver value. Hospitals have so many problems today; what customers perceive as value is shaped by several factors: Shrinking margins and cost contraction means fewer dollars to spend; the need to balance the quality of care with operational efficiency; and measurable patient issues like length of stay, infection control, safety, mortality, and morbidity. Delivering value in the healthcare industry has never been more important, nor more complicated. The very definition of *value* is shifting from *product-centric* to *customer-centric*. Indeed, today good product quality is merely a threshold requirement.
>
> "The sales job is shifting from *specialized* to *generalized*. Traditionally, healthcare providers like hospitals and healthcare centers were very tech focused. They wanted best-in-class technology and product capabilities; we made sales with new *best mousetraps*, regardless of price; after all, payment was on a cost-plus basis. There has been a dramatic shift in focus to efficiency—cost reduction and cost avoidance. Major changes in reimbursement models to quality metrics like patient outcomes have changed (and will continue to change) purchasing behavior dramatically.
>
> "The *rubber meets the road* at the FLSM. Our best FLSMs not only are fully aware of the sweeping environmental changes our customers face, they derive the implications for individual customers. Working with their sellers, FLSMs use those implications as raw material from which to fashion value for customers."

Another sales leader put it this way:

> "FLSM competence starts with industry knowledge. They understand where solution opportunities occur; articulate what we do that customers value; have enough

connections to open doors to get to the right person; know how the system works; understand customer challenges; speak their language; and develop innovate solutions. And help individual sellers navigate these customer mazes."

Securing deep customer knowledge is important for all FLSMs in all industries, but deep customer knowledge alone may be insufficient. In addition, it may be necessary for FLSMs and their sellers to have deep understanding of their customers' customers. Only then can they provide the products/services that help customers be successful in their markets, and hence *pull through* the firm's products. One FLSM in telecommunications told us:

"You have to know as much about your customer's products, and those of your customer's customer, as they do. More importantly, you probably need to understand how they fit into their market space."

A key element of business acumen is deep insight about customers. FLSMs must understand not only functional needs, but also various competitor and environmental pressures on customers, and the economic realities they face. In healthcare, for example, FLSMs must understand customer relationships with payers, and be able to *connect the dots* in the economic system, so all parties are *singing from the same song sheet*. FLSMs in this industry must understand how all the mechanisms and contracts between providers and insurers work, and be able to articulate that story well and effectively. FLSMs/sellers must be sufficiently immersed in customers' businesses before they tell them what they need—sometimes customer personnel are too busy to understand what they are missing. In a statement that should function as a goal for all FLSMs, one FLSM told us she frequently says to customer executives:

"Here is a key issue that you are not addressing; let me show you how."

Competitors

In this section, we have focused heavily on understanding customers. But we must not forget the firm develops value propositions to secure customer agreement to purchase firm products/services, *in the face of competitors attempting to do the same thing*. It therefore is incumbent on the firm to provide FLSMs and sellers with good competitor data.

At a global level, some firms support the salesforce with output from some competitive/business intelligence group. One sales leader reported:

"We have a really good business intelligence group at corporate, so that is a significant benefit for us."

But the sales leader went on:

"We could always stand to benefit from specific market and value proposition data from competitive landscaping."

What the sales leader is essentially saying is that, at a general level, the salesforce knows what competitors are doing, but has little data regarding competitor actions at specific customers. We did not focus specifically on this issue in our interviews, but our general sense is that sellers and FLSMs do not, generally, have good handles on competitive activity at their current and potential customers.

As we discussed in Chapter 2, there is a big difference between generalized value propositions developed by the marketing department, and specific customer-focused value propositions that enable the salesforce to win deals for the firm. The same is true for competitors: It's one thing to know generally what competitors are pitching; it's quite another to understand how specific competitor sellers/FLSMs are operating at particular customers, or in particular geographic areas. Regardless, FLSMs should encourage their sellers to do the best job they can to secure understanding about who/ what they have to beat at customers in their territories, so as to win business.

Certainly, sellers/FLSMs may secure some of this information by being observant in customer visits and asking appropriate questions. Our general observation is that individuals in customer firms vary widely in their predisposition to discuss competitor activity. Astute sellers/FLSMs learn who (and who not) are good competitor information sources.

Several years ago, one of us (NC) visited IBM to sell an executive education program on behalf of Columbia Business School. The meeting, with a dozen or so IBM executives, took place in a conference room arranged in a classic U-fashion. Several minutes into the presentation, NC noted the name cards in front of the participants. They were in the format *Jack Smith—Dell Computer*; *Jane Andrews—Hewlett-Packard*; *Roland Johnson—Hitachi*. NC halted his presentation, picked up one of the name cards and asked a question:

"Who are you guys?"

The answer:

"We are shadows; these are the firms we are shadowing."

IBM was operating a sophisticated *shadow system*.[2] The full-time job responsibility of these executives was to know as much as possible about the firms they were shadowing, using whatever information sources they could identify. The insights these executives developed were fed into IBM's strategic decision-making process.

FLSMs can adapt this system for their sales districts. The FLSM compiles a list of required competitive information (and updates this list over time). The FLSM also appoints individual sellers to *shadow* specific competitors. Sellers secure data about the various competitors, then send it to those competitors' shadows. The shadows become experts on their competitor targets; they periodically share information and insight with the entire sales team. The FLSM directs and manages this process.

 ## Do the Math/Make the Business Case

Time and again in our interviews, we learned of successful FLSMs *making the business case* for individual deals. The overarching issue was demonstrating the translation from *functional* benefits/ values into *economic* benefits/values. Strategic acumen points the way to this translation; but the FLSM must have business acumen to *do the math*.

We touch on this translation in Chapter 2. Recall what Marty Homlish told us about SAP's traditional focus on functional value and the transition to economic value that he engineered:

"We used to talk about successful implementation like this: 'Customer XYZ implemented SAP Supply-Chain Management. They had to do it in 100 days, but they went live in 99

days and only had one critical crisis [i.e., *functional* value].' But that was not the issue. The real story was: 'Customer XYZ implemented SAP Supply-Chain Management. As a result, it reduced its on-hand inventory from 2.8 months' supply to 2.1 months', and its on-the-water inventory from one month to two weeks. And customer XYZ saved $500 million [i.e., *economic* value].'"

Similarly, in the sports-arena example, SAP had to show a positive ROI for its customer, based largely on various revenue enhancements, for instituting the new customer service initiative.

We also see this functional-to-economic benefit/value translation played out in Cisco's *Telepresence* sale to the retail bank. *Telepresence* offers many *functional* benefits/values—bank customers can talk to a specialist almost immediately—no appointment necessary; bank branches free up infrequently used office space; bank specialists do not have to travel to branches, hence eliminating travel time; the bank offers specialist expertise in previously unserved remote locations. These functional benefits should bring increased revenues. Some operating costs may rise; other operating costs may fall. Does investment in *Telepresence* make sense for the bank financially? That was the core question.

Certainly, the bank had no easy way to make this determination. After all, *Telepresence* was a game-changer, an innovative approach outside the bank's experience. Yet, senior bank executives required an affirmative answer to the *economic value* question before moving ahead. Securing this answer was a job for the FLSM/seller team.

A key part of business acumen is *doing the math*—figuring out the net of increased/decreased revenues, cost reductions/increases, and customer investment. This *net* must represent a positive customer ROI, and otherwise improve its ability to reach objectives. Cisco could not have sold *Telepresence* to the retail bank without promising a positive ROI. To reach such a conclusion, the FLSM/seller had to *identify* and *understand* the financial implications of each element involved in shifting the bank's approach to providing specialist consumer advice, from face-to-face to *Telepresence*.

In many *Telepresence* sales, Cisco FLSMs/sellers must conduct deep analyses of customer operations. A global natural resources firm made a major investment in *Telepresence* for its global operations only after detailed analysis of executive travel patterns and related airline, hotel, other travel expenses.

One FLSM at a distribution firm explained his approach to *making the business case*:

> "It's always difficult to come in at a higher price, but we make product deliveries frequently. The customer may get a better price direct from the manufacturer, but delivery is only three times per year. The working capital savings in [more frequent] buying from us far outstrips savings from a lower price."

FLSMs may have to develop creative ways of *doing the math* so both firm and customer win. These approaches may involve unusual payment structures like risk-sharing deals, and shifts from periodic payments to continuous/recurring revenues. As software as a service (SaaS) proliferates, tech firms must contend with such changes: Revenues are immediately reduced as customers reject capital expenditures in favor of continuous payments via cloud computing. If customer reluctance to make capital expenditures expands to other industries, FLSMs will find themselves on the front line of constructing new types of deals.

Of course, *doing the math* has two parts. First, the FLSM/sellers must show customers that their purchase will show a positive ROI. Second, the FLSM must ensure the firm earns decent profit margins. In a very real sense, pricing partitions value between supplier and customer. By its action in producing/delivering products/services, the firm creates value—some value goes to the customer, some value is retained by the firm. High price—high value to the firm; low price—high value to the customer. One sales leader put it this way:

> "In our firm, the FLSM gets very involved in contract negotiations. We create a lot of value but the FLSM has the job of dividing up that value between the customer and the company. It's a difficult job, but we train our FLSMs for that."

One FLSM affirmed his detailed engagement with customers:

> "Although I have a strong team, I spend a lot of my time looking for creative ways to structure deals."

Making the numbers work can be a major part of the FLSM's job. One FLSM selling into the banking industry told us:

> "I spend 25 percent of my time repairing spreadsheets, looking at the numbers, trying to make them work for this particular customer or prospect. I also work with senior management, getting the price. If there is a legal issue in the contract, I will spend time with the legal department. That's usually time well spent; there's a reason people call our legal guys the *sales prevention* department."

One Philips Medical Systems (PMS) FLSM highlighted the focus on detail that enabled PMS to win a multimillion-dollar contract:

> "With our consultative approach, we work hard to navigate and deeply understand customer needs, and the regulations and organizations they must deal with. The contract winners don't necessarily have the lowest prices; rather, they help resolve the customer's many issues. We often reveal problems by challenging product utilization, and investigating issues like service, maintenance, training, and upgrades related to new government regulations or reimbursements. Many different things come up: We work hard to identify these up front, so we can better position ourselves versus competition. A lot of times we can package stuff to provide that value. For example, a customer may have budgeted an upgrade—we may wrap that into an offer at no cost. Or, we may train the biomed organization. Of course, that comes out of margin, but it allows us to look at customer needs more holistically."

Promising to deliver functional benefits/values to customers continues to be extremely important, but is increasingly insufficient. FLSMs must lead the charge to ensure they and their sellers can make the translation from functional benefits/values to economic benefits/values. *Doing the math* is central to building the customer's business case, and is a core element of business acumen.

Enhance the Firm's Face to Customers

Sellers are the firm's everyday face to customers; FLSMs are typically less frequent, but more senior, firm faces who appear at select customers periodically. When working with customers, sellers and FLSMs benefit from brand image of the firm/business they represent—Chapter 3. By the ways they behave, FLSMs can also enhance these organizational brand images. Organizational brand images are more generally a responsibility of senior management/marketing—Chapter 10. Successful brand-image development eases the way for sellers/FLSMs to gain entry to, and work with, customer personnel. The seller should not enter the customer as a blank slate, but rather with a positive aura built up over time.

But brand enhancement is not solely the domain of senior management/marketing. The sales organization has a critical role to play; no role is more important than the FLSM. In our research we found brand enhancement happened most effectively via close-in FLSM interactions with the customers, where listening and learning were the primary objectives. Successful FLSMs we met wanted to know from customers:

- Did you get what you expected from our firm?

- How could the experience be improved?

- What went well and should be continued/expanded?

- How could we add more value?

We noted three broad types of interaction between FLSM and customers.

Check-in Meetings. FLSMs ride with sellers to interact with customers. FLSMs observe seller-customer interactions, while listening for clues regarding customer satisfaction and possible opportunity. This was the most common form of regular FLSM-customer interaction. One FLSM reported:

> "When I travel with my reps I have multiple agendas. Of course, customer meetings always provide opportunities for seller coaching. But I try to show the customer it's not only the seller that has their interests at heart. My presence demonstrates that our entire firm is concerned that we treat them well."

Formal Annual Reviews. FLSMs sit down with customers (usually with the seller present) to review annual activities, assess relationship strengths/weaknesses, and plan for the new year. Interviewees considered such meetings highly effective as a way to secure direct, constructive feedback. One sales leader provided her perspective:

> "I insist each of my FLSMs provide me with a list of customers with which they will conduct annual reviews. I review the lists and make additions and subtractions. My stated reason for customers is that together we can plan for the future. But my unstated agenda is to engage these customers in closer relationships."

User-Group Meetings. FLSMs form a community of customers that meets regularly to discuss common issues. Customers offer advice to each other, and to the firm (vendor). Nonusers/prospects may occasionally be added to the guest list. Such communities are highly effective (though not without risk if not well managed).

One FLSM for a higher-education software firm described an Ohio-based group:

> "We generally have about 200 people at this user group, hosted by one of our clients. It's a great way to meet customers in a more relaxed environment. The actual users show up, not just the IT folks, so we can familiarize them with what we do. Each of our user groups is very serious; they elect a board of directors and a president. The users run the conferences, arrange the schedule, or figure out the learning tracks. We support these groups with our product experts."

FLSMs have the responsibility for building on firm/business brand image, and educating customers about the organization and its products/services. Another device used by several FLSMs we talked with was *lunch-and-learn* sessions involving current and potential customers. Successful FLSMs implement this process to drive brand development. But, rather than firm employees delivering messages that enhance the brand, current customers present their own experiences. Such participation in these sessions demonstrates their enthusiasm and commitment toward the supplier. Current customers provide unbiased information to potential customers. As one FLSM told us:

> "Lunch-and-learn sessions can be enormously productive. I organize events and manage the process, but current customers do the heavy lifting for the firm."

Of course, sellers do not necessarily start off with a positive brand image, or even a blank slate. Indeed, the slate may be dirty! Under previous leadership, the firm may have been involved in shady business practices, faced lawsuits, received bad press, endured quality/delivery problems, been subject to a consent decree. As one FLSM told us:

> "When I became FLSM, we had a lot of baggage. Our problems are well behind us, and we continue to provide great technology. But people have long memories; there was a very bad taste among several executives at our major customers. I spent a lot of time at customers with my account managers, working to dispel those negative feelings. I have great account managers, but I needed to support them and bring a managerial perspective to these discussions. By and large, I think we've done a pretty good job with key customer executives. Most of them understand that bad stuff happens; they know we are working very hard to recover our reputation."

Senior management has a core responsibility for firm/business brand image, but so do FLSMs. Whereas senior managers exert their influence largely via managerial decisions and public pronouncements, FLSMs work with customers face-to-face. In their various customer interactions, at all stages in the buying/selling process, FLSMs have enormous opportunities to win customers' *hearts and minds*, enhance the firm's brand image, and create substantial value. By the same token, firm failure, especially at the *implement* and *use* stages of the selling process, can cause significant damage. FLSMs should work hard to ensure this does not occur.

 Drive the Sale

Perhaps it was once the case that sellers made sales, and FLSMs managed sellers at arm's length from customers. It may also have been the case that some FLSMs deliberately kept the largest customers for themselves, while managing sellers who dealt with less lucrative smaller customers. Those behaviors may still occur in some domains. Generally, our sales leaders told us sellers were responsible for individual customers, but FLSMs were frequently involved directly in making deals and contract negotiations, especially where large revenues were at stake.

There are two core reasons for this aspect of FLSM role evolution.

The Changing Customer DMU

As noted previously, in many firms, responsibility for purchase decisions is moving horizontally—across functions, into individual businesses—and vertically—up the organizational ladder. Indeed, senior executives are becoming part of the DMU in situations that would have been unthinkable a few years ago. Reasons for these evolutionary trends (noted earlier):

■ **Democratization of technology.** As computing power has increased, and the Internet has become ubiquitous, decisions previously made by experts, like corporate IT professionals, are moving into other functions/businesses.

■ **The 2008/2009 recession.** Enhanced uncertainties and desire to manage costs/investments more closely have led senior managers to become more involved.

■ **Suppliers avoiding procurement.** In many firms, procurement organizations have significantly upgraded their competence, and introduced *strategic sourcing* and *vendor management* programs. Hence, suppliers must broaden their scope of customer contacts.

■ **Greater procurement professionalism.** Many firms have realized that potential procurement savings are enormous. Hence, they have staffed-up with high-caliber procurement professionals, and reorganized their procurement departments.

■ **Strategic selling.** Enhanced strategic acumen has allowed FLSMs and their sellers to develop higher-level value propositions. These value propositions require responses from more senior customer executives than conventional product/service-based offers.

The totality of these factors leads to one inevitable conclusion—the selling job is getting tougher. In many cases, sellers will be unable to apply organizational acumen to fully navigate customer organizations. Nor will they have the necessary business acumen to make optimal deals for both the firm and customer. Quite simply, the FLSM must get involved.

Greater FLSM involvement requires new thinking, new approaches, new ways of doing things. In the continual search to identify opportunities, and provide customers with greater value, some attempts will fail. FLSMs must develop a culture within their districts that rewards creativity, but also accepts the inevitably failures that will occur. And they should model such behavior for their sellers.

Shift to Economic Purchasing Criteria

As noted earlier, customers increasingly want to know the economic consequences of their purchasing decisions. Hence, sellers must shift focus from *functional* benefits/values to *economic* benefits/values. But, it's one thing to explain product features/attributes, and how they provide functional benefits/values—less frequent errors, significant time savings, happier workers, whatever. It's quite another to figure out the economic benefits/values of those functional benefits/values, and to calculate metrics like customers' total cost of ownership (TCO), profit, ROI.

In many firms, seller training focuses initially on product attributes/features—functional benefits/values. The transition to economic benefits/values is more complex and difficult to learn. It takes time and experience to become truly facile with required financial-analytic techniques. There are many cases where the seller does not possess the training or ability to make the required calculations. An FLSM with appropriate financial ability can take on such tasks, and be successful. A telecommunications FLSM said:

> "We are facing increasing pressure from customers for economic justification of our products. That's not a simple task, as we have to translate many sources of value into dollars and cents. My guys are pretty well trained but, frankly, sometimes the complex calculations are beyond them. They know when they're getting out of their depth, so I come in to structure things up. I trained in finance, so I can add a lot of value directly by taking all the positive elements of our offer, turning them into economic values for the customer, and helping to close the sale."

What FLSMs Should Do

A core feature of business acumen is for the FLSM to decide how involved to get in seller/customer deals. Some FLSMs prefer a hands-off approach; others like to get in the action, especially if they possess critical skills that individual sellers lack. Regardless, FLSM time is a scarce resource, so they should only get deeply involved with the *right* deals at the *right* customers. Said one FLSM in medical diagnostics:

> "I separate the big deals from the smaller deals, so I can focus my efforts where it's most valuable. But I make sure my sellers have the tools to do the job."

FLSMs should have a consistent approach to deals, large and small, regardless of whether they get deeply involved with the customer or whether this responsibility rests with the seller. We heard often that competition is continually getting tougher. The medical-diagnostics FLSM told us:

> "I always take the opportunity to differentiate ourselves on everything. You have to do those in-depth cost analyses to vet out every ounce of value where we can prove our worth, so that, ideally, we can avoid customers going to an RFP. I drive this cadence hard with the reps, so they do what they have to do. I make sure I continue the momentum—keep the reps thinking: What can I do to separate myself; what can I do that's creative—technically, financially—continually thinking of better solutions and outcomes for the customer.

"I didn't make my numbers year after year by just driving the deals that were on the table. I always try to find where I can shake something that's not loose, but maybe can get in before everybody else. Maybe I can find a gap the customer doesn't even realize is a gap, and just make it bigger than they realize. Maybe I build a financial model on how to get them from the current *it's-not-so-bad* state—'I didn't know I needed this'—until they feel the pain—'I can't live without it.' And I make them realize there's a plan to move from *now*, to a positive future state. I want them to say to themselves: 'I can have more value and it will cost me less.' This approach is very different from just waiting for the RFP.

"You can't do something for yourself unless you're doing something better for the customer—you have to find what that win is for them."

This FLSM is showing great business acumen. Armed with his firm's broadscale value propositions, he delves deeply into customer situations, seeking places to add value and ways to differentiate the firm from competition. The FLSM works this way where large deals are possible. But the FLSM also works hard to ensure his sellers approach their customers in exactly the same way.

Speaking more generally, FLSMs must become more directly involved in the actual selling process. The shift to tougher selling environments and increased focus on economic, rather than just functional, benefits/values requires a deep experience level that many sellers do not possess. Certainly, seller training is imperative, but FLSMs, with their superior business acumen, must be prepared to *step up to the plate*.

Keep Tabs on Progress

A critical element of business acumen is knowing how well you are doing, and taking steps to keep on track, bring you back on track, or generally do better. All firms we interviewed set quotas for FLSMs and their sellers. Most quota setting was top down, often originating in a corporate finance group, then reaching FLSMs via the sales management structure. We found very little evidence of formal bottom-up/top-down quota setting for FLSMs. In some cases, FLSMs had limited influence in setting district quotas via lobbying their bosses, but this was not common.

Generally, quota setting for individual sellers was also top down, essentially breaking down the FLSM quota. In most cases, FLSMs had no influence on these territory quotas; in other cases, FLSMs had limited ability to modify individual seller quotas at the margin; in a few cases, FLSMs allocated the district quota among sellers/sales territories.

Regardless of the actual quota-setting processes, at the end of the day, FLSMs had a *number*—a revenue quota they had to meet. Individual sellers also had their own numbers/quotas. (Sometimes the firm set subquotas in terms of products and/or market segments.) Achieving these performance targets was important for the firm, but also important for FLSMs and sellers alike in determining take-home pay and other benefits.

The ability of FLSMs to achieve quota is, of course, critically dependent on how FLSMs interface with sellers. In Chapter 5, we discuss team building and the role of coaching and training in improving sellers' intellectual capital. Here, we focus more directly on managing quota achievement.

Quota achievement is only really possible if the FLSM has a good idea of where sales opportunities exist, within the district and within individual sales territories. In one fast-growing software firm, the sales leader focused especially on the balance in securing revenues from current customers and acquiring new customers:

> "Every year, my best guys hire well, ramp their people up well, leverage company resources—and balance their portfolios. They know where the big deals are, but they also make sure their sellers get both run-rate business and single-growth business. They've this great ability to have balance in their business. The guys who do incredibly well know how to mine their base. They simply know which sales execs and which customers they should always be minding, and really know how to get some new logo [customer] stuff.
>
> "Failure occurs when an FLSM is over-tilted to get new logos, and they just don't quite make it; they can't bring it in; they get folded under the deal pressure. Or, guys start to depend too much on their installed base, and manufacture deal after deal after deal. One day they just run out of capacity and they haven't developed their new logo business. The guys that have a balanced portfolio with their installed base and white space kill it here."

Relatedly, from another sales leader:

> "The successful people in this company, up and down in different segments of the business, truly understand, from the beginning of the year, *how to balance* short-term actions with longer-terms objectives."

More generally, the best FLSMs focused laser-like on quota achievement. They develop regular schedules for keeping on top of seller performance. One FLSM told us:

> "I keep very close tabs on my quota attainment, and quota attainment by each of my guys. I also check their sales pipelines—what they have committed, and what they're working on but not yet committed. I track by month and by quarter: I have a half-hour weekly call with each seller on Monday morning. Then I have a team call on Thursday. On Friday, I brief my manager. In these calls, we review opportunities in the pipeline, and see what help we can provide individual sellers. This is all pretty rigorous.
>
> "In these various interactions with my people, we go through a strategic planning process for major deals that are coming up with customers in their territories. Our goal is to create a shared roadmap with individual customers on how they will adopt our products and technologies over a three-year period. So, I brainstorm next steps with my people; we create action plans together. That may involve getting inside the customer to do user surveys, or identifying executives we should be talking to.
>
> "We also have quarterly business reviews: We take a couple of steps back and ask questions of each account executive one by one: 'How are you going to do this year? How are you going to hit/exceed your number? What opportunities are you working on? What have you done year-to-date? What are you going to do in the current quarter? Next quarter? What business development are you doing in your territory? What key customers are you working with? What is competition doing? How are our new products being accepted?'

> "The guys who are doing really well look forward to these reviews and planning sessions. Those that aren't doing well hate it. But I believe it helps all of them; and it helps me in deciding where to spend my time in the field."

A focus on quota attainment is critical, but perhaps more important are the factors that drive revenues. Revenues already earned are history; at any point in time, what really matters are future revenues, and how to earn them. One FLSM with a medical-supplies firm put it this way:

> "The guys that hired me as an FLSM taught me to spend really little time, in my first meeting with each team member, looking at sales numbers. If I look at a sales number, and it's low, I feel, '*oh crap*', but it's too late. That number's already out there; it's too late to change it.
>
> "I spend a lot of time analyzing the factors that make a rep successful. What are the key performance indicators; what makes someone successful; and then I measure the whole team against those factors. It can be many different things: how many quotes they write in a month; how many doctors they see in a day; how many referral meetings they hold in a month; how many nights they spend in a hotel. Some factors are hard to measure; that's why the FLSM's duty is to get it and analyze it. I'm very big on analyzing and trying to establish what my good people are doing, and then make those deliverables for everyone. It helps identify key issues early on and correct them. After all, I can measure these things on a daily, weekly, or monthly basis, and give fast feedback.
>
> "The first thing a typical poor-performing rep will say is, 'Poor me, I'm out there every day, but I just have a terrible territory that's different from everyone else's.' But if I have key performance indicators, I guarantee I can find somewhere they're deficient in what they're doing. I've rarely seen people fail who were out there doing the right things day in and day out."

One telecommunications FLSM not only focused on his personal numbers, but required his sellers to do likewise with their numbers, then push for reasons:

> "I make sure my people understand what they sold, what they lost, and why they lost— price, product, service? I want to know what additional services we sold and lost—what came in the front door versus what went out the back door. Not only how much, but why. I try to take off my blinders; I encourage my team to do the same. I want the sale, but I also want to understand what is going on within that customer. What potential sales are we missing; where do we risk losing current business. I want to see if a particular product is growing; if a product that should be growing is flat."

A useful way to conceptualize the things sellers *do every day* is by using an input ➠ intermediate ➠ output framework—Figure 4.2:

- **Input**—Actions that sellers take in pursuit of sales.

- **Intermediate**—Customer actions/state-of-mind changes that may lead to sales.

- **Output**—Performance variables like sales revenues, profit contribution, profits.

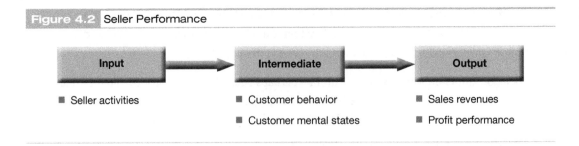

Figure 4.2 Seller Performance

As our medical-supplies FLSM noted, as far as *output* variables are concerned: "It's too late." Those sales numbers are already in; they're history. Hence, we focus on areas where FLSMs can make a difference—*input* and *intermediate* variables. Because of our focus on quota attainment—*output* variables—we reverse the chronological order and start with *intermediate* variables.

Intermediate Variables

Perhaps the most common source of intermediate performance measures is the increasingly popular sales-pipeline analysis. Pipelines essentially track customer behavior through the selling process, from opportunity identification to sales revenues, using intermediate measures. (Indeed, the most effective sales pipelines go beyond the sale—*output* variable—to also measure customer satisfaction with the purchase—*implementation* and *use*.)

Sales Pipelines. The sales pipeline comprises various measures related to stages in the selling process. Customers move from prospects (potential customers) to buyers. Pipeline analysis tracks firm success as customers traverse these various stages, and is critical for sales forecasting. Figure 4.3 illustrates the sales pipeline for a large tech firm.

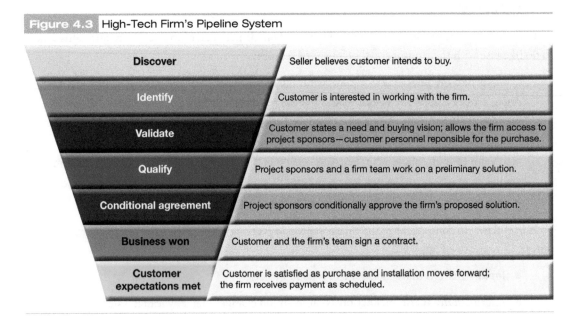

Figure 4.3 High-Tech Firm's Pipeline System

For pipeline systems to work appropriately, FLSMs must ensure their sellers enter each potential opportunity into their individual pipelines, and estimate sales revenues. For various reasons, sellers often resist entering pipeline data: Experienced/successful sellers cannot be bothered; in some Eastern cultures, an opportunity that exits the pipeline is a personal failure, and a cause for shame, so the pipeline's opening stage is empty. Regardless, FLSMs (supported by sales leaders) must make entering pipeline data mandatory. FLSMs must insist that, periodically, sellers update each opportunity with a refined sales forecast. If customer plans change, or the customer eliminates the firm as a potential supplier, the opportunity exits the pipeline.

FLSMs must aggregate pipeline data from individual sellers, and constantly track opportunities by sales territory. They must also track percentage of opportunities moving from stage to stage, starting with total sales leads/opportunities discovered.

Sales-pipeline-velocity measures can be very helpful for gaining insight into potential sales— Appendix 8. FLSMs can then project expected sales revenues by individual territory, and by their entire districts. Perhaps more importantly, FLSMs can identify where seller performance is on track, and where it should be improved. These analyses allow FLSMs to direct sellers where and when to focus their efforts—securing leads, validating opportunities—and where the FLSM should expend coaching effort and/or intervene personally at specific customers with specific sellers.

One FLSM emphasized her firm's commitment to pipeline management and how she implemented the system:

> "We are much more regimented on updating our forecasts than we were in the past. We used to focus on the annual number. So, you could not sell anything for a couple of quarters because you were chasing a couple of big deals that came in during the fourth quarter, and still be successful—have a great year. The end of the year was all that management cared about.
>
> "Today, we are monthly driven and quarterly driven. If you have not updated that opportunity in the last six weeks, there's a conversation about that. If it's a commit, you should have updated that opportunity every two weeks. Those types of metrics we are definitely using.
>
> "We expect you to bring in multiple transactions a quarter, and we track that very closely. I have direct influence and control over what accounts you hold. I really work very hard and diligently to make sure everybody has enough opportunity and accounts to be successful."

A second FLSM also discussed the change in approach to future business at his firm:

> "We have a weekly or biweekly call for what we call *forecast* and *pipeline* reviews. *Forecast* focuses on the current quarter—we do a good job; all our FLSMs are very current-quarter focused. At forecast reviews, we're looking at the deals—plans to close deals: 'What do we need to do to get this business?' 'What does the forecast look like?' 'How are we trending?' In the past, the general approach has been: 'Next quarter is next quarter; I just have to get through this quarter.'
>
> "But now we're shifting the conversation, shifting the mindset. There has to be a balance of current quarter and *pipeline*—looking into the next quarter. We make sure we

build the pipeline, so we always enter any quarter with enough demand. The conversation is different: 'How are we advancing?' 'What are the next steps to a win?' 'What do we have to do next to get that deal ready?' 'What is the compelling event?' So, it is really balancing these two directions."

Many firms now implement software from Salesforce.com and others to track and manage sales pipelines. These applications have many tools—for sellers to better analyze customer data, and for FLSMs to gain greater insight into seller performance. Regardless, lack of a corporate system—purchased or proprietary—should not impede FLSMs from developing and managing their own pipeline systems for their sellers and districts.

Other Intermediate Measures. An alternative term for *sales-pipeline measures* is *macro-intermediate measures*. Pipeline measures focus on a series of macro-stages that customers traverse (or not) on the way to an agreement to buy. But much customer behavior occurs between these stages. In part, the seller's job is to influence these customer behaviors; we label these measures micro-intermediate.

Examples of micro-intermediate measures are legion—commitment to engage in co-op advertising; agreement to place the firm on an approved supplier list; agreement to conduct factory trials; acceptance of firm proposals; agreement to accept retail displays; agreement to meet with a firm's subject-matter expert; agreement to join a customer advisory board; agreement for a high-level firm-customer meeting. These measures reflect seller progress in moving the customer from stage to stage through the sales pipeline, and/or help develop the firm-customer relationship. (Some of these micro-intermediate measures may function as macro-intermediate measures in some pipeline systems.)

These micro-intermediate measures are particularly important; they represent the sorts of granular areas where FLSMs can coach sellers on steps that move customers through the sales pipeline, and/or strengthen relationships. These measures are the crucial link between *input* variables and *macro-intermediate* (*sales pipeline*) measures.

Input Variables

What intermediate variables do not reveal is what sellers actually *do*. Seller behavior is an input to intermediate variables and the pipeline system. How sellers spend their time is a critical driver of intermediate-variable performance and, ultimately, of output-variable performance. Seller inputs are the crucial seller variables FLSMs can direct and manage. FLSMs must decide what they want sellers to do, then make sure they act accordingly. Specific activities FLSMs may require from sellers are many—make calls on specific current/potential customers, interface with customer service/technical service personnel, write sales-territory/account plans.

Sales Plans. Sales-territory plans and individual account plans—aka *sales action plans*—are fundamental to constructing an effective pipeline-management system. Typically, FLSMs work with individual sellers a few months prior to the operating period to identify opportunities and expected DMUs/DMPs, establish required resources, and generally formulate calendars for customer meetings. During the operating period, the sales action plan, continuously updated, functions as a framework for the FLSM to direct, lead, and manage individual sellers. One FLSM explained his approach:

> "The sales action plan drives from individual account plans: 'Where is the business?' 'How much of that spend can we get?' Strategic: 'How are we going to approach that spend?' Tactical: 'What meetings do we need?' 'With whom?' 'What tools are necessary?' 'What day-to-day activities must I do to work those strategies to capture those revenues?'
>
> "We do twice-a-year reviews, but I do a one-on-one monthly meeting with each rep. We go through the account plan. We compare the plan to their sales funnel. We make sure that opportunities in the funnel match opportunities in the sales action plan. 'Should we adjust the plan?' 'Should we adjust the opportunities?' 'Are our 30-day and 60-day forecasts still on target?' 'Are we moving the dial to where we need to go?'"

FLSMs should be very clear about required seller behavior, measure actual behavior, isolate discrepancies, take corrective action, then move ahead. When sellers do not act as required/planned, FLSMs should pursue one course of action. If sellers have acted as directed/agreed, but anticipated customer actions—intermediate variables—did not occur as planned, FLSMs should undertake quite different actions. Table 4.1 shows some basic input measures.

Table 4.1 Evaluation Methods: Input Measures

Measure	Value	Limitations
Calls per day	Identifies level of calling effort	Measures quantity of calls, not quality
Calls per account	Identifies level of calling effort	Measures quantity of calls, not quality
Calls per new account	Identifies where time is spent; link to sales strategy	Should be used together with calls per existing account
Calls per existing account	Identifies where time is spent; link to sales strategy	Should be used together with calls per new account

Working Full Time. In the foregoing discussion, we assumed sellers were spending their time attempting to make quota, achieve firm objectives, and generally work for company success. Certainly, some selling jobs are defined as part time, but the question to consider is the following: Are nominally full-time sellers actually working full time? Do they score well on working hard?

For sellers whose pay is predominantly variable, this may be a less serious issue at a tactical level—no sales, no pay—but may, nonetheless, have serious strategic implications related to inadequate market coverage. Regardless of seller compensation arrangements—commission, bonus, salary, combination salary plus incentive compensation—an important FLSM task is to ensure their sellers put in a full day's effort, and do what they are supposed to do. When we raised this issue in our interviews, the typical response was:

> "Our sellers are professionals. We have great FLSMs; they all work very hard. Lack of effort is not a problem for us."

We certainly hope our FLSM and sales leader readers can confidently agree with this statement. But we have seen cases where sellers did not put in full effort, and FLSMs had to take action. From an FLSM at a firm selling to independent retailers:

> "I came into a situation where the former FLSM was a long-time firm employee; sales leaders had not wanted to address the poor performance in his district. New sales leaders pretty soon realized there was a serious problem with this FLSM; he accepted early retirement, and I was appointed his replacement. Right away, I had to deal with a couple of problems with long-tenured sellers. The most senior seller was close to retirement and was just coasting, not really motivated by money, and with too large a territory. But the most serious immediate challenge was an independently wealthy guy who was effectively working part time, focusing on a smallish group of favored customers and ignoring significant sales potential.
>
> "Once I got my facts together and met with him, he acknowledged the situation and promised to improve. I accepted his apparent sincerity, and in the late fall and winter, both his activity and sales results trended in the right direction. But in the spring, the golf course proved too seductive. I had to fire him."

This problem also occurs in high tech. A highly paid account manager for a well-known high-tech firm made the following offer to representatives of a small start-up:

> "When I was [a self-employed consultant], I did a lot of work improving your operations; I think you were pretty happy with my contributions. I'd really like to see you guys succeed, but I know budgets are tight. Anyway, I have landed a well-paid (mainly salary) sales job. What I suggest is you hire me on a one-day-per-week basis to continue what I started. I can do my sales job four days per week, and save one day for you."

What a great offer for the start-up, but not so good for the high-tech firm. If the start-up agrees to the proposed deal, the high-tech firm will only receive 80 percent (4 out of 5 days per week) of the effort for which it pays its seller. (The start-up's chairman turned down the offer on ethical grounds.) FLSMs must ensure they receive the expected 100 percent effort and time commitment from their sellers. They must set expectations for input-variable behavior, and ensure sellers act accordingly.

Administrative Tasks. One critical element of keeping tabs on progress, indeed of doing all aspects of the FLSM job well, is spending time wisely. Many sales leaders testified to the high demands of the FLSM job. In Chapter 7, Personal Acumen, we highlight personal drive and hard work as critical characteristics of successful FLSMs. But it's one thing to work hard doing stuff; it's quite another to spend time doing the *right* stuff.

Time spent doing administrative work is time *not* spent keeping tabs on progress, coaching sellers, and generally getting up/keeping up to speed on all aspects of *strategic, organizational, business, team-building, resource,* and *personal* acumen. We believe that, in many cases, administrative demands, imposed on FLSMs by senior management and sales leaders, are too onerous. Indeed, in Chapter 8, we call on firm/business leaders to *remove the crap,* reduce administrative demands, and streamline processes.

Regardless, FLSMs have a personal responsibility to take control of their own time allocations. One FLSM in medical technology spends significant time in the field taking part in customer training with his sellers. He told us:

> "I spend much of my time in the field with my sales reps in day-long customer-training workshops. We probably do at least one every other week, and that's a really important part of my job. Unfortunately, I feel I spend way too much time right here; right in front of my desk, doing administrative work. [Yesterday, for example], I read 73 emails and sent 48."

But it's not just the amount of time doing administrative tasks, it's what type of time. One sales leader explained:

> "There's a corporate focus and emphasis on how FLSMs manage their time, so we are getting much more granular about that. But it's not just a question of total time spent in certain activities. For example, people often say they spend 15 to 20 percent of time on email, right? But I'm noticing that top performers batch their email, morning and late afternoon, as opposed to throughout the day. I think that relieves their minds to just do their work during the day, and be more efficient. Also, those who are great at forecasting spend a bit more time on forecasting."

Not only should FLSMs be concerned about spending their own time wisely—not getting pulled away from critical tasks involved in exercising *strategic, organizational*, and *business* acumen—they should also ensure they take steps to maximize the time their sellers spend making sales. Effective FLSMs affirmatively take steps to remove administrative tasks from sellers, often taking these on themselves. We address this issue in Chapter 5, Team-Building Acumen.

 ## Influence Market Offers and Firm Behavior

In Chapter 1, several sales leaders commented on both the importance and the difficulties of the FLSM role. These sales leaders told us the fundamental challenge of being an FLSM was its position as a boundary role, sitting between senior management on the one hand, and both sellers and customers on the other:

> "The FLSM has one of the most difficult jobs in the company—new initiatives, new messages, new KPIs [key performance indicators]—all being driven down to that person. And every customer issue bubbling up from the other end. Above and below, everything converges on the FLSM."

> "The FLSM *makes the wheels turn*. [The problem] is that he's pulled in two directions—down to the reps and up to senior management. It's a push-and-pull job. The FLSM's challenge is to stay close to the sales team and their customers, but also have the right focus internally."

"FLSMs are the *meniscus* between how things *rub* together, or don't. The overall link between the corporation and the salesforce is so crucial. It's imperative that FLSMs are the most talented people in the management team."

These comments showcase the FLSM's two roles: Pass instructions from the top of the organization on to sellers—top down—but also negotiate seller and customer concerns with sales leaders—bottom up. Of course, sales leaders and other senior executives also receive feedback directly via personal customer interactions, and periodically from customer satisfaction surveys like *Net Promoter Score* (NPS).[3] Regardless, securing direct feedback from boundary-spanning personnel, who interact with customers on a day-to-day basis, has a very different valence. In this section, we emphasize the second element of top-down/bottom-up communication—what comes up from the bottom. These issues may be tactical or strategic.

Tactical Issues

Tactical issues come in many shapes and sizes. We illustrate the sorts of issues with reports from different FLSMs about failures in four specific areas.

- *Delivery and pricing.*
  "Our quarterly reviews also isolate problems. For example, we've had some trouble with recent new product rollouts—basically on delivery. We send that information back up the line. Similarly, with pricing; we're the first to hear if marketing has been too aggressive; so, we send that information into the system."

- *Field marketing.*
  "We get great support from our field-marketing organization. They work with our sellers to do a real deep dive into customer issues, and understand what value means to them. Then they help the sellers deliver that value with our current array of products and services."

- *Accounting.*
  "We had a major customer that had not paid a relatively small invoice. Neither I nor my seller knew about this situation; it was handled in accounting. Over there, they operate with a set of protocols. Regardless of what other payments a customer is making, if an invoice is unpaid, after a certain time, the message goes out: Halt deliveries.

  "So that's just what happened. The customer's unpaid invoice hit the stop-delivery date, and a low-level employee pulled the switch. (Actually, she was just doing her job.) The customer was furious; I had to sort out the situation and try to repair the damage. I calmed the situation down, but we also got the system changed. Now, no delivery stoppage is implemented without the salesforce being involved."

- *Customer service.*
  "We had a great relationship with one of our major customers, so much so they invited my seller and me on a tour of their plant. It was a great visit, but when we came back

from the factory and were walking though the offices, we saw some products from one of our chief competitors. This really surprised us. We believed we were the sole-source supplier. We gave them tremendous service; our technical service people were essentially on call for them.

"The specific product was a portable analyzer. Customers' technical people used the product to figure out the chemical composition of various products: Did aluminum alloys have the right percentages of rare earths? Did the paint on children's toys contain lead? But these machines are a little delicate; if a technician knocked one over, the customer would send it back for reconditioning. We have a department that deals with returned machines.

"When we questioned our customer about the competitor products, they essentially said to us: 'Your products are the best, but we often have problems with reconditioning. Sometimes the machines come back right away; other times we have to wait several weeks. So, we decided to diversify our risk by getting a second supplier.'

"Right away, I got in touch with our reconditioning department. It turned out, they operated a FIFO [first in, first out] system. That was the reason for the variable response times. I spear-headed an agreement, via our sales leaders, to speed up reconditioning overall, and to prioritize damaged machines from our most important customers."

These tactical situations are annoying and can cause serious problems for the firm-customer relationship. The FLSM should be prepared to get involved and work with sellers/customers on isolating and addressing these issues. The FLSM should also work internally with the appropriate internal functions to minimize reoccurrence of these operational problems.

Strategic Issues

What is far more serious than tactical matters are strategic issues. Market research data secured by the marketing department may provide an incomplete market understanding. Marketing's attempts at market segmentation may be ineffective—marketing does not construct *good* segments, or does not target those segments where the firm has the best chance of winning. Or, the firm's systems and processes for addressing customers may lead to serious brand damage.[4]

One of the most serious problems concerns misreading customer requirements, leading to poor product development decisions. Then, the offers sellers make do not fit customers' needs, priorities, problems, pain points. Recall what we heard from an FLSM at a U.S. technology firm—Chapter 2:

"We have not sufficiently listened to what customers say. We have not absorbed their feedback and incorporated it into our product development cycle. So, we have not created products that really fit their needs. Right now, we do not have enough to sell, so we're trying to piece together everything and anything. It's a very difficult position.

"We have a situation where two or three large customers provide the firm with 60 percent of revenues. We built products based on what these guys asked us to build. We did not build products based on a vision of where we thought the industry was going. We did not lead the market, but some of our competitors did.

"Some of our smaller customers are more innovative than the big guys…. Field sales passed their requirements up the ladder. But because of our focus on the large customers, we do not have products for our smaller, more innovative customers. What's even worse, the big guys are now trying to innovate and follow their competitors, so we don't have good products for them either. Essentially, we're trying to force square pegs into round holes."

Clearly, this firm failed to act appropriately in the product development process. FLSMs passed customer requirements *up the line*, but nothing good happened—the firm made a serious *strategic* error for which it paid a very high price. Did the FLSMs do their job? Or should they have done more? Should they have exhibited greater *managerial courage*—Chapter 7—to secure more attention to market realities with product development decision makers/influencers?

That was not the situation in all the firms with whose sales leaders and FLSMs we met. One FLSM explained:

"I will do face-to-face with a large client. They'll come up with an idea and we'll research it. I work with product management to identify a couple of partners we can work with. (Later we may seek executive approval together.) The partner may expand the idea, even bring in other partners. We're very open to customer ideas on new products, but we cannot take every innovation and run with it—we just don't have the bandwidth."

Sellers and FLSMs secure some of the best information about future customer needs, priorities, problems, pain points of anyone in the entire firm. It is insufficient for FLSMs just to pass this information *up the line*. If FLSMs are really convinced their information is really important, but firm response is inadequate, they should be prepared to sufficiently escalate the matter to secure the appropriate response from senior leaders.

Summary

Chapter 4 focuses on the third of six acumen dimensions effective FLSMs must possess—*business acumen*. The core of business acumen is to make deals—to secure a very granular understanding of customers and their needs, priorities, problems, pain points. FLSMs must possess the capability to add value at a fine-grained level. Only such deep understanding allows FLSMs and their sellers to actually deliver the appropriate values and make deals.

The business acumen challenge is growing in depth and scope. Customer DMUs and DMPs are evolving in the face of significant competitive and environmental pressures, and the resulting evolution in firm and customer strategies. *Organizational acumen* is necessary to identify and address the appropriate customer contacts. FLSMs must exercise *business acumen* to identify customer needs, priorities, problems, pain points, then bring value both to the customer overall, and to individual DMU members. Increasingly, the FLSM must be able to make the translation from *functional* benefits/value to *economic* benefits/value, do the math, and make the business case for the superiority of firm offers over competitors'.

The FLSM has a general responsibility to enhance the firm's brand, but a specific responsibility to make sometimes difficult decisions of when, and how, to be involved in the actual sales process, versus giving sellers autonomy. The FLSM must keep tabs on progress by monitoring input, intermediate, and output variables, at both individual seller and overall-district levels. The FLSM uses sales pipeline and other systems to diagnose issues, then direct, lead, and manage sellers as appropriate. Finally, the FLSM ensures that information from the field reaches appropriate internal personnel, so as to influence the firm's tactical and strategic decisions.

Endnotes

1. A *cath lab*—catheterization laboratory—is an examination room in a hospital/clinic with diagnostic imaging equipment for visualizing heart arteries and chambers to treat any stenosis or abnormalities. Cath Lab, Wikipedia, retrieved July 5, 2018, from https://en.wikipedia.org/wiki/Cath_lab.

2. The *shadow* system gets its name from the British parliamentary system. The governing party has a cabinet comprising (among others) a prime minister and foreign secretary. The opposition party appoints a *shadow* prime minister and *shadow* foreign secretary.

3. Net Promoter Score (NPS) has become a popular customer satisfaction measure, relatively simple to administer. F.F. Reicheld, "The One Number You Need to Grow," *Harvard Business Review*, 81 (December 2003), pp. 46–54.

4. A classic example occurred in 2017. In order to accommodate its employees on an overbooked flight, United Airlines ejected a paid, seated passenger against his will. The resulting uproar led to congressional hearings, and significant damage to the United brand.

Chapter 5

Team-Building Acumen

The fourth dimension of the sixfold acumen framework focuses on the front-line sales manager's (FLSM's) ability to build and sustain a high-performing sales team. This simple statement masks many challenges and complexities. In-place FLSMs must continually improve their sales teams. Incoming FLSMs may start with a clean slate—new business start-ups or opening a new sales district; more likely, the FLSM takes over from an existing FLSM who is moving on. Regardless, the FLSM's key challenge is to employ **team-building acumen** to *build, lead, and manage a high-performing sales team comprising a group of individual sellers.*

Of course, melding a group of sellers into a high-performing sales team is a core acumen dimension. But FLSMs must also identify key resources throughout their companies, and bring them to bear on firm-customer relationships. Resources may reside at more senior organizational levels, or in other organization functions. We address these team-building efforts in Chapter 6, Resource Acumen.

As discussed in Chapter 4, the FLSM may become deeply involved in individual selling situations. Indeed, for certain strategic customers, it may be appropriate for the FLSM to assume the lead selling role. More generally, individual sellers develop and maintain key day-to-day relationships with customers; the FLSM either plays a supporting role in the firm-customer relationship, or leaves the relationship more or less entirely in the hands of individual sellers.

In some firms, the FLSM's challenge to develop high-performing teams is built into the organizational fabric. One FLSM shared the support he received:

> "Our firm has culture pillars for everyone in the organization to abide by—employee ownership, transparent communication, encouraging innovation, empowerment, *teamwork*. I reinforce these pillars with my field managers. I believe adopting these behaviors will help their success—with direct customers externally, but also internally, with the people they interact with every day."

Team-building acumen comprises six dimensions—*assess current seller talent; secure effective sales talent; enhance sellers' intellectual capital; leverage firm resources; manage the seller team day-to-day; build an effective sales-team culture*—Figure 5.1.

One sales leader reported on a recent meeting he attended:

> "I just came off four days of our North American sales meeting and awards ceremonies. One of our front-line sales managers just got her 36th consecutive month of top sales performance ranking—that's pretty hard to do, right? The performance measure is not total sales, but sustainable, ongoing performance. In addition, more people in her team have been promoted than anybody else in the entire North American organization. She is

Figure 5.1 Team-Building Acumen Dimensions

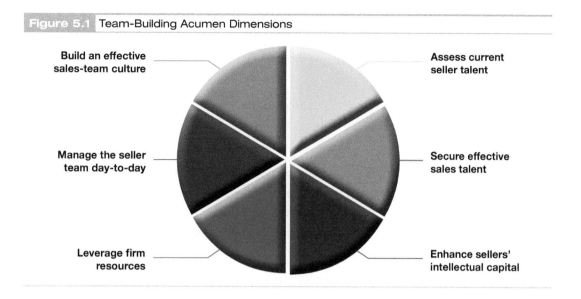

Build an effective sales-team culture

Assess current seller talent

Manage the seller team day-to-day

Secure effective sales talent

Leverage firm resources

Enhance sellers' intellectual capital

not using magic to make all this happen. She's a good leader, and people like to work for her. She teaches them well."

Clearly this type and level of performance is something for FLSMs to strive for.

A common theme among our respondents was the importance of building a strong team of sellers. One FLSM believed two factors were important for his success. First, passion for the FLSM job—Chapter 7; second, having a strong, dedicated team of sellers. The FLSM commented:

> "Having a strong team of motivated players is so vital. I am successful because my team is successful. We support each other—this is a two-way street. I have very knowledgeable self-starter salespeople. When you take that type of individual and challenge them—'This is your business'—you just let them spread their wings. Of course, you put in a lot of coaching and support; we have weekly strategic dialogues to talk through approaches. We focus on who, how, and when to communicate certain messages. But those sellers are absolutely key to my success."

The successful FLSM helps sellers develop the knowledge, skills, abilities (KSAs) necessary to succeed. The FLSM uses various approaches for sellers—assessing, coaching, modeling behavior—and mandates that they take advantage of company training and other systems and processes designed to enhance their capabilities. The FLSM encourages and promotes individual seller initiatives designed to increase their intellectual capital. And, the FLSM conducts periodic performance reviews to encourage some types of behavior and to modify others.

Successful FLSMs are very clear about the sort of sales teams they want to develop:

> "I want salespeople who are experienced in the field, and have a history of success. When I sit down with them, I want to see excitement; I want to see passion; I want to see a high energy level. I want them to convince me they are highly motivated to succeed;

that they're a self-starter. I need to know that they're going to be getting out the door just as early every day—working just as hard, making every call count, driving the business—as they are when I'm with them. This is the kind of job where a passion for customers really can be critical to success."

"They must have the skills to accomplish their goals. They must be able to close business, to find new business, to manage their territory, and to develop account relationships."

"Our world has changed. The days of the successful lone-wolf seller are over—I'm not interested in those types of people. I want sellers who can plan and strategize about their territories, about their customers, and who are willing to accept my steering them to help achieve their goals. They have to know, viscerally, that time is their scarce resource, and plan their calls effectively."

"I want to get the sense that they have a drive—anything less than success is unacceptable; that they are willing to do whatever it takes to ramp quickly to succeed. We kissed a lot of frogs before we hired the quality we wanted."

Of all the various components required to *build, lead, and manage a high-performing team of sellers*, perhaps the most crucial is having the *right* people, in the *right* places, at the *right* times. Commenting on FLSM roles, one sales leader told us:

"Ultimately, it's about the people underneath you. The FLSM is never the one in the spotlight here. You always want your rep to be. The rep should always be the star. It all comes down to having the right people."

One FLSM strongly echoed this perspective in driving success in his responsibility area:

"It's just about having the right people on the bus. Getting the right people that can handle very complicated customer situations. People that are self-motivated, competitive, assertive, do not give up, and understand accountability. Then work as a team to move the sales process forward."

When an FLSM joins a new business or opens a new district, the initial team-building task is recruiting, selecting, and hiring individual sellers. But for FLSMs who are taking over an existing group of sellers, the first order of business is to assess current sales talent. We discuss this dimension of team-building acumen next.

 ## Assess Current Seller Talent

In most cases, an incoming FLSM is taking over a functioning sales district, comprising several sellers, each with a performance track record. Perhaps the new FLSM is replacing a star FLSM whose district has seriously outperformed all peer districts; the former FLSM has been promoted to greater responsibilities, or hired away by a savvy competitor. Conversely, the district may have performed disastrously; the FLSM was fired, and sellers are depressed, dispirited, and looking for other jobs. More likely, the situation faced by an incoming FLSM is somewhere in between these extremes.

Whatever the situation, the incoming FLSM must assess the inherited sales talent and make serious decisions regarding which individual sellers should remain, and who should be removed. The FLSM must look very carefully at the reasons for prior seller performance. For example, *lone-wolf* sellers may have driven high district sales performance in the past, but such behavior may be unacceptable to the incoming FLSM (or to sales leadership). Conversely, poor sales performance may simply reflect a history of poor management. Regardless, thoughtful assessment of current sales talent is crucial.

As one sales leader put it:

> "Each incoming FLSM is dealt a set of cards (sellers). They have to decide which cards to hold, and which to discard. Then, they must be very careful to rebuild their hands."

One successful healthcare FLSM told us:

> "The FLSM must manage out the misfits, and get the *right* people in place. In my case, this was the major accomplishment that turned this district around."

Notice the term *misfit*. An FLSM may remove a seller for reasons other than poor performance. One FLSM told us:

> "I have this really incredible relationship with my sales team, yet I am also the sales manager who has released more employees than any other sales manager. I demand integrity, but they also have to fit the culture I've developed. Be ready to put themselves out for their fellow team members. If that's not there, no matter their own performance, they're gone."

And from an FLSM at a medical-diagnostics firm who not only replaced sellers, but arranged new positions, sending a powerful signal regarding concern for individuals:

> "Last year, we totally reorganized the salesforce; the majority of FLSMs took on new sales territories. I now have 14 direct reports, but I had to build a new team. I managed eight out and rehired eight [former employees]—some had previously left; others had been let go. This rebuilding was probably the best thing I did. The folks I managed out were not the right fit; I found other places for them to go where they are probably happier as well. Getting the right people is probably my major accomplishment that turned this place around."

Removing a seller can mean several things, ranging from an internal transfer to a position better suited to the individual's talents, to termination. The FLSM should not make precipitous decisions, but neither should ambiguous situations be left to fester. FLSMs' decisions should be made on the best available data; securing that data may require weeks or even months of observation. And the FLSM must, of course, follow the firm's human resource (HR) procedures if firing is the ultimate decision.

One FLSM recounted how she followed tough HR procedures and ended up in a good place all around:

"Our HR requirements for letting someone go are pretty intense and very document-heavy. When I took over, I had an underperformer; she was definitely affecting the team's morale. But the prior documentation was outstanding; so, it took a while. I sat down with her and said, 'Let us just be really real, because you do not seem happy: What is going on? What tools do you need? What support have you not been getting?' During the conversation, it turned out she was not happy. She knew she was hired in over her head. She had let it go so long, now she had a bad reputation and felt it could never be repaired. We did a mutual separation; it was a very positive experience actually. We were happy; it was a win-win. Then we hired the correct person for the job.

"But I also had a quite different nonperformer situation. This person had a bad temper. It was challenging, but you just have to stand your ground, and make sure you have HR involved. You speak to the person, but make sure you have the documentation."

Prior performance or longevity often earns the seller significant support in high places, so removal may be difficult. Yet, if the FLSM truly believes change is necessary—performance has declined, or the seller is unable/unwilling to make necessary changes—now is the time for courageous action—Chapter 7. The FLSM should be absolutely clear about the *right* course of action, then *go for it*. The FLSM may face tough sledding in the near term, but managing a sales team with weak or unenthusiastic members is even more serious in the long run.

More likely, the FLSM inherits a sales team in which individual sellers possess both positive and negative attributes. If the FLSM removes a seller whose negatives outweigh the positives, then territory sales are immediately at risk; they could be subject to sharp decline right away. The actual sales trajectory depends in part on the time it takes to place a new, competent seller in the field. Of course, it may be difficult to find this person, and there is no guarantee that a new hire will be an improvement. On the positive side, with a now-empty slot, the FLSM has a clean slate to fill with a newly selected seller. The FLSM must balance positive and negative factors before making the retain/remove decision.

An important source of data about individual sellers is the departing FLSM. This person has the most intimate view of individual sellers—attitudes, behavior, performance. But, to a very large extent, individual seller performance depends on the relationship between seller and FLSM. A seller who performs at a high level with one FLSM may perform less well with another. One successful FLSM with a social networking firm told us her experience when taking over her current sales district:

"Both my immediate predecessor as FLSM and his predecessor told me that [one particular seller] should be the first to be let go. Essentially, they'd given up on her—she did not regularly meet her numbers. It turned out that customers adored this seller. She is a very compassionate person, and was a fantastic advocate for customers within our firm. But because of her extensive customer focus, she just could not push our products unless she was convinced they benefited the specific customer. So, I worked with her for about a year. I showed her how to get deep insight into customer needs, then understand how our solutions satisfied those needs. In this way, she could be true to her customer-advocacy philosophy, and also earn revenues. I did one-on-one sessions and joint calls until she was comfortable advocating our products. She is now one of my most successful sellers; it's been an amazing transformation."

On assuming her new position, this FLSM could have simply taken the advice of her predecessors: let the seller go and hire a new seller. (Note, however: These predecessors had not followed their own advice!) Regardless, the FLSM's time investment to understand the root cause of the seller's inadequate performance, then her work to resolve the problem, clearly paid off.

Relatedly, a poorly performing inherited seller may just be in the wrong selling job. For example, if the FLSM requires sellers both to secure revenues from new customers—*hunting*—and to secure increased revenues from existing customers—*farming*—a particular seller may simply be in the wrong role. One FLSM for a software firm explained her experience:

> "When I took this job, one person had not been doing much. I spent a lot of time understanding what she was good at. I wanted her on my team, but she was in the wrong job. I shared my assessment: 'This seems to be your interest, let's go figure it out.' Today, one year later, she is my top performer."

Certainly, assessing individual team members is critical when assuming an FLSM position. But continual assessment is vital. The FLSM may make a hiring mistake, or an apparently good seller's performance may atrophy for a host of reasons. The FLSM's challenge is especially difficult when the seller is in another country and deep understanding of the seller and work environment is difficult to secure. As an FLSM at a global software supplier explained, sometimes physical presence is necessary to pick up on a misfit in culture or work style:

> "Just recently, I took a one-week trip to Asia. In that short time, I learned what would have taken six months to understand otherwise. I took quick action and let go an account manager who was not a good fit. Without that trip, we could have had several months of poor interactions with customers that would have taken even more months to repair."

In a Chapter 2 case study, an IBM FLSM ignored the corporate mandate to focus efforts on service revenues at a specific customer, a large bank. The FLSM believed that this customer offered a good opportunity to earn substantial revenues from sales of mainframe computers. The FLSM resisted significant internal pressure to replace a seller. He told us:

> "I knew that the bank had installed a lot of servers from different suppliers. They did not work well together; it was clear to me and to my seller that many different influences had led to this hodgepodge of procurement decisions. The situation cried out for IBM mainframes, but it just took time to nail down the banks' evolving DMU [decision-making unit] and DMP [decision-making process]. Meanwhile, other parts of the IBM organization were screaming for service revenues, and there was pressure on me to have the seller fired. I resisted, and she kept working the bank. Eventually, we got the breakthrough we were seeking, and IBM revenues from mainframe sales to this customer were very significant."

Building a high-performing sales team is crucial, but sometimes a shift in corporate direction can impede the best-laid plans. In such situations, the FLSM's job is usually clear: Embrace the strategy and make it happen! One FLSM relived the difficulty of managing the boundary between senior management and sellers in his sales team:

> "I hired this one guy to fill a slot in my district. He was ramping up pretty well and showing a lot of promise in his territory. Then corporate decided to develop a specialized salesforce and gave me a headcount reduction. I looked at all my people on various metrics, and this guy came out on the bottom. Not surprising really as he was just getting going. So, I had to fire him. That was hard, really hard. Corporate didn't let me off the hook, not even a little bit."

 ## Secure Effective Sales Talent

The FLSM must operate with the best possible set of individual sellers that can be molded into an effective sales team. Typically, those individuals are some combination of inherited sellers from the previous FLSM, and newly hired sellers. To put in place a fully functioning sales team may take many months.

Building and maintaining a sales team at full strength is critical. The FLSM may have this problem when assuming district leadership, or from any number of causes in the normal course of business—seller performance declines, internal transfers, promotions, resignations.

The core issue for the FLSM is to minimize the delay in returning the sales team to full strength. When vacancies appear, for a limited period, the FLSM and/or other district sellers may step into the breech, but this solution is generally suboptimal, and unsustainable for more than a limited time.

Hiring the right sellers is a *crucial task* for FLSMs. As one successful FLSM told us:

> "Personally, I think my strength is hiring the right people; that is key. You can be a great coach, but if your team is not good, it does not matter."

The FLSM should maintain, or have access to, an *inventory* of potential sellers. In some firms, senior leaders plan for empty seller slots; they centralize recruiting by maintaining a *bench* of qualified internal candidates, ready for promotion/transfer to the selling role. In many cases, these benches reside in customer service, marketing, related functions. Some firms put more effort on outside hiring, yet also centralize the process. One FLSM reported on the support he received:

> "We have a recruiting team. They focus on salesforce-specific recruiting—organized by different types of sales team, different geographies, or both. Their job is to find quality candidates, do the first screen. They initiate a selection process for candidates they feel are worthy. Of course, at the end of the day, I get to make the choice."

Another sales leader told us:

> "Overall, we have a preference for internal hires, because we want to offer career opportunities to people in functions like marketing and customer service. On the other hand, we are concerned about becoming insular. So, we are always looking outside as

well; these hires bring new ideas into the firm. This internal/external balance has worked well for us."

The sales leader for a global service provider explained how he had evolved the recruitment/selection process at his firm:

"We have made huge changes in recruiting sellers. We have taken FLSMs out of the front end of the hiring process—all of the preliminary interviewing, testing, and screening. Actually, we outsourced all of our hiring and recruiting to a third party. That may sound odd; but we still let FLSMs have the final say on a yea or a nay for hiring a sales rep."

In other firms, the system is totally decentralized; FLSMs have the sole responsibility for filling empty seller slots. In this situation, constructing a network, and continually identifying and interviewing potential candidates, is the best way for FLSMs to build a seller inventory. Continually updating this inventory avoids, or at least minimizes, the timespan when the district is understrength, and suffering the consequences of lost revenues. Constructing a seller inventory is time-consuming work, requiring constant effort.

One FLSM for a higher-education software firm shared his perspective:

"It's hard to find really good people. It's probably the hardest part of my job, having good people I can bring in if someone leaves my organization. I'm always looking. I keep tabs on good people, and keep in touch with them. I see them at higher-ed conferences—have coffee, breakfast, or go out for a drink—just to keep us top-of-mind if they're ever interested. That includes good people who have left us. They find *the grass isn't greener*, and sometimes they come back after a couple of years."

The best FLSMs do a great job in hiring exceptional sales talent. One sales leader at a global technology firm expressed a very strong position on the importance of this part of the FLSM's job:

"Every great FLSM I've known exerts a *magnetic* pull for great talent. I've traveled the world and it's amazing how consistent I find it—certain FLSMs have all the best people on their teams—year in and year out. It's just amazing. And that's because people go to work for managers they're drawn to. There's just no price you can put on that as a company. It's just so valuable and something that a firm can't live without."

Other sales leaders made similar comments:

"In my experience, great FLSMs have a seventh sense for discovering great salespeople and matching them to needed roles. They do the homework, check backgrounds, and get the right profiles. It's like a *secret sauce* to find the right people, and understand who has a collaborator profile."

"Successful FLSMs are not necessarily the smartest people, but they have the ability to *get the right people and keep them*, guide them, build them, and develop them."

Some FLSMs picked up on this sales leader's assessment:

> "I only want to hire people that are smarter than me, and who have that drive to be successful."

> "I am not the smartest person in the room; I do not understand our technology better than anybody else. But I can identify the right people for the right jobs, get them on the team, and keep them. Some people say it's like a seventh sense; that's not the answer academia expects, but it is! I do my homework, talk to all the past managers, look over their past 10-year history. That homework and my sense for successful sellers have worked very well for me."

In decentralized situations, the HR department may play various roles, like validating and processing FLSM selections. Other times, aggressive HR departments can make the selection decision difficult—FLSMs must either *suck up* those setbacks, or escalate the decision.

The authors do not take a position on centralized versus decentralized recruiting systems, so long as FLSMs have the authority to make the final selection decision. What we do believe very strongly is that each FLSM must be in a position to swiftly fill an empty seller slot, right when it occurs. Otherwise, the opportunity losses from failing to keep the salesforce at full strength are too great.

 ## Enhance Sellers' Intellectual Capital

It's one thing to secure great sales talent; it's quite another to turn a set of individual sellers into an effective sales team. All things equal, the more competent and better prepared individual sellers are, the more likely the sales team will be successful. Notwithstanding the availability of firm resources, FLSMs must take responsibility for enhancing seller expertise—*intellectual capital*. They must use whatever resources are available, not least of which is their own experience.

In Chapter 2, we showed how seller Lily King wowed the CEO of a major customer she met by happenstance on the New York–to–Boston shuttle. Recall how the CEO described the flight to an aide:

> "I just had a most interesting conversation with Lily King.... I was amazed at her degree of customer resonance—how much she knew about us, our customers, our competitors, and the issues we and the industry are facing. Lily raised some topics I had not even thought about; the conversation gave me a couple of directions for things we should take a look at."

Increasingly, customers want ideas on how to improve their organizations, be more competitive in their markets, and improve their financial performance. A prerequisite for sellers is to become very familiar with the customer's industry, and the challenges industry and customer face. Good insight is core to *strategic acumen*. Not only must FLSMs possess good strategic acumen, they must also work hard to ensure possession by their sellers.

We heard about the strategic acumen requirement several years ago from a seller for an Indian high-tech outsource provider. The seller had been unable to make progress in securing higher-value sales from a long-time customer. He met the customer CEO at an industry event and expressed his frustration:

> "I think we're doing a good job for your firm in providing low-cost services. Your people seem highly satisfied, and our revenues are increasing. But I'm having difficulty getting traction with our more complex and higher-value services. What should I do?"

The CEO's response was very simple and direct. He said:

> "Surprise me!"

As the firm's value propositions evolve, the FLSM must ensure these values resonate with customers, and are then translated at a more granular level into customer-specific values—for the customer organization and individuals in the DMU—*business acumen*. And, of course, identifying DMUs and DMPs—*organizational acumen*—is also critical.

But understanding value propositions and making these translations for the appropriate customer personnel are not jobs for FLSMs alone. Rather, the FLSM must work with individual sellers to ensure they also understand the firm's evolving value propositions, and can make them come alive for customer DMU members. It's one thing for the FLSM to secure strategic, organizational, and business acumen; it's quite another for the FLSM to enhance these acumen dimensions in their sellers.

In today's business environment, sellers must be sufficiently prepared to bring value to the table, right from the first meeting. One FLSM at a higher-education software firm told us:

> "The major change in the past 10 years is that today people have so little time. They will not give you a second chance if you don't show them it's worth meeting with you, and working with you on an ongoing basis. Today we use LinkedIn and other Internet resources to do our customer research, so we align with their business goals right from the get-go."

Enhancing the strategic, organizational, and business acumen of individual sellers is important for two quite different reasons. First, individual sellers will be far more effective in their jobs. Many of their customers will never meet the FLSM, so sellers alone must formulate and execute on firm value propositions at customer DMUs. Second, FLSMs have a responsibility to enhance their direct reports' intellectual capital, and prepare them for potential advancement in the firm. One sales leader told us:

> "We are very serious about intellectual capital development for all our employees. Of course, this is absolutely critical in the salesforce, where our account managers interact daily with customers. Indeed, we expect the FLSMs to foster and encourage learning by all our sellers."

Intellectual Capital Elements

A useful way of thinking about intellectual capital development is as *stocks* and *flows*.

- ▪ *Stocks—How to be a better seller.* Intellectual capital stocks comprise a potpourri of selling, planning, time-management, and execution skills that are fundamental to successful selling.

■ *Flows—Keeping up-to-date.* Intellectual capital flows embrace the ability to deliver value to customers as their needs, priorities, problems, pain points change, and firm value propositions evolve. FLSMs and their sellers must possess deep customer, competitor, industry, and firm knowledge.

An easy way to distinguish between stocks and flows is to imagine a seller who leaves the firm for an equivalent position in a completely different industry. The *stock* of intellectual capital accompanies that seller to the new job, and can be put to use right away. The *flow* of intellectual capital comprises those items that were important for success in the current job, but have little or no value in the new position.

It follows that intellectual capital *stocks* build over time, have a long half-life, and provide value throughout a seller's career. By contrast, intellectual capital *flows* have a relatively short half-life, and must be continually replenished.

The challenge for the firm is to put in place systems and processes that enhance sellers' intellectual capital—*stocks* and *flows*. We discuss two broad approaches next—training and coaching.

Training

In many firms, the broad responsibility for enhancing seller intellectual capital stocks rests within the sales organization, possibly in a sales-operations or sales-enablement department. In other firms, this responsibility sits in a learning-and-development department within the HR organization. Sometimes the firm offers training programs at specific points in a seller's career, like onboarding; sometimes the FLSM identifies gaps and proposes specific training. The major responsibility of the FLSM is to *identify individual seller's training needs*, then ensure sellers take full advantage of learning opportunities. Executing on training requirements may not be a simple matter: Day-to-day selling responsibilities tend to place longer-term investment in personal growth/intellectual capital development at a lower priority.

Intellectual capital flows, by contrast, typically rest with both corporate and sales leaders. All play major roles in feeding data on evolving firm value proposition and new products/services to the salesforce. They also deliver broadscale data on customer, competitor, and industry trends. Methods vary: formal seminars, online training, podcasts, regularly scheduled interactive broadcasts, idiosyncratic announcements, all-hands calls, and so on. FLSMs have the responsibility for mandating that team members set aside time to take advantage of what sales leaders and corporate are delivering. FLSMs must also ensure their sellers understand, and adhere to, firm policies and procedures.

Intellectual capital flow training is particularly important when significant change occurs in the firm's product/markets—affecting products/services, market intelligence, value propositions. There is just more *stuff* for sellers to get their heads around. One sales leader concentrated on evolution of the firm's product portfolio:

> "Training has been absolutely critical for us. We have many long-tenured sellers. The firm's evolution has put tremendous pressure on them. We have added many products, both from internal development and from acquisitions. Our sellers really have more products than they can manage; essentially, we're having to *teach old dogs new tricks.* FLSMs must ensure their sellers get up to speed on all our products, then stay there by tapping into the extensive training resources the firm provides. Our sellers have to be a

jack-of-all-trades. What's really important for them is the first meeting. They have to get through that; for the second meeting, they bring in a specialist."

A second sales leader focused on the evolving customer DMU:

"We've moved out of IT [information technology]; our sellers now deal with people like the enrollment manager, financial aid, the registrar, and alumni relations. Our sellers have to know what these people are interested in; what are their *hot buttons*; what is changing around them; how other institutions are addressing these changes. And what does that *talk-track* look like? What are some good opening questions? How should sellers lead customers through a conversation?

"We train our sellers to take the customer through the conversation, validate their challenges, then show how we have some competitive differentiation. When I travel with my sellers, I let them go through the process, and interject where necessary. Then we debrief after the call. But for individual sellers, it takes a long time to do this smoothly."

Although corporate investment generally drives the firm's major formal training approach, there may be additional avenues for skills improvement—industry associations, community colleges, online education. The FLSM's role is to support and encourage sellers to take advantage of these training opportunities. One FLSM reported on her practice regarding external resources:

"Over and above the mandatory training we provide, my people go to an external coach to improve themselves. I also support taking external courses, so long as they are making their numbers."

Coaching

Notwithstanding the FLSM's ability to secure strategic, organizational, and business acumen, perhaps the major FLSM responsibility is to coach sellers in these acumen dimensions. In developing their KSAs, sellers should improve performance. One FLSM provided a powerful metaphor for his approach to coaching:

"I am teaching them [sellers] to fish. If they need help, I'll pull them back into the boat. But sometimes I'll step back and let them do it on their own. Then they can rise up to the challenge, step forward and push their comfort boundary, and build more confidence."

Many sales leaders and FLSMs believe coaching is a critical (if not the most critical) characteristic of the FLSM job. One sales leader stated this most succinctly:

"The key [FLSM] leadership role is to focus on the coaching piece. Of course, I coach in private, but, when appropriate, I praise in public."

Coaching requires observing seller behavior, frequently during joint calls, providing feedback and modeling required behavior, and following up. Of course, FLSMs make joint calls for many different reasons, but one important purpose is to observe sellers in action. As one FLSM put it:

"I inspect what I expect."

Successful FLSMs travel constantly with sellers; three days per week is not unusual for our FLSM interviewees. They spend large amounts of time one-on-one, and significant time together calling on customers. And they constantly talk on the telephone. Each interaction provides opportunities for coaching—reinforcing current behavior, providing opportunity feedback to suggest modifications. One successful FLSM told us:

> "The only way to develop my team is to spend time with individual sellers. I have a scheduled weekly review call with each seller for at least a half hour, plus as-needed calls on a day-to-day basis. And I take a two- to three-day field ride with each seller once per quarter."

Building on what we reported about the FLSM role in Chapter 1, one successful sales leader told us:

> "At our firm, the FLSM role is to *model, express,* and *reinforce* the behavior we require. It starts with the onboarding training for the new hires, so they learn the concepts we require. FLSMs are expected to role-model what they ask from their teams. They should reinforce that by seeing all the good happenings in their teams, and calling it out when they see it. Indeed, recognition and rewards are crucial."

And from a sales leader at Oracle:

> "I remember growing up in the organization, and I used to see sales management in the office a lot. You need to get out there. I want the guys out there, so they observe, and they teach. If you're going to be a leader, you must learn how to teach. Your job is to teach."[1]

Several sales leaders and FLSMs emphasized the importance of consistency in coaching. Good coaching behavior was not sporadic, not even regular, but continuous. The underlying notion expressed was that virtually every FLSM-seller interaction provided an opportunity for feedback, and that the FLSM should let no opportunity go to waste. One sales leader advised:

> "The *coaching* goal should be continuous improvement via constant feedback. The FLSM should provide clear perspective, infuse enthusiasm, and give a pat in the back when it's deserved. Innovation is great, but the FLSM should aim for continuous improvement from the sales team."

When developing their coaching approaches, FLSMs should incorporate the following elements.

Accompany Sellers in the Field. Individual customers present different problems and opportunities for developing and communicating benefits/values that meet DMU requirements. A core FLSM skill is to work with sellers to address these problems and opportunities in the field. One FLSM emphasized this perspective:

> "The most important thing is to ensure your reps have the skills and guidance to drive opportunities forward, to manage a territory, and to understand their customers. I make sure my team knows what they need to do, and how to achieve their goals—to close business, to find new business, and to develop account relationships.

"I coach them. 'Do you feel strong in pre-call planning?' 'Do you feel strong in uncovering customer needs?' 'Okay, you do. That's great. Let's make some calls.' So, we make some calls, then we debrief. 'What do you think went well? Where do you think you could improve?' This is a continuous activity; there's always something to learn, to do better."

And from another FLSM:

"When I was appointed FLSM, following many years being a successful seller, I saw for the first time how other people do the selling job. I saw how differently they did things, saw things, or did not understand things. So, I had a lot of coaching work to bring them up to speed."

One sales leader's firm focused heavily on time management. She collected granular data on how FLSMs spent their time, and shared an interesting result from her studies:

"When we do 360s, we ask reps: 'If you had one person to take to a meeting, would it be your manager?' Because they'd be useful, right? The answer is yes, for those managers who spend time coaching. Managers who spend less than 15 percent of their time coaching don't get the same type of scores. So far, we see 20 to 25 percent of time coaching, including feedback, as a good number."

Assess Various Coaching Approaches and Use as Appropriate. We should not get the idea that coaching consists only of wisdom that FLSMs pass on to sellers to get them to change their behavior. Evolution in the business environment demands that FLSMs continually update their own intellectual capital, staying ahead of evolving trends and continually reevaluating how best to lead and motivate their sellers.

In Chapter 2, we discussed how DMUs are changing in many customer organizations. The SAP and Cisco case studies showed decision making moving out of IT into many different functions. A higher-education software firm identified a similar trend. One FLSM told us:

"Decision making is moving away from IT to users and administrators—on the business side of the house. To be successful, we have to be more than an inch deep and a mile wide. We have to be able to talk to these people, not just IT. So, for example, I'm trying to find out the full extent of the registrar's job—what are they trying to achieve? How can we help? And the same for the vice president of finance, and so forth. My job is to coach my sellers to figure this out, so we know the right subject-matter experts to bring in."

The FLSM went on:

"I coach my guys in basic *blocking and tackling*—follow up, be prepared, be respectful of those people and their time. To get an appointment, you have to work at it, be persistent. It's a pain, but you have to figure out a way—maybe someone in IT can get you a meeting. You've got to want to do it; you have to be driven to do it. I make sure I have the *right* people on my team, then I coach the hell out of them."

Another FLSM elaborated on *blocking and tackling*:

> "In sales, you spend a lot of time finding the gaps, developing a solution, selling the solution. Then you reach the call-to-action stage, and salespeople forget to count—how to make the customer more money, or cost the customer less money. I coach my guys to find the gaps, then fill those gaps with the best solutions. But our customers are not generally great businesspeople; we have to show them how that solution makes/saves them money."

Two FLSMs elaborated on their general approaches to coaching sellers:

> "We have a lot of seasoned salespeople, but they can always use improvement. Oftentimes, I just sit and listen to what they say, see how they react, and the different things they do within their accounts. I just coach on how they should have handled something a little bit differently, or what they could do to improve on some characteristic or other. Maybe there's a deficiency they should address, so I just provide some insight from my experience during many years of selling."

> "I want them thinking all the time: 'What is it I can do to separate myself from the competition?' 'What can I do to be creative financially?' 'What can I do to be creative technically?' 'How can we make this bigger?' 'What are new and better ways of getting the sale done? And done faster?'"

Of course, it's insufficient for FLSMs just to reinforce good behaviors and point out bad behaviors, and to secure appropriate behaviors via rewards. The FLSM must *lead* sellers to make the necessary changes by motivation. Said a telecom sales leader:

> "The FLSM has got to be a motivator, instructing the right things to the sales team."

But presumably not according to the model used by Alec Baldwin's character in *Glengarry Glen Ross*![2]

Some FLSMs were at pains to point out the focus on seller behavior with customers. One FLSM told us:

> "I tell my people, they should sell like they want to be sold to. They should treat customers with respect, with integrity. I work hard to instill those values in my team."

One valuable way for FLSMs to coach sellers is to highlight positive examples of one seller's actions to other team members. One healthcare sales leader illustrated how his best FLSMs coach sellers using this approach:

> "Our FLSMs have regular calls with the entire sales team. They use these opportunities to illustrate when a sales rep makes a specific contribution, or aligns his/her activities with a corporate initiative.
>
> "Right now, we have a corporate initiative to secure toeholds in diagnostic labs where we have no presence. This foot-in-the-door objective is to get placement of a single instrument; then we get some of our diagnostic tests run. The FLSM doesn't just

congratulate the rep on the phone. Rather, with the entire team listening, the FLSM ties together the steps the rep went through to gain the customer's trust. The FLSM shows how the customer was willing to accept the placement, and sign a contract. The FLSM also focuses on how the rep's success ties into the corporate goal and initiative, and how this success helps steer the firm's future direction."

Another sales leader made a similar observation about seller recognition:

"We make sure we're using our recognition and awards appropriately, not just sparingly. If we're seeing a lot of good stuff, we urge our FLSMs to call it like they see it."

An important element of intellectual capital sellers must develop is *the ability to fully comprehend what is going on* with a customer, what the customer is actually saying. As one FLSM put it:

"Oftentimes, a salesperson will not be able to see the *forest for the trees*. FLSMs can stand at 30,000 feet from the transaction, and see things the seller does not.

"One time, I made a joint sales call to a bank president. The president bragged about one area where we'd worked together, then began to complain about three or four other areas. When we got in the car to drive away, the salesperson looked at me and said: 'Well, he is really happy.' I was thinking: 'We are in trouble if we don't fix some things right away.' I heard the three or four negatives; my seller did not.

"That ability to really understand comes from experience, but also from coaching. FLSMs can help develop that skill in their sellers."

Certainly there are many areas for which coaching by FLSMs is valuable for sellers. FLSMs should develop a coaching cadence—a series of frequent interactions between FLSMs and sellers. Said one sales leader:

"We expect our FLSMs to develop a coaching cadence, so their sellers develop expectations about their learning from their managers. Any particular FLSM may operate with several cadences depending on the seller's profile. For example, an FLSM would have a different cadence for rookies than for very experienced sellers. And we give FLSMs pretty strong advice on what are appropriate cadences."

Work with Sellers Individually. As is evident from the discussion thus far in this section, training is an activity that can involve multiple sellers at a time; by contrast, coaching is typically a one-on-one activity. We emphasize this distinction by presenting two examples that exemplify coaching's individual nature.

One FLSM was living through an organizational transformation from a traditional geographic salesforce to two salesforces—hunters and farmers. Although change was necessary across the board, the new required behavior was against the nature of some individual sellers. This FLSM explained the situation with one of his sellers:

"We have this one seller who is a really great hunter. When we formed the hunter/farmer sales organizations, our sales leaders wanted him to join the hunters. But I became a farmer-FLSM, and he wanted to work for me; sales leadership agreed. But *farming* is different from *hunting*. So, we sat down, and I said: 'Here are the things you need to work on and do better to excel in this role. It's different from being a hunter.' So, we're still struggling. I have to get him to really acknowledge the problem; after all, you can't fix it until you acknowledge it."

Some issues involving seller behavior are solved simply by providing perceptive feedback. In cases like the foregoing, it may be necessary for the FLSM to work with a seller over some considerable time period to secure the necessary change. One FLSM in the social networking services industry provided a second example of successful over-time coaching with an individual seller:

"This guy is one of my most knowledgeable, sharp, and creative sellers. His ideas on solving customer problems are always spot on, but he had challenges *packaging* the delivery of his sales message, and wasn't making his numbers. I did some joint calls and saw right away that he had a very aggressive style. Before he met with customers, he had figured out their problems *and* the solution, and he was mostly on target! He would present the whole thing on a well-prepared set of PowerPoints, but it wasn't working.

"We talked about his approach. His immediate reaction was almost disappointment in himself: 'It's not my intention to be aggressive.' He just hadn't seen that he was misaligned with customers; he wasn't allowing them to go through the discovery stage themselves.

"As I continued to go on joint calls, he changed his approach. Same preparation as before, but now he went through the discovery stage alongside the customer. Together they identified problems, and then developed solutions. Everything was the same; just the approach was different. Now the customer felt part of the process. This shift was easy for my guy; he took the change very well, and the new approach was very successful. He continued to do the analytical and pre-work, and he loved talking to customers. After one meeting the customer told us: 'This was the most beneficial meeting we've had with your firm in a year and half.' The transformation was amazing."

By all accounts, this seller possessed ample strategic and significant business acumen—"one of my most knowledgeable, sharp, and creative sellers"—but was having trouble in customer engagement. So, the coaching process pushed this seller way outside his comfort zone, but to successful performance.

Pave a Two-Way Street. Coaching should not just be something FLSMs impose on sellers. Rather, FLSMs should create a culture in which sellers reach out to their FLSMs for advice and counsel. One sales leader was quite explicit with a golfing metaphor:

"If you're a novice, or even a well-established golfer, and your numbers aren't there, you seek out a coach to help improve your game. There's always some way to improve. We want our sellers, even the most experienced guys, to seek coaching from their FLSMs, no matter how experienced they are. And we want our FLSMs to be competent to help them."

Another sales leader compared coaching sellers to football:

> "All great football teams have great head coaches, but I think the key role is the offensive coordinator. He knows the players better than the head coach. The offensive coordinator works with his players to improve their performance. He knows what his players can do. He must get the *right* players on the *right* field at the *right* time. But he also knows what the head coach wants to have happen. I'm like the Vince Lombardi for my sales team, but I'm only going to get the result I want if my offensive coordinators—the FLSMs—do an outstanding job for me."

Coaching can be a two-way street in a second sense—coaching for FLSMs from their sellers. One FLSM described her philosophy:

> "Some days I'm going to call you out on some strikes, but other days I'm going to call you out for your batting average, or your fielding skills—I'm a coach. But you're also a coach for me. You can help me be a better coach; tell me what I'm doing that works for you, and where I could do better."

Coaching sellers is a critical skill FLSMs must possess. Corporate has a significant responsibility in making sure the FLSMs it appoints possess, or quickly secure, the skills to do this task well— Chapter 8.

 # Leverage Firm Resources

As just noted, the corporate infrastructure can play an important role in improving sellers' intellectual capital—*stocks* and *flows*. Corporate management, and especially sales leaders, have the responsibility to provide tools and other resources to help FLSMs and their sellers succeed. In dealing with the corporate and sales management hierarchies, we consider three core issues.

Ensure Value for Sellers

FLSMs have the responsibility to ensure that tools and resources made available to the salesforce do, in fact, have value for sellers.

We are all familiar with complaints from marketing departments:

> "Our group develops tons of leads [or brochures or other sales materials] for the salesforce, but they never seem to use them appropriately, nor follow up as they ought to."

The salesforce responds:

> "We get all these leads from the marketing department, but they're useless. Marketing doesn't seem to have any idea about the sort of customers we deal with, or the day-to-day problems they face. If we had to rely on what marketing gives us, we'd be spinning our wheels chasing imaginary customers with useless sales materials."

Clearly, this sort of mal-integrated situation is highly dysfunctional, but it's less rare than we would like to think. FLSMs should push back against such wasted resource, either directly with marketing or via the sales management hierarchy.

One specific resource FLSMs should tap into is the firm's procurement organization. In the Preface, we showed that many firms have recognized the strategic importance of procurement, staffing this department with talented executives. These executives construct more effective procurement organizations, and develop systems and processes to enhance procurement performance.

Hence, sitting within the firm is a great resource, available for FLSMs/sellers to learn about procurement organizations and the challenges they face. Learning from their firm's procurement executives may provide useful insights into customer behavior. Said one FLSM:

> "Every so often, when we have a team meeting, I invite in one of our procurement people. They give us a briefing about what is going on in procurement. It lets my guys see what pressures procurement organizations face, and how they deal with them. It's a perspective we are not normally exposed to on a day-to-day basis. My guys find these sessions very helpful."

Of course, procurement is not the only internal resource that can provide value to FLSMs/sellers. We discuss extended firm teams—*resource acumen*—in Chapter 6, but for now we merely alert readers to the fact that many firms' functional areas face similar challenges that customers face. These internal functions can be a valuable resource for FLSMs and their sellers.

Ensure Sellers Use Provided Value

On the positive side, many firms do a great job of developing events, materials, promotions, and tools for the salesforce. Sales leaders drive development, either within the sales organization, or via collaboration with marketing or some other organizational unit. After ensuring that these resources are valuable for sellers, the FLSM's job is to make sure sellers use them, overcoming any resistance to innovations and new behaviors. As three different sales leaders put it:

> "We expect our FLSMs to leverage the mix of behaviors and tools. The best FLSMs maximize the tools and utilities that are available to them."

> "FLSMs must ensure that they and their sellers leverage the whole company—corporate-wide events, executive calls, intimate dinners...."

> "FLSMs must secure company assets to build their sellers' competence, and enhance their credibility when they are face-to-face with customers."

In Chapter 1, we emphasized the importance of senior management creating systems and processes that FLSMs can tap into to enhance intellectual capital for both themselves and their sellers. Salesforce.com is not only a product innovator, but also an innovator in constructing an environment where their FLSMs can be successful. One Salesforce.com sales leader told us:

> "The thing I cannot emphasize enough is that we sell a *branded experience*. That's pretty unique. The FLSMs who do really well here know how to leverage all the branded things

we do, from *Dreamforce*[3] to customer-on-customer dinner events—they are like nothing I've ever seen in the industry.

"At these dinners, we may have around 30 CIOs [chief information officers] or other C-Suite members, from current and potential customers. A couple of Salesforce.com execs get the session off, and then our guests just sell to each other—it's really unique. The core outcome is educational, but we also personalize our relationships. Our success is derivative of those FLSMs who can pull off those events.

"Successful FLSMs must know how to leverage company resources. The guys who do really, really well here do it year in and year out. And you see the rising stars coming through and learning how to do it. But I see guys fail, and fail miserably, when they try to do it on their own. They try to bring a very traditional sales model to their districts, and they just get blown up."

Firms develop a variety of approaches for reaching individual customer executives. The FLSM's role is to get sellers to persuade customers to take part. Webinars are increasingly popular; so are events that provide opportunities for seller-customer interaction away from the workplace. Individuals attending events are typically more relaxed, and maybe more open to sharing information. Events may also present opportunities to meet with executives who are otherwise difficult to reach in the normal course of business. One FLSM in higher-education software reported:

"We create day-long *one-to-many* events on topics of industry-wide interest, as and when they come up. We bring in a senior executive as a keynote speaker. Sometimes a customer will host an event for fellow customers; other times we arrange and pay for a dinner event at a good restaurant. Just recently, we did a day-long event; we managed to get 15 minutes with the CIO of an organization with more than 20 geographically dispersed facilities. We'd been trying to track this guy down for several weeks, then suddenly, here he was."

Ensure Sellers Get What They Need

Corporate management/sales leaders may deliver valuable tools and resources to FLSMs and their sellers. But FLSMs also have the responsibility to feed ideas into the sales management hierarchy, especially when it comes to sharing tools and materials that can enhance sales performance, both for individual FLSMs and for the salesforce in general.

As one example, we came across a pharmaceutical firm that developed a drug for use by hospital cardiologists. The drug was significantly more expensive than alternatives, but provided better care for certain types of patients, and offered considerable financial value for hospitals—it decreased patient length of stay, both in intensive care and overall in the hospital. Although the firm developed a solid value proposition, estimated financial savings depended on several individual patient- and hospital-specific characteristics.

A creative FLSM developed an algorithm including these factors. Based on this tool, the firm designed a software program that all FLSMs and sellers could use to show individual hospital customers their precise expected financial savings from adopting the drug. Revenues reached hundreds of million of dollars annually.

▶ Manage the Seller Team Day-to-Day

So far in this chapter, we've discussed several issues concerning preparing sellers to address customers in their territories. Now we turn to three specific areas concerning where FLSMs should expend effort.

Run a Tight Ship

To be able to provide the appropriate attention so as to *build, lead, and manage a high-performing team of sellers*, the FLSM must construct a personal management structure that optimizes time spent with sellers. In our interviews, we did not speak to a single FLSM with spare time on their hands. Each FLSM was challenged to meet tough performance standards, but usually had insufficient time to do what had to be done. Most FLSMs developed a target weekly schedule. Schedules tended to vary by salesforce and district characteristics, but many followed a similar pattern:

- Monday—in the office, focus on the sales team: all-hands phone conversation, phone calls with individual sellers—looking forward to the week ahead, and managing the seller side of the vertical internal boundary.

- Tuesday through Thursday—in the field, joint calls with individual sellers.

- Friday—in the office, focusing on managerial tasks: internal administration/reports, discussion with boss, and otherwise managing vertical and horizontal internal boundaries.

Most firms (especially publicly traded) are managed on a quarter-by-quarter basis; after all, Wall Street examines quarterly results. Clearly, sales results are a key element. One FLSM explained how this quarterly focus translates into interactions with his sellers:

"Early in the quarter, I spend a lot of time with my team—analyzing territories and coaching them: 'Let's dig into your territory.' 'Let's see what your top opportunities are.' 'Are existing customers going to buy more, or can we bring new customers on board?' I focus on three things—size of the prize, degree of difficulty, time to close: 'What are the main initiatives we're going to focus on?' 'What do you need to do?' 'Do you feel comfortable talking to this customer, that customer?' 'Let's make some calls together.' I just want to make sure we're on the right track. We work on the skills they need to be successful that quarter.

"Later in the quarter, it becomes hectic: 'What customers should we visit, or get on the phone?' 'Who should we put contracts in front of?' 'What must be done to close this quarter?' At this stage, I'm spending more time with my manager discussing what I need to close the quarter, and also doing a lot of administrative stuff—forecasting, writing reports."

One FLSM in healthcare shared his approach:

"What's really important to me is making sure my team has a very defined roadmap and game plan. I spend a lot of time with my team early in the quarter, to make sure they're equipped with the tools they need to succeed. And then I monitor and measure. So, say, I get my rep to prepare for three joint calls; then we make those calls. Afterwards, I say: 'What did you learn?' 'What are you going to apply in the future?' A little while later, we make three more calls; I see if they're doing what they learned; if they have the tools they need. They have to demonstrate they learned."

Protect Seller Time

In Chapter 1, we noted that one difficulty for FLSMs is the boundary role they occupy between sales leaders/senior sales managers on the one hand, and their sellers on the other hand. A key part of the FLSM's job is to *protect* sellers from unreasonable demands from senior management—like ad hoc requests for information. Senior managers may have a *need to know*, but fulfilling these requests can be very time consuming for sellers; time better spent addressing customer needs, priorities, problems, pain points. Sometimes, it seems, senior managers fail to understand the impact of their requests on FLSM/seller time.

A particular problem occurs with performance expectations as senior managers push for short-term revenues. One FLSM confided:

"They want everything expedited. It's your normal sales organization! 'We need that order yesterday.'"

Another FLSM described his experience:

"You get pressure from senior management: 'Hey, bring the numbers; bring the numbers,' and you can lose focus very easily. To a certain extent, it's okay at the end of the quarter, if you need to push. But you can't change your overall strategy in a *knee-jerk* manner. I push back as much as I can; I want to hold true to my beliefs. The front-line manager has this push-pull job, but the big thing is to stay true to team members, and to make sure they are operating as they should to grow and develop the business."

The selling job often comprises many individual tasks. Typically, some tasks are sales related; others are more administrative in nature. From the firm's perspective, it would make sense to free up seller time to focus on selling activities. Other functions—finance, human resources, sales operations—can take responsibility for repetitive tasks.[4] Improved systems and processes may also play an important role. One FLSM explained a problem that he helped resolve:

"One of the big time wasters my sellers had to deal with was calls from customers enquiring about their orders. They were often frantic about delivery. Our production process consists of several discrete steps, so my sellers would have to call various production units to find out the current status: 'That order, we finished it last week'; 'What order, never heard of it.' I was able to convince senior management we had a problem. So, we developed a web-based system that shows the current production stage and estimated delivery time; customers can go online directly and find out what they need to know. It wasn't cheap, and our sellers still get a few calls, but we secured a significant increase in selling time."

Effective FLSMs make a point of protecting their sellers from activities that reduce selling time. Three FLSMs told us:

> "I take care of most of the admin requests on my own, without getting the sales reps involved, without sending out one of those *action-required* messages. Salespeople really dislike administrative duties and requests. So, I try to keep my team protected as much as I can, to let them do what they signed up for—go out and sell and produce the results."

> "I position myself at the customer interface. I literally will work with people who process orders on a daily basis—right up to our COO [chief operating officer], and everyone in between. A lot of what I do involves problem solving, keeping orders moving, and providing customers with status updates. I really spend a lot of time facing *inward*, so I free up time for my guys to face *outward*, and maximize their selling time."

> "Our sellers work in a global technology space; they have to navigate a lot of complexity. I step in and take on admin tasks. I get involved in conflict resolution—within our company, with our partner community, with our customers. These guys carry big quotas—anything that stops them selling is a bad thing. So, one of my jobs is to minimize that, and clear the clutter."

The requirement for FLSMs to protect seller time may become even more important as corporate initiatives take their toll on organizational capacity. One FLSM recounted his experience:

> "There are several groups that have to work together. But this doesn't happen as well as it used to since our reorganization and reduced headcount. Many problems I am solving (or helping solve) for my sellers arise simply because you have to push some work from one group to the next group to the next group, to get buy-in and resolution. So, I am making the internal alignments happen. It feels like we now have a lot of silos, instead of the way it was before."

The FLSM can play a major role in reducing silo-thinking, and pushing/arguing for these sorts of solutions.

Of course, notwithstanding the extent to which FLSMs free up time for sellers, the way sellers spend their time is critically important. They make choices every day: Which customers?—Phone or visit? How to schedule customer visits? Which products? Which solutions? Work on current opportunities or seek new opportunities? When to bring the FLSM? FLSMs should ensure sellers make good choices—aligned with district strategy and firm strategy.

One FLSM reported on a detailed time study his firm had conducted:

> "We didn't learn anything new, but we got good confirmation on what we believed. The best salespeople spent the most time in front of customers. A second major bucket was time building cross-functional relationships with internal partners. Third was account-planning activities. The findings confirmed that the behaviors we were looking for actually aligned with the data."

Understand Sellers as Individuals

A fundamental truth that all FLSMs must recognize—noted previously in the coaching section—is that sellers are individuals, each with their own issues and motivations. Hence, there is no single way to develop, lead, and manage sales talent. Rather, FLSMs should use an individual approach for working with each individual seller. As one FLSM told us:

> "An individual approach is harder, but it generates motivation and loyalty from people."

Other successful FLSMs echoed these sentiments:

> "The way to get the most and best out of the team is to treat them as individuals. I'm able to read my team members and decide what buttons I can push, and what buttons I need to back off."

> "You can't use a *cookie-cutter* approach; you have to treat each seller differently. Everybody may have similar goals, but get there a little bit differently."

> "I am involved in more coaching than day-to-day issues—trying to help sellers navigate their accounts. I'm there to bounce ideas off, and to provide an escalation point if they are stuck. It varies from rep to rep. I have a couple of new reps where I am more involved; I talk to them more than my more tenured reps."

> "Leadership must be displayed in a humble way, in the leader's ability to evaluate, and acknowledge, people's differences and styles."

> "An effective FLSM recognizes what people need and does not treat all of them in the same way."

> "You just have to be able to manage the personalities, manage the emotions, and their strengths and weaknesses. You must be able to read people, and to respond and react."

> "You must treat your people as individuals. You must recognize when you need to give and when you need to take. If you do this well, you make the relationship better, that person better, and the business better."

The sales leader at a major high-tech firm shared his perspective:

> "A prerequisite for super FLSMs is their ability to retain top talent. Retention has a lot to do with connection to the people as individuals, creating the right goals and *individualized-development* plans, focused on taking their competencies to the next level. I ask my FLSMs: 'Do you have *individualized, personal development* plans for all your people?' 'Have you meaningfully differentiated between your star performers and your low performers?' I've tried to guide my activities this way over many years of managing, both directly and in managing front- and second-line managers."

And an FLSM at a social media firm was very clear about the reason for her own success, but recognized she could not assume her sellers possessed similar world views:

> "One of the things that I have always believed is that I am successful because of the drive that I have, *but I cannot assume* that everybody who works for me has that same level of drive or the same motivation. So, I have to understand what their motivations are in order to help develop them in the right way. That means I manage every single person differently. I manage based on what their needs are versus what mine are, and it is harder."

The sales leader at another firm agreed with the need to understand each seller's world views, in this case regarding younger sellers:

> "The FLSM's job must change a little. You have to have empathy for different behaviors; millennials want different things than our traditional sellers. So, we're building that into our diversity training. (Of course, we see the same thing on the customer side!)"

For several FLSMs, managing sellers as individuals took on a genuine *Theory Y* perspective of care for sellers as individuals, and was perceived as a central success characteristic.[5] *Care* does not imply a liberal softness, but rather a real concern for the well-being of individual sellers and their job performance. One FLSM told us:

> "For me, *care* implies being able to put on the account manager's shoes, but *not* practice micromanagement. I do not get too heavily involved with the reps in dealing with their customers, but neither do I allow the reps to run the business with lack of transparency so I cannot provide support."

A closely related notion to *care*, and treating sellers as individuals, is *transparency*—the notion that there should be no secrets, that individual sellers have the right to know what is going on and where they stand performance-wise. One FLSM at a leading global high-tech firm was convinced transparency with sellers was a fundamental prerequisite for FLSM team building and success. He told us:

> "I believe the important issues for being a successful FLSM are transparency and trust. *Transparency* leads directly to *trustworthiness*. When performance is great, I'm the number 1 cheerleader. For poor performance, I am quick to share concerns and indicate gaps. My guys always know where I stand. I set high expectations, then get the team to achieve high results. I always give the *why* behind the *what*. My communication style is straightforward and clear."

Another FLSM, with a medical-diagnostics firm, speaking about both members of his seller team and individuals from other firm functions, put it this way:

> "The FLSM role is by far the most challenging and difficult position I have seen in my 15 years of field sales. The FLSM role requires a great deal of flexibility and psychological skills and approaches. You must be able to have those candid heart-to-heart conversations with individual team members, and to wear a lot of different hats. You must

develop the right mix of friend and inspector with each of them. A chameleon can do the job well!"

Focusing on sellers as individuals is not just a matter of sellers today, but of where sellers will be tomorrow. In so many firms, the pressures of today crowd out concerns about tomorrow. The sales leader at a major software firm focused on this issue:

"Most sellers today in the firms I know don't have development plans, so they cannot see the future. It's been like this for years, although my firm requires it. Unless people have development plans, they cannot see the future. We have annual development goals, required actions to meet those goals, and we track progress. For the people who are not going to make it here, we start working them out of the sales organization."

If the firm does not have a formal process, FLSMs must build personal-and-career development activities into how they treat sellers. This may mean finding a seller an alternative position in the firm if that is warranted. One FLSM provided an illustration:

"Last night, one of my solid performers had a baby, so she's not going to be traveling for a while. I was able to find her a position in inside sales. She is a very valuable account executive and employee."

More generally, the FLSM should understand the personal ambitions of sales-team members. Although the FLSM has elected to pursue a managerial career-path, many sellers prefer to remain as individually contributing sellers. As sellers, they avoid the many pressures faced by FLSMs in today's corporations and, furthermore, do not have to take an immediate pay cut! Two FLSMs provided their perspectives:

"Understanding what is important to my sellers individually is very important—getting promoted, or never wanting to do the job I am doing. It may be leaving the team and going to another team, or just getting the biggest paycheck. What's critical is knowing what they want, and keeping them fulfilled."

"In general, my success is not helping a salesperson sell the next widget, although making quota is very important. My success is when one of the managerially ambitious sellers gets promoted."

Managing the seller team day-to-day is a complex and challenging undertaking. FLSMs are more likely to do this job well, and achieve high performance, if they build an effective sales-team culture.

 ## Build an Effective Sales-Team Culture

We heard time and again that, although FLSMs should treat sales-team members as individuals, the team as a whole must be more than a group of individuals—more than the sum of its parts. Following Peter Drucker's famous admonition— "Culture eats strategy for breakfast"—FLSMs should construct a positive culture where team members share a common purpose, and individuals are mutually supportive. This is not a trivial issue, as we heard something like the following several times:

> "Bad culture happens; you should not just react to it. You have to work at developing good culture, so it evolves in a positive manner."

Indeed, one FLSM told us:

> "In our business, there's lots of technology and technology change; that part is easy. It's the people part that's hard."

So, how should FLSMs go about building a positive sales-team culture? An effective culture comprises four dimensions—Figure 5.2.

Figure 5.2 Creating a Positive Culture

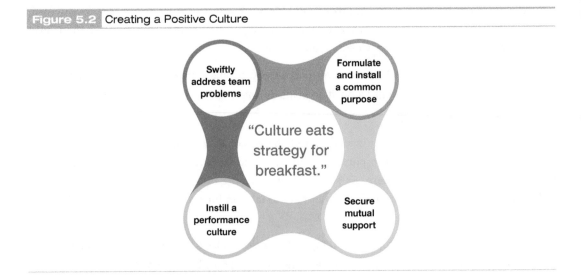

Formulate and Install a Common Purpose

A core aspect of the FLSM's job is to *formulate and install a common purpose* in the seller team—a calling, a reason for coming to work every day—over and above financial and other personal rewards. The FLSM should craft a vision (or mission), and act as a role model in pursuing that vision (mission). The sales leader at a biotech firm put it this way:

> "The FLSM must instill a sense of *mission*, higher purpose for sellers, so we are truly a *purpose-driven organization*. Our CEO says: 'At heart, we are people caring for people.' The firm's mantra is: *Good medicine is good business*. FLSMs must instill a sense of care and responsibility, and make sure our solutions are good for both the patient and the hospital. Our firm is an excellent place for sellers who genuinely want to serve others, and make their living out of it."

And from the sales leader at a global technology firm:

> "FLSMs are a key conduit of the company's culture. They really are the *cultural-ministry officers* for the firm. Along with attracting talent, that ability is worth its weight in gold.

They are the ones who give the presentations, who stand in front of people, who communicate what the firm is about, who help win. Ultimately, they are the ones who make it real."

There are many ways to develop and reinforce team culture. The sales leader at Salesforce.com told us:

"FLSMs in our district offices integrate corporate and local initiatives, whether it's lunch-and-learn events, C-Suite dinners, or training (for customers and our sellers). We back up these professional events with boxes at local sporting events—for customers and district personnel. Taken together, these activities serve as the *cultural hub* for the local sales team. They facilitate customer engagement, and transfer knowledge among account executives and other internal teams."

Secure Mutual Support

Developing a *common purpose* is one element in transforming a group of individuals into an integrated team striving to achieve team objectives. *Secure mutual support* is another. But mutual support can occur only if the FLSM's leadership style encompasses support for team members. As one FLSM put it:

"I truly try, and believe, my job is to support and help my team be better at what they do. They are in the trenches with their peers every day. I am very jealous of their time. I try to protect them from any extra work, busy work, extra emails. If I can deal with [the busy work], I do, so they can do their jobs."

Strong personal support from the team leader—the FLSM—sets the conditions for mutual support among all team members. As one sales leader observed:

"Effective FLSMs build a successful team dynamic. The way to know if an FLSM is successful is whether the team is cohesive and mutually supportive. That means not taking sides with someone to the detriment of someone else."

One FLSM at a leading global technology firm took a similar position but used a *family* metaphor to emphasize mutual support. She opined:

"We have a great team in place. You have to create the team and the environment to forge success. In my experience, if you build the right team, success will come. You must treat people with respect, trust, and care. The FLSM must be compassionate, as we expect results. In my branch, we treat everyone as a family member; after all, we spend more time at work than with our families."

Mutual support starts at the top. Team members must believe they have the full support of their FLSM. One FLSM was quite emphatic:

"Developing credibility with individual salespeople is really crucial. You have to make sure they understand that you are looking out for their careers, and their goals for that particular year."

FLSMs can take several specific actions to inspire mutual support among their sellers:

Reinforce Day-to-Day. One way to encourage mutual support is to build it into the fabric of the workplace. One FLSM from a software firm told us:

> "I hold an hour-long telephone meeting at 7:30 a.m. every Monday morning, before the week starts. We talk about last week. It's not tactical, more like word on the street; what customers are saying; what are the new selling tools, product features, and so forth.
>
> "We also have Monday morning mochas. I started these years ago in a different role. We may focus on a particular product, or I'll bring in a product or industry expert. My goal is to create an environment where my sales team is always thinking."

Other FLSMs told us about scheduled all-hands calls with similar agendas:

> "In my weekly calls, I read out the numbers—district overall, and each seller individually. Then each rep reports on the situation with his/her top three opportunities, including top three issues/challenges. When they've all reported, I open it up. The reps reach out for each other's experience: 'How did you do that?' 'Where did you start?' They take off flying and educate each other."

All-hands meetings by telephone are important team-building activities for many FLSMs, especially when team members are widely dispersed geographically. Physically meeting together is difficult, so some FLSMs take every opportunity to meet as a team. As one FLSM told us:

> "We all travel to sales meetings and conferences. Then we take an extra day for either a business meeting, or some team-building exercises."

Encourage Mutual Sharing. When individuals work together as a team, they share—experiences, ideas, information, expertise. The FLSM's job is to encourage and facilitate that sharing. One FLSM explained how he used technology to share information among team members and increase the sense of shared mission:

> "Each and every day, my reps are picking up information about market changes, technological developments, competitor actions. I make sure they share this information with me and all other team members. They just post it online to the entire team, so everybody is plugged in and staying abreast of what is going on in this fast-moving environment. Then we take up the most important items in our weekly calls."

Some of the most important interactions among team members occur in the absence of the FLSM. One FLSM positively encourages such interactions without his participation. He provided his perspective:

> "Let's share best practices; let's share innovative ideas. If something is working in your territory, you don't have to send it to me; send it to the team. I don't have that silo mentality among my guys. They really do try to help one another. There's a great camaraderie among them."

Develop Specialists. In many salesforces, within their fields of responsibility, sellers are *generalists.* If help is required for a particular issue/problem/pain point, the seller's first stop is often the FLSM. One FLSM in the healthcare industry sought to develop a culture of specialist excellence throughout his sales team:

> "I have this rep in Charlotte who's a real good analytic type—he's my *analytic champ.* I have another guy who really understands sales process, sales strategy, business development—he's my *champion of sales strategy and the deep processes.* Then I have someone who's really good at marketing, helping accounts market themselves—she's the *marketing champ.* And I have somebody who's really good with general practitioners [GPs]—growth and sustainability; she's a GP *whisperer,* my *GP champion.*
>
> "In some cases, I observed the person was outstanding in a particular area, so I said: 'Okay, you are the champion.' In other cases, I just appointed them. So, I said to my new guy: 'You have only been here six months. You have not really developed a big strength yet, but I want you to get really good in helping coach customer-treatment coordinators, and financial coordinators, on patient consulting, insurance, finance. I want you to get really, really deep and develop expertise. I'll take you as far as I can, but I'm going to partner you with people across the country who can help you, who are really strong in that area. I want you to be the resource for my team on that. You will be my *patient consulting, insurance, and finance champ.*'"

This FLSM added:

> "One important benefit of this approach is that there are certain sellers who prefer to secure information from a peer, rather than from their manager. I'm just fine with that, so the more positive peer interaction the better, as far as I'm concerned."

And one higher-education software FLSM shared his experience with product specialization:

> "I noticed Jack had sold several *Clover* products, so I asked him to be the go-to guy on our team for *Clover.* Then I had this other *Buttercup* product, and I asked Jill to lead the brigade on *Buttercup.*"[6]

By turning team members into champions, these FLSMs deepened the intellectual capital of the sales team overall. But the FLSMs also created climates of best-practice sharing among individual sellers; hence, they developed their team cultures. Recall how, as we noted in Chapter 4, the *shadow* system for gaining insight into competitors employs a similar approach.

Foster Peer Coaching. One important way in which a sales team works together is peer coaching of sellers. Certainly, FLSMs should be coaching, but peer coaching can be very effective. Said one sales leader:

> "We often find sellers learn best from each other; we spend a lot of time trying to figure out how to make that happen."

One approach is to appoint experienced sellers in adjacent territories as mentors for new hires. We heard about a success story from one FLSM in healthcare:

> "I have one rep who had no previous sales experience. He's very strong technically, very sharp, very bright. I worked with him very closely on his selling skills; he also took some courses. Then I placed him with one of my senior reps. Customer calls used to be very bland, like he was using a script—he was nervous, scared. But after nine months, it was a complete turnaround—like he's a different person. His pre-call planning is great; he knows exactly how to interact with customers—what questions to ask, what next steps. But this didn't come just from me; it came from his mentor rep, and other reps on my team. Of course, training helped. Bottom line: We're a team. I want my reps to learn from each other; after all, they're in the trenches together every day."

Instill a Performance Culture

A further cultural dimension is *performance*. Notwithstanding elements of *common purpose* and *mutual support*, or perhaps because of them, the FLSM must *instill a performance culture*. The FLSM and team do what it takes to reach their performance targets.

Of course, some firms drive such cultures from the top by annually eliminating the bottom 10 percent of performers, and developing payment systems heavily skewed to incentive compensation. Regardless, FLSMs typically insist on high individual performance to remain members of the sales team. Indeed, FLSM acceptance of poor/mediocre performance may have a significantly negative effect on otherwise successful team members. Conversely, individual high performance may spur sellers to greater efforts, so as to emulate their peers. FLSMs should foster a culture of high performance expectations and continuous improvement.

Compensation systems raise an interesting issue. It is axiomatic in salesforce management that the firm rewards sellers for achieving the results it requires; hence, successful sellers earn commissions, bonuses, and/or salary increases for hitting/exceeding sales targets/quotas. However, even though virtually every sales leader and FLSM we spoke with emphasized the importance of sellers acting as members of a team led by the FLSM, rarely did we find any direct financial incentive for such behavior. Certainly, as noted above, sellers receive various types of indirect reward for team-building behavior, but not financial rewards.

There was one exception. An FLSM in telecommunications explained how seller compensation works among his sellers:

> "Each seller has responsibility for their individual sales component, but part of their compensation is based on total revenues across the entire district. We make that linkage explicit, so we are all contributing to the cause. My guys are paid 50:50, salary/incentive compensation. Of the 50 percent incentive, 75 percent is individual performance; 25 percent is based on total district performance. That gives us a common thread."

Many compensation experts object to basing compensation on *input* variables (working together) versus *output* performance (sales revenues). Regardless, the telecom FLSM is conducting an interesting experiment.

Swiftly Address Team Problems

As noted, our respondents were, overall, highly positive about teams and teamwork. They saw building and managing the seller team as a critical FLSM function. Indeed, the title of this chapter is *Team-Building Acumen*. But we should not assume that all is sweetness and light among team members.

Some team members are more team-focused than others. Some team members do more than their fair share of mentoring; some avoid such responsibilities. Some team members are more diligent than others in providing information about market changes. Some team members are givers; others are takers. The FLSM's job is to manage these different contribution levels, and make them even out. The FLSM should avoid distrust and acrimony, push for positive team-member behavior, and *address team problems swiftly*. One FLSM in telecommunications provided his perspective on team-based issues:

> "I insist to my guys that, if we have an internal issue, we get it out today. We want to invest our energy, expertise, and experience selling, servicing, and solving customer problems. We do not want to burn that energy internally in battles that really do not mean anything."

Perhaps the greatest challenges arise when compensation is involved. As with any potential problem that may affect team solidarity, pro-action is generally preferable to reaction. This FLSM described a difficult situation that arose among his team members, and how he dealt with it:

> "One of my sellers did a great job of relationship building with a new contact at our account. She picked up a lead, followed through, and won a significant order for high-margin products. Some products were delivered and installed in her geography, but others in geographies where teammates had responsibility. Hence, she would be compensated for a portion of the order; her two teammates also received partial compensation.
>
> "I recognized there was a potential problem. So, I got all three together and we thought it through. I started with a little pep rally for all the work the seller had done, then we talked it through, including the logistics. We took time to deal with the impact on compensation plans, to make sure up front—this is how it's going to work; this is how everybody will be treated fairly; this is the best way to help. I try to anticipate the potential of human nature."

Summary

Chapter 5 focuses on the fourth of six acumen dimensions effective FLSMs must possess—*team-building acumen*. The chapter focuses on the seller team. The goal is very straightforward—*build, lead, and manage a high-performing team of sellers*. Team-building acumen comprises six dimensions—*assess current seller talent; secure effective sales talent; enhance sellers' intellectual capital; leverage firm resources; manage the seller team day-to-day; build an effective sales-team culture*.

Entering the FLSM position for an existing team, the FLSM must assess each individual seller, then decide who should stay and who should go. Whenever new sellers are required, the FLSM must staff the team with the best available talent. FLSMs are responsible for the performance of their direct reports; they must select appropriate individuals. The FLSM should strive to increase overall team competence by improving members' intellectual capital—*stocks* and *flows*. The FLSM should ensure team members take advantage of corporate training and other resources to the fullest extent possible, and spend significant time coaching sellers.

The FLSM should run a tight ship: Be very clear with sellers about what is expected, but provide as much help and guidance as needed, in a structured manner. Acting as a boundary spanner, the FLSM should protect sellers from unreasonable demands from senior managers. In managing sellers, FLSMs should treat team members as individuals.

FLSM/seller teams should be greater than the sum of their parts. The FLSM should develop a team purpose that all members can buy into. Such a purpose should provide seller motivation, and generate mutual support among team members. Finally, the FLSM should instill a performance culture, and swiftly address team problems.

Endnotes

1. N. Capon and G. Tubridy, *Sales Eats First*, Bronxville, NY: Wessex, 2011, Chapter 1, p. 4.

2. *www.axcessvids.com* [code 950v]

3. *Dreamforce* is an annual event that Salesforce.com stages for current and potential customers.

4. For information on sales operations, Appendix 7.

5. D. McGregor, *The Human Side of Enterprise*, New York: McGraw Hill, 1960.

6. Person and product names disguised.

Chapter 6

Resource Acumen

The heart of the front-line sales manager's (FLSM's) job is to achieve/exceed performance targets. To achieve success, the main vehicle the firm provides the FLSM is the ability to build a team of sellers—Chapter 5. In addition, the FLSM should secure and work with other resources to support sales-team efforts in attaining sales revenues. Individuals in other firm functions/organizations/business units have important roles to play in aiding, and generally supporting, the salesforce in this task.

Foreshadowing our discussion of leadership in Chapter 7, one sales leader at Cisco highlighted the importance of team building for modern sales organizations:

> "[The challenge is] developing leadership that can learn how to be collaborative, that can learn how to reach across the sales organization and share its collective talent.... It might not be you or your team's expert who needs to speak to the customer. It might be someone in a completely different group or different country."[1]

We firmly believe the salesforce *owns* the firm-customer relationship; hence, by definition, when individuals from other firm functions/organizations/business units interface with customers, they are members of the FLSM's *extended team*. Close to home, the FLSM may be involved with other sales teams (field/inside), and customer-facing functions like customer service, logistics, marketing, technical service. Further afield, FLSM responsibilities may extend to more distant functions like accounting, procurement, production/operations, R&D, and supply chain. Finally, the FLSM may corral customer personnel as resources to help achieve objectives. The FLSM's challenge is to use **resource acumen** to *meld these resources into an extended team.*

Extended-team members may have formal dotted-line relationships to FLSMs or other sales executives in a matrix-type organization structure. Alternatively, these resources may just be members of some other organizational function without any formal relationship to the salesforce. Indeed, they may not even be corporate employees: Perhaps they work for distributors, partners, complementary-product suppliers, or even customers.

Let us be very clear. For the FLSM to manage the set of extended-team relationships between firm resources and customers is not a straightforward task. As an Oracle sales leader explained:

> "Over time, the customers fan out. They build relationships with the support organization; they build relationships with the development organization; they build relationships with the marketing organization. So, when they need something, they don't need to go through the account team. They can go right to the executive in marketing that they've been working with, or the executive in development or the executive in support."[2]

Building an extensive web of firm-customer relationships is great, but the seller/FLSM's task of overseeing the entire firm-customer relationship web becomes more difficult the larger and more spread-out the resource web. If the seller/FLSM does not do a good job of managing these relationships, there is a very good possibility that the *left hand will not knowing what the right hand is doing.*

To fulfill overall customer needs, and deliver benefits/values to satisfy individual decision makers/influencers, requires resources. *Resource acumen* focuses on resources *within* the firm (or some other entity), but *outside* the FLSM's sphere of authority/responsibility. The FLSM's job is to secure agreement from key stakeholders to make these resources available to drive sales revenues. Required resources embrace various types of sales ability, customer/technical-service expertise, field marketing, value engineering, senior management involvement, but also resources—like R&D—that are organizationally more distant from the salesforce.

Individual sellers may find it difficult to reach the levers of resource-allocation power within the firm. FLSMs with high levels of resource acumen work with their sellers to identify critical resources, then do what it takes to align those resources with opportunities at customers. *Business acumen* focuses on figuring out what resources are required; *resource acumen* focuses on securing those resources.

Typically, as noted earlier, FLSMs both oversee, and participate in, the process of building and maintaining the firm-customer relationship. Many other organizational functions may also get involved to conclude deals. The firm often employs administrative procedures in the *implementation* stage of the selling process, to fulfill orders/contracts without direct salesforce involvement. FLSMs/sellers become involved in ordering, fulfillment, and payment only when problems like late delivery, defective products, or payment delays arise.

One FLSM at a telecommunications firm provided a classic example of the importance of extended teams in his firm, and the role he plays:

> "We have a business unit for hardware; there are multiple people we deal with. Then we have business units for software and wireless. A commercial management team helps with financials and deals; and various other organizations, from multiple business units, support selling solutions. So, overall, we deal with many different people. My sellers do a lot of work themselves; they come to me when things are not getting done, to hold people accountable, and make sure they support our efforts."

Another FLSM, at a software supplier to the banking industry, emphasized the importance of various firm organizational units providing service to customers:

> "Decision-making units and decision-making mechanisms are much more educated nowadays. The whole conversation with medium-sized banks is around services. The reason that banks switch suppliers is not because they can get better products elsewhere. The key question is: *How is the current provider treating me?* Service lapses enable us to win new business. Conversely, we work extremely hard to keep our existing customers very happy."

To build a successful extended-firm team and direct the *right* resources to the firm-customer relationship, at the *right* time, the FLSM should ensure that sellers treat non-seller-team members with respect. Part of that respect shows in the manner and care with which sellers prepare communications for these peers. One telecommunications FLSM shared how he instructed his sales team:

> "When you do an analysis, or make a presentation that will be used internally, make sure you take the time to polish it up. Anything you write, anything you present, is a reflection of your communication skills. Take the time to make sure it's precise, even to the extent of laying out information on the page—key information in the top third of the page."

To specify this element of resource acumen, one FLSM stated the issue most succinctly:

> "It's all about who you know to get things done."

Resource acumen comprises three dimensions—*permanent customer-facing resources, temporary firm-wide resources, customer resources*—Figure 6.1.

Figure 6.1 | Resource Acumen Dimensions

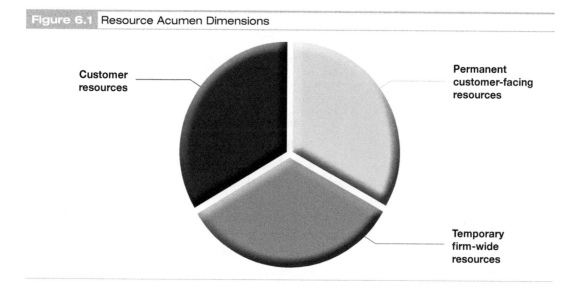

Customer resources

Permanent customer-facing resources

Temporary firm-wide resources

 ## Permanent Customer-Facing Resources

The FLSM may have important roles to play in working with many different types of firm resources that support the firm-customer relationship. As an illustration of resource acumen, one FLSM at a healthcare firm explained the breadth of the internal relationships he maintained:

> "We have a team of sales coordinators; they generate quotes and do many administrative tasks for us. We work closely with our contracts department, especially for system-wide deals; they evaluate terms and conditions to make sure we're able to adhere to them. Of course, we also work closely with our customer care and technical support departments. Supply chain is another important group—to make sure products are available. Then

> there's reimbursement and regulatory compliance, to make sure our products, and what we say about them—materials, sales tools—match regulatory guidelines."

FLSMs and team members often embrace resources from several different functions, organizations/business units.

Selling Resources

FLSMs may have key roles to play in different types of selling effort, over and above their directly managed sales team. Interviewees discussed several types. Perhaps the most common were situations where the firm had both a field salesforce and an inside salesforce.

Coordinating Field and Inside Salesforces. Many inside salesforces were traditionally telephone-based—telemarketing/telesales—but many have moved to a hybrid model, primarily using the Internet and live-chat systems for voice and interaction, depending on the industry. We identified three situations where FLSMs were involved in coordination efforts with inside-sales resources:

- **Prospecting.** The inside salesforce is responsible for identifying and screening potential customers (lead generation). Those leads meeting certain agreed-upon criteria are passed to field sales. As one FLSM put it:

  > "We work very closely with our telemarketers. We ask them to focus on certain market segments, and certain geographies, and we give them criteria for passing over leads. They are measured on number of generated leads, but we insist on strict adherence to the agreed-upon criteria. I don't want my guys spinning their wheels with lousy leads."

- **Independent selling.** The firm segments customers by size. Below a certain sales revenue level, inside sales is responsible. Above that level, the firm addresses customers with a field salesforce. One sales leader reported on his firm's experience:

  > "We sell though retail, so our field sellers spend most of their time visiting stores. There's a broad customer size range, from a few big-box retailers at one extreme to many small mom-&-pops at the other. A few years ago, we realized two things: First, we weren't spending enough effort with our larger customers; second, the cost to serve our smaller customers was very high relative to the revenues we received.
  >
  > "So, we reorganized. We developed an inside telephone-based salesforce for all our smaller accounts; the field guys could then spend more time with larger customers—that increased attention has been quite successful. The other thing we found out concerned our smaller customers; even though they lost our field sellers and now had telephone reps, their customer satisfaction levels improved! The reason? Frequently, it took the field guys a couple of days to get back to a small customer who wanted to talk about an issue; the sellers had bigger fish to fry—

larger customers. But the telephone guys are always there, so customers get an instant response. Overall, this sales reorganization has really worked."

■ *Joint selling.* An inside-sales organization works directly with field sales; inside sellers are teamed with field sellers who lead the account strategy. Each seller-pair works together to make sales. One field FLSM described his firm's process:

> "My guys work very closely with the inside salesforce. It would not be uncommon for an outside person just to call the inside person and say: 'Hey, I got an email from customer XYZ, they are interested in product ABC; do you mind following up for me.' And they just take it from there.
>
> "In general, our compensation system is low on salary and high on commission and bonus. We split commissions with the inside guys. We have some products where it's 25 percent inside seller, 75 percent outside seller; others are 75:25, and some are 50:50."

In a fast-growing medical-technology firm, field-sales interaction with inside-sales teams emphasizes the FLSM's supervisory role. In this firm, inside sellers report to an inside-sales supervisor, corresponding to the field-sales FLSM. The FLSM must manage interactions with inside-sales partners both at the seller level and at the managerial level.

Coordinating Multiple Field Salesforces. Working with an inside salesforce is one thing, but FLSMs may have to coordinate with other field salesforces. For example, in addition to a traditional geographically organized salesforce for most products, the firm may offer a specialized product(s) requiring specialist selling expertise. A specialist salesforce acts as an overlay to the traditional salesforce; traditional sellers may have responsibility for bringing in specialists to opportunities they identify. One sales leader explained:

> "As the environment has changed, we have had to develop new product/solution sets for our customers. So, we set up a new salesforce, also geographically organized, but with fewer people, so the sales territories are much larger. One responsibility for our traditional sellers is to identify opportunities for these new offerings, so we can bring in the specialists. Our FLSMs are central to this initiative."

Sometimes, FLSMs are assigned to coordinate major account coverage where multiple sellers report to individual businesses. These sellers are naturally keen to make sales and earn revenues for their specific businesses, but the FLSM may have to exercise considerable skill in counseling/cautioning aggressive sellers for the greater good of winning a contract embracing multiple businesses. As an FLSM in this situation told us:

> "No seller likes to be told to hold off on a customer when they can smell business. I just give them enough examples to make it credible—why they need to slow down. It's really all about influence without authority."

The FLSM followed up with an example:

> "One of our businesses sells hardware; another sells disposables that work with the
> hardware. Our hardware has a strong value proposition and significant differential
> advantage over competitors. But the disposable product is pretty much a commodity. For
> our disposables unit to sell its products on a stand-alone basis is tough. I try to arrange
> things so the customer places orders for hardware and disposables at the same time.
> Then I can design very attractive combined hardware/disposable offers. But to do that I
> may have to get hardware sellers to slow down so the customer's purchases are in sync."

Each of these cases—coordinating field and inside sales, and coordinating multiple field sales-forces—requires FLSMs/sellers to engage with some other organizational unit within the firm that has customer-facing responsibilities. Within the sales district, the FLSM is responsible for managing this extended-team effort.

Other Resources

In many firms, organizational functions other than sales are involved with customers on a regular basis.

Service. Customer/technical-service relationships are common. These relationships are typically valid and necessary but, as they proliferate, the possibility of *crossed wires* with field sales accelerates. FLSMs have the responsibility to ensure all customer-facing/firm representatives are *singing from the same song sheet*. Consider what a sales leader at a higher-education software firm told us regarding his FLSMs' use of resource acumen:

> "Each of our FLSMs oversees about half a dozen direct reports, but that's only part of
> the job. We also have a service organization that interfaces with the same customers,
> and functional experts who frequently interface with customers also. Our sellers are
> charged with overseeing the entire selling/servicing effort, including cross-functional
> people involved in specific deals. FLSMs work with sellers to minimize overlap, and stop
> our people falling over each other at individual customers. The FLSM functions as an
> escalation point for the entire sales-and-service effort."

In the fast-growing medical-technology firm, in addition to extensive interactions with inside sales, the FLSM told us:

> "My internal interactions do not stop with the inside-sales folks. I have frequent
> interactions and alignment meetings with sales enablement, sales operations, sales
> training, and marketing."

Marketing. Marketing departments do many different things, ranging from highly strategic—develop value propositions—to highly tactical—produce brochures, manage events. Marketing departments have many skills and resources that can aid the salesforce in reaching its objectives. In some firms, close interaction between sales and marketing is forced by appointment of a chief revenue officer (CRO). (Reporting to the CRO are all *permanent* customer-facing functions like marketing, sales, service, *last-mile* logistics.) In other firms, there should be high-level conversations between marketing and sales leaders on marketing support for the selling effort.

Regardless, FLSMs have the responsibility to work with marketing when needed to support their sellers; they should be forceful in securing the support they require. Unfortunately, as one FLSM described, the support isn't always there:

> "We're not that engaged with marketing; we don't find them terribly useful! They work on big events, but that's really the only support they provide."

Some FLSMs improve that kind of situation by engaging marketing executives in selling activity. Including marketers in sales calls, for example, can teach marketing about *bad* leads, and work on harmonizing criteria for *good* leads. In part, the goal is also to bring MQLs (marketing-qualified leads) and SQLs (sales-qualified leads) into sync.

Regular contact with the marketing department may play an important role in cementing relationships with customers, and even directly persuade *potential* customers to become *actual* customers. At a medical-diagnostics firm, for example, one element of the corporate value proposition concerned future tests the firm planned to introduce. When such a test cleared all regulatory hurdles, the firm would begin the selling effort. To implement this approach, FLSMs had to ensure they and their sellers were fully cognizant of what tests were in development, and when they would be released for sale. Said one FLSM:

> "Future tests are an important selling point for us. Marketing provides this information to the entire salesforce via 90-minute to two-hour monthly calls. Sometimes the timing is inconvenient, but I absolutely insist that my sales team attend each of these presentations. They have to be fully up-to-date."

Other Functions. The FLSM may have to become involved with various firm functions in the *implementation* and *use* stages of the selling process, when issues/problems arise. Examples: delivery/logistics when the firm fails to keep delivery promises; manufacturing if product quality dips below acceptable levels. The FLSM may also have to work with accounting, as a collection agent, if recalcitrant customers do not pay their bills on time. But the FLSM may also get involved if the firm's accounting function puts the firm-customer relationship at risk. We return to an example from Chapter 4 in which, without the FLSM's knowledge, the firm's accounting department halted all deliveries to a major customer that had not paid a relatively small invoice:

> "The customer was furious; I had to sort out the situation and try to repair the damage. I calmed the situation down, but we also got the system changed. Now, no delivery stoppage is implemented without the salesforce being involved."

The bottom line: Many individuals representing a variety of firm functions/organizations/businesses interface with customers on a regular basis. *Murphy's Law* has broad applicability—stuff happens! The FLSM must be ready and willing to get involved with many different individuals throughout the firm to modify systems and processes, do damage control, and get the firm-customer relationship back on track, as and when necessary.

Problems with Managing Permanent Customer-Facing Resources

In Chapter 3, we presented the huge success one FLSM achieved following a casual customer contact in a men's room. The FLSM managed to involve specialist resources that ultimately solved a tough customer problem. A more difficult situation occurs when the FLSM must orchestrate several different types of firm resources for ongoing commitment. Then, it's not a question of persuading a single individual or group (function) to participate in some customer-focused endeavor, but rather integrating participation by multiple entities.

Perhaps the FLSM must orchestrate participation of several different functions within a business, or orchestrate several businesses within a multibusiness corporation. We discussed the following situation in Chapter 2: Some years ago, an FLSM at a global healthcare firm faced such a challenge, and failed. The idea was simple and elegant. The healthcare firm comprised many individual businesses, each offering specialist products for use in hospital operating rooms. The FLSM's proposal was to create and sell a product bundle comprising products from multiple businesses. Customer research had shown that, at the right price, such a bundle would have considerable value for hospitals, and would be difficult for competitors to replicate.

However, the FLSM was unable to convince sales leaders in critical businesses that the proposal was worthwhile. Notwithstanding arguments about increased revenues and enhanced brand equity for the firm, several businesses balked. The most severe criticism concerned necessary price reductions to make the proposal work. The FLSM believed the core problem was the firm's highly decentralized structure. Senior executives focused on reaching performance goals for their individual businesses, and were far less concerned for the firm overall.

Operating as a team in pursuit of firm objectives is no simple task for FLSMs. In many firms, marketing departments appoint product managers to develop strategy and implementation plans for individual products/product lines. Product managers typically strive to meet objectives—sales revenues, profit, profit contribution; their ability to achieve desired results is, at least in part, a function of selling effort. In some firms, multiple product/product-line objectives are tightly integrated with salesforce objectives; in other firms, salesforce objectives are only loosely integrated. In these latter cases, internal competition among product managers, aided by loose managerial controls, can frustrate the exercise of resource acumen by FLSMs. A senior executive at a major book publisher voiced her disapproval:

> "We have made life really difficult for FLSMs trying to get all members of their teams on the same page and working together. Our sellers carry the entire product line. Product managers are strongly incentivized to meet sales targets for their books. As a way to secure disproportionate selling effort on their product portfolios, some product managers devise incentive schemes for sellers. In seeking to optimize their personal earnings, sellers play havoc with FLSMs' attempts to develop coherent team efforts. We have to get past the internal dissension these schemes cause, so our FLSMs have more control over doing their jobs."

As we have noted several times, the FLSM job is not an easy one. Building a fully functioning seller team is one thing; integrating various functions, organizations, and businesses that interface with customers on a regular basis is quite another. In this section, we illustrated some of the positive ways FLSMs can work with individuals in other customer-facing roles, but we also noted problems. FLSMs with good resource acumen will secure positive cooperation, while minimizing the negatives.

 # Temporary Firm-Wide Resources

Virtually every version of *Selling 101* demands that sellers probe customer needs. The basic goal is to isolate those needs, so the seller can show how firm offers satisfy them better than competitive alternatives. When sellers succeed in this task, sales revenue follows. In an increasingly complex/changing world, the seller may realize that current firm offers do not completely satisfy some emerging customer need, problem, priority, pain point. The customer-focused seller/FLSM may believe, nonetheless, that such an emerging customer need can be creatively addressed by the firm. It's just a matter of identifying the required expertise/resources, then bringing it/them to bear on the matter.

Functional Resources

In some firms, the salesforce requires additional support only after the seller/FLSM has identified and validated a sufficiently attractive opportunity—this task is often a key FLSM/seller responsibility. After validation, the FLSM's resource acumen challenge is to secure the appropriate firm resources, and meld them into a team to prepare a proposal and win the business. Of course, in most cases, availability of required resources is limited.

The medical-diagnostic firm we discussed earlier has a well-developed system for addressing major deals. The firm uses customized sales automation software to track each customer's equipment and reagent purchases—from the firm and other vendors—to judge deal size. Mathematical models help understand how to price, and calculate potential profitability. The firm attempts to be smart by participating in deals with the right amount of vigor, and committing scarce resources carefully. The seller and FLSM complete the review process, jointly with the total solutions design manager (TSDM). For deals that make the cut, the FLSM and the TSDM work on a strategy to win the business. The TSDM represents a different organizational unit, matrixed with the salesforce. This organization provides resources to design and develop customer solutions. Individual resources from the TSDM's organization may spend up to 18 months working on a specific deal.

The seller and FLSM together figure out the anticipated customer decision-making unit (DMU) and decision-making process (DMP). Then the FLSM and the TSDM together select team members and schedule customer interventions. Securing these internal agreements is critical for moving forward successfully. As one FLSM put it:

> "My relationship with the TSDM is absolutely critical for securing the *right* resources at the *right* time. These deals are so complex, the field-sales organization can't do them on its own. The *solutions team* concept really works, but the TSDM has limited bodies he can allocate. So, I make sure I maintain a good relationship with this person. Of course, getting some big wins doesn't hurt; it helps the TSDM meet his numbers, as well as ours in the district.

"Actually, we try to construct the solutions team well in advance. We say: 'Hey, this deal's coming up next year'; then we form the team. We're two to three years out projecting deals to focus on, and trying to align resources for the accounts. We even try to set a calendar with an account: 'This is what's going to happen over the next 18 to 24 months as you go through your decision process.' Of course, not all prospects are willing; they want to wait for their RFPs to come out. That's counterproductive—they miss out on being fully educated, but we have to live with their decision. We do the best we can.

"There's always been a chemistry specialist per district to help *smoke out* quality problems, but customer needs and our value propositions have evolved over the years. So, today's solutions team likely has an automation specialist, information-management specialist, instrument specialist, and a workflow specialist. There's also an enterprise account manager specialist [EAMS] whom I can bring in to work on large deals. My EAMS has the most experience to address instrument complexity. Then, in addition to these specialist members of a solutions team, from time to time I bring in their bosses. So, the internal management of resources that I don't control gets pretty complex."

Contracts are for several years, so each individual seller sees only one or two big deals annually. But each FLSM manages several sellers, and so may participate in half a dozen deals simultaneously. Because, in general, FLSMs are much more experienced than individual sellers, they must be deeply involved in each deal. And, of course, the FLSM has far deeper customer knowledge than any specialist resource. The FLSM went on:

"My job is to meld the set of individual specialists into a team, so we put forward a seamless face to the customer. In fact, I must secure and manage several such teams, each with a different composition of specialists. If we want to win many of these deals, I must take control. The core problem I face is that all these individuals reside in separate organizations. Each organization has its own priorities, and they don't always line up exactly with mine. Also, in any particular specialty, individual specialists possess different skill sets, and have different experience levels; and we have many different personality types.

"The specialist manager may assign specialist A for a particular deal, but I'd rather have specialist B, because I know specialist B would have a better working relationship with other solution-team members, and do a better job. It's a constant battle to optimize team membership, so I can be sure what needs to get done, actually gets done. I have to make sure the group of individuals really works well together. Then I help my sellers manage these resources over the period we're working on each deal—that could easily be for 18 months. After all, although they *work for me*, they report to a different organization.

"What I generally like to do is keep successful teams together to work on multiple deals—I don't want to continually reinvent the wheel. But the specialist organizations often seem to think their specialists are interchangeable. To up my chances of fielding the best possible teams, I make certain I have good relationships with managers in the specialist organizations. These guys call the shots when it comes to appointing specialists. I have to make sure I'm not at the bottom of the totem pole when they make their allocation decisions. Sometimes, I have to escalate to my senior management to put pressure on the specialist organizations, so I get the people I need."

In a Chapter 2 case study, we discussed the 15-year, multimillion-dollar deal that Philips Medical Systems (PMS) concluded with Georgia Regents Medical Center (GRMC). Once the local account manager shared the opportunity he had unearthed by talking with GRMC's CEO, the FLSM took on the role of *point person* to share details of the opportunity internally across the PMS organization.

The FLSM's local team acted as coordinator of the entire PMS effort; team members provided significant relationship value by maintaining customer confidence in PMS as the process unfolded. Regardless, most of the detailed work and problem solving for the deal was undertaken by a *deal team*, constructed and led by the FLSM. This deal team ultimately comprised a diverse group of more than 20 PMS employees, most of whom brought specialist expertise during the 18-month development and negotiation process. A PMS sales leader put it this way:

> "The GRMC opportunity would never have come to fruition if the FLSM and his local team had not known how to engage the broader Philips organization to solve customer problems. Opportunities are becoming larger and more complex, especially in healthcare; the capability we need to address them meaningfully simply does not exist in local teams. So, the ability to access and use resources at the *right* time, in the context of the *right* strategy for that customer, is a core skill for our FLSMs and their front-line account managers."

The sales leader added:

> "It's not so long ago that we had a number of highly successful do-it-yourself-cowboy-solo salespeople. Those days are over. PMS does not lend itself to that sort of selling anymore. Increasingly, the key FLSM (and account manager) skill is being able to interface and engage with the entire Phillips organization."

A key characteristic of working with permanent customer-facing resources and securing temporary nonhierarchical resources is the absence of any solid-line authority/responsibility relationships. Sometimes there are dotted-line FLSM-to-specialist relationships but, mostly, formal relationships do not exist. As one sales leader put it:

> "We're in the realm of managing without authority."

And from one FLSM at a software firm:

> "Things are getting more complicated, so I'm bringing in subject-matter experts [SMEs] more frequently to have those complicated technology conversations. I assign the team that's going to work on a particular deal—the most appropriate people to support my sellers—based on background, geography, all sorts of things."

There is no doubt that FLSMs may have to develop temporary teams incorporating resources from several organizational functions when the selling process embraces *ideate* or *design*. When deals are being concluded (especially at high price tags or if government bodies are involved), there may be an important role for the legal department in negotiating contract details. In such cases, FLSMs should have good relationships with firm lawyers, with FLSMs and legal working together for the good of the firm. Unfortunately, this is not always the case. As one FLSM confided:

> "Legal is like this big old vulture sitting on top of the roof, looking over the entire neighborhood. It flies down and scoops up when it feels like having a meal."

The core message is very clear. As customer DMUs and DMPs evolve, along with increased complexity in customer needs, the firm must bring an increasing variety and depth of skills/resources to the firm-customer table. Someone has to identify those resources, negotiate internally to secure them, then create a functioning team—*resource acumen*. That is becoming an increasingly important FLSM responsibility.

In addition to securing temporary resources for specific pre-sale selling situations—*ideate, design, close*—FLSMs may have to interface with quite different resources in the *implement* stage of the selling process. And if problems occur in the *use* stage, another set of resources may be involved. As one FLSM at a major software firm noted:

> "Certainly our team is involved postsales as well as presales. Typically, post-sales, there is an implementation partner that is largely responsible for implementation success. We also offer support-solution teams that help to ensure success while customers are under contract."

We came across several cases where the customer required assistance that did not directly relate to the firm's products/services, but the firm did possess expertise. In effect, the firm used its expertise to deliver *consulting* advice as a means of relationship building. Again, the FLSM was the *point person*. One FLSM in wholesaling reported:

> "Our account managers today are ten times busier than they were 20 years ago—their world is so much more complex. When I started, it was mostly price and product. Today, it's more consultative. I had a dealer that wanted help in its warehouse: I sent in an expert from head office; he looked through warehouse processes, and how the warehouse was laid out. He made recommendations to improve productivity and reduce pulling errors.
>
> "Dealers ask for credit help: 'I need somebody to look at my financials; my DSO [days sales outstanding] is running 45 to 50 days—that's a problem.' We'll fly in, take a look, and make recommendations. We also get into branding and marketing—that's a big deal, so we send in a team. It's more than just a logo refresh; it's all about the entire company—what your people say from the time they answer the phone, to your warehouse operations, and how your drivers interact with customers."

In an ideal world, where the firm operates as a customer-centric, externally oriented organization, FLSMs secure resources from and work with other firm functions in a highly collaborative manner in pursuit of serving customer needs. Regardless, the harsh reality is that few firms enjoy such a positive culture. In any event, functional resources are typically scarce—functional members face many demands. Although freely given cross-functional collaboration is an ideal for which firms should strive, FLSMs may have to *shake a few trees*—use resource acumen—to get what they need to serve customers. As one sales leader observed:

> **"One thing I think our sales organization does very well is this: If it needs something from product development, it doesn't say, 'Development didn't give it to me.' It gets in their face and says, 'We've got to make this happen for the customer.'"**[3]

Top-Management Involvement

A particularly important resource the firm may bring to the firm-customer relationship is top management. The FLSM faces two quite different situations. On the one hand, FLSMs may want to introduce senior managers into customer organizations as a means of enhancing the customer relationship and/or to accomplish specific goals. On the other hand, a senior manager may wish to meet with a customer's senior executives—the FLSM/seller may have to make the necessary arrangements to ensure the visit has a positive outcome. Of course, such visits should not occur without seller/FLSM knowledge. Indeed, the FLSM should ensure the senior executive is fully briefed before the visit and, if neither FLSM nor seller attends, that seller/FLSM are fully debriefed afterwards.

Certainly, as noted in Chapter 4, some senior managers will not visit customers. These executives take the position that customers are *not my problem*. They believe the salesforce has the responsibility to earn sales revenues; they have their own responsibilities and day jobs. If the salesforce believes it needs help, maybe the salesforce needs different people!

Figure 6.2 identifies four types of senior management involvement with customers, based on two core high/low dimensions—*revenue seeking* and *relationship building*.[4]

Figure 6.2 | Senior Management/Customer Relationship Roles

Revenue Seeking

	Low	High
Relationship Building — Low	Loose Cannon	Deal Maker
Relationship Building — High	Social Visitor	Growth Champion

Loose Cannon—low revenue seeking, low relationship building.

Loose cannons—aka *seagulls*[5]—seem to be ubiquitous in many corporations. Loose-cannon/customer interactions are short-lived, and not particularly focused on revenue generation (at least not in the short term). Loose-cannon behavior typically occurs when a senior executive meets with a customer, but has no (or minimal) prior interaction with the seller/FLSM. Sometimes, sellers/FLSMs only discover about the interaction long afterwards—often from customer executives! Not only was the senior executive not (or poorly) briefed, the executive may commit the firm to actions without full awareness of complexities in the firm-customer relationship. Many times the executive may fail to advise the seller/FLSM of these agreements.

Social Visitor—low revenue seeking, high relationship building.
Executives acting as *social visitors* demonstrate supplier commitment; they create trust through long-term personal and professional relationships. Though less negative than loose cannons, the social visitor has its own set of risks and rewards. Whereas loose cannons can be positively destructive for the firm-customer relationship, the social visitor's impact ranges from mildly positive to mildly negative. The social visitor specializes in relationship building via *meeting and greeting*. Typically, the firm arranges meetings for senior customer executives—educational events on company premises, cocktail parties at trade shows, trips to sporting events. The social visitor works the crowd, engages in conversation about industry issues, and builds personal relationships with individual customer executives. Rarely do such social interactions cause harm. But customer executives may wonder why these interactions are all they see of senior supplier executives. Indeed, they may feel mildly negative about lack of relationship depth, and be frustrated about missed opportunities for meaningful discussion.

Deal Maker—high revenue seeking, low relationship building.
Deal makers stabilize shaky relationships and/or secure deals. Senior executives can have a major positive impact as deal makers. FLSMs actively managing sales pipelines know what deals customers are deciding on a week-to-week basis. For many opportunities, the customer's critical deciding issue is not so much the value propositions that sellers/FLSMs offer, but whether the firm will live up to its commitments. Seller promises go so far; FLSM promises go further; but often, only a senior executive can fully commit firm resources. The deal maker is very revenue focused. In many customer organizations, middle managers negotiate deals and make purchase recommendations, but senior managers have the final word. We have observed cases where top management intervened in the buying process/reversed previously agreed-upon purchase decisions. Senior executives are uniquely placed to fulfill the deal-maker role.

Growth Champion—high revenue seeking, high relationship building.
Unlocking new growth opportunities and serving as role models to inspire sellers/FLSMs are the main purposes of *growth champions*. They represent the most positive customer-facing behavior for senior executives. Senior executives acting as growth champions play a critical role in driving revenue and profit growth. Well-planned, well-organized, well-executed executive involvement at customers can pay huge dividends.

Key issues for FLSMs: Be knowledgeable about predispositions and capabilities of senior executives. Proposed actions for FLSMs concerning senior executives with these tendencies:

- Loose cannon (seagull)—Keep away from customers in your district.

- Social visitor—Use relationship prowess as appropriate. Manage customer expectations as regards business involvement.

- Deal maker—When the going gets tough, bring in as needed.

- Growth champion—Get close; involve with customers as appropriate.

Questions for readers: Can you identify loose cannons, social visitors, deal makers, growth champions in your firm? What specific approaches will you use to harness the positive features of senior executive involvement with your customers, and minimize potential negative effects?

Customer-Formed Teams

When the customer must make a difficult decision with broad applicability, it may choose to form a team of internal experts to make the decision, or make recommendations to higher organizational levels. Sometimes, customer firms invite potential suppliers to nominate one or more personnel to join such a team/task force. This is a special case in which FLSMs using resource acumen may play an important role in making available firm resources to help drive sales and enhance the firm-customer relationship. Clearly, having a seat at the table provides the supplier with an *inside track* regarding future sales revenues. The FLSM can play a major role in making this happen.

This situation played out in the PMS-GRMC relationship. The PMS FLSM was the *point person* for the interorganizational relationship; he managed to have a PMS representative sit on the GRMC executive team that worked on the deal. This aspect of the innovative partnership was extremely helpful in pushing the deal along. The PMS person became aware of issues/problems in real time, and was able to quickly secure responses to matters that arose.

We saw another example in Chapter 3. Recall that an FLSM ran into a customer executive in the men's room at the customer's offices. Based largely on the FLSM's *organizational acumen*, he secured significant information on a serious problem the customer's firm was facing. Armed with this information, the FLSM used his *resource acumen* to identify SMEs in his firm, then persuaded them to visit the customer to scope out the problem. A joint firm-customer task force worked on the problem for about one year to come up with a satisfactory solution for the customer. That solution earned millions of dollars revenue for the FLSM's firm.

Generally, securing positions on customer teams is a great way to influence customer decision making in the firm's favor, but the FLSM must be careful. Consider the case of an FLSM at a major tech firm. He arranged for an SME to join one of his customer's task forces for a major project that could lead to millions of dollars in revenues. The FLSM made the arrangement, but failed to follow up with the SME on a regular basis. One day, the FLSM ran into his key customer contact, who said:

> **"Your SME's forgotten who he works for. He keeps pushing your competitor's product. I told my guys to get an expert from your firm because I want your product."**

After apologizing, the FLSM called the SME's manager. The manager defended the SME. He responded:

> **"They [SMEs] have to show clients they aren't just pushing our products. They have to demonstrate objectivity to build credibility."**

The FLSM told us:

> **"I understood this position up to a point, but the customer did not want objectivity; it wanted assistance with our product. Neither the SME nor his manager would do what I wanted them to do, despite several telephone calls. Regardless, the committee chose our product, despite the SME's recommendation for the competitor.**

"This incident taught me a big lesson. Getting my people onto a customer team is great, but I have to keep on top of what is going on; otherwise the situation could blow up in my face. In this case, I was lucky, but now I make sure this will never happen again."

Typically, the FLSM is not involved in the customer's decision to form a task force. Regardless, when such formulation occurs, the FLSM should be ready to offer the appropriate personnel resource(s) to take a seat at the table, aid customer decision making, and place the firm in a strong position for future revenue generation. Then, the FLSM should monitor task force progress to ensure that supplier personnel resources placed on the task force are both pulling their weight as members and appropriately advancing the firm's interests.

 ## Customer Resources

The third type of resource acumen with which FLSMs must be concerned mainly comprises customer personnel. There are many different occasions where individual customer employees can enhance the firm's agenda. A popular version is customer user groups. We all know about Macintosh user groups, and the Harley-Davidson owners group, HOG. But FLSMs may also form local user groups. Recall what one FLSM for a higher-education software firm told us—Chapter 4—about an Ohio-based group:

"We generally have about 200 people at this user group, hosted by one of our clients. It's a great way to meet customers in a more relaxed environment. The actual users show up, not just the IT [information technology] folks, so we can familiarize them with what we do. Each of our user groups is very serious; they elect a board of directors and a president. The users run the conferences, arrange the schedule, figure out the learning tracks. We support these groups with our product experts."

Such user groups are an efficient way of providing product/service information to a broad group of customer personnel. This sort of format enables customer personnel to talk to their peers about the supplier and its products/services in a relaxed atmosphere. Hence, these customer individuals, acting as high-credibility emissaries, are valuable firm resources.

The ability of customer personnel to act as high-quality firm resources is exemplified by Salesforce.com. As we noted earlier, lunch/dinner-and-learn events are specifically designed so that current customers act as *sellers* for Salesforce.com. As we reported in Chapter 5:

"At these dinners [sometimes lunch-and-learn sessions], we may have around 30 CIOs [chief information officers] or other C-Suite members, from current and potential customers. A couple of Salesforce.com execs get the session off, and *then our guests just sell to each other*—it's really unique. The core outcome is educational, but we also personalize our relationships. Our success is derivative of those FLSMs who can pull off those events."

In a related initiative, one FLSM set up a blog for his business associates—direct-seller reports, internal-firm contacts, and customers. By building credibility with customers, the FLSM believed they would become advocates for the firm. He told us:

> "I decided to set up this blog. I populate the blog with industry information—a report here, an article there—information on what our firm is doing, and some commentary by me. I work hard on keeping it up-to-date, so scarcely a week goes by without something new. What I'm trying to do is create a sort of extended team, comprising my sales organization, the firm overall, and customers in my district. An increasing number of customers are subscribing, so I think I am getting some traction."

In these examples, firm employees play a major role in securing customer resources. Indeed, the FLSM may be highly involved in persuading personnel from many different customer organizations to come together in space and time to act as resources for the firm.

Summary

Chapter 6 focuses on the fifth of six acumen dimensions effective FLSMs must possess—*resource acumen*. Resource acumen concerns working with and securing resources to support the selling effort. The FLSM integrates these resources into an extended team that secures sales revenues, and builds the firm-customer relationship.

Resources comprise three broad types—*permanent customer-facing resources, temporary firm-wide resources, customer resources.* Permanent firm customer-facing resources include individuals from organizational functions that interface with customers on a regular basis. Typical functions are sister sales organizations—field sales, inside sales—customer service, logistics, marketing, technical service. Since the salesforce *owns* (or should own) the firm-customer relationship, FLSMs should be deeply involved with individual relationships between customers and members of these firm organizational units with which they interface.

In the second broad type of firm, the FLSM plays a major role in scoping out temporary resources, and securing necessary agreements, when these are required to address customer needs, priorities, problems, pain points. Securing these resources generally advances the firm-customer relationship. Of special concern is managing senior executive interactions with customers. These interactions can be extremely positive if well-managed, but they can also be matters for concern.

A special case of securing firm resources concerns customer teams/task forces. The FLSM should work hard to identify when customers form such task forces, then seek to add firm personnel as members. But the FLSM should also monitor the progress of the task force overall, and the firm's members in particular.

In the third broad dimension of resource acumen, using customer resources, the FLSM may create situations where personnel from different customers act as critical resources to advance the firm's agenda. When FLSMs are successful in this task, customer personnel play an important role as highly credible information sources about the firm and its products/services.

We generally think of the FLSM as focusing efforts outward to secure customer revenues. FLSMs lead, direct, and manage sellers to make their individual quotas and so make district quota. But to achieve high performance may require significant internal resources. To secure these resources, FLSMs must also face inwards to secure these resources, using high levels of resource acumen.

Endnotes

1. From N. Capon and G. Tubridy, *Sales Eats First*, Bronxville, NY: Wessex, 2011, Chapter 1, p. 14.

2. Capon and Tubridy, *op. cit.*, p. 18.

3. Capon and Tubridy, *op. cit.*, p. 17.

4. N. Capon and C. Senn, "Customer-Centricity in the Executive Suite: A Taxonomy of Top-Management–Customer Interaction Roles," *Strategy and Communication for Innovation*, Nicole Pfeffermann and Julie Gould (Eds.), New York: Springer, 2017.

5. The seagull flies in, makes a *deposit*, then flies off, never returning to the same place!

Chapter 7

Personal Acumen

Chapter 7 is the last of six chapters concerning acumen dimensions for successful front-line sales managers (FLSMs). *Strategic acumen* and *business acumen* focus, respectively, on strategy and implementation. *Organizational acumen* and *team-building acumen* focus, respectively, on external (customer) and internal (sales team) organizational issues. *Resource acumen* is concerned with additional resources FLSMs can secure and bring to bear on the firm-customer relationship. In this chapter, we turn our attention to *personal acumen*, a group of personal attributes that are consistent with high FLSM performance.

Many sales leaders and successful FLSMs we interviewed had their own perspectives on the personal qualities necessary to be a successful FLSM. This chapter attempts to capture the broad sweep of insights our interviewees provided. We focus on five specific aspects of **personal acumen**—*leadership, personal drive and hard work, creativity and risk taking, managerial courage, managerial style*—Figure 7.1.[1]

Figure 7.1 Personal Acumen Dimensions

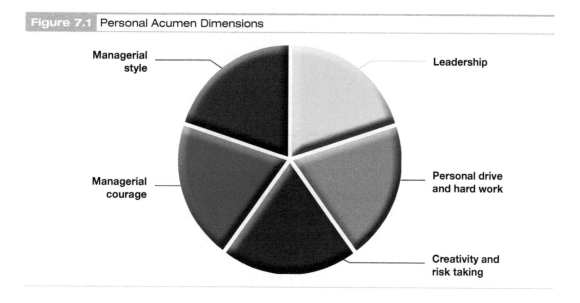

 Leadership

"Sales leadership: There is no substitute."[2]

Of all the personal attributes sales leaders believed were important for being a successful FLSM, there was absolutely no disagreement on the most important—*leadership*. One sales leader expressed his belief about the FLSM position:

> **"Successful battles aren't won without field generals that are empowered. The FLSM is the field general."**

This is extremely evocative language. To continue with the military analogy, we are not talking about the U.S. joint chiefs based in Washington, D.C., London, or other capital cities. We are talking about some of the greatest battlefield leaders: Eisenhower, Montgomery, Patton—World War II; MacArthur—World War II, Korea; Petraeus—Afghanistan. These field generals fought enemies for territorial gain on the battlefield; FLSMs fight competitors for market share gain and customer revenues in the marketplace.

As one sales leader told us:

> **"Subordinates do what managers *tell* them to do, but people *follow* leaders."**

Perhaps we should retitle this position (and this book) as the *front-line sales leader* (FLSL) rather than front-line sales manager (FLSM).

The mark of a great leader is the ability to engender *followership*. People do what the leader requires, not because they are *told* to do so, but because the leader *asks* them. Leadership subsumes many individual characteristics we discuss later in this chapter, but here we highlight two critical leadership characteristics for FLSMs.

In recent years, the life sciences industry has seen several mergers between firms focused separately on instruments and consumables. In one such merger, a newly formed account management group was responsible for sales of instruments, consumables, and services, to existing accounts and new target accounts. Each seller now sold a much broader product line than before the merger. The sales leader reflected on the important leadership role played by FLSMs in the transition:

> **"To be successful, this salesforce transition depended on leadership and engagement from energetic FLSMs. We charged FLSMs to assess sales talent; identify cross-selling opportunities; coach sellers to reach all decision makers; deliver new, more compelling messages; leverage elements of the new sales-incentive plans to drive greater focus on instrument lead generation; coordinate opportunity pursuit. We engaged FLSMs early in the transformation to help make territory- and compensation-design decisions. They drove seller buy-in; that, in turn, accelerated the transformation process. Our FLSMs became more complete managers by leading their sales teams to succeed in a new, more complex selling environment."**

Lead from the Front

All sales leaders and FLSMs we talked to believed FLSMs should spend significant time in the field working with sellers and customers. At its essence, *lead from the front* (and not from the back) means not asking sales-team members to do anything FLSMs would not do themselves.

> *The Air Force captain addressed his men: "I want each of you to do 100 push-ups." When the men hesitated and looked apprehensive, the captain set down his cap and did 200 push-ups. The men followed suit, and did the best they could.*

Leading by example, in collaboration with rank-and-file sellers, is especially important in today's fast-changing and ever more complex market environments. Sellers must take the lead identifying opportunities and coordinating complex resource sets to craft compelling value propositions for customers. They best learn needed skills by observing and emulating their FLSMs who lead from the front. Leading from the front defines how the most successful FLSMs venture into risky territory, and transform markets by creating new ways of addressing customer needs, priorities, problems, pain points. In our interviews, both FLSMs and sales leaders embraced the *lead-from-the-front* approach.

Two FLSMs provided similar perspectives:

> "It's important to have the competencies and the drive to get the job done. But I think it's also critical to *get out in front* of your team, and not stay behind the desk. This is important for motivation, but it's also impossible to fully understand the marketplace unless you do."

> "Leading by example really helps. As long as I'm out there beating the street, up at night, and promptly returning emails, that emulates the expectations we have as an organization. That comes through, and it's easy to ask for things to get done."

Sales leaders opined similarly:

> "They [FLSMs] have their *sleeves rolled up*, go down *in the trenches*, make things happen, correct things if they slip off the course."

> "Building the sales team is critical, but each FLSM must step into their own confidence zone. They have to kind of break away from the camaraderie of the sales reps, so they can truly lead."

> "The best FLSMs don't manage from behind a laptop; they are in the trenches, which is key."

> "Leadership has certain characteristics you can spot almost immediately. When we look at promoting sellers to be FLSMs, we see who appears able to *lead from the front*."

> "Historically, there are different styles of leadership. But the one that appeals the most to me, and that I think is most applicable to our sales organization, is *not leading from behind*; it's *leading from the front*. It's getting out there with the troops and saying, 'I'm not going to ask you to do anything I'm not going to do. If you're going to do this, I'm going to do it with you.' I think that's really important."

> "There are some fundamental principles to sales excellence: The *right* products/services, the *right* sales models and strategies, the *right* talent, the *right* incentives, the *right* behavior, and the *right* culture. At the core is the *right* leadership. You can either *lead from the front* or you can lead from the back. Our people *lead from the front*."

Without question, sales leaders and FLSMs believe *leading from the front* is critical to becoming a successful FLSM.

Act Like It's *Your* Business

Leading from the front implies deep involvement in the field: spending time with sales-team members in the heart of the battle for customers. One approach to leading from the front we heard from the sales leader at a major software firm was that FLSMs should encourage their sales team to act like *this is your own business*. Relatedly, FLSMs expressed the view that they provided sellers with their own *franchises*, in the form of sales territories, and a set of products/services with which to satisfy the needs of current and potential customers in those territories.

> "The primary tool for creating compelling customer value is fostering, in the sales team, that members should act like *this is your own business*. This is a major FLSM responsibility. We use this approach to drive leadership initiatives throughout the ranks, from FLSMs to sales reps.
>
> "I can't imagine being a sales leader on any level and not having the mentality that you're the one who's judged, you're the one who's accountable, you own it. So, act like it's your own business. If you were running a small shop on the corner, what would you do to survive in tough times? If you have that mentality every day, you're going to make something happen. You almost will it to happen.... If you sit there and say: 'It's not my job'; 'it's not my responsibility'; then the organization fails, the company fails, customers fail."[3]

One FLSM in telecommunications echoed these sentiments:

> "My challenge to my team is you run your responsibilities like it is your business because, at the end of the day, it is your business."

Not only do FLSMs and sellers have this *ownership* responsibility, to push the metaphor further, all other organization members are *shareholders* (joint owners). After all, if FLSMs and sellers fail in their responsibilities, as we noted at the beginning of this book, *no one gets a paycheck*.

We address many aspects of leadership in this chapter, but above all else, those being led must know where they are supposed to be going. The desired approach: Be authentic, direct, self-aware, straightforward. One FLSM captured this perspective:

> "I am very direct; my reps always know where they stand. I always hear them out, and make sure they understand the dialogue. They have really opened up, and they trust me when I throw new ideas at them. I am also vulnerable; I let them know I don't have all the answers, but want them to come up with new approaches. Then, of course, there's accountability; at the end of the day, we are all accountable for the numbers."

Servant Leaders

Successful FLSMs know their success is directly related to their sellers' success. Hence, they do what it takes to make their sellers successful. Indeed, some firms embrace the idea of *servant leadership*. The sales leader at a global services firm captured this idea very well:

> "We work for the sales reps and the customers. Our more successful sales managers around the world have one critical ingredient other than intellect, drive, and reflection of our values. It's that when they get up in the morning, they truly believe they work for the sales reps and customers."[4]

The sales leader at a social media firm emphasized that the best FLSMs treat their teams well:

> "They are leaders through *servitude*. What I see (and try to facilitate) in the successful FLSMs—you would almost think the FLSMs report to the account executives."

We noted in Chapter 5 how the sales leader at a medical-technology firm appreciated the leadership qualities of one of his FLSMs:

> "[She] just got her 36th consecutive month of top sales performance ranking—that's pretty hard to do, right? The performance measure is not total sales, but sustainable, ongoing performance. In addition, more people in her team have been promoted than anybody else in the entire North American organization. She is not using magic to make all this happen. She's a good leader, and people like to work for her. She teaches them well."

Just in case there is any doubt, we repeat the quotation from the start of this section:

> "Sales leadership. There is no substitute."

 # Personal Drive and Hard Work

Perhaps the most striking personal acumen dimension our interviewees noted was *personal drive and hard work*. The FLSM job is not for diffident wallflowers; indeed, it is quite different from most other sales management positions. Successful FLSMs spend an enormous amount of time in the field with sellers and customers, typically involving large amounts of travel and time away from home. They also spend significant time internally with sales leaders/senior sales managers and other functional executives.

Several FLSMs were very clear about the fundamental underpinning of their success:

> "One of my things that I have always stayed true to is that I am successful because of the drive that I have."

> "I am very driven. I don't take over a customer, but I'll do what it takes. If a customer has a managerial shake-up, I'll dive right in. I'll work with my seller to figure out the new DMU [decision-making unit] and DMP [decision-making process]. But I make sure the delegation piece and the trust piece are on track."

One FLSM for a medical-diagnostics firm echoed this perspective:

> "There is no *silver bullet*, but I believe the critical element in the FLSM profile is a great work ethic—a never-give-up attitude. The perspective must be that there is always a way. A '*No!*' from the customer may not necessarily mean *no*. It may actually mean '*Not right now!*' There may be another way. The FLSM must be able to discern these distinctions. Timing is critical; the FLSM must be in the *right* place, at the *right* time, with the *right* people."

FLSMs not only have to work hard, they also have to work smart. Certainly, FLSMs in general understand the importance of time as a scarce resource, for themselves and for their sellers. The really successful FLSMs also know what things to do, and what things to let slide. One FLSM focused on his major time waster:

> "There are way too many meetings; each one is important because somebody called it. I can be double/triple booked—it's unmanageable. Some meetings are critical; they affect revenue, so you have to be on that call. But you're not always sure which ones those are."

Of course, many other activities, often initiated at senior organizational levels, can get in the way of FLSMs' direct focus on securing revenues. We address this issue in Part II of the book.

Passion and Engagement

Regarding working hard and smart, one FLSM put it this way:

> "You have to have *passion*. The FLSM must be passionate about success and passionate about your people. I have responsibilities for the company, but I am also cognizant of quality of life for my people. I do not ask them to do anything that I would not do myself. I have this really incredible relationship with my team. They will go the extra mile for me when I really need it.
>
> "Another way to put this is *engagement*. The FLSM must be *engaged* with each seller individually, and *engaged* with customers also. When things go well, the FLSM feels that viscerally. The same when things go badly, ready to jump in with sellers, as needed, to turn a situation around. That engaged FLSM is passionate about results, for sellers individually, and for the team."

One sales leader also focused on *engagement* as a substitute for *hard work* terminology:

> "From what I have seen over the years, there might be a couple of profiles of exceptional FLSMs. But to pick one core characteristic, it's *engagement*. These FLSMs are really engaged—each is a coach, and a leader, and to my way of thinking, *engagement* leads to trust."

The focus from sales leaders and FLSMs alike regarding hard work/passion/engagement was not isolated. We heard the same theme from an FLSM in telecommunications:

> "Anything you do, you need to be passionate—to be fully invested. I am going to put everything I've got into this job. My challenge is not to beat my peers, but to achieve everything I possibly can in my field of responsibility. I have set a very high standard for my performance. I try to translate my motivation, my passion, and my expectations—and paint that vision—for my team members. I try to reinforce with them: 'This is who we are; this is what we are responsible for; we have an opportunity.' And you must communicate your vision of what we can accomplish as a team."

The FLSM's job is not just Monday through Friday. Consider how one FLSM described his frequent Sunday evenings:

> "One of my best sellers ever asked me if I could spend 30 minutes to an hour with her on Sunday evenings. So, I coach her. It's a good use of my time. You have to have those types of understandings, even though it's at an unconventional time."

Furthermore, it's not just a matter of FLSMs working exceptionally hard at well-defined tasks. As we heard, there's a lot of unpredictability in the FLSM job:

> "FLSMs have to be on the ball and be ready to act when stuff comes up. They must know exactly what to do, and how to do it. They must step in and make a block, or intercept a pass, or run the correct play when called upon to do so."

We conclude with a word of caution one FLSM offered to those considering FLSM positions:

> "In this job, you have to be willing to put in a lot, a lot of hours, and sacrifice at home. The work/life balance is what it is, and it is transparent here. When I accepted the role, I knew it, and I was told it; but you do not appreciate it until you are in it. It's a great job, but you really have to put in the hours."

Keep Up-to-Date on the Business

An important part of FLSM passion/engagement is deep understanding of the ongoing progress of their districts, their sellers. In Chapter 4, we discussed *business acumen*, including such topics as pipeline management. Here we focus on the personal characteristic of keeping on top of performance measures at the district and individual-seller levels. The FLSM who acts with passion and engagement not only has a plan, but knows how current performance stacks up against planned results—both for the district overall and for individual sellers.

One sales leader told us:

> "My best FLSMs know their sellers' pipelines and opportunities cold. When they talk to/ travel with sellers, there's not a lot of time spent bringing them up to speed. They are continuously on top of all of their territories, so they can spend valuable time on more productive pursuits."

One successful high-tech FLSM reflected on the process he used to stay on top of progress in individual territories:

> "Every month, each account manager gave me an updated spreadsheet of opportunities they were working on. I transferred these data into my own spreadsheet, typically four or five pages. Typing the spreadsheet entries myself solidified the information in my memory; it was always at my fingertips. I also wanted each of my sellers *to know that I knew* the status of every potential transaction. Whenever I talked to a team member, I would always make sure we discussed what was happening on their deals, and what our next steps were."

So, personal drive and hard work are critical, but FLSMs must be totally on top of the business in their districts. One sales leader at a high-tech firm, selling to end-user customers via channel partners, was adamant:

> "A key characteristic for FLSMs is to know their business. They know their people, and they know their customers. They don't need two to three weeks to be ready for the business review. They understand their business, and the processes, and work well with the channel, understanding how much value the channel brings."

Keeping up-to-date on the business—aka monitor and control—is a critical part of the entire plan-act-review process. The FLSM spends sales resources—seller time—day in and day out calling on customers. Knowing the results of those efforts is crucial. FLSMs can then lead, direct, and manage changes in approach, as necessary. Having performance results at their fingertips is a critical part of the FLSM job.

 ## Creativity and Risk Taking

Creativity concerns the formation of something new and valuable.[5] We view creativity as related to curiosity, always asking questions to get to the root cause of an issue,[6] then seeking new and innovative solutions. Creative FLSMs are self-aware; they understand that *you never know what you don't know.* Creative FLSMs recognize that change is a given, a way of life; they have the flexibility to react to change occurring in their environments, but also to drive change through their creative actions. One sales leader reflected:

> "During the past few years, we've had a couple of major transformations in our salesforce. Our most successful FLSMs have taken these changes in their stride. They have been able to adapt to the transformations senior leadership imposed, and have responded creatively to the uncertainties those transformations generated. Our less flexible FLSMs had great difficulties with these changes, and are no longer with us."

Related to creativity and risk-taking concerns is allocating resources toward a goal, but recognizing that failure may occur. In our discussion of *strategic acumen,* we noted FLSMs must be able to take marketing-developed value propositions and find new and unusual ways to address customer needs, priorities, problems, pain points. The successful FLSM spends considerable time with sellers working on customer issues. A major value-add from FLSMs, for sellers and customers alike, is to generate new and creative ways of addressing these issues. In doing so, the FLSM delivers high value to customers, but also to the firm. Consider an example from FedEx, a global leader in package delivery.

CASE STUDY FedEx

Since its founding in the early 1970s, CEO Fred Smith has consistently stated that FedEx's (formerly Federal Express) value proposition was trust: trust in FedEx's ability to solve problems for customers with urgent shipping needs. Armed with that value proposition, a FedEx licensee's FLSM in Central Europe creatively won a significant contract. The licensee had a weak market position, but was nonetheless invited to bid on a new project—ship physically heavy, time-sensitive cargo (medical-equipment components, semifinished items, electronics) from a small Central European city for global delivery within 48 hours of pickup. The FLSM takes up the story:

> "We knew this project would be difficult for any carrier as the factory was in a small city, three-and-one-half-hour drive (90 miles), on poor roads, from the main national airport. What made the project especially difficult for us was that we had no established ground pickup operation in that area. Anyway, I went to the city to check things out, and spotted an abandoned airfield, unused since World War II. I approached city officials; they agreed to reopen the airfield on a partnership basis, and to provide maintenance and other services, so long as we made a several-year commitment. The city was interested in employment opportunities and tax revenues.
>
> "This arrangement allowed us to operate a small feeder plane for pickup from the local factory at the end of the workday. When the feeder plane reached our national hub, we put the cargo onto skids for transfer to the wide-body flight headed to FedEx's global network, within 30 minutes of the factory pickup. Later that same evening, the cargo was off around the world.
>
> "This high-value solution won us a multiyear, multimillion-dollar contract. At the time, no carrier made local pickups by plane directly. Because of the three-and-one-half-hour drive to the national airport, no other competitor could get cargo into their global system that same evening. So, we had a strong competitive edge—one day faster delivery than the best available alternative."

The FLSM's solution was truly creative. Starting from a competitive disadvantage that seemed insurmountable, the FLSM created a sustainable differential advantage. As it turned out, the solution was the starting point for a long-term customer-FedEx partnership. FedEx earned significant brand equity in the local market, and later acquired the licensee.

The key point about the FedEx case study is that the FLSM's creative insight built on the firm's corporate value proposition. FedEx operated planes from the national airport that linked into its global delivery system, offering tremendous value to customers. But that value was relevant only if cargo reached the national airport in time to catch the evening flight. That would never have happened without the FLSM's creative insight.

One FLSM reported on creative action he had taken on the spur of the moment, when a sales leader did not exhibit patience. (Later in this chapter, we identify *patience* as an important characteristic for successful FLSMs.) On that occasion, the FLSM's sales leader had insisted on being part of the customer meeting that was likely to make the final decision about a major contract. The FLSM takes up the story:

> "In previous customer meetings, I had more or less secured agreement on terms. But with my boss present [in this final meeting], the customer surprisingly got very tough, and

insisted on significant price concessions that would have cost us several million dollars in lost margin. My boss was so anxious to make this deal work and secure the revenues that he was about to agree to these new terms. I couldn't object to his decision in such a meeting, so all I could think about was ending the meeting. So, I faked a heart attack. The meeting ended abruptly. I returned alone a few weeks later and signed a deal at close to the original terms I had negotiated."

Unusual behavior? Certainly. Creative? We think so.

The digital revolution has provided many opportunities for creative ways to engage customers. As we reported in Chapter 6, one FLSM delivered customer value using his *team-building acumen* (enhancing sellers' intellectual capital), *resource acumen* (corralling customer and firm resources), and *personal acumen* (creativity)—all by simply creating a blog:

> "I populate the blog with industry information—a report here, an article there— information on what our firm is doing, and some commentary by me. I work hard on keeping it up-to-date, so scarcely a week goes by without something new. What I'm trying to do is create a sort of extended team, comprising my sales organization, the firm overall, and customers in my district. An increasing number of customers are subscribing, so I think I am getting some traction."

Not only should FLSMs exercise creativity and risk-taking behavior personally, they should encourage such behavior in their sales teams. Constant experimentation is necessary so that the firm in general, and the salesforce in particular, can continuously improve. That way, the firm keeps pace with—or better yet, anticipates—evolving customer needs, priorities, problems, pain points. One FLSM in high-tech explained how one of his sellers made a high-risk creative bet that paid big dividends:

> "An industry group organized a benefit for *Women in Technology*, in the form of an auction. The CRO [chief revenue officer] of a large company, where we had no business, donated a one-on-one lunch for the benefit. My rep bid $3,000 *from his own pocket*, and won the lunch. Eighteen months later, we closed a multimillion-dollar deal. There is no way that we would have approved such an expense, but this rep managed the entire sales cycle perfectly."

Compensation is another area where creativity and experimentation can put the FLSM ahead. In Chapter 5, we noted how one FLSM backed up his focus on teamwork with a compensation system that rewarded sellers for working together as a team—75 percent of incentive compensation was based on individual performance, but 25 percent on team performance. The FLSM explained how this innovative system came about:

> "I worked out the team-based incentive-compensation element with my boss. Of course, we have standard compensation packages, but I was able to convince him that this plan would enhance teamwork and hence overall performance."

This particular creative idea demands more attention, for compensation is a critical topic for both sellers and sales management. First, virtually all interviewees confirmed that their firms compensated sellers individually, with a significant proportion based on quota attainment. Second, all interviewees attested to the importance, for FLSMs, of building a strong sales-team culture. Since people in organizations generally do what they are paid to do, sales leaders place FLSMs in a tough position. Essentially, they say: "You go ahead and build a sales team, but we'll implement organizational arrangements (the compensation system) that make it difficult to build a team culture." Firms need more creativity in this area, both from FLSMs and sales leaders.

A corollary of creativity and risk-taking is that failure will occur. To build a culture of creativity and risk-taking among their sellers, FLSMs must confront failure. They must turn failure into an opportunity for learning, and for improving intellectual capital, throughout the sales team. One FLSM told us:

> "I encourage my guys to take sensible risks when the prize is worth it. Of course, things don't always work out. So, we talk about it: 'What went wrong?' 'What could we have done differently?' Then I make sure we share that learning with the team."

Creativity and risk-taking are key characteristics of successful FLSMs, but they also should foster that behavior in their sellers. One FLSM at a biotech firm commented on a seller who had clearly learned these lessons; he had grown revenues in his territory four times faster than his peers:

> "This seller's big message to the salesforce is, 'You shouldn't wait for your manager [FLSM] to tell you what you are doing right and not doing right. You have to become a master of your craft.' The seller also tells them: 'The process is never done. I still have to make improvements. I have to learn from you [peers], too.' And he queries them on what they do and how they are successful."[7]

 ## Managerial Courage

Courage is the choice and willingness to confront agony, pain, danger, uncertainty, or intimidation.[8] We all met courage (and lack of courage) as children, confronting (or not) the playground bully. *Managerial courage* is the exercise of courage in managerial settings.[9] Managerial courage is tactfully dispensing direct and actionable feedback to others, without being intimidating. Managerial courage deals head-on with people problems and prickly situations.

The opportunities for FLSMs to exercise managerial courage are legion. At a fundamental level, FLSMs must construct high-performing sales teams. Deciding whether to remove a seller may take considerable managerial courage—suppose the seller has performed well historically and has good connections with senior managers. Notwithstanding solid reasons for taking such a decision, it may be highly courageous. Consider also the FLSM we noted in Chapter 5 who decided not to follow the advice of her two predecessors and fire a seller who turned in below-par performance; that decision required managerial courage.

As noted in Chapter 1, the FLSM spans two boundaries: internal—between corporate management/ sales leaders, functional executives, and sellers; external—between the firm and its customers. The FLSM does not act merely as a postbox, passing information back and forth across these boundaries.

Rather, the FLSM must balance the various demands from each side of these boundaries and frequently make tough decisions. As we learned in Chapter 1, this may not be an easy task:

> "[The FLSM's problem] is that he's pulled in two directions—down to the reps and up to senior management. It's a push-and-pull job. The FLSM's challenge is to stay close to the sales team and their customers, but also have the right focus internally."

So, let us suppose the message from the field does not match the message from senior leaders. Senior leaders tell the salesforce to focus all selling efforts on product X, but one seller's customer wants product Y. What should the FLSM do? One sales leader from a global conglomerate was very clear:

> "Never let a sales budget or headquarters stand in the way of doing good business. Make the case for good business, and we'll find a way to do it. But you have to make the case. You have to put it all together. You have to show the profitability and the return. And if you show us, we'll find a way."[10]

By way of illustrating this perspective, a Chapter 2 case study described the situation when IBM top management required that selling efforts be focused on services, but an IBM FLSM and his seller (account manager) believed there was a significant opportunity at a bank customer to replace out-of-date servers with IBM mainframes. Despite the corporate edict, this FLSM and his seller pushed ahead with potential mainframe sales. Furthermore, the FLSM challenged the seller's direct-line manager, who wanted to fire the seller because of her failure to implement instructions from corporate. The FLSM escalated the decision, and prevailed in retaining the seller. IBM ultimately made large mainframe sales to the bank.

This FLSM's actions—fighting against blanket implementation of the corporate direction, challenging the seller's direct supervisor—took significant managerial courage. Because of the FLSM's boundary-role position, this sort of conflict situation is not rare. Senior managers frequently request FLSMs/sellers to act in certain ways but, typically, they are not privy to the granular customer-level data possessed by FLSMs and their sellers. Of course, in many cases, FLSMs can work out these conflicts with sales leaders—but not always. There will be situations, as in the IBM illustration, where a corporate decision may disadvantage a customer *and* the firm. In such cases, FLSMs must possess the managerial courage to challenge corporate decisions.

We also saw managerial courage in Chapter 3, when a FedEx FLSM received a telephone call from a customer seeking information on sea freight. The FLSM provided counsel and advice on sea-freight options, rather than attempting to persuade the customer to switch to FedEx's air-freight service. The senior executive with whom the FLSM was traveling was not pleased. The FLSM justified his advice on the basis that sea freight was best for the customer. He quickly received validation for his decision in the form of a large unrelated contract.

One sales leader emphasized the fast-changing, highly competitive environment his firm faced, and focused on the necessity of acting with incomplete information. Following General George S. Patton's famous dictum, "A good plan violently executed now is better than a perfect plan executed next week," this sales leader opined:

> "They [FLSMs] have to have the courage to make decisions quickly. There's not enough time in today's world to check, and recheck, and double check. You have to have instinct, and your instincts must be based on experience."

One FLSM in healthcare emphasized the importance of staying close to his sellers, and pushing back on senior management demands, when that was the right thing to do:

> "If FLSMs don't stay close to the reps, they get sucked in higher, and become less effective. Their job is to keep the team humming—right focus, right guidance—otherwise they won't produce. But you get pressure from the top to deliver the numbers; it's easy to lose focus. Leaders want a knee-jerk change of direction; but I know that's negative in the long-run—I'm much closer to the action. So, I push back—hard! I have to be true to my beliefs. After all, that's why they put me in this job."

Managerial courage is not just a competency to exercise periodically, but rather is a skill to use daily. FLSMs continually make decisions. First and foremost, they have to decide if they have the authority to make a particular decision, or whether that decision should be escalated higher in the sales organization. Some decisions must be escalated, but FLSMs typically have considerable latitude over many district-level decisions. Indeed, for all sorts of reasons, it may be difficult to get an escalated decision made that supports the FLSM's perspective. As a general rule, FLSMs should feel empowered, and develop the managerial courage to make tactical decisions themselves.

Managing Up

One specific aspect of managerial courage is *managing up*—the ability to tell the boss that something isn't working and should be changed. Many employees accept that the hierarchy makes the best decisions, so they fail to question. But not always. One sales leader reported the behavior of an FLSM in his organization:

> "An important element of our sales effort is product presentation; we have product specialists who do this job for us. That organization makes several presentations per day—week in and week out; these people are very important for us. One of our FLSMs came to me and said: 'Our presentations are terrible.' The problem: The audience was often accounting and finance types; if the numbers didn't add up perfectly, it freaked them out, even though such discrepancies had little to do with the thrust of the presentation. So, we fixed it, and our presentations are now the best in the industry. Frankly, initially, I didn't want to redo the presentations as it was a big job, but it was the right thing to do, thanks to my FLSM who successfully managed up."

As a general rule, FLSMs should follow the instructions they receive from sales leaders and corporate management. But senior executives do not always get it right. Surprise! When FLSMs have good reasons to believe they know better—based on superior data from customers and/or sellers—they should exhibit managerial courage, and not be afraid to push back.

If readers have any doubt about the wisdom of this assertion, think back to our Chapter 2 discussion of the U.S. technology firm that experienced product development issues. Despite receiving feedback from its FLSMs, product development efforts were off base. Should the FLSMs have exhibited greater managerial courage and pushed back harder? Had they done so, the firm might have avoided disaster—as one of the FLSMs put it: "[W]e don't have good products.... Essentially, we're trying to force square pegs into round holes."

Managerial Style

One of the attributes that our respondents consistently identified as the hallmark of a successful FLSM was the *right managerial style*. We heard myriad opinions regarding managerial style for successful FLSMs. The appropriate style (rather styles) comprises several attributes: *micromanagement—NOT, flexibility, empathy, unselfishness, listening and communicating, patience, humility*. Sales leaders and successful FLSMs variously focused on some attribute combinations more than others. Regardless, there was very clear agreement on what managerial style was unacceptable—*micromanagement*.

Figure 7.2 Managerial Style

Micromanagement—*NOT*

We heard much commentary from sales leaders and FLSMs about micromanagement; it was a consistent theme. Three sales leaders expressed similar views, but in somewhat different ways:

> "I want my FLSMs to strategize with their sellers, and help each of them to deal with pitfalls as they arise, using their judgment and experience. We have to get away from directive styles and trying to micromanage everything."

> "The managers [FLSMs] reporting to me need to empower their people to step up and make mistakes, and learn from them."

> "One consistent theme I see with stronger performers is they prioritize. They make that transition from individual contributor to leader. They are not in the details on every single deal or every single customer. Some FLSMs are struggling because they can't let go. Successful FLSMs know what they have to *stop doing*, and let the sellers do their thing."

Similarly, FLSMs also felt negatively about micromanagement:

> "I am not opposed to people making their own decisions. I am not a micromanager telling them what to do. I tell them where we have to go, and tell them: 'You can pick the path to go there.'"

> "The key to developing a successful sales team is to support and co-work with team members. What not to do—act bossy."

Following up on the *bossy* notion, one FLSM at a healthcare services and data provider was uncomfortable with the term *boss*:

> "Sure, I'm the boss, but that's just a title. The consulting part of the seller's job is very complex, and takes a lot of time, effort, and psychological skill to work with clients. What's important for team success is respect for the reps as friends and peers. The way to get the most and best from the team is getting them to be happy individuals, and successful executives.
>
> "An ability to be a servant leader is the most important aspect. Not following, but walking alongside team members—definitely not a micromanager who opposes people making their own decisions. I am his manager, but more I am his ally. I am his peer; there is no ego. We are equals. That is just the way it works for us. My guys hate micromanagement. By and large, they want to be trusted; they want support when they need it. But: 'When I don't need it, leave me alone.' This perspective works for me: 'As long as your numbers are there, I'm going to let you do it your way.'"

Finally, from a highly successful FLSM at a software firm selling to the banking industry:

> "I do not believe my taking over the sales cycle is in the best interest of anybody, especially not my sellers, and probably not the customer. My practice is to be in at the beginning—I want customer executives to have a name and a face—most often this is a meet-and-greet affair. Then I get involved at the end, when we're into contract negotiations—these are increasingly complicated, so I'm getting more involved. But in between, I stay out of it, though I give very solid, very active support—day and night—to my guys as they work through the process—it's typically a 9- to 18-month cycle."

We found universal agreement that the appropriate way to manage sellers was not to *tell* them what to do but, rather, to *mold* them to behave in ways the FLSM believed was appropriate. Two interrelated skills dominated the responses—*coaching* and *modeling behavior*—Chapter 5.

Flexibility

In the Prologue, we highlighted several tectonic shifts that have greatly influenced how successful sales organizations must behave. These factors are causing many firms to modify their sales strategies and transform their sales organizations. The net result is that many people in the sales organization must change their behaviors, not the least of whom are FLSMs. Sales leaders told us that these strategic and organizational evolutions frequently led to substantial turnover for both sellers and FLSMs.

Many sales leaders commented on *flexibility* as an important characteristic of successful FLSMs. When sales strategy and/or sales organizations change, many FLSMs are able to evolve their skill sets to match these evolutions; but some are not. The sales leader at a medical-technology firm explained what occurred when two salesforces merged into a single sales organization:

> "The FLSMs probably had one of the harder transitions. There were marketplace changes, changes in the product portfolio, and changes in how the new organization worked—especially support systems for sellers. If an FLSM cannot support the team, s/he loses credibility. As it turned out, we lost at least 20 to 30 percent of our FLSMs. Despite our best efforts, they just could not make the transition; they did not have the base knowledge to support their people. Those changes occurred very early, because it was apparent very quickly where people could, and could not, fit into the new organization."

As a second illustration, consider the telecommunications firm facing major customer evolution—Chapter 2. The core issue for this firm was the requirement to shift from selling *boxes* to selling *solutions*. The FLSM emphasized the importance of being *flexible* and shifting to a new selling model, but bemoaned other parts of the sales organization:

> "I adapt, and I am flexible; my team has changed quicker than others. There are still sales teams just selling boxes; that is kind of scary. As a company, everybody knows we cannot just sell boxes anymore; you have to change. Something has to be done; it must happen top-down. Some sales teams are still selling on relationships, but those are very narrow. Those sellers have just been doing the same thing for a long time."

Change is an increasingly important element in daily life—personal and professional. FLSMs face change on a daily basis, but more substantially on a periodic basis when the firm evolves its sales strategy and/or sales organization. FLSMs must have the flexibility to roll with those punches.

Empathy

The sales job is a lonely profession. Sellers are often alone for many hours per day, driving to appointments, sitting in waiting rooms, and then, frequently, facing rejection. Successful sellers must be able to deal with rejection, pick themselves up, and go to the next appointment. FLSMs must have deep understanding of this way of life and display empathy with their sellers. Frequently, of course, FLSMs understand the lonely nature of the selling job as they were previously sellers themselves.

Two FLSMs demonstrated their similar understanding of the seller's job:

> "You got to be there to pick them up, and not beat them down. You must be somewhat of a cheerleader, a positive influence."

> "You have to have the ability to put yourself in the account manager's shoes, but not practice micromanagement. Getting into those shoes does not mean prohibiting the rep from running the business, nor withholding support."

But empathy is not just a one-way street from FLSM to sellers; it's also important for FLSMs and sellers to display empathy for customers.[11] We saw customer empathy most explicitly from a medical-supply firm where the sales leader told us:

> "Sellers have significant empathy for patients through the long sales cycle. We pay special attention to empathy and patience [discussed below] in the onboarding process. We make sure all our sellers acquire and express these concepts—they aren't necessarily part of selling elsewhere."

Regarding the seller team, we heard time and again that FLSMs should treat their sellers as individuals. One FLSM remarked (using similar language to an FLSM we reported on in Chapter 5):

> "My team is still here because of the respect I give. You have to treat everybody a little differently, based on their needs. As a leader, you must recognize when to give, and when to take. You must not treat people all the same. I have a problem with a rigid process that cannot be changed to help a person be better."

And from another FLSM:

> "You have to be conscious about the types of questions you ask, and how you ask them, based on each individual and their drivers—acquiring things; material growth; money for their families; bonding and being part of a team. You have to incorporate those drivers into making that person feel supported and engaged. That made a huge difference with my team."

Revisiting our Chapter 5 discussion on personal development plans, FLSMs should also have empathy for sellers' futures. Some successful sellers, earning high compensation, are happy to devote their careers to selling. But others have different ambitions, and want to move up the managerial ladder in sales or some other function. FLSMs have a responsibility to understand their team members' ambitions and guide them in the direction they want to go. They may offer (or arrange for) additional coaching and advice on how to prepare for the future, while simultaneously performing as a seller at a high level. As one FLSM told us:

> "I make it my business to keep on top of my sellers' individual goals and ambitions— where they want to go. I have an open-door policy; it takes a lot of time, but it's the right thing to do. Then I make sure they get the right sort of visibility within the organization."

One sales leader at a global package-delivery firm focused on the changing demographics of the salesforce:

> "As millennials started to enter the workforce, the sales manager's job changed a little bit. You have to have more of an *empathy* aptitude for behaviors. Millennials want different things than our traditional Gen-X or baby-boomer salespeople. So, we are adapting our training and education curricula to build an empathic sales management cadre."

We also noted in Chapter 5, in the context of treating sellers as individuals, that *care* does not imply too-liberal softness; neither does displaying empathy. The sales leader at a banking software firm explained:

> "I create a challenging environment that hopefully reps respond to in terms of wanting to be successful, and grow their careers. But I also try to have *empathy* for the things that they're working on, or struggling with, or trying to improve on."

The best FLSMs give tough love. They set high expectations but have empathy for the challenges and problems their sellers face. They help sellers succeed by providing significant resources, including their own time.

Unselfishness

Unselfishness was most frequently mentioned in the opposite sense as a characteristic FLSMs should avoid—*selfishness*. Several respondents identified FLSMs who put their own careers ahead of supporting members of their seller teams. Said one FLSM at a high-tech firm:

> "I see this all too frequently, FLSMs who are always managing upward instead of coaching their own teams. I believe in honesty and straightforwardness; these FLSMs are overly focused on their own careers and their sellers suffer."

Another FLSM recounted the actions of his replacement as FLSM:

> "I was in the position for about eight years with great sales and profit growth. I always resisted customer pressure for price reductions, but I would drop price if customers would increase their total purchases. Although the firm measured FLSMs on both sales revenues and profits, it seemed to focus more attention on sales revenues where FLSMs were concerned.
>
> My successor knew about corporate's joint concerns, but he also knew that corporate focused mostly on sales revenue growth. He knew that if he could increase revenues quickly, he would be in line for a big promotion. So, he cut prices and increased revenues; he was out of that position in a couple of years, with a new big job. His actions served him personally very well, but not the firm. His replacement inherited what turned out to be a big mess. Even though I'm no longer involved, I'm advising the new FLSM on how to turn things around, but it's going to be a long and difficult job."

One sales leader asserted the virtue of *unselfishness* in the transition of great sellers into FLSMs:

> "All of our best managers check their egos at the door. That's one of the things that doesn't translate well from one of your best salespeople into your best sales managers. If you can't get rid of the Michael Jordan—'I've got to be the best player on the floor'—mentality, then you can't be a manager. You have to let your best sellers shine. FLSMs must display *unselfishness* to let this happen."

One FLSM described his approach to working *for* his team:

> "Everything that I do and everything that I am looking at, everything I have learned and everything that is coming my way from the company, I am always thinking how do I turn this into execution in view of my reps."

Highly unselfish!

Listening and Communicating

There was broad agreement among our interviewees that *listening and communication skills* are critical for FLSM success.

Listening. *Listening* is a key skill for both FLSMs and sellers. FLSMs should always be seeking insight, ideas, and issues from the field—both from sellers and from their customers. As one sales leader put it:

> "Both FLSMs and their sales reps have to be excellent *listeners*—it's part of the FLSM's job to coach this skill. We see our FLSMs as *dialogue facilitators*. To do this job well, the FLSM must also have judgment, patience, and presence. Customers must see them as real and authentic. Of course, FLSMs must also be excellent communicators in an unselfish way—inclined to share. But it all starts by being a great listener."

One sales leader told us:

> "We get many of our best ideas from sellers, who get them from customers. Well-coached sellers hear, see, and sense what excites the customer. The FLSM is critical in making this happen."

To reinforce the point, we note that Sony's cofounder and most famous CEO, Akio Morita, said: "Wisdom is not the sole possession of management." Pursuing this theme, sales leaders at two global technology firms told us:

> "You don't always have to please sales reps ... but you have to listen to them ... to keep a sales organization functioning at a high level."

> "A culture of listening helps positive change to occur.... [This requires] open communication, where nobody gets punished [for raising difficult issues]."[12]

Because of their greater experience, FLSMs should secure greater depth of insight when meeting with customers, especially on joint calls. We saw in Chapter 5 that one FLSM in banking software was a more effective listener than the seller. Recall what the FLSM told us:

> "One time, I made a joint sales call to a bank president. The president bragged about one area where we'd worked together, then began to complain about three or four other areas. When we got in the car to drive away, the salesperson looked at me and said: 'Well, he is really happy.' I was thinking: 'We are in trouble if we don't fix some things right away.' I heard the three or four negatives; my seller did not."

One sales leader in social media emphasized the importance of FLSMs being open to feedback and communication, then taking appropriate action:

> "Our best FLSMs come from a lot of different technical backgrounds, but what sets them apart is their flexibility and how they deal with change. Not only are they good at communicating to others, they have a desire to learn, and learn continuously. They seek feedback from their teams, not just from HR's periodic 360-process, but all the time. They ask continually: 'What can I do better? Is this a good level of support?' They want to make sure they meet their team members' needs. They use specific examples: 'When we were closing this deal, was my support adequate?' 'How could I have supported you better?' They take that feedback and incorporate it into their development plans so they continue to grow. And, they act to improve team performance. These FLSMs are good communicators, but they are also very willing to be communicated with. That feedback could come from lots of different places—customers, direct reports, bosses—but they are always open to it. All our most successful FLSMs do that regularly."

Another FLSM reported on his practice:

> "I have an open-door policy. I want my salespeople to bounce ideas off me, brainstorm potential solutions to problems. I try to manage in a way that will help them to become better, and help them become more successful. I trust my people; I think that comes across."

Listening is fundamental to being a good communicator. Many sales leaders and FLSMs highlighted the importance of communication skills. One FLSM strongly emphasized the listening dimension:

> "Only by being a good listener can I decide what action to take. Good listening helps me decide whether I should amplify an issue, or whether I should mute it down."

Communicating. Our interviewees broadly agreed that FLSMs should have great interpersonal and communication skills—and be not just good communicators but also advocates for their sales teams. Said one FLSM:

> "I have a long track record of credibility in this business. I can say: 'I've been there and done that.' I am an advocate for my guys. My long history in this position buys me a lot when my team needs something."

One telecommunications FLSM cautioned about the type of communication, noting the vast increase in electronic communication:

> "Electronic communication is now very popular, but I think the key dialogue must be more personal. What particularly challenges me is selling to a millennial. That generation may be totally comfortable doing everything by email. That represents a change in how we communicate; that's a vital issue in sales."

One sales leader used a blog to enhance both listening and communication, in particular peer-to-peer communication among sellers:

> "I established an internal blog; all senior management must log on and read it. So, [our sellers] recognize a couple of things. Number one: They can communicate in any way they want—not necessarily my preferred method. (It's not a memo from my office.) Number two: They know I read it, and management reads it. They get answers on it from management and from other sales reps. So, you don't just say you listen; you demonstrate that you listen."

It should come as no surprise to readers that our interviewees placed a high stock on great communications skills. FLSMs should take advantage of the increasing variety of communications modalities, and work hard to *up their games* in the communications arena.

Patience

Does this sound like a familiar request from corporate? "We want increased revenues, and want them right away—this quarter (or yesterday)." One FLSM paraphrased a typical request he received:

> "'The end-of-quarter performance measurement is approaching, and Wall Street is watching. Can't you shake something loose from one of your customers? What about customer Y; can't you push them to bring that big order forward by a couple of weeks?'"

To our FLSM readers: If you are an FLSM at a listed firm, you have probably received this sort of request. We do not object to such requests from corporate leaders. After all, part of their job is managing market expectations. But the potential for sellers/FLSMs to modify customer DMPs may be limited. Cutting prices for an end-of-quarter sale may do the trick in the short term, but such actions may play havoc with long-term pricing strategy.

Patience is a critical attribute for FLSMs. Of course, a core FLSM responsibility is to motivate sellers to bring in revenues, but the FLSM must also display patience—and communicate that patience upwards in the organization. Long sales cycles are a fact of life in many markets, and becoming more common as solution selling replaces product pushing. FLSMs and their sellers must coordinate their efforts with the rhythm of customer decision making. One sales leader in healthcare equipment told us:

> "When a customer considers buying a piece of our equipment, it's a long sales cycle. To make this sort of sale really requires patience. You must adjust to the pace of the customer's needs. We look for this quality when we appoint FLSMs. And we expect our FLSMs to model the appropriate behavior, and impart that behavior to their sales teams. *Patience* is needed to run long sales processes."

Another sales leader at a major manufacturing firm explained how his firm had built *patience* into its company culture, at least partially:

> "In our best FLSMs and their teams, there is an ethos of *let's take the time to do it right*. Suppose we lost a piece of business. We might not win it back tomorrow, because we

just lost; it's going to take time. But by taking the time to do it right, we believe we're going to win. There's a sense of patience. We don't want to wait forever; we're going to come back and patiently attack the situation, and win our fair share and more, but over time."

Note: This sales leader is focusing on the *use* stage of the selling process. The firm lost the sale to competition. In this case, the sales leader combines *patience* with a *never-give-up* attitude: The lost sale is just a temporary bump in the road, and will be put right, all in good time.

Humility

The job of leading and managing a team of sellers requires a very clear understanding of what each team member brings to the table. Diversity is a positive team attribute. Having the *humility* to understand (and act upon) the power of a diverse team is fundamental to FLSM success—both for the seller team, and for permanent and temporary extended teams. The sales leader at a global package-delivery firm had a very strong position on diversity:

> "Considering this whole notion of diversity, inclusion, and the humanity of leadership, I believe we are just on the fringes right now. This is one area where the sales manager's job today and tomorrow is going to be very different."

At root, FLSMs must have a visceral sense that they are not necessarily the smartest people in the room, nor should they have this expectation. Certainly, each FLSM should strive to exhibit the qualities discussed in this chapter, but they must be comfortable with and, indeed, celebrate and surround themselves with team members who possess unique expertise.

One software FLSM provided her perspective:

> "I am looking for people that have long industry tenure. These guys are *much smarter* than me. They drive new business—they are tenacious. They can do more in one week than most people do in a month."

And from another FLSM:

> "We have really quality people; I am often doing more learning than teaching. I take information from one seller who is doing something very effectively, and cross-pollinate to other sellers. I am like a bee going from flower to flower, and pollinating those folks."

We note in Chapter 5 that a major cause of failure in recruiting and selecting FLSMs is to appoint the best salespeople to those positions, without serious consideration of other factors. Rather, the sorts of people who make effective FLSMs are those who possess the required set of leading, directing, and managing skills. To these individuals, it is not important to be the smartest members in their teams. Their job is to hire and develop the smartest people. FLSMs must be comfortable with their choices, and have the humility to let them shine.

A Top Seller's Perspective

To this point we have deliberately focused on the positive elements of managerial style, but sometimes all is not sweetness and light. We believe most FLSMs do the best they can for their teams to make them successful. However, for one reason or another, that does not always happen. Here are three anecdotes we secured from a highly successful and experienced seller, at a global services firm, about what attributes the seller values in a FLSM. First, the bad news:

> *Negligent manager.* "Now, I know the email workload is a real problem for FLSMs, as is the excessive reporting, admin processes, formal online training, certifications, on top of tech changes, traveling, and environmental complexity. But one of our guys handled it *so poorly*. We had a large holiday party with families. After showing up for just 20 minutes, he disappeared to do his email. It was so-so-so embarrassing—poor managerial and people skills. And the firm created that behavior; it's probably the same in all large companies!" [We discuss this topic in "Remove the *Crap*" in Chapter 8.]

> *Bottleneck manager.* "This is the most toxic of all managerial styles I've come across in my career, especially in large companies. *Bottleneck managers* keep work, relevant updates, and/ or opportunities from their teams. Then, they use these instances to hammer their own people. Oftentimes, this behavior is driven by personal insecurities, or political playing around to serve hidden agendas. I had an FLSM who would send me invitations to quarterly reviews with top global prospects two weeks after the meetings. Or, I wouldn't be told about a new product roll-out, then be kicked for not submitting correct reports."

On the other hand, comments in a more positive light:

> *Umbrella manager.* "These guys really work for the team. The FLSM acts as a *buffer*, keeping team members safe from admin, from silly HR formal processes, and from being kicked by senior management when it's not warranted, and maybe taking the bullet when it is.
>
> "My ex-boss literally said to me: 'Keep your focus on real stuff—customers and real problems. Be great at what you do (sales more than double quota while the industry was really suffering), and I will keep an umbrella above you—for any admin, miscellaneous, ridiculous HR stuff, or crappy trainings, and superior management stuff.' I got out of a whole lot of stuff because my performance was superior—it was making results for the entire European region look astonishingly good. But I was lucky; he was an exceptional boss, smart, savvy, bold, and none of the more senior managers messed with him. He was a long-time employee and had an impeccable reputation."

Summary

Chapter 7 focuses on the last of six acumen dimensions effective FLSMs must possess—*personal acumen*. Personal acumen comprises several types of behavior superior FLSMs possess: *leadership, personal drive and hard work, creativity and risk taking, managerial courage, managerial style.*

Clearly, there are many ways to exhibit leadership—leading from the front, and acting like it's your own business are two important ways. Passion and engagement, and keeping up-to-date on the business are critical elements of personal drive and hard work. Opportunities for creativity and risk taking are abundant; and FLSMs have many ways to demonstrate managerial courage.

Finally, FLSMs must develop their own managerial styles. We found strong objection to micro-management, but wide agreement that certain types of behavior are highly beneficial for successful

FLSM performance—flexibility, empathy, unselfishness, listening and communicating, patience, and humility.

Strategic acumen, organizational acumen, business acumen, team-building acumen, resource acumen are all important for FLSM success. But FLSMs can only realize the true potential of these acumen dimensions if they also possess high levels of *personal acumen.*

Endnotes

1. These *personal acumen* dimensions focus on FLSM *behavior.* Hence, they are quite different from other approaches to describing individuals, like the *Big Five* personality dimensions—*extraversion, agreeableness, conscientiousness, neuroticism, openness.* R.R. McCrae and P.T. Costa, "Validation of the Five-Factor Model of Personality across Instruments and Observers," *Journal of Personality and Social Psychology,* 52 (1987), pp. 81–90. However, readers will observe some overlap between the *Big Five* and the FLSM dimensions we discuss.

   For interested readers, *Big Five* definitions and discussion: K. Cherry, *The Big Five Personality Traits,* April 11, 2018, *https://www.verywellmind.com/the-big-five-personality-dimensions-2795422*; Big Five Personality Traits, Wikipedia, retrieved July 29, 2018, from *https://en.wikipedia.org/wiki/Big_Five_personality_traits.*

2. From N. Capon and G. Tubridy, *Sales Eats First,* Bronxville, NY, Wessex: 2011, Chapter 1. Adapted from a line spoken by the Tom Cruise character in the movie *Risky Business*: "Porsche. There is no substitute."

3. Capon and Tubridy, *op. cit.*, pp. 10–11.

4. Capon and Tubridy, *op. cit.*, p. 16

5. Creativity, Wikipedia, retrieved July 25, 2018, from *https://en.wikipedia.org/wiki/Creativity.*

6. Total quality management (TQM) methodology asks five *Whys* as it seeks the root cause of an issue.

7. Capon and Tubridy, *op. cit.*, p. 11.

8. Courage, Wikipedia, retrieved July 25, 2018, from *https://en.wikipedia.org/wiki/Courage.*

9. H.A. Hornstein, *Managerial Courage: Revitalizing Your Company without Sacrificing Your Job,* New York: Wiley, 1986.

10. Capon and Tubridy, *op. cit.*, pp. 11–12.

11. *Empathy* has long been suggested as a positive characteristic for sellers to display for customers: D. Mayer and H.M. Greenberg, "What Makes a Good Salesman," *Harvard Business Review,* 42 (July–August 1964), pp. 119–124; L.E. Dawson, Jr. and C.E. Pettijohn, "The Effects of Empathy on Salesperson Effectiveness," *Psychology & Marketing,* 9 (July 1992), pp. 297–310; D.A. McBane, "Empathy and the Salesperson: A Multidimensional Perspective," *Psychology & Marketing,* 12 (July 1995), pp. 349–370.

12. Capon and Tubridy, *op. cit.*, p. 23.

Part II

Top Management and Sales Leadership Responsibilities

In Part I of *The Front-Line Sales Manager – Field General*, we presented a sixfold acumen model—*strategic, organizational, business, team building, resource, personal*—for identifying the requirements for high-performing FLSMs. That's all well and good, but FLSMs operate in an internal environment created by a management cadre comprising top management, sales leaders, and senior sales managers.

Given the critical importance of earning sales revenues, the senior management cadre only has one job—set FLSMs up for success. To achieve this end, senior management must make decisions and allocate sufficient resources in several areas.

Diagnosing the Salesforce Problem

The high-level corporate executive met with the national sales vice president (NSVP) at the firm's most seriously underperforming business. The following conversation ensued:

Senior corporate executive: "Please explain to me the core essence of your job."

National sales vice president: "I direct and manage four regional sales managers. In turn, they each direct and manage four to six district sales managers/front-line sales managers [DSMs/FLSMs]. Each DSM/FLSM has six to ten sellers directly reporting to them. So, I'm in charge of the entire salesforce—22 sales managers and 160 sellers."

Senior corporate executive: "I understand that, but what is the core essence of your job?"

National sales vice president: "In a nutshell, it's to make sure my salesforce, including all the people I just mentioned, runs smoothly."

Senior corporate executive: "You're fired!"

National sales vice president: "What? ..."

Senior corporate executive: "What you just told me describes part of the NSVP job. But you did not address the core essence of leading, directing, and managing the salesforce hierarchy. The central task for sales leaders is to make your DSMs/FLSMs and their sellers successful. You scarcely mentioned them.

"I've talked to several functional heads within this business. I believe the core reason for poor performance results from lack of understanding about what really drives sales revenues. Highly competent and highly motivated FLSMs are the key. After all, sales revenues are earned by FLSMs and their direct reports—sellers. I have to find someone to be NSVP who really believes this fundamental truth at a visceral level, and can act accordingly. Believe me, you're not the only sales leader in this industry who misunderstands how salesforces are supposed to operate. When I get the right person, it will give this business huge competitive advantage."

After reading this vignette, you may wonder: How many sales leaders really understand the critical relationship between FLSM performance and firm success? Sales leaders should also know it's a tough job, primarily because of the double boundary-role positions the FLSM occupies: between the firm and its customers; and between individual sellers and sales leaders/senior sales managers and other firm functions. FLSMs are pulled in many different directions. FLSMs told us:

> "The FLSM role is by far the most challenging and difficult position I have seen in my 15 years of field sales. The FLSM role requires a great deal of flexibility and psychological skills and approaches. You must be able to have those candid heart-to-heart conversations with individual team members, and to wear a lot of different hats. You must develop the right mix of friend and inspector with each of them. A chameleon can do the job well!"

> "Our firm's performance rests on the backs of what my fellow FLSMs and I do. We have to meet our numbers, but that's not easy. Competitors are good and getting tougher. We get support from sales leadership, but negotiating between their demands and what my guys are picking up from customers can be pretty stressful."

Throughout this book, we assert that the FLSM role is not only critically important, but also very challenging. Notwithstanding those challenges and difficulties they face, for the firm to be successful, FLSMs must perform at a high level. Superior sales revenue performance is a FLSM responsibility, but not a responsibility of FLSMs alone. Sales leaders, senior sales managers, corporate executives, and functional heads—customer service, logistics, marketing, technical service—also have major responsibilities. They must play their parts to create the conditions that enable FLSMs to secure superior performance. Indeed, we believe the core job of these senior executives is to set FLSMs up for success.

Since corporations are only successful to the extent they attract, retain, and grow customers, a heavy weight of setting FLSMs up for success rests with sales leaders/senior sales managers. They are most responsible for creating the conditions for FLSM success, and securing support from top management and functional heads.

We have argued, we hope persuasively, that FLSMs and their sellers are responsible for earning sales revenues for the firm. It follows, therefore, that more senior sales managers and sales leaders are *non-revenue-generating overhead*. That's right, you heard correctly. For the most part, sales leaders/senior sales managers are *non-revenue-generating overhead*. That doesn't mean they don't add value; of course they do. But it's important to understand what value they *must add* to set FLSMs up for success.

Perhaps the overarching challenge for sales leaders is to secure and allocate resources. Corporate management has the job of allocating corporate resources throughout the firm. Corporate leaders face many demands on resources—from different businesses, different functions, different geographies. Sales leaders, wherever they sit within the firm's organization structure, must make compelling arguments to corporate so they receive the appropriate resources to execute the sales job and secure high levels of sales performance.

Regardless of how successful they are in securing resources, sales leaders must allocate the resources they secure to areas within the sales organization they believe will secure the best short-, medium-, and long-term performance. Of course, a core argument of this book is that one area for serious investment is in FLSMs. But it's not simply a question of where to allocate resources; sales leaders must carefully examine where resources are being spent today, and decide not only where resources should be maintained and increased, but also where they should be reduced or eliminated.

In order to make these decisions well, sales leaders should ensure they possess great data and insight into their sales organizations. Most sales leaders have systems and processes to provide disaggregated performance data; they should be sure to collect and analyze these granular data from throughout their sales organizations. One sales leader reported on his firm's process:

> "We do an annual anatomy assessment. We get measures from the sales reps on about 20 different components—from the way our executives interact in a sales situation (could include our president and our CEO), and how our presentations go. It's like going in for your annual physical. That's very, very important. How do you know to improve if you really aren't measuring it? So, we want our direct sales team to let us know as a leadership team how we're doing to support their needs. Some sales leaders have a hard time hearing bad news; I don't. I want to know if there's something our folks are not getting. I don't want to have them say, 'I would have gotten my number if I'd had this.'"

Using data systems like this and other analytic approaches, sales leaders should act boldly. *Wait and see* is not a good recipe for success in today's complex and fast-changing business environment. Bold experimentation is probably a better approach: Find out what works and *scale* it; find out what doesn't work and scrap it.

In Part II of *The Front-Line Sales Manager – Field General*, we identify several specific areas where top management/sales leaders should allocate resources, and where they must excel, to optimize FLSM performance.

- ▪ *Chapter 8* focuses directly on the FLSM, particularly on four areas directly related to securing a group of high-performing FLSMs.

- ▪ **Chapter 9** addresses two fundamental management areas—sales strategy and sales organization structure.

- ▪ *Chapter 10* is concerned with three broad sets of decision areas where the *right* actions by top management/sales leaders can have a major impact on FLSM performance.

Focus on FLSMs

Chapter 8 comprises discussion of the four elements concerned with developing and maintaining a group of high-performing front-line sales managers (FLSMs)—*appoint the* right *FLSMs; mold superior FLSMs; improve FLSM performance; remove the* crap—Figure 8.1.

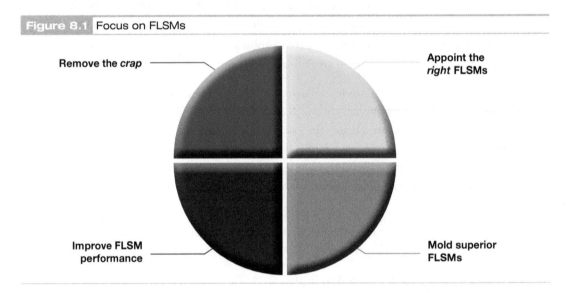

Figure 8.1 | Focus on FLSMs

Appoint the *Right* FLSMs

The starting point for setting FLSMs up for success is making sure the *right* people occupy these positions. Given the performance challenges and boundary-role difficulties we have noted throughout the book, high-potential FLSM candidates are not easy to find. Sales leaders have the difficult task of identifying candidates who either possess, or can reasonably be expected to acquire (in a relatively short time), the six types of acumen required for success—*strategic, organizational, business, team building, resource, personal.*

Arguably, the medical industry is undergoing as much change as any industry, but the challenges faced by these sales leaders are cautionary for all sales leaders. One sales leader in the medical-technology field gave us his views:

"FLSMs and front-line service managers are the two toughest jobs in the firm—tougher today than a few years ago—and the toughest to fill with the *right* people. These people are charged with developing, training, maintaining, and strategizing for three times more products than they had before. The impact of making a bad call on hiring AEs [account executives] is pretty scary; FLSMs are shooting in the dark on some elements of their jobs. They feel uncomfortable with fast-changing regulations, and the many things they have to do today. The risks they take are much higher than they've ever been."

Questions for sales leaders: Are you *in the same boat* in appointing FLSMs? Does this sales leader capture how you view the recruitment and selection process for FLSMs? Are you challenged to find these *supermen* and *superwomen* to appoint? Does the *attrition problem*, discussed next, make the challenge even more difficult?

The Attrition Problem

The task of recruitment and selection is typically not simple, especially if the firm does not have a succession plan for new appointments when current FLSMs leave. Sometimes the firm has plenty of notice regarding FLSM vacancies—planned promotions, job changes, retirements. But less well-planned internal movement or FLSM resignations can leave sales leaders scrambling.

Indeed, in recent years, the world has changed in many ways, particularly in the nature of relationships between firm and employees. Long gone are the days when individuals would expect to spend their entire working lives with a single employer and, correspondingly, the firm could expect long-term employee loyalty. The labor market has become much more efficient, as firms like CareerBuilder, Glassdoor, and LinkedIn reduce the friction for both recruiters and those being recruited—filling positions and changing jobs, respectively.

Of course, if sales leaders can make the market less efficient by doing a better job of FLSM retention, so much the better. As one sales leader told us:

> "We work on creating FLSM *stickiness* to the organization. Our approach is more appreciation, and providing more tools to get the job done. We put a lot of effort into training for FLSMs and their teams. We pay them pretty well. But we should really do things like stock options, so they have *skin in the game*."

If you are a sales leader reading this chapter, there is a high likelihood that one of your successful FLSMs is being recruited by a competitor and will quit within the next 12 months; far higher than it was five years ago. Certainly, you can work on incentive structures and managerial development programs to reduce FLSM attrition. But those actions will not completely stop the drain. As a sales leader, *you must expect FLSM attrition*, and plan accordingly.

Just as FLSMs should place potential sellers on *the bench*—put them in *inventory* ready for appointment when a vacancy occurs—so should sales leaders *inventory* potential FLSMs. The most obvious pool of potential FLSMs is current firm sellers. Sales leaders should periodically review all sellers to identify those with FLSM potential. For these sellers, sales leaders and/or senior sales managers should design work assignments and training programs to prepare them for FLSM positions when they open up. Of course, the salesforce is not the only source of internal candidates—customer service and marketing organizations may also contain potential FLSM talent.

Sales leaders may decide to search for/appoint FLSMs from outside the firm. Sales leaders should engineer opportunities to meet potential candidates. They should always be looking for attractive FLSM candidates, and develop a list of potential appointees, ready to call when a vacancy occurs.

In some firms, identifying candidates for potential FLSM vacancies is part of a broader corporate succession-planning initiative. One sales leader explained:

> "Every director has a succession plan; every manager has a succession plan. They must say who could replace you tomorrow. I want two candidates. I want to know why they can replace you. This is a very formal process; HR [human resources] helps us. Candidates can come from inside or outside the firm. We do a lot of mixing and matching; we just want the best managers in those positions."

The major message from the foregoing is very clear: Sales leaders fail when they do not plan for FLSM attrition. Hence, when vacancies occur, they may scramble and take the path of least resistance—appointing the most successful seller.

Appoint the Best Sellers?

The harsh reality is quite simple: The seller job is quite different from the job of *directing, leading,* and *managing* sellers. Sellers must have a laser focus on their customers. By contrast, FLSMs must be concerned about all their direct-reporting sellers. FLSMs must also forgo the emotional highs of making sales; those experiences belong to sellers. This is not to say that the best sellers may not become great FLSMs; certainly, many do. Yet to promote solely based on great sales performance ignores a host of other factors—the six acumen dimensions at the heart of successful FLSM performance.

The sales leader at a medical-device firm reported her experience, and her dilemma:

> "A couple of years ago, we created 12 district manager positions [FLSMs]; they didn't previously exist. We appointed our top salespeople. Today, only two are still with the company. And we ask ourselves: Were they really district managers? Were they truly *people leaders*? Or, were they just super territory managers [sellers] who stepped in to do the selling job for their people, rather than really lead? To grow, we need some strong leadership, and I don't know if *super sellers* can get there."

Two other sales leaders essentially agreed with the problem of promoting the best salespeople:

> "Most of our best salespeople never make it into management roles because they do not have the skill sets to be a good leader."

> "Our FLSMs are internal people. Most of them were good salespeople. They may not have been the very best we had, but they were all good salespeople, and they were all good leaders."

But you say, surely sales leaders know about the potential problem of appointing the best sellers to FLSM positions. Maybe they do but, unfortunately, day-to-day pressures can get in the way of optimal decision making. The harsh truth is that many sales leaders do not plan as they should. One sales leader admitted:

> "The best FLSMs are focused on their teams and team success, not on themselves. Those managers that focused on themselves are gone. That's because most of them were great salespeople. But, generally, great salespeople do not make good sales managers."

The authors have seen many examples of the destructive effect such appointments can have: The firm loses a successful seller and gains a poor FLSM. District performance plummets, and sellers resign. Out of frustration, the new FLSM (the former high-performing seller) also quits, and the FLSM vacancy remains unfilled in the now poorly performing district.

Who was at fault? Who is to blame? The locus of responsibility is very clear—sales leadership. The core message: Plan carefully for new FLSM appointments. Select the *right candidates who possess, or can reasonably be expected to acquire, the six acumen dimensions* to become high-performing FLSMs.

One FLSM had an interesting perspective on salesforce composition and how he became an FLSM. Referring to his career as a seller, this FLSM told us:

> "I did it, and I knew I was good at it, but I wanted to share it. That would bring more people like me into the organization, and make the company better.
>
> "Some people just like selling; they like that jazz of going out and being with customers. They do not want to manage people, and would probably not be good at it. Then there are people who are great at selling, and love to teach selling, and love to share how they sell. They become the good managers. That's my story. I really liked what I did, but I wanted to share with others."

Sales-Leader Approaches

Notwithstanding the focus of this book—*six acumen dimensions* for high-performing FLSMs—the approaches actually used for selecting FLSMs varied markedly across our interviewees. Among those approaches expressed by sales leaders (some noted previously) were the following.

Leadership.

> "Essentially we look for leadership—you can spot it almost immediately. Most of our salespeople never make it into sales management roles. They do not have the skill sets to make good leaders. We have a pretty rigorous process: All FLSMs have to identify two candidates to replace them, and why. (We do this right up the line to vice presidents.) The replacements can come from anywhere in the organization, or outside. We do a lot of mixing and matching."

Track Record.

> "What's most important to me when I'm appointing a FLSM is their prior performance, wherever they have been. Perhaps in sales, but it could also have been in operations."

This sales leader added:

> "They also must have the financial and technological savvy to *talk turkey* in deal negotiations, and be highly motivated."

Industry Background.

> "In this industry, experience is key for FLSM appointments. That person can share what is or isn't working for sellers in the industry—sharing best practices and not-so-best practices. And making sure we're doing everything within guidance and compliance. That would be very tough for someone coming in from the outside."

And from two other FLSMs:

> "I have been in this industry for 15 years. I know how it works. I know people at our customers. I know people in our customers' customers. I even know people at our competitors. When there are problems, I know what to do, who to call. I can't imagine anyone being a successful FLSM without deep industry experience."

> "I think that one of my strengths is that I came from the banking industry. I started as a teller after college, and worked my way through the organization for 15 years, before I switched careers to become a vendor. So, I have deep knowledge of the industry—how people think, how people act. I think that gives me a real advantage."

Referrals.

> "The FLSM job is so important; I am extremely careful in putting people in that position. My best appointments have come from referrals. When a person I respect suggests someone—a hands-on manager with field experience—and when they have seen firsthand the leadership qualities I require, those candidates are always well worth looking at."

Replace the *Wrong* FLSMs

Just as important as selecting the *right* FLSMs is deselecting the *wrong* ones. Certainly, monitoring FLSM performance is an ongoing responsibility for sales leaders and senior sales managers, notably the FLSM's boss. If the appropriate senior sales manager is convinced the firm has made an appointment error, or if FLSM performance has atrophied, the firm should replace the offending FLSM as soon as possible.

Replacement possibilities spike when the firm makes serious changes in sales strategy. Such changes may require new organizational arrangements—Chapter 9. These *transformations* may also require different behaviors from many individuals, including FLSMs. Some FLSMs are able to make these transitions; other FLSMs may be unable to do so.

The consultant to one firm making a strategic change recounted his experience:

> "The client was a leading supplier of building materials for the residential market. Faced with declining demand, the chief revenue officer [CRO] formulated a new strategy,

focused on architects. This approach would disrupt the traditional distribution system. Though confident in the new strategy, executive leadership realized many FLSMs were resistant to change, even vocal opponents. These FLSMs did not care to disrupt the status quo relationships with traditional channel partners. Accordingly, the CRO took time to rewrite the FLSM job description, then personally assessed each individual FLSM; one-third did not make the cut. Together with newly appointed FLSMs, the entire set of FLSMs was now enthusiastic supporters of the new strategy. Although delayed, implementation was highly successful. As the housing market recovered, the firm enjoyed several quarters of above-market growth."

In an illustration we presented in Chapter 7, one medical-technology sales leader explained his experience when his firm merged two somewhat specialized salesforces into a single generalized salesforce:

"The FLSMs probably had one of the harder transitions. There were marketplace changes, changes in the product portfolio, and changes in how the new organization worked—especially support systems for sellers. If an FLSM cannot support the team, s/he loses credibility. As it turned out, we lost at least 20 to 30 percent of our FLSMs. Despite our best efforts, they just could not make the transition; they did not have the base knowledge to support their people. Those changes occurred very early, because it was apparent very quickly where people could, and could not, fit into the new organization."

The core message for sales leaders: Plan for FLSM vacancies—expected and unexpected. Make FLSM appointments *very* carefully. Search for early warnings of FLSM failure, and replace sooner rather than later when performance problems arise.

 ## Mold Superior FLSMs

So, we seem to have pretty good agreement among the sales leaders we interviewed. Not only is the FLSM job one of the most important in the salesforce (maybe even in the firm), it's also one of the most challenging, and difficult to do well. Indeed, as we showed in previous chapters, to perform the FLSM job at a high level requires significant *strategic, organizational, business, team building, resource, personal acumen.*

But simply appointing *the best* people is insufficient. To be an effective FLSM is a tough and ever-changing job. As change occurs on multiple competitive, environmental, and firm strategic and organizational dimensions, FLSMs must operate in a continuous learning mode. As one sales leader put it:

"One of the most important things we have seen about what makes a successful FLSM is not what they come into the job with, but what they learn while they are in the job—how they grow and develop from the feedback they receive."

Sales leaders have a serious responsibility to *take the raw material of current and potentially exceptional FLSMs*, and make sure they continue to grow in the job.

Perspectives on Training FLSMs

We commence this section with some differing perspectives we identified on training FLSMs.

The Importance/Investment Disconnect. Sales leaders know that poorly prepared FLSMs cause serious problems in their districts. Hence, well-run firms go to considerable lengths to prepare newly appointed FLSMs for their positions. Then, these firms continue to allocate significant training resources to enhance the intellectual capital of their FLSMs. Right? Wrong!

At least in the firms we talked to, there seemed to be a significant disconnect between FLSM job importance and investment in skills development. Whereas sales leaders agreed that the FLSM job is both critically important and difficult to do well, our research revealed little overall organizational commitment to FLSM growth and development. The following is typical of what we heard from several sales leaders:

> "Our training is not where it needs to be—not near enough. We have some basic product training, but it's essentially the same for FLSMs and sellers. We send out product bulletins when we have product or capability or rack-rate pricing changes, but as regards to FLSM training, we really have to do more."

From sales leaders and FLSMs alike, we did not find the level of investment corresponding to the centrality of the FLSM role. Perhaps the situation is not as bad as the report one of us received several years ago from a newly appointed FLSM in the insurance industry:

> "I was a successful salesperson when the firm promoted me to FLSM. Our salespeople are on 100 percent commission, so they are very self-motivated. In my new job, I was responsible for a couple of hundred individual producers. That's quite a span of control, so it's not an easy job. You'd think that I would get some level of management training. Right? Think again! Management brought several new FLSMs to the New York head office. They gave us a two-day dog-and-pony show. That was it; nothing else. Then I was on my own."

But we heard the following from sales leaders at a global package-delivery firm and a medical-technology firm, respectively:

> "The FLSM is the highest leveraged position we have in the organization—and the one we give the *least attention* to—it's an oxymoron. The FLSM has the highest leverage of any job."

> "[Our] problem is a *lack of training*. FLSMs have to make difficult decisions without having been in the business for a long time. A great challenge for any company with a wide, diverse product line is high risk. Because there are no training budgets any longer, this places great pressure on FLSMs. We have to act quickly and make decisions in a very tough environment, where we don't have oodles of experience."

It's not that senior leaders do not recognize the problem. In many firms, FLSM development just doesn't rise to the level of importance required for serious action. From two sales leaders:

> "The FLSM position is one of the most difficult jobs in high-tech, because quite often they are learning on the job. And I think companies struggle with putting the right leadership development programs in place, and in thinking about how you enable excellence in those roles. All those things are really, really, really challenging, because those FLSMs bear a huge weight on their shoulders."

> "[FLSM training] is an unattended area. I don't know if that's by intention, but the sales community has kind of skipped this managerial category."

FLSM Training Successes. Designing and executing development programs for FLSMs may be very challenging, but firms that put in the effort and allocate resources are pleased with the results. The sales leader at a software firm told us:

> "Companies forget to develop the FLSM as much as they do sales reps. Scale comes from the first line. If salespeople aren't managed well, it's a mess. We have improved attrition and increased retention because we make our FLSMs more aware. We give them better tools to manage their teams, and better conversations to coach. Our field leadership is incredibly important. We're going to continue to develop them at an equal rate as we develop anybody else in the organization."

Two other sales leaders offered similar perspectives:

> "We are putting our FLSMs though training on the most common and effective solutions across the enterprise, across the world. Along with that, we are pushing pricing decisions down to FLSMs, and providing them with necessary training and with learning and development tools for their sellers. Of course, we also hold them accountable for pricing-file yields, in addition to revenue growth."

> "As the firm has grown over the years, our products, services, and customer solutions have grown dramatically, and continue to increase. So, we put our FLSMs through educational and development training on the most common and effective solutions that work across the enterprise. Then we give them an easy spot to find them."

And two FLSMs expressed positive sentiments about the training their firms provide to enhance their intellectual capital:

> "We get considerable training—some internal, some external. In the past couple of years, I did an internal in-house course on developing reps, and a second on managing remote reps. Then I did an external course on sales leadership."

The Bottom Line. Sales leaders agree on the critical importance of the FLSM job. They believe FLSMs drive sales revenue performance. They also agree it's difficult to be a highly successful FLSM. But, in many firms, there seems to be a large gap between sales-leader comprehension of this reality, and firm willingness to invest in their FLSMs. Yet, perhaps we should not be too quick to blame corporate management for this lack of attention in FLSM training. It's difficult to believe senior executives would decline to invest in FLSMs, if sales leaders made a strong-enough case for its importance.

Notwithstanding the serious importance-investment disconnect we observed in many firms is that some firms both recognize the importance of the FLSM position *and* invest in training resources to improve FLSM intellectual capital. Both sales leaders and FLSMs report positively on the results from these investments.

Train FLSMs

Here we usefully revisit the two types of training we discussed for sellers in Chapter 5, suitably modified for FLSMs—intellectual capital *stocks* and *flows*:

Stock Training. Stock training is geared toward improving FLSMs' ability to better perform the FLSM job, regardless of firm or industry. Many firms provide stock training for sellers, focused largely on selling skills. Many fewer firms provide stock training for FLSMs. Stock training programs for FLSMs have very different focuses and content than comparable training programs for sellers.

What is the focus of stock training for FLSMs? The answer is straightforward: Concentrate on the six acumen dimensions of the FLSM job—*strategic, organizational, business, team building, resource, personal.* Of course, these dimensions are not independent. Neither should be the training. Not only must FLSMs develop strategic, organizational, and business acumen, they must also possess sufficient coaching skills—team-building acumen—to ensure their sellers also develop these skills.

Flow Training. Flow training focuses on the job at hand for both FLSMs and sellers. The goal: Keep FLSMs and sellers up-to-date with important business issues—external and internal:

- ***External:*** environmental change (PESTLE forces), competitive threats, industry trends, and implications for the firm, customers, and customers' customers

- ***Internal:*** sales strategy evolution, customer solutions, new product introductions, pricing algorithms

The goal of flow training is to enhance FLSM and seller abilities to have intelligent conversations with customers about issues of joint concern. As a result, *ideation* and *design* selling processes improve, and the firm secures deeper relationships with customers. Whereas stock training occurs periodically, flow training is regular and ongoing, often delivered internally by sales leaders and subject-matter experts.

For some FLSM positions, knowledge, skills, and abilities (KSAs) attained in a totally different industry are sufficient, along with moderate flow training, for an incoming FLSM to *hit the ground running.* In other industries, product and/or customer complexity is so great that significant flow training is a serious requirement. Regardless, formal training is a critically important element in molding FLSMs to secure superior performance.

Coach FLSMs

So far in *The Front-Line Sales Manager – Field General*, we have said little about the FLSM's boss, a more senior sales manager—possibly regional sales manager (RSM), national sales vice president (NSVP), or sales vice president (SVP). One key responsibility of this individual is to improve the competence of directly reporting FLSMs. Typically, an FLSM's boss has more extensive managerial experience than the FLSM; the more-senior person should be in a good position to provide counsel, feedback, guidance, modeling, and general coaching for improved FLSM performance.

We should not underestimate the amount or type of coaching FLSMs may require. One sales leader made the interesting link between a particular FLSM coaching requirement and time spent in the office doing administrative tasks:

> "At the FLSM level, we focus and emphasize more time in the field, and less admin time. I think some of our FLSMs may not feel confident in their own skills, so they spend time on admin stuff or in meetings, rather than with their reps. It's not because they don't genuinely want to be in the field; I just think they are not incredibly confident about their coaching skills. But we are going to do something about this."

Questions for sales leaders: How much time do your FLSMs spend in the office? Should they be spending more time in the field coaching their sellers? Does their coaching competence need enhancing? What are you going to do about it?

In Chapter 5, we discussed seller coaching by FLSMs, but seller coaching and FLSM coaching start from very different places.

How to Coach FLSMs. FLSMs have significant information on what they need to coach so seller performance improves. Generally, FLSMs spend, on average, three days per week in the field with sellers visiting customers. They are also frequently in contact by email, telephone, Skype, and other means. FLSMs possess significant information on their sellers; they have many opportunities to coach as part of the normal workday.

By contrast, FLSMs see their bosses infrequently. Rarely do bosses observe FLSMs interacting directly with sellers. Hence, the FLSM's boss must use more traditional managerial processes— management by objectives (MBOs)—to identify FLSM performance, and coach for improvement. We address performance measures—*intermediate* and *output*—in the next section. Typically, FLSM bosses have access to *output* measures—sales revenues/quota attainment—and, increasingly, to *intermediate* measures within pipeline systems. Performance versus objectives/targets forms the basis for coaching about identifying opportunities.

The key piece that's missing is *input* performance—what FLSMs do on a day-to-day basis; how they spend their time; and how they interface with sellers. FLSM bosses can secure these sorts of data by 360 feedback, then coach based on results. Several sales leaders reported on their experiences:

> "I can see there are gaps about how often our FLSMs are truly doing their one-on-one coaching with their reps. Some are more prepared than others. And some did not know their numbers in certain areas. That is a big piece that I am going to be working on."

"From our studies, we identified several coaching needs for FLSMs: coaching sellers, conducting effective one-on-one meetings, conducting effective team meetings, forecasting, time management. There were also basic things like: 'Who do I go to if I have this problem?' We wrapped this into onboarding [discussed below]."

"On an annual basis, we have an outside provider survey our sellers; they provide data on their FLSMs. We aggregate these data, then provide feedback to our FLSMs. The raw data are highly confidential as to source—I don't know, and I don't want to know. We take the confidentiality and the entire process very seriously. It's very valuable.

"As an example, a couple of years ago, one of our best FLSMs received some feedback on his coaching that really surprised him. So, his manager started coaching him on his coaching via a series of one-on-one sessions. The FLSM was determined to improve and now, a couple of years later, his coaching is top notch."

"So, there are some expectations around enablement and then there are expectations around what we would call performance management, the coaching element of the front-line manager's role. Everybody has a development plan in place, right? Are we doing quarterly discussions? What is that coaching framework? So, we are actually reintroducing something that we had done away with. We call it leading sales excellence.

"How to have the right conversations; how to do your business reviews; what are the kind of questions you should be asking your team? We call it *inspect what you expect*. It is not micromanaging; it is around the coaching conversations, when you should have those conversations."

"We recognize that we need to do a better job teaching our front line. We have set the expectations, but now it is showing them how to do what we expect if they do not have the skills right now. So, there is an enablement component for our front-line leaders that we are actually rolling out this quarter and next, because we recognize that we have not done a good job of helping our managers be the best they could be."

"Of course, FLSMs have to do managerial stuff—running reports, submitting forecasts. But they must drive leadership qualities through coaching. Team members must understand their team's value to the firm; their organizational role, and how they relate to the strategy. Each seller on the front line must feel connected to the organization, so they can say, 'I make a difference.'"

"As the sales leader, if I want to coach my FLSMs on how they coach, I need to see them in action. I need to sit in the car and watch them coach after the sales call."

One of the firms we interviewed had developed a very thorough approach to FLSM coaching. The sales leader explained:

"We talk about coaching *cadences*, when the coaching takes place—weekly, monthly, quarterly, biannual, and annual planning interactions. Each cadence is a series of frequent interactions for the front-line management to learn, so they can coach their sellers. Each cadence focuses on different things, but there is considerable overlap. For example, a business plan is set annually, but is updated one other time a year. The most sought-after skills for FLSMs to acquire are *knowledge*—competitive, product, customer; *negotiation skills*—our deals can get up to $20/50/80 million in total contract value, so that's really important; *CRM [customer relationship management] related*—territory management, time management, forecasting, account planning; *rules of how we do business*—fundamentals about how we behave in the market, and how management is held accountable for those behaviors."

For FLSMs to achieve high performance levels, coaching by sales leaders and senior sales managers is a critical piece of the puzzle.

Onboard FLSMs. Perhaps the most crucial times for FLSM coaching occur when the FLSM is first appointed and when the firm makes a significant salesforce organization transformation. In either case, the FLSM is facing a new environment, so *onboarding* training and coaching are critical.

For newly appointed FLSMs, the onboarding process should relate directly to their backgrounds. FLSMs appointed from outside the firm require somewhat different coaching than do those appointed internally. Internal promotions from the salesforce require different coaching than do those appointed from other functional areas. And a seller promoted to an FLSM position in an unfamiliar district may require different coaching than does a new FLSM who must now lead, direct, and manage sellers who were formerly peers. One sales leader shared his perspective on a challenge he faced with a newly appointed FLSM:

> "I have one manager who is a little more relaxed in his demeanor and mannerism; he was a sales rep. Now that he is the manager of that region, he needs to step into his own confidence, and break from the camaraderie of the sales reps to be the leader. That is a bit of a challenge, but we will work through it, and I believe he can do it. So, we just need to work on that."

For current FLSMs who face salesforce transformations, training and coaching take a different course. Earlier in this chapter we noted the medical-technology firm that merged salesforces and subsequently lost 20 to 30 percent of its FLSMs. But this attrition was not a result of lack of sales-leader effort—indeed, FLSM losses could have been even greater without the training and coaching efforts the firm provided. The sales leader explained:

> "Throughout the transition, we coached FLSMs extensively. We coached them on our new approach to managing opportunities, including special manager-coaching workshops; we put these on around the world. There were also one-on-one coaching calls, and online support through an e-learning platform. We also did extensive FLSM training on the new product portfolios and new marketplaces FLSMs were addressing, similar to our efforts with sales reps. But there were additional meetings and group sessions for FLSMs.
>
> "We supported FLSMs with a corporate change-management program, dealing with the softer side of change—what their team was going through; how each team member would accept change differently. This intervention focused on how to deal with the field reps and get them through the change.

"We communicated constantly; I believe people have to hear something seven times before they internalize it. Overall, our coaching efforts went above and beyond, so FLSMs could really support their sales reps."

A Coaching and Learning Culture. Just as coaching is a critical element of the FLSM's job—to improve seller performance—so should coaching be a key part of the FLSM boss's job—to improve FLSM performance. But the firm must work harder to enact FLSM coaching than seller coaching. FLSMs are typically geographically separated from their bosses, and observing FLSMs in action is not a regular daily activity.

Sales leaders have a responsibility to develop a coaching culture throughout the entire sales organization—not just for FLSMs and sellers. The sales leader at a global services firm bemoaned the *administrative* culture that had gradually seeped into the FLSM role at his firm. He told us:

"We are doubling down on our efforts to provide these sales managers with the appropriate tools, and the appropriate time utilities, to act as coaches to their various sales individuals as part of our *coach-to-learn* initiative. We want them to have much higher impact as coaches. It's a philosophical change for us as we try to shift the *bell curve* to the right.

"In the middle of the curve, you see a lot of our performers between 95 percent and 105 percent [of quota]. Then you have the extreme left—poor performers; and extreme right—exceptional performers. We just want to move the curve to the right. By creating a different mentality, a different philosophy [and change in the role of the FLSM], we think we can move that curve."

Another sales leader emphasized that, in her salesforce, there was a strong expectation that not only FLSMs but their regional sales director (RSD) bosses should also spend time in the field:

"Our RSDs are very active coaching the FLSMs. I want RSDs to coach the FLSMs on how to coach. So, I need them to sit in the back of the car after the sales call and watch FLSMs coach the sales rep, then provide coaching to the FLSM."

Sales leaders should insist on a significant coaching effort for FLSMs; this is clearly a priority for the global business-services firm. After all, that's the nexus of sales-performance leverage.

Finally, coaching is a low-key, low-direct-cost, but potentially high-value activity. FLSMs carry a heavy responsibility; they must make decisions quickly, often with limited information. One sales leader offered an insightful view on FLSM decision making, with an improvement option:

"Our FLSMs must make decisions rapidly on their own. For this to occur, the firm must create a culture that has deep respect for the sales function. Lacking that respect, folks won't make those decisions; they won't give you their best thinking. So, my responsibility is to create that culture. I make sure my FLSMs get exposed to senior management on a regular basis. I want my FLSMs to feel part of the executive team, and that they have received the credentials from senior leaders, to make those tough decisions on their own, without having to check.

> "I want my guys exposed to the head of marketing, to the head of operations, and to the head of R&D. And I want those people to understand that the FLSMs are an extension of me. Building these relationships is very powerful; without them it's paralyzing."

Over and above the learning FLSMs receive from exposure to senior firm leaders, they also secure good connections internally, and hence improve resource acumen. But FLSMs can also learn from their peers. As we saw in Chapter 5, effective FLSMs collect and disseminate best practice among their sales teams. One sales-leader responsibility is to leverage seller and FLSM best practice among all FLSMs.

Retain High-Performing FLSMs

So, you've done a great job of molding a group of superior FLSMs; what could go wrong? They could quit! We expect to lose some superior FLSMs to other managerial positions within the firm, some to higher levels in sales management, others to different functions. But to have a top-flight FLSM leave to join a competitor, or pursue some other opportunity, is a serious blow.

Most FLSMs we talked to expected to receive less financial compensation than their star sellers. There seemed to be an implicit deal that accompanies FLSM promotions from the seller ranks— higher managerial status, but lower take-home pay. Sales leaders know this trade-off; most likely they accepted the same deal earlier in their careers. But sales leaders should take care that these most valuable of managers do not become disaffected over money.

One FLSM, speaking of herself and her peers, told us:

> "You have to get some more buy-in with us because, at some point, we become free agents. The work is great, not complaining one bit. But if I can say: 'I can work 60 percent of my current pace, and make more money as an account executive, at this or another firm,' maybe I should rethink my career."

In Chapter 1, we provided many quotations from sales leaders attesting to the importance of the FLSM role, but we should not forget that many of these leaders also recognized the difficulties. Certainly, this is an important issue when addressing FLSM retention and unplanned turnover. One sales leader recognized the critical nature of this reality:

> "The FLSM position is the most underappreciated job in the entire organization—the dirtiest job. You get your hands very dirty, dealing with strategic-customer conversations, down to: 'How come I didn't get credit on this return?' 'How come you're raising prices on my contract items, but the manufacturer's price didn't go up?' Then there are policy changes from the top that must be implemented at the customer. It's a cliché, but it's where the rubber meets the road. It's the most underappreciated, but the most important position we have: When the firm decides to do something with a customer, or to a customer, it's the FLSM's job to get that done. And those conversations are very difficult."

Important yet underappreciated seems a recipe for disaster. The sales leader went on:

> "Retaining our FLSMs is very important, so we pay them pretty well. But I don't think that's sufficient. They're pretty tough cookies, but I think some TLC and recognition goes

a long way. So, I send notes or cards on anniversaries, or: 'I noticed your district was up 5 percent.' I think everybody wants to be noticed, and it doesn't have to be big stuff. I don't use email; I send a personal card, so the spouse/significant other says: 'Wow, that's a pretty decent company you work for.'"

For most sales organizations, unplanned loss of a high-performing FLSM is an unfortunate event. Regardless, superior HR planning can minimize the negative effects of such defections. The replacement FLSM quickly moves into leading, directing, and managing the sales team, and rebuilds customer relationships. But for some firms, departure of any FLSM—high-performing or not—can have much more serious, and immediate, consequences. We revisit what the sales leader for a distribution firm told us:

"We have two main businesses, let's call them A and B. In the A business, if we lose an FLSM or a seller, we don't miss a beat; the customer's not going to make any significant moves. But in the B business, if we lose an FLSM, or even a seller, they'll take probably 50 percent of the business with them. Because they *own* the relationship. So, my customer is more my FLSMs and their sellers, rather than the real customer—that's not a good feeling."

Retaining high-performing FLSMs is a critical sales-leader responsibility. During our interviews, we observed a serious disconnect in some firms between assertions of FLSM importance (high) and attention to FLSM development and compensation (less so). To lose a high-performing FLSM is a serious setback. Sales leaders should ensure they do what it takes to minimize unplanned FLSM attrition.

Improve FLSM Performance

One of the oldest saying in management is the following: *If you can't measure it, you can't manage it. If you can't manage it, you can't improve it.* Nowhere is this statement more true than in the salesforce—for individual sellers, FLSMs, and further up the sales management hierarchy. What sales leaders strive to improve is *sales performance*—quota attainment—at every level.

When people talk of performance, they typically mean **output performance**—sales units/revenues, profit contribution, bottom-line profits. But in order to secure good *output* performance, it's important to earn good **intermediate performance**: the critical middle layer of outcomes in performance measurement. Achieving good intermediate performance does not guarantee good output performance, but good output performance is unattainable without good intermediate performance. In turn, the firm will not secure good intermediate performance without doing the *right* things (FLSM activities)—good **input performance**. When we talk of improving FLSM performance, we focus on all three performance types—*input, intermediate, output*—Figure 8.2. We address these items in reverse order.

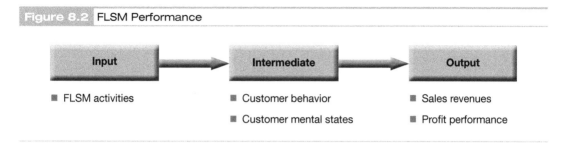

Figure 8.2 | FLSM Performance

Output Performance

All FLSMs have a number (or several numbers) they have to meet, typically stated as a sales revenue goal/quota, or sometimes as profit (or profit contribution). The overall goal for the sales organization typically derives from the firm/business strategy via the chief financial officer. Salesforce goals should be **SMART**:

FLSM goals are typically that portion of the total salesforce goal for which the FLSM is responsible. FLSM goals are annualized, but may be broken out by quarter (or even monthly, weekly). There may also be subgoals, like revenues from new products, new customers, or individual product/market segments. Some goals relate to specific strategic situations/initiatives. Examples:

- *Current customers buy on price.* Goals—profit margin, customer retention.

- *New product/market entry.* Goals—customer acquisition, revenues from new products.

Related to the Chapter 4 discussion on seller performance, we term these measures *output* variables. Generally, sales organizations do a good job of measuring FLSM success/failure regarding output variables. But, as noted above, knowing whether or not an FLSM secured (or did not secure) good output performance does not help much to sustain/improve this performance. Successful output performance derives from successful intermediate performance. In turn, successful intermediate performance derives from successful input performance. Now we explore both.

Intermediate Performance

We employ the same distinction between two types of intermediate measures that we introduced in Chapter 4—*pipeline/macro-intermediate* measures and *micro-intermediate* measures.

Pipeline/Macro Measures. We introduced pipeline issues in *business acumen*—while discussing the FLSM task—*keeping tabs on progress* of individual sellers. (Figure 4.3 shows a high-tech firm's pipeline system.) Of course, the pipeline system for sellers should roll up to the pipeline for FLSMs. Hence, FLSMs can assess individual seller pipelines and, by aggregation, secure an overall view of district health.

In addition to output quotas, sales leaders should set macro-intermediate (pipeline) quotas for FLSMs—based on overall salesforce objectives/quotas. We do not expect individual sales-district quotas to exactly mirror overall salesforce objectives/quotas; after all, individual sales districts have different characteristics/opportunities. But sales-district aggregates should roll up to salesforce numbers overall.

Careful setting of intermediate quotas provides sales leaders with a powerful means of monitoring FLSM performance. By this means, sales leaders can direct FLSMs to work with sellers to place effort in specific areas where improvement is required.

Table 8.1 illustrates a simple six-step sales pipeline—*sales leads discovered* (step 1) to *business won* (step 6), for a given sales territory. The table shows three numerical rows:

- **Row A:** total territory sales revenues (from Total Sales Leads Discovered [step 1] to Business Won [step 6])

- **Row B:** potential sales revenues at each pipeline stage stated as a percentage of total potential sales revenues in all discovered leads

- **Row C:** potential sales revenues at each pipeline stage stated as a percentage of potential sales revenues at the prior stage

The figures in rows B and C form the basis for intermediate quotas.

Table 8.1 Sales Pipeline Illustration—Sales Revenues

		1 Total Sales Leads Discovered	2 Opportunities Identified	3 Opportunities Validated	4 Opportunities Qualified	5 Conditional Agreements Made with Customer	6 Business Won
A	Territory total	$76 million	$28 million	$17 million	$13 million	$10 million	$8 million
B	Percentage of total potential sales revenues	100%	37%	22%	17%	13%	11%
C	Percentage success from previous stage	100%	37%	59%	77%	76%	85%

The sales leader for a high-tech firm explained how he used sales-pipeline measures to improve FLSM performance:

> "We've given up doing reports with PowerPoint decks; we manage our FLSMs directly from dashboards, linked to pipeline measures. Do they have a *clean* pipe or a *dirty* pipe [deals that haven't moved]; what is their *pipeline coverage*? What are their ACV [annual contract value] and bookings; what is their *close ratio* to the pipe coverage? When *close rates* get off-kilter with coverage, we know we've got an issue.
>
> "This is how it works: Suppose we know our close ratio in a 90-day period is 50 percent, then our pipeline coverage must be 2X—that is, 2.0/200 percent. If an FLSM has a $15 million quota, the pipeline would have to be $30 million [15 × 2].
>
> "As the quarter progresses, the coverage plan changes, because stuff moves, comes in, goes out, whatever. We know by the linearity of a week whether or not we've got enough pipe (if our close ratios stay consistent) for the revenues we need to deliver. This is really critical; our FLSMs have to know their pipeline metrics inside and out. We use these metrics to coach our FLSMs.
>
> "We have this down to a science. One of my guys worked with an FLSM who had a $12 million forecast; he told the FLSM his revenues would be $12.1 million. They put a bottle of wine on the number; it came in at $12.11. And my guy didn't even know the deals. He said, 'I could see it in the math of your coverage.'"

The sales leader describes what is really a first-cut analysis. He told us he typically goes deeper to look at deals at different pipeline stages. These more granular measures reveal the velocity with which individual opportunities travel through the sales pipeline—Appendix 8.

Micro Measures. These intermediate measures concern various types of customer behaviors that lead to performance on pipeline measures. Examples include commitment to engage in co-op advertising; agreement to place the firm on the approved-supplier list; agreement to conduct factory trials; agreement to specify the firm's product; acceptance of firm proposals; agreement to accept retail displays; agreement to meet with a subject-matter expert; agreement to join a customer advisory board; agreement for a high-level firm/customer meeting.

Sales leaders may set quotas on any of these micro-intermediate measures, assess performance, and hence modify what FLSMs demand from their sellers.

Input Performance

Related to the discussion in Chapter 4, *intermediate* measures do not reveal what FLSMs actually do. FLSM behavior is an *input* to intermediate measures and the pipeline system. How FLSMs spend their time is a critical driver of FLSM intermediate and output performance. FLSM **inputs** *are the crucial variables sales leaders can direct and manage.* Sales leaders must decide what they want FLSMs to do, then make sure they act accordingly.

Examples: Sales leaders may require FLSMs to spend more time in the field, traveling with sellers and meeting customers; do a better job of pipeline management; conduct dedicated coaching sessions;

demand greater use of sales tools; secure access to customer C-Suites; spend less time on administration; make decisions on myriad other activities.

The sales leader from a global package-delivery firm stated his requirement that FLSMs spend less time on administrative tasks:

> "We had allowed our FLSMs great flexibility and independence, so there was little consistency/harmonization across the firm. Now we are going to manage just a limited number of things. Empirical items—number of sales calls, number of pricing files submitted; learning and development goals related to online modules, periodically updated. We test understanding and are considering certification. Essentially, we're professionalizing the entire selling operation. For the FLSM per se, we're shifting strongly to an enhanced coaching role. Right now, our standard is three days per week in the field, but we're thinking of raising that to three and one-half days. On the *output* side, we focus on yield from pricing files submitted, and revenue growth. That's it. We're doing this in the U.S., but are going to roll it out globally."

Sales leaders should isolate discrepancies, then work to modify FLSM behavior.

The sales leader at LinkedIn offered an interesting perspective on salesforce culture, and a key driver of FLSM behavior:

> "In our sales culture, we have a strong focus and emphasis on admin—*less*; time in the field—*more*. I have observed that FLSMs tend to spend more time on administrative tasks and in meetings, and less time in the field, when they are less confident in their managerial skills. So, we work on building confidence. It starts with FLSM onboarding—meet and learn from current, successful FLSMs. We have a buddy-manager program—proactive outreach to show new guys how the job is done. We also form communities of new-manager cohorts, so individuals do not feel alone—they get together for one hour monthly to discuss challenges and solutions. We prepare an issue agenda in advance, so they can give thought to solutions, and avoid the process degrading into a gripe session."

Another sales leader was excited about a new system his firm was implementing:

> "Up to now, FLSM measurement was just revenue achievement; we also had a few seller surveys of FLSMs through HR—part of our standardized 360 process. Now, we're getting data on where our FLSMs are spending their time—leadership, coaching of sellers versus managerial versus administrative activities. We're getting a much better picture of how they and their sales teams are working—much better transparency."

Finally, one FLSM provided his firm's approach to monitoring sales-manager performance that embraced both intermediate (pipeline) and input measures:

> "Ultimately, it comes down to hitting your numbers. But we have multiple other KPIs [key performance indicators]—number of activities sales-team members are using, like marketing programs; number of opportunities reps create; how quickly opportunities are

moving through the funnel [sales-funnel velocity]; number of lost accounts; number of new accounts; utility of sales tools."

Developing Trends

One trend we identified seemed related to greater use of input and intermediate variables in FLSM monitor-and-control processes—increased use of CRM and related tools. More generally, some firms are wrapping input and intermediate measures into management by objectives (MBO) systems. One sales leader identified the sorts of MBO measures his firm used to monitor FLSMs:

> "We look at how well the FLSM is managing the district—things like number of sellers promoted, number of sellers resigning, open-territory weeks, seller inputs into their sales funnels, sales-plan completions, sales-plan quality, use of marketing programs, use of sales tools like online presentations, and things of that nature."

Relatedly, one FLSM in higher-education software reported her experience:

> "I am graded on how well I hire and retain individuals; how I motivate them and keep things moving forward—not just sales, but various things like account plans. I am measured on team performance in keeping plans updated, and being current with pipeline information. And I am accountable for making sure all sellers attend training programs."

For the firm to succeed, FLSMs must perform at a high level. Certainly, sales leaders should monitor FLSM output performance. But monitoring output performance does nothing to *improve* that performance. Sales leaders influence *output* performance only by focusing efforts to monitor and control FLSM *intermediate* and *input* performance. Insufficient effort placed in these monitor-and-control activities, and lack of coaching for improvement, represent a serious sales leadership failure.

In addition to improvements in monitor-and-control systems, we observed increasing use of field data, driven largely by sales-operations departments. By combining multiple data streams into a *data lake*, and employing data scientists to search for meaningful relationships to sales performance, firms are identifying best salesforce practices. These practices are swiftly passed to FLSMs and their sellers. Said one sales leader:

> "Our analysts may find that in a few territories, sellers are performing especially well with a specific product at a particular type of customer. Then we look for commonalities in how those sales are made, and feed that to FLSMs to coach their sellers. We're at the beginning stages of these efforts, but corporate is making a big IT bet on the CRM systems we believe will spur our ability to feed the revenue-growth engine."

In reality, the FLSM position is often transient. Sellers may remain in place for many years, or even an entire career; FLSMs are often *passing through* on their way to higher-level positions in sales, marketing, or general management. Indeed, success in the FLSM role is often a good predictor of success in more-senior managerial positions. A useful approach to codifying actions for improving FLSM performance is the FLSM Playbook.

FLSM Playbooks

When FLSM turnover is nontrivial, sales leaders should build what amounts to an FLSM Playbook. Related to, but quite different from, a seller playbook—Appendix 10, the FLSM version captures essential practices of the FLSM job. Hence, newly appointed FLSMs can quickly learn what to do and achieve rapid competence.

Generally speaking, the new FLSM must get up to speed quickly. It's not a good idea for *field generals* to take a long time to find their footing. Traditionally, such playbooks, where they existed at all, were literally three-ring binders. Today, they may take the form of frequently updated documents on a shared drive, or even cloud-based applications. In whatever form they take, FLSM Playbooks typically comprise several components—*performance indicators*, *diagnostics*, *meeting cadence*, *second-line coaching*:

- **Performance indicators.** Critical metrics include both *leading* and *lagging* indicators. Leading—intermediate variables—offer insight into likely future revenues and quota attainment via current performance in variables like those in pipeline systems (discussed above). *Lagging*—output variables—sales revenues and/or quota attainment.

- **Diagnostics.** Assuming a robust array of performance indicators, the FLSM Playbook should provide a framework for FLSMs to spot deviations from expectations. The playbook should also identify approaches to assess corrective options. Among these options are actions for bringing underperformers back on track.

One seller's pipeline performance was insufficient to attain sales revenue quota. The FLSM's task was to determine why the seller was set to underperform; and what changes were required in input variables. Was the seller:

- making enough sales calls?
- covering the *right* accounts?
- discussing the *right* products?
- calling on the *right* decision makers/influencers?
- discussing the *right* solutions?

The correct diagnostic framework must be established for FLSMs, based on recent best practice. In this way, rookie FLSMs and incumbents can easily replicate an approach comprising the best current thinking.

- **Meeting cadence.** FLSMs must spend significant chunks of time in the field with their sellers—stars as well as underperformers. The content of *ride-withs* varies across sellers. The FLSM extracts best practices from stars, but suggests corrective action to underperformers. Regardless, the framework and frequency of discussion topics should not occur at the discretion of individual FLSMs. Rather, FLSMs should base their meeting cadence on past wisdom and best practice. Sales leaders should embed meeting cadence in the FLSM Playbook.

- **Second-line coaching.** Particularly for new FLSMs, second-line managers should also follow a meeting cadence for visits with their directly reporting FLSMs. As noted above, second-line managers should both observe and offer support and coaching. Over time, such meetings should continue, but the content shifts from inspection/coaching to discussion/joint learning about what is working and why. The support structure flexes to the incumbents' abilities.

The *FLSM Playbook* is a valuable tool that great sales organizations offer their FLSMs. Great FLSMs have a flair for execution. They are the *can do, get it done* people. They are inclined to action, and willing, even eager to *run the plays*. Generally, providing a playbook gives FLSMs a tool that they are delighted to use.

 # Remove the *Crap*

Sellers/FLSMs secure sales revenues only when they actively engage with customers or otherwise work on customer-related issues. Generally, they do not enhance sales revenues when they are securing data for marketing, responding to sales-leader requests for performance metrics, spending time in internal meetings, or working on a host of other administrative tasks sellers/FLSMs are frequently asked to complete. Nor do they earn sales revenues when they labor to complete necessary tasks with long-out-dated systems and processes.

Reduce Time Wasters

For head office/marketing-department personnel who require market-oriented data, it all seems so easy: Just put out a request to the field. After all, as they see it, "Sellers are in a position to secure and provide what we need to know. They are in the field every day." The bottom line: There are many ways to fritter away time.

Of course, FLSMs will spend time on activities that do not immediately generate revenues. Coaching and training are obvious areas, along with briefings from internal stakeholders on the economy, industry evolution, competitor activities, other environmental trends, firm strategy, new product introductions, and the like. But, it's the responsibility of sales leaders to monitor the time drag on these non-revenue-producing activities. According to The Alexander Group benchmarking data, across all salesforces, the majority of sellers spend only one-third of their time on direct, customer-focused activities. In fact, even best-in-class firms rarely exceed 40 percent.

Related to this seller-time issue, the sales leader at a global package-delivery firm told us how the FLSM culture at his firm had evolved:

> "As we grew over the years, the number of solutions we offer has climbed well into three figures. Furthermore, we are awash in data. Although senior management focuses on five or six key metrics, that's only a fraction of what's available for FLSMs to examine. Literally, they have access to hundreds of reports, tons of data. Then again, we pushed a lot of stuff out to the field—slow payers, high complaint ratios—for FLSMs to chase down. And, of course, senior management was always asking for more information. The dominant culture for FLSMs became *administrative*. Sales leaders and other top managers were a significant part of the problem.
>
> "But we're changing. We've streamlined the accounts receivable process, and we have a sales-manager playbook. Any request to the field must be cleared through the playbook, and that must be signed off by me. I'm making sure we're not polluting/corrupting the sales effort with administrative stuff. I am determined to significantly cut down administration from the FLSM job."

Forecasting future sales for sales leaders is another major time sink for many FLSMs. Of course, sales leaders and senior management require sales forecasts for many internal and external constituencies. Regardless, given FLSMs' scarce time, we are forced to wonder if firms have identified the appropriate trade-offs between time spent by FLSMs on continual sales forecasting, and time spent on selling activities. Consider what two FLSMs told us:

> "I spend a lot of time on paperwork; forecasting is a good example. I do that every month. When you have 11 guys that you are forecasting for, you need to have several good conversations before doing the forecast. Between preparing the forecast, and briefing my boss, it really burns up a lot of time."

> "I spend about five to six hours per week on forecast calls—with my people, my boss, my boss's boss—and preparing for those calls."

Now, consider what we heard from one FLSM. It may seem extreme, but we think you'll get the picture:

> "My week began by collecting sales data from my 17 direct reports. I spent half an hour on the phone with each team member in turn, going through each and every sales opportunity to identify the sell-cycle stage, and to discuss the plan for moving the opportunity to the next cycle. We'd discuss success probabilities and how much revenue was at stake. That task consumed all of Monday. On Tuesday, I had a call with the person responsible for sales in the Eastern U.S. to pass along these data—an all-day affair. Wednesday was a repeat of Tuesday, but with the person responsible for industry sales—another whole day. Thursday, similar to Tuesday and Wednesday, but with product executives. That left Friday for doing whatever else I needed to do. The following Monday I started all over again. Collecting and passing on the data became my whole job."

In this regard, *sales leaders have two specific responsibilities:*

- **Develop a scarce-time culture.** Throughout the salesforce, from the top of the organization to individual sellers and FLSMs, sales leaders should communicate the value of time. In particular, sales leaders should clarify the sorts of activities FLSMs/sellers should avoid, and emphasize the best use of their scarce time resources. Sales leaders should continually remind FLSMs/sellers of the importance of spending time with customers—identifying and supporting decision makers and influencers—and generally working on customer issues and making sales.

- **Protect sellers and FLSMs.** Setting up and reinforcing a scarce-time culture is one thing; protecting FLSM/seller time is quite another. Sales leaders have the power to restrict information requests, meetings, and all manner of time-killing activities that reduce time spent with customers, and on customer-related issues. They should not hesitate to exercise this power.

One sales leader put it this way:

> "The best FLSMs understand that coaching and supporting sales reps is their primary role. Of course, they have to do managerial things—running reports, submitting forecasts, and all that stuff. But really driving leadership qualities through coaching, making team members understand their value to the firm, and connection to the strategy is crucial. The best FLSMs focus on coaching leadership qualities. We emphasize the leadership dimension of the job, not the managerial dimension."

A few years ago, a large high-tech firm realized it had a significant scarce-time problem within the salesforce—insufficient seller-customer face time. The major problem was communications from more senior levels to more junior levels. When a senior manager called, the junior manager would drop everything to respond right away. Also, sellers wanted advice, decisions, information, and resources from managers. Internal communications were sporadic, time-consuming, and frustrating. The tech firm realized its approach was extremely wasteful of time. The firm implemented strongly enforced mandatory guidelines to manage communications throughout the salesforce, limiting the length of each conversation type and restricting level-skipping communications.

- Monday: 30 minutes—Salespeople and FLSMs

- Tuesday: 60 minutes—FLSMs and RSMs

- Wednesday: 60 minutes—RSMs and zone sales managers

- Thursday: 60 minutes—Zone sales managers and SVPs

- Friday: 2 hours—SVPs and executive management

Result: With internal communications streamlined, seller-customer face time at this firm increased considerably.

Improve Systems and Processes

In addition to removing direct assaults on FLSM/seller time, sales leaders should automate processes where possible to remove roadblocks to effective organizational functioning. One such roadblock in many salesforces is a requirement for approvals. Such approvals may lead to slow customer-response times, and jeopardize potential deals. The sales leader at the global packaging-firm explained the changes his firm had made regarding approvals for pricing decisions:

> **"We have streamlined and accelerated the pricing system. FLSMs now have more responsibility/authority for pricing decisions. Of course, we hold them accountable for yield management and revenue growth. We back this up with learning and development tools for their individual sellers."**

The core message from this example is that pushing authority/responsibility down through the sales organization is a sure way to reduce approval time. There are, of course, many arguments on both sides of the centralization/decentralization decision. We identified organizational benefits from greater empowerment in Chapter 2.

Sales leaders also have a responsibility to ease the FLSM's burden of completing regular administrative tasks by ensuring that firm systems and processes are up-to-date and easy to use. Consider the complaints of one successful FLSM:

> **"Everything we do to track things is difficult, if not unbearable—filing expense reports, filing a requisition for a new hire, doing employee reviews. The systems are not intuitive—you literally have to relearn every time. To build a quote and put it into the system is super tedious—it's the bane of most salespeople's existence."**

The core message for sales leaders: You hired FLSMs and sellers to earn sales revenues. Use your positions of authority/responsibility to get the organization out of the way, out of the dark ages, and let FLSMs and sellers do the jobs they were hired to do—increase sales revenues.

Summary

Chapter 8 is the first of three chapters in Part II of *The Front-Line Sales Manager – Field General*. This chapter focuses on the ways in which senior managers/sales leaders can build a group of high-performing FLSMs. The starting point is appointing the *right* FLSMs. Three issues are critical here. First, plan ahead so that vacancies—expected and unexpected—can be swiftly filled in a measured way. Second, be very clear that the competencies for being an outstanding FLSM—*strategic, organizational, business, team-building, resource, personal acumen*—are very different from those that make an outstanding seller; do not unthinkingly promote your best sellers to FLSM positions. Third, minimize your need to appoint new FLSMs by doing what is necessary to retain your current high FLSM performers—minimize attrition probabilities.

Regardless of current performance, all FLSMs are capable of continuous improvement. Firm leaders should invest in *stock* and *flow* training for FLSMs—both for improvement and for retention. Sales leaders and more senior sales managers should also invest the time and effort to coach FLSMs. An important coaching focus should be performance versus objectives. Of course, measuring quota attainment is critical, but this measure concerns *output* variables. From a coaching perspective, *intermediate* variables (what customers do) and *input* variables (what FLSMs do) are far more important for securing performance improvement.

Finally, senior management and sales leaders should focus on two broad areas that increase seller time with customers and on customer-related issues, and allow FLSMs more time to support their sellers. First, they should invest in systems and processes that make it easier for sellers/FLSMs to do their jobs. Second, they should minimize the requirement for administrative work, so FLSMs can concentrate their efforts on the most important part of the job—their sellers.

Chapter 9

Strategy and Structure

Management theory tells us that two of its most important concepts are **strategy** and **structure**. In this chapter, we address strategy at three different levels before turning to the sales organization structure. Specific topics—*articulate and communicate firm strategy*; *evolve sales strategy*; *ensure value propositions are compelling*. Then we turn to *make the* right *salesforce organization structure changes* for increasing salesforce effectiveness—Figure 9.1.

Organizational Issues

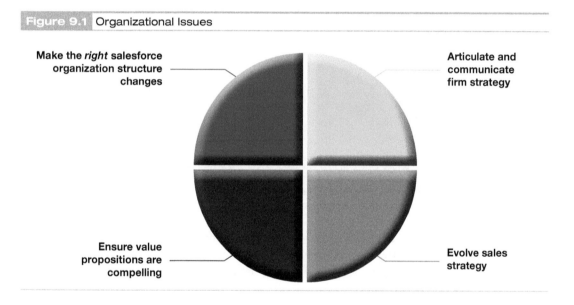

Make the *right* salesforce organization structure changes

Articulate and communicate firm strategy

Ensure value propositions are compelling

Evolve sales strategy

 ## Articulate and Communicate Firm Strategy

In Chapter 2, we presented a vignette about Mike Smith, a seller for a new line of household textile fabrics from the Wongyang firm. While awaiting his appointment at a potential customer—Furnzen—by chance, Mike ran into Hillary Stein, Furnzen's CEO. Ms. Stein, who was under time pressure, asked Mike for the elevator speech on Wongyang. Recall that Mike was unable to respond effectively.

Setting aside the possibility that Mike is simply incompetent, there are two likely reasons for Mike's failure. First, Mike's managerial hierarchy did not educate him about Wongyang during onboarding training. (Mike had been with the firm about one year.) This could be a front-line sales manager (FLSM) failure or a failure at more senior levels in the salesforce. Second, senior corporate management failed to articulate and communicate firm strategy. Either way, there is a serious problem. In

Appendix 6, we lay out one strategy framework that has served us well—*vision, mission, growth path, timing of entry, market/market-segment strategy*. An abbreviated form of this framework is in Table 9.1.

Table 9.1 A Growth-Strategy Framework for FLSMs and Their Sellers*

This strategic framework comprises five elements: **vision**, **mission**, **growth path**, **timing of entry**, **market/market segment strategy**.

Vision	*Vision* is a description of the firm's ideal future state—not too broad, nor too specific, nor easily achieved. Corporate vision concerns the entire firm; business vision focuses on an individual business. Well-developed visions are outward-looking; aspirational yet realistic; but do not raise customer expectations beyond the firm's ability to deliver.
Mission	*Mission* is more specific than vision. Mission guides the search for opportunities.** A well-developed mission keeps the firm focused in a limited arena where success is likely. Mission avoids dispersing firm energy and resources in multiple directions. Mission states what the firm/business will do—and, by omission, what it will not do!
Growth Path	*Growth path* is more focused than mission. Growth path is specifically concerned with trade-offs between expected financial return and risk, as the firm applies competencies/resources against potential opportunities. Figure A6.1 in Appendix 6 shows the growth-path matrix's two dimensions—market, product/technology. Broad approaches to growth are market penetration, product growth, market growth, product/market diversification.
Timing of Entry	*Timing of entry* concerns when to seize an opportunity. We identify five product life-cycle stages—introduction, early growth, late growth, maturity, decline. We further identify four entry options, one for each of the first four stages: *pioneer*—blazes trails and create new markets via consistent and extensive R&D; *follow-the-leader*—enters rapidly growing markets on the heels of pioneers; *segmenter*—enters established markets in late growth by adding value for specific market segments; *me-too-er*—enters mature markets with limited product lines—Figure A6.2.
Market/Market-Segment Strategy	For each chosen market, marketing conducts segmentation studies and selects one or more market segments to address with its products/services. Customers in any market have broadly similar needs, but finer-grained needs differ from market segment to market segment. The firm targets one or more market segments. Key elements in the product/market-segment strategy are:
	■ *Objectives.* *Strategic objectives* specify broad direction; *operational objectives* focus on results: How much? By when?
	■ *Positioning.* The heart of the product/market-segment strategy, *positioning* comprises four core elements: *customer targets*—specific organizations, decision makers/influencers where the firm will expend effort; *competitor targets*—organizations offering related benefits/values to the firm; *value proposition*—the basic reason(s) customer targets will purchase/recommend firm products/services rather than competitors'; *reasons to believe*—why customer targets should believe the firm will fulfill promises made in the value proposition.
	■ *Implementation.* These elements are the tools marketing possesses for executing the product/market-segment strategy. These tools are broadly known as the marketing mix or the 4Ps—product, promotion, price, distribution (place). Other implementation elements comprise requirements from the firm's functional areas.

* Adapted from N. Capon, *Managing Marketing in the 21st Century* (4th ed.), New York: Wessex, 2017, Chapter 7.
** These *vision* and *mission* definitions are not universally accepted. What we note as a *vision*, some firms call a *mission*.

In addition to strategic issues, FLSMs and sellers should also know about other firm-wide initiatives that do not necessarily involve strategic changes. An example comes from the sales leader at a global package-delivery firm:

> "Each year we engineer waste out of our system and reduce transit time between two cities. We want to make sure our sellers and FLSMs know about that."

There are four critical reasons why senior corporate management should ensure FLSMs/sellers are well aware of the firm's strategic directions and other company-wide initiatives:

- *FLSMs/sellers can better present the firm to current/potential customers.* This is the issue represented by the Mike Smith vignette. Although company-offered attributes/features and benefits/values are important to customers, they also want to know if the firm is a supplier they can trust and do business with. Is the supplier going to be around in a couple of years? FLSMs and sellers should be able to provide a thumbnail sketch of the firm to anyone who is interested, not necessarily the details, but a quick overview. For multibusiness firms, these data concern the specific business, but also the firm overall. Such data are important to firms selecting suppliers.

- *FLSMs/sellers will better understand the realities of resource availability.* Senior management has the responsibility to provide direction regarding product/markets the firm currently serves, and those it intends to serve in the future. This information is especially important if future directions differ from past practice. Such articulation is important for fast-growing firms with aggressive internal-growth ambitions, firms undertaking acquisitions, and firms divesting businesses. Articulation is also important when the firm has a leadership change. As soon as possible after taking over, the new CEO and the leadership team should clarify what offerings and practices will continue, and what will be new. FLSMs/sellers need to know where the firm is placing its resources, so they can prepare for the future. They must be able to help customers learn where the firm can help them succeed moving forward.

- *FLSMs/sellers are better able to develop partnership relationships with customers.* Many firms seek to avoid procurement pressure for lower prices and better terms by becoming involved with customers at the *ideate* or *design* stages of the selling process. These interventions typically involve high-level discussions of customer strategy. Inability to articulate their own firm's strategic direction can initiate a crushing credibility deficit for FLSMs/sellers. They must be extremely familiar with the Table 9.1 strategic framework (or an alternative). Only then can they fulfill the requirements one CEO articulated:

> "We have a responsibility to our customers to help them think through strategically important issues. We want to sell to high-end executives on the basis of outcomes that matter to them. We can only accomplish this task if our salesforce truly understands where we are headed."

■ *FLSMs/sellers are better able to pursue opportunities.* Many large firms have multiple sales-forces—there are many different arrangements. Sometimes two salesforces sell different products to the same customer. Other times, salesforces sell different products to different customers. In these, and other organizational arrangements, sellers may unearth opportunities for members of a sister salesforce, but only if they have good understanding of firm strategy. (Of course, compensation for such opportunity identification is a separate issue.)

In the Chapter 2 vignette, Mike Smith was unable to articulate the essence of his firm's strategic direction. We suggested this was a serious failure by Mike and his FLSM. But the root cause may have been a senior-leadership failure to articulate firm direction. Senior management not only has the responsibility to articulate firm direction, it must also make sure that direction is widely communicated within the firm, especially to the salesforce. One sales leader expressed frustration with his current situation, contrasting it with CEO behavior at a former employer:

> "One thing we really struggle with is what I call our short elevator speech. We do not have a real firm handle on that; it shows in our sellers' inability to make a concise statement of what the firm stands for. At one firm where I used to work, the CEO was frantic about this issue—he'd get into the elevator and demand you produce it. For anyone that could not, there was hell to pay—not just for that person, but all the way up his or her managerial hierarchy. This is not a trivial issue; we have made several large acquisitions and significantly enhanced the product portfolio. We have to do a better job of articulating who we are, how big we are, what is our capability set, and that we can do the things the big guys can do."

Some firms take educating FLSMs and sellers about future firm plans very seriously. The best example we came across was Cisco's quarterly *Top 400 Seller Board initiative. Senior corporate executives meet with sellers (client managers/client directors) for two-way conversations. In these meetings, sellers/ FLSMs learn about Cisco's development plans.*

Top management has the responsibility to develop firm strategy. But top management and sales leadership also have the responsibility to articulate that strategy, at least in broad strokes, throughout the salesforce. The salesforce is the firm's primary vehicle for communicating with customers. Customers planning their futures want to know about their suppliers' futures. For this and other reasons we just articulated, communicating firm strategy to FLSMs and their sellers is a crucial responsibility for senior managers and sales leaders alike.

 ## Evolve Sales Strategy

In previous chapters, we discussed evolution in environmental pressures, markets, customers, competitors. These changes demand evolution in firm strategy at several different levels, not least in sales strategy.

Sales strategy devolves most directly from market strategy. We noted in Chapter 2 that *market strategy concerns market segmentation*, the choice of which segments to target for effort, and how to address them—Table 9.1. Of course, the firm may address several different markets and/or segments, with different products/services.

At a general level, strategy focuses on allocating scarce resources to achieve objectives; *sales strategy concerns allocating scarce sales resources to achieve sales objectives*—typically stated in terms of sales revenues. The core sales resource to allocate is seller time/effort.

Design Sales Strategy

The starting point for allocating sales resources should be the several objectives that are part and parcel of the firm's various product/market-segment strategies. Indeed, negotiations among and between sales and marketing executives play a key role for integrating marketing and sales efforts. Based on sales objectives emerging from those discussions (or otherwise decided), sales leaders make sales time/effort allocation decisions.

In addition to marketing-driven sales objectives, sales leaders may base sales time/effort allocations on variables that do not enter (or enter only peripherally) into the product/market segmentation process. Variables like *customer industry, customer size,* and *current versus potential customers* are three favorites for sales leaders. (Such dimensions may be orthogonal to marketing-driven product/market-segment decisions.) These sales-based approaches to customer grouping may represent the best way for sales leaders to think about achieving sales revenue objectives, and hence making sales time/effort allocations.

Sales leaders should develop sales objectives both for marketing-defined product/market segments, and for groups formed from sales-leader dimensions just discussed:

- **Customer industry**—financial services, government, healthcare, manufacturing. Many salesforces set sales objectives and allocate resources for specific industries.

- **Customer size**—small, medium, large. Many firms break out key/strategic accounts for special treatment—separate sales objectives and resource allocations.

- **Customer status**—current, potential. Many firms set sales objectives, and allocate resources, separately for current customers and potential customers (including former customers—winbacks).

Sales leaders should make sales-resource-allocation decisions corresponding to the various market segments/sales-defined customer groups it decides to target. As a practical matter, because of the potential complexity for integrating product/market-segment objectives and sales-leader-defined customer group objectives, sales-leader-defined objectives often take effort allocations.

Sales leaders should not only develop sales objectives and resource-allocation guidelines for the salesforce as a whole, they must also *push allocation guidelines down to organizational control units*—zones, regions, districts (FLSMs), individual sellers. Since sales objectives and sales time/effort allocations are intimately related, FLSMs/sellers cannot meaningfully allocate time/effort unless objectives are clearly stated—both overall and for specific market segments/customer groups.

The firm has many alternatives for organizing the allocation of sales resources. At a high level, it can decide to outsource sales effort to one or more third-party providers—agents, brokers, independent representatives, distributors. Typical criteria for making this decision are control, flexibility, cost. (A major advantage of outsourcing the selling effort is that virtually all costs are variable. The firm only incurs costs when the outsourced supplier makes sales; fixed costs are low or zero.) Other firms employ their own salesforces, with organization structures that evolve over time.

Implement Sales Strategy

There are several ways to implement the sales strategy. Consider a small national salesforce with a national sales vice president (NSVP), several district sales managers (DSMs/FLSMs), and sellers.

Suppose also that the NSVP has determined that 60 percent of selling effort should be allocated to current customers, 40 percent to potential customers. The NSVP has three broad options for implementing the sales-resource-allocation decision:

- **Allocate at seller level.** Require each seller to allocate 60 percent time/effort to current customers, 40 percent to potential customers. FLSMs are responsible for ensuring compliance by sellers in their territories.

- **Allocate at district level.** FLSMs are responsible for the 60:40, current:potential customer time/effort allocation. FLSMs may specialize sellers by redefining territory boundaries and/or designing overlapping territories, based on opportunities and seller expertise. (An illustration of this approach is on p. 218.)

- **Reorganize the salesforce.** Reorganize the salesforce into two separate salesforces: One salesforce has responsibility for current customers; the other salesforce is responsible for potential customers.

Sales leaders must decide which approach to take; each option has pros and cons. The first two options involve implementing the sales strategy within the context of the current district-level sales organization. The second option permits significant reorganization within the district. The third option requires *sales transformation*—a new sales organization. The foregoing illustration is a relatively straightforward example of sales-strategy implementation in a simple sales organization. Many firms have far more complex problems to solve.

Regardless of which approach sales leaders elect, they must *clarify sales objectives for various levels (control units) in the sales organization*. Lack of clear objectives is frustrating and self-defeating for FLSMs/sellers. Consider what we heard from one FLSM:

> "Our fiscal year started two and a half months ago—we're almost at the end of the first quarter—and I still don't have a quota. Of course, my guys don't have theirs either."

Senior managers/sales leaders in this firm have created a situation that rendered FLSMs clueless. The FLSM went on:

> "I think it rolls down from our CEO to the COO [chief operating officer], then to the sales SVP, then works its way down to individual VPs, and eventually to the FLSMs and our sellers. I assume some VPs are negotiating with the SVP, or maybe the SVP is negotiating his total number with our COO. I just don't know what is going on, but it's pretty demoralizing."

We agree. Come on, senior managers/sales leaders—get it together; get with the program!

Ensure Value Propositions Are Compelling

In many firms, the responsibility for developing value propositions for product/market segments rests with marketing. Ideally, the marketing organization conducts marketing research, then works with R&D to ensure new products/services meet customer requirements. As discussed previously, once the firm has decided to enter a specific market, marketing has the responsibility to segment that market, select a segment(s) to target, then develop strategy for the target segment(s). Since, by definition, customer needs differ from market segment to market segment, so too do firm positioning statements, including value propositions. The value proposition is the heart of the market-segment strategy—Table 9.1.

The job of FLSMs/sellers is to take marketing-developed value propositions, and/or create new value propositions based on combinations of what marketing develops, and turn them into compelling offers for specific customers—*strategic acumen*. FLSMs and sellers face two problems:

- ▪ *Marketing develops value propositions for market segments, not for individual customers.* Hence, even the best marketing-developed value propositions must be *massaged* to satisfy the needs of individual customers.

- ▪ *Marketing is not typically involved with customers on a day-to-day basis.* Despite best intentions, marketing is removed from the daily challenges customers face. Not so for sellers/FLSMs. Whereas sellers/FLSMs may lack the broad view that marketing possesses, they face the reality every day of how marketing-developed value propositions interface with customer needs, problems, priorities, pain points.

A major responsibility of sales leaders is to collect and synthesize data from customers across the salesforce; these data should enter the product development process. By the same token, marketing executives have the responsibility to secure insight from the salesforce, so the value propositions they develop are embraced by FLSMs/sellers, and are likely to excite customers. Marketing should act consistently to avoid earning the salesforce perspective that they are just *ivory tower* types, with limited understanding of what customers really want.

In those firms where the boundary between sales and marketing is contentious, sales leaders may have to push strongly for their points of view to receive the hearing they deserve. Failure to push the salesforce perspective sufficiently can lead to disaster; recall from previous chapters the *square pegs into round holes* results in one U.S. technology firm. This firm's new product development and value proposition was a total failure. Sales leaders did not push hard enough. They failed in their responsibility. Sales leaders in general should ensure this type of situation does not occur. They must set FLSMs up for success, not for failure.

As another illustration of senior management failure, we heard from one FLSM about the travails he and a fellow FLSM faced:

> "Jason and I worked together for these last two years pushing our development, pushing every aspect of our company to get ready for this. Because we learned about it before the industry thought it was going to be a big deal. But, essentially nothing happened within our firm. Now competitors are talking about it, and we've lost the head start we were planning for."

Notwithstanding these failures, senior management often does a fine job. Consider the situation at one firm:

In one business of a major distribution firm, the customer relationship was *owned* by FLSMs and their sellers, not by the firm. The business was highly transactional; competitors did not differentiate their offers in any meaningful way. Hence, when an FLSM or seller left the firm (resigned or was fired), on average they took 50 percent of the business with them to their new employer.

The distributor developed a new value proposition focused on providing consulting advice to help customers expand their businesses. The firm backed up this strategic change by evolving the sales organization to make sales-resource-allocation decisions at the district level. One long-serving FLSM explained:

> "We put customers in three different categories, based on size—large, medium, small—but implemented the new strategy at my—FLSM—level. I have seven sellers reporting to me; each used to have their own sales territory, but I changed that. Now, my key account guy covers the entire district, focused on the largest customers. I split the district in two for middle-size customers, so two salespeople each focus on half the district's geography. I also split the district into four parts for sellers serving smaller customers. Sellers overlap geographies and travel time has increased, but we now better match specific customer types with my sellers' skill sets."

The sales leader took up the story:

> "The challenge is to evolve the relationship, so the customer puts trust in the firm rather than in individuals—sellers/FLSMs. We have to create stickiness, so the business stays with us. We are now doing things in the distribution system to improve our offers. We are working with customers to help them expand sales in their local markets—sort of like consulting. This approach offers very different value from just supplying products. The customer conversation bears no relationship to the traditional transactional sale."

In the previous section, we noted that at Cisco's quarterly *Top 400 Seller Board* initiative, senior corporate executives present the firm's development plans to sellers/FLSMs. But, at these meetings, Cisco's top brass also learns the reality of customers' experiences with Cisco products and solutions—the good, the bad, the ugly (if any). Cisco's sellers are not shy in passing on feedback to senior managers. The former director of this initiative told us:

> "These guys have full responsibility for very large customers, generally one-to-one relationships. I put the same top management cadre—CEO, operating committee, developers—in front of them as for our *Global Customer Advisory Board*. So, these sellers have the ability to influence major decisions—they are the internal voice of the customer. We also conduct mini-versions of this initiative in different countries around the world; after all, infrastructures differ from country to country."

Evolving the Value Proposition

More generally, senior firm management has the responsibility to provide the salesforce with compelling value propositions. In many industries, the environment faced by customers is growing increasingly competitive, complex, and difficult to navigate. Hence, pressures on the firm to be nimble, to innovate, and to develop new products/services are greater than ever. Some firms are doing a better job than others in providing sellers with compelling value propositions.

The sales leader at a well-known global electronics firm described how a critical insight led to a major change in the value proposition the salesforce offered to customers, and the impact on the salesforce:

> "At the time the firm was struggling with supply-chain issues—inventory turns were too slow; top management wanted to increase turns and hence increase ROI [return on investment]. In the salesforce, we realized our major customers had the same problem. Our sales strategy had always focused on high product quality, but we supplemented that message by focusing on our customers' ROI. No more *sell in*—stuffing the channel; but *sell through*—manage customer inventory. We trained our sellers in supply-chain management, brought in promotional experts to consult with customers, and changed compensation. Within a couple of years, critical seller metrics became based on *sell through*, not on *sell in*. Customers loved our shift in value proposition."

In the banking industry, reduced margins (driven by historically low interest rates) have caused many bank failures. Pressure on bank vendors to reduce prices is intense. One FLSM at a bank software vendor told us:

> "Some 200 banks closed in the U.S. last year. The intense price pressure we face led our two major competitors into significant layoffs; we managed to avoid that. Relatively few banks consider changing systems in any given year; four or five of us are going after that business. There's a limit to reducing prices, so we have developed some products that help banks earn revenues. That reduces the pricing pressure somewhat, and gives our guys a small advantage."

The message from this bank vendor is very clear—*enhance customer value.*

We noted in Chapter 2 that in many industries, it's no longer good enough just to deliver good *functional* benefits/values; the firm must also deliver good *economic* benefits/values. And, as we saw in both the Cisco and the SAP case studies, economic value requires more than just reducing customer costs/investments: Economic value must also involve customer *revenue enhancement*. A focus on revenue enhancement requires different data and analytic tools, for now the firm must learn about its customers' customers and about its customers' market challenges, and help figure out solutions. Senior management, and especially marketing, have a responsibility to *rethink* the fundamental underpinnings of the firm's value propositions.

Sales leaders also have a responsibility to develop new value propositions for FLSMs and their sellers, by integrating individual value propositions developed by marketing—sometimes by separate marketing organizations in different product groups/businesses. In most firms, marketing departments within individual product groups develop value propositions based on their particular products/services, then hand them over to the salesforce to sell. The salesforce may receive several of these value propositions from one or more product groups. Sometimes value propositions are independent of one another and, as noted in Chapter 6, product groups may compete internally for seller time.

But there may be opportunities for the salesforce to integrate several marketing-developed value propositions into a more all-encompassing value proposition for customers. In Chapter 2 we noted that some years ago, a leading healthcare firm produced several different products used in hospital operating rooms; each product line was the responsibility of a separate product group, and each group developed individual value propositions. In this firm, sales leaders designed an all-encompassing value proposition around the notion of one-stop shopping for hospitals. Unfortunately, this value proposition did not gain traction with the product groups.

But this example is a forerunner of the multimillion-dollar deal Philips Medical Systems (PMS) forged with Georgia Regents Medical Center (GRMC). As we noted in a Chapter 2 case study, PMS offered GRMC a comprehensive range of consulting and maintenance services, advanced medical technologies, and operational performance planning, at a predetermined monthly price. As part of the multimillion-dollar deal, PMS agreed to provide GRMC with rapid access to new equipment, new technologies, and educational resources. Included were imaging systems, patient monitoring, clinical informatics solutions, lighting, consumer products.

Sales leaders should assess value propositions coming out of marketing as *raw material* for their FLSMs/sellers. In the foregoing we see two attempts to form sales-driven value propositions, one that didn't work (leading healthcare firm) and one that did work (PMS). Many times, those value propositions will be well developed and ready for sellers to execute. Other times, value propositions will need work to fashion more compelling customer-need-satisfying offers. That is a sales-leader responsibility.

Bottom line: FLSMs must display good *strategic acumen*. They must work with broad value propositions developed in marketing and/or at high organizational levels, and make them come alive for specific customers. FLSMs' ability to accomplish this task is directly related to the quality of the value propositions they receive. Corporate management and sales leaders must be flexible and open to change; they have a significant responsibility to work with marketing or otherwise provide FLSMs/sellers with *compelling* value propositions.

 ## Make the *Right* Salesforce Organization Structure Changes

Earlier in this chapter, we addressed the evolution of sales strategy. Following agreement on sales objectives, sales leaders have the responsibility to *design*, then *implement* sales strategy. Since it is axiomatic in management theory that structure follows strategy, a core sales-leadership task is to decide if the sales strategy can be implemented within the current sales organization structure, or whether there should be a change. If an organizational change is called for, what should the new sales organization look like? We outline the various options:

- **Unspecialized salesforces**
  - *Unconstrained*—sellers sell all products to all customers, anywhere.
  - *Geographic*—sellers sell all products to all customers, in a defined geographic area.

- **Specialized salesforces**
  - By *product*—separate salesforces sell different products/product groups.
  - By *market segment*—separate salesforces sell to different market segments—industry verticals.

- By *customer type*—separate salesforces sell to different organization types. Example: health-care—payers, physicians, patients.

- By level in the *distribution channel* (important subset of customer type)—separate sales-forces sell to distributors and end-user customers.

- By *current buying relationship*—separate salesforces sell to current customers—farmers, and to potential new customers—hunters.

- By *customer importance*—a separate sales force has responsibility for key/strategic, and/or global customers.

Of course, many of these specialized salesforces are organized geographically.

When the environment is relatively stable, and the firm has designed and is implementing a successful sales strategy, there may be little need for organization structure changes. But if the environment is changing and becoming more complex, and consequently the firm's strategy is evolving, sales leaders should continually consider new organizational options. For FLSMs/sellers to perform at high levels, both sales strategy and sales organization design must be effective. After all, *the sales organization defines the nature of the selling task*. In this section we address several issues concerning sales organization transformation.

Unspecialized Salesforces

Two quite different types of unspecialized sales forces remain in wide use today. In **unconstrained** sales organizations, individual sellers sell all firm products to all customers, anywhere. This organization structure is very popular in the life insurance industry. In **geographic** organizations, sellers again sell all firm products to all customers, but within defined geographic areas. This approach has the benefit of low cost; many small and growing firms use this sales organization—it is probably the most common of all salesforce structures.

Specialized Salesforces

For firms with simple product lines offering limited customer benefits/values, well-trained sellers typically possess the required intellectual capital to do their jobs. They are competent to sell the firm's entire product line to all target customers. But when the firm's product line expands and/or customer needs become more complex and diverse, life becomes more difficult. Individual sellers are less able to satisfactorily represent the entire product line to all customers—the required bandwidth is just too great.

At some point, it may become necessary to implement a *sales organization transformation* (below). For example, the firm may split the single salesforce into two or more salesforces. Hence, the required intellectual capital required by an individual seller is much reduced, and selling ability increases.

A less-traumatic approach may be to add **specialists**. In this approach, each seller has access to a cadre of specialists. Specialists can be called upon when intellectual capital requirements exceed the seller's abilities. Specialists have various competencies—product, industry, market, solutions, technical, value engineering, workflow. Specialists exercise their supporting role via a variety of organizational arrangements.

Several sales leaders spoke about the value their specialists provided. The following observation was typical:

> "We rely pretty heavily on our specialists. They must deliver value to, and complement, our sellers. That means they are much more than just warmed-over sellers with a new title."

When intellectual capital requirements exceed the capacity of sellers, sales leaders must act. Adding specialists can solve the intellectual capital problem, but they can be expensive. Sales leaders employing specialists are aware of this problem:

> "In our bank, we have specialists to back up our sellers. But we deliberately minimize their headcount. We do not want the availability of specialists to be a crutch for our sellers. We know that specialists may be critical on some occasions—that's why we introduced them. But we also want our sellers to be competent to hold not only the first conversation, but the second conversation also. Then they can bring in the specialist if it's really necessary."

> "The account managers need to get the ball past midfield. They can't simply hand it off on their own 20-yard line."

> "When you put specialists in the deal you want them to add rocket power to the process, not act as training wheels for the account manager. Training wheels just add to cost without adding any value."

A more significant change than adding specialists is full-scale organizational transformation.

Sales Organization Transformation

In our research, we isolated several examples of firms that made sales organization transformations. In each case, the organization/structure change resulted from an evolution in sales strategy.

Higher Education. A higher-education software firm operated a traditional geographically organized salesforce. The firm earned revenues from repeat and new product sales to existing customers, and net-new sales to new customers. Overall, the firm had a 50 percent success rate with net-new opportunities. This performance was a problem. One FLSM told us:

> "When you're working with a prospect, it gets very intense. They take a lot of time and focus, and pull the account executive away from other work with existing customers in the territory. When you're chasing *net-new* business, it's very exciting; winning that new deal is really thrilling. To get new business from existing customers is a totally different ball game. You don't just show up and put out your hand for a new contract. It's a tough job to get a contract renewed, and to *sell in* our new products. We were not putting in the effort that was needed.
>
> "Our guys were putting in 50 percent effort for a 50 percent win rate on *net-new* deals—they are very competitive—that had a six- to nine-month sales cycle. Correspondingly, they were short-changing their regular clients. This was not a good

equation. So, the firm made the decision to split the geographically organized salesforce into two. One salesforce now focuses on current customers—*farming*; the second salesforce focuses on new customers—*hunting*. Each of these salesforces has its own geographic organization; six months or so after the first sale, the *hunter* hands over new accounts to a *farmer*."

Medical Technology. At a medical-technology firm, we saw a quite different organizational transformation—from two salesforces to a single salesforce. The sales leader explained:

"We used to have two salesforces, each addressing different markets—life sciences and molecular diagnostics. Salespeople reported through totally separate organizations and did not talk to each other, even if they had responsibility for the same customer. Indeed, in the vast majority of cases, these two salesforces were calling on the same macro-customer, just different individuals in different departments, depending on the products for which they were responsible. For any single macro-customer, we might have three or four sellers calling—the assigned salesperson plus specialists. So, we merged these salesforces and, of course, we cut the geographic size of sales districts and territories. Each salesperson was now responsible for the entire account relationship, and had many more touchpoints than in the previous organization."

This reorganization made the salesforce more efficient as regards travel time, but raised serious issues of salesforce competence—intellectual capital—in product groups for which a seller did not have experience. The sales leader continued:

"We did several things to make this integration successful. First, we standardized sales training around a single approach to opportunity management. This approach allowed us to address customers holistically, versus the previously fragmented approach of multiple salespeople; it was an important part of our change-management process. Second, we heavied-up on product training: diagnostics training for life sciences sellers, life sciences training for diagnostic sellers—not just the product mix, but also things like billing, insurance, reimbursements. Third, we formed several specialist groups to support our sellers and FLSMs; they are now responsible for the entire customer relationship.

"It turns out, we have done a sufficiently good training job. Sellers and FLSMs negotiate 90 percent of our contracts; they only bring in specialists for contract negotiations at the most complex 10 percent of cases. We have seen a lot of synergies by having one salesperson responsible for the account, especially at large accounts that buy the entire product line. We are penetrating deeper into the customer organization, focusing on their real problems, and getting to be seen as a partner, not just as a vendor."

Media. In a third example, we observed a major media firm facing an evolving media-buying landscape. This evolution resulted, in part, from fast-changing digital technology. The firm operated as a collection of distinct magazine brands, with separate salesforces and go-to-customer strategies for each brand. Sellers for various sales teams frequently called on the same customer individuals, but were unable to leverage benefits from the broad brand portfolio.

To address customization demands, and based on customer buying patterns, the firm created several *brand portfolios*. Sellers, organized by customer industry, now sold brand portfolios rather than individual brands. Sales leaders allocated resources—rules of engagement, sales playbooks, sales compensation plans—to enable FLSMs to execute the new strategy. The sales leader commented:

> "Our FLSMs were critical in translating the new strategy to the redefined sales teams. We tasked FLSMs with executing the new sales playbooks and ensuring the new rules of engagement were clearly understood. We gave FLSMs a large mandate to drive revenues within their own teams, but also to find and leverage opportunities across sales teams. We developed a process for FLSMs to share feedback and perspectives from customers to improve future strategy and structure iterations. We positioned FLSMs as leaders who would make the new strategy a reality."

Once again, we see how sales strategy and sales organization decisions set the stage for execution. Sales leaders have the responsibility to develop sales strategy and the related salesforce organization structure, so FLSMs and their sellers can execute. The structural decision has major implications for all aspects of building a competent, motivated, well-supported force of sellers, and the FLSMs that lead, direct, and manage them.

Cautions for Sales Organization Transformations. Notwithstanding the above success stories, organizational change is a tricky business, especially in the salesforce. In many cases, salesforce reorganization involves geographic relocation for at least several people. Long gone are the days when the family breadwinner (male) would simply accept relocation, uproot his family, and move to a new city. Today, many two-income families are much more location-inflexible, with more options given the more active talent market, especially for high-performing sellers.

Consider what occurred at Xerox some years ago. Xerox's salesforce was geographically organized; individual sellers had sales responsibility in specific geographically defined territories—a fairly classic sales organization structure. Incoming CEO Rick Thoman (former IBM chief financial officer) developed a new vision for the Xerox salesforce. Thoman viewed the seller's role as not just selling products, but as analyzing an entire customer business and identifying the best way to manage the complex flows of data, graphics, and images. Thoman believed salespeople could develop intellectual capital by industry; hence, a salesforce organized by industry would be a much more effective way of allocating sales resources. Territories in general would be larger than previously, but sellers would be more effective.

Good idea? Maybe. Indeed, we would typically applaud a CEO getting involved in the firm's sales activities. But Xerox made the change before sellers were trained in the new model, and did a poor job of switching accounts among sellers. Unintentionally, Xerox orphaned previously well-served customers. Many sellers resigned rather than relocate; competitors hired disgruntled Xerox sellers. Xerox fired Thoman after only 13 months on the job.

The issue regarding the classic Xerox disaster was not about the appropriate sales strategy, nor the sales organization design to implement the strategy. The key issue was how to *get there from here*. Organizational change, especially in the salesforce, is a big deal. Sales leaders should figure out the best organization structure to implement the strategy, but also have a very clear idea of what it will take to make the transformation work, without major disruption. Then, sales leaders should put in place the systems and management-change processes that make it happen.

Conflict among Salesforces

A particularly serious problem can occur when the firm goes to market with multiple salesforces, possibly via multiple **distribution channels**—for example, wholesalers and retailers. A serious problem occurs when both wholesale and retail sellers try to sell to the same customer. One sales leader commented:

> "Internal channel conflict is increasing. We have become so hungry for revenues, and we have so many hunters in the market. Our retail and wholesale sellers are cannibalizing each other. Sometimes it becomes very difficult to retain people. Retail sellers tell the wholesale side: 'You stole my deal.' Sellers do not take the view that *the firm* won the deal, not the competitor. Indeed, some sellers resent the fact that we try to sell through multiple channels. I try to keep that resentment factor down, but make sure the firm wins. I hear the good, the bad, the ugly—sellers are always worried about compensation, so I'm frequently dealing with requests for quota adjustments."

Sales leaders must become aware of these potential internal conflicts, and put in place systems and processes to avoid (or at least minimize) them. This sales leader seems to be managing the problem, but in general, sales leaders faced with a potentially dysfunctional situation must make adjustments to sales strategy and/or sales organization.

Sometimes these overlapping seller situations are less about compensation conflicts than they are about rational presentation of the firm to its customers. Indeed, deep organizational-design issues may drive salesforce conflicts.

Some years ago, Lucent (now Alcatel-Lucent, owned by Nokia) pushed authority and responsibility for product development deep in the firm. But getting business units to cooperate was difficult. As one illustration, several businesses developed variations of the *softswitch* telecommunications device. Each business unit had its own salesforce selling its product. One customer said:

> "I am confused on what Lucent is actually offering, because I've heard different descriptions of the same solution from different Lucent teams."[1]

Such conflicts are devastating for the firm's brand image, and highly wasteful of corporate resources. Sales leaders must take whatever steps are necessary to avoid such conflicts, and address them vigorously as and when they occur.

Territory Design

The key issue that sunk the Xerox initiative was territory design and change.[2] Most firms we interviewed told us that sales leaders and senior sales managers, not FLSMs, made territory-design decisions. Furthermore, territory design was infrequently modified, unless there was an overall organizational transformation. On such occasions, the firm should design new territories based on factors like balanced number of accounts per territory, account size (spending potential), likelihood of purchase, workload, travel time, and the like.

One structural change we observed in a few firms concerned *hunters* and *farmers*. To drive growth, these firms had taken a classic geographically organized salesforce and created two separate salesforces based on **current buying relationships**: salesforce A—*hunters* to secure new customers; salesforce B—*farmers* to build and strengthen relationships with existing customers.

At the higher-education software firm (discussed above), winning net-new business at a new customer was a multimonth process. One FLSM with salesforce B (farmers) observed:

> "For the guys [in salesforce A (hunters)], it's tough to walk away from those customer people. They get to know them really well throughout the six-month to one-year sales process. We're new to this so we'll have to see how this transition works out, and whether our guys [salesforce B] can pick up on the relationships our *hunters* have developed, and run with them. We have a very high year-to-year customer retention rate, so I'm pretty sure it's going to work. Along with this shift, we did a lot of territory realignment in my region, but this seems to have worked out OK."

A related form of separation occurs in fast-growing firms. As one FLSM put it:

> "There's not one FLSM who doesn't start with a hole in their business—we just keep growing. You could have a solid team of six, suddenly you've got a solid team of four, because they had to split sales territories. The split-conquer-divide mentality is not dead, especially if you're in certain hot growth areas."

Sales leaders must make territory split and combination decisions carefully, but the core message is very clear. Sales leaders should continually monitor sales performance, and make necessary territory-design adjustments.

The Vertical Dimension

Thus far in this section we focused on what we may call the *horizontal* features of the sales organization—the various organizational options noted above. Now, we turn to *vertical* issues—the responsibilities of various management levels in the salesforce hierarchy. The focus of this book is on the *front-line sales manager* (FLSM), but what about the job responsibilities of more senior sales managers—managers of FLSMs, sales VPs, and senior sales VPs? An information-services provider addressed this issue head-on. The sales leader commented:

> "We have a mixed bag when it comes to sales leaders and employee development. Because of this, we are making our processes more formal and more consistent—both agendas and responsibilities. We will hold people [FLSMs] accountable and tell them: 'Look, your job is people management; if you can't develop new people, you are in the wrong job.'
>
> "We are preparing job capsules—defining jobs with a lot of detail. Before, we never really defined what it meant to be a VP—how many direct reports; how many accounts; how much revenue under management; key talents and skills required; lines of communication; how to spend time. We just did all that.
>
> "In some places, I'm not sure we need a VP. Looking at the org chart, some VP positions just seem dumb. We have too many expensive 'chiefs' for the number of workers. In the past, we made too many intuitive staffing and structural decisions, instead of working under a strategic umbrella. At the end of the day, we'll have fewer VP positions, and some current VPs will be VPs no longer."

Reflecting our discussion of specialists (above), this sales leader was also concerned about various groups that supported FLSMs and their sales teams:

> **"Also, we've not done a good job designing optimal support structures and defining responsibilities."**

The issues this sales leader is addressing relate strongly to an assertion we made early in this book: FLSMs and their sellers earn sales revenues; senior salesforce members are non-revenue-generating overhead. And some senior salesforce members are very expensive.

That's why we advocate a *zero-based budgeting approach* to the sales management hierarchy. Sales leaders should be very clear about the value senior sales management positions add. Their core task is quite straightforward: Set sellers/FLSMs up for success. That is the acid test for any sales-management position. The sales leader at the British subsidiary of a U.S. technology firm told us:

> **"We did a thorough analysis of our salesforce. As a result of the findings, we removed an entire layer of salesforce management. This organization had grown up over time, but the value was just not there."**

Another vertical dimension concerns the underlying geographic basis for sales organization design. With a single exception, sales organizations we examined were organized geographically; indeed, our experience tells us this is the default option. The exception was organization by **customer importance**: In this design, the focus is on key/strategic/global accounts, regardless of geographic location. The customers may have regional, national, or global scope.[3]

In geographically organized salesforces, FLSMs (district sales managers [DSMs]) in contiguous geographic areas report to a regional sales manager (RSM). RSMs report to a national sales VP (NSVP). (In large sales organizations, RSMS may report to geographically organized zone managers.) *Question:* Is geography the best underlying basis for a sales organization? Certainly, geography makes all sorts of sense at the district level. After all, we expect FLSMs to spend several days per week in the field working with sellers. Geographic proximity is vital for FLSMs to do their jobs well.

But what about RSMs (and more senior sales managers, if any, up to the NSVP)? The geographic structure dates back to at least the 1950s, when travel was much more difficult than it is today. Now we have better roads, better cars, national air transportation; we also have much-enhanced communications—telephone service, Skype, video conferencing. Furthermore, with increased data availability, salesforce monitor-and-control systems are much improved. *Question:* Do FLSMs and their bosses need to be geographically proximate, or is there a better way? We believe this is a serious question sales leaders should pose for their sales organizations.

Suppose a sales organization comprises 25 districts. These district FLSMs report to five RSMs with geographic-region responsibility; the RSMs in turn report to the NSVP. An evaluation of the FLSMs reveals the following: 12 FLSMs can be relied on to achieve quotas—they do so year after year; 7 FLSMs are close to attaining quota, but rarely do so; 6 FLSMs don't get close to quota attainment—some are rookies.

How should these variously performing FLSMs be managed?

- **High performers** (12)—always achieve quota. Managerial prescription: Get out of the way. These FLSMs know what they are doing. They require minimal guidance. These FLSMs should report to a single RSM.
- **Moderate performers** (7)—almost achieve quota. These FLSMs need coaching to identify their weaknesses. They are close to succeeding, but they need to identify what is missing and work on it. Partition these FLSMs into two groups, each reporting to an RSM.

■ **Poor performers** (6)—nowhere near achieving quota. These FLSMs require considerable help if they are to get close to succeeding. Maybe some are candidates for transitioning out of their positions. Maybe the rookies are having trouble adjusting to their new FLSM position. Partition these FLSMs into two groups, each reporting to a RSM.

In effect, these new RSM responsibilities mirror (but more formally) those FLSMs who appoint sellers to be experts in some area or other—Chapter 6. We do not suggest this option as the only organizing principle for senior sales managers. Rather, we should like sales leaders to *think out of the box* and question the geographic basis for salesforce organization at higher levels than FLSMs. They should explore innovative alternatives that may work for their salesforces.

Outside and Inside

A final nontrivial topic for sales leaders is the balance between *outside sales* (on-the-road field sellers) and *inside sellers* (telemarketing/telesales). After all, inside salesforces are typically less expensive than field sales. Inside sellers may work in tandem with field sellers as members of sales teams—Chapter 6, or they may act more or less independently. Regardless, sales leaders must decide whether to invest in inside sales, the specific nature of the inside-sales role, and the extent of allocated resources.

One common challenge occurs when the firm examines its customer base and decides it would be more effective to serve smaller customers with an inside (rather than an outside) salesforce. The sales leader at a firm selling into distribution shared his story:

> "We used to address all our distributors with field sellers. We looked at our payroll, applied an 80:20 rule to distributors, and decided to serve many smaller distributors with inside sales. So, we cut our districts from 10 to 6; headcount dropped from 70 to 50. We focused our outside sellers on their top 40 distributors, rather than 90.
>
> "We had to hire people to work the phones and stay connected to the smaller distributors. It wasn't easy. We were slow to hire, so some small distributors were in limbo in the transition; they got upset and dumped on field sales—the lightning rod for distributor complaints. Some people lost their jobs through realignment. We had to replace [a person with] 14 years of experience with a new 30-day hire and hope they could grow quickly. It wasn't pretty, but we had to do it."

Field sales is expensive. Many firms are investigating alternative ways to leverage sales resources for interactions with current and potential customers. Sales leaders have a responsibility to investigate alternative ways to market. These include various uses of traditional telemarketing/telesales, as well as newer Internet *chat-based* options.

Developing sales strategy and designing the appropriate structure for the sales organization are critical sales-leader tasks. Neither of these jobs is easy. Certainly, caution is appropriate, especially regarding organizational-design evolution. Sales transformations are typically highly disruptive, particularly for long-time employees who may face many work and personal changes; some may end up leaving the firm. But in the face of environmental change, competitive challenges, and firm strategy evolution, inertia may ultimately be a more serious problem. If transformation is deemed necessary, sales leaders must ensure design changes are well planned and well executed—seamlessly, and with added value for customers.

What sales leaders must avoid are mismatches between sales strategy and the sales organization. When these elements diverge, sales leaders must grasp the nettle and make the tough decision to enact a sales transformation. Sales leaders must develop the *right* sales strategy, design the *right* organization structure, to meet or exceed sales objectives. After all, that's why we pay them (or should pay them) the big bucks.

Summary

Chapter 9 is the second of three chapters in Part II of *The Front-Line Sales Manager – Field General*. This chapter focuses on key management topics—*strategy* and *structure*. We address strategy at three levels. First, at *firm/business-unit* level, it's important that firm strategy be clearly articulated and communicated to FLSMs/sellers. Generally, customers want to know the direction in which their suppliers are headed; FLSMs/sellers should be able to articulate firm/business strategy, at least at a general level.

Second, *sales strategy*. Sales leaders negotiate sales objectives with senior firm managers. Then, sales leaders must make resource-allocation decisions so as to achieve those objectives. The key resource is seller time/effort: How much selling effort on this market segment? How much on that market segment? How much selling effort on new products versus existing products? How much selling effort on potential customers versus current customers? If sales strategy involves a major change, organization structure changes may be necessary.

The third strategic element concerns the *value proposition*. Marketing should develop a positioning statement for each market segment the firm decides to target. The heart of the positioning statement is the value proposition. Marketing-developed value propositions are the raw material sellers/FLSMs use to persuade customers to buy. Of course, sellers typically massage these value propositions to make specific offers to customers; they may also develop new sales-driven value propositions by combining value propositions developed by marketing. Regardless, *marketing-developed value propositions must be compelling*.

Salesforce organization structure is the final element in the strategy-structure paradigm. The sales organization drives what sellers/FLSMs do on a day-to-day basis, and should be consistent with the sales strategy. Many design options are available. The firm may add specialists to an in-place sales organization, or may undertake an organizational transformation. Organizational transformations may be necessary, but they require considerable skill and effort to complete effectively.

Sales leaders should also examine the requirements for senior sales managers—FLSM bosses and above—to ensure the structure and job descriptions provide the greatest bang for the buck. Finally, well-functioning field sales organizations can be very effective, but they are expensive. Sales leaders should evaluate telemarketing/telesales options and selling efforts via the Internet.

Endnotes

1. "The Genesis of a Giant's Stumble," *The New York Times*, January 21, 2001. In 2006, Lucent merged with Alcatel; in 2016, Nokia acquired Alcatel-Lucent. *Softswitch*—a component in software that connects telephone calls across a network or the Internet, like VoIP or Skype.

2. The classic article is W. Talley, Jr., "How to Design Sales Territories," *Journal of Marketing* (January 1961), pp. 7–13. For a more recent paper, A.A. Zoltners and P. Sinah, "Sales Territory Design: Thirty Years of Modeling and Implementation," *Marketing Science*, 24 (Summer 2005), pp. 313–331.

3. N. Capon, *Key Account Management and Planning*, New York: Free Press, 2001; N. Capon, D. Potter, F. Schindler, *Managing Global Accounts* (2nd ed.), Bronxville, NY: Wessex, 2008.

Chapter 10

Broad Leadership Responsibilities

Chapter 10 comprises three broadscale topics for consideration by sales leaders and other top management. Appropriate investment and effective decision making in these areas can improve front-line sales manager (FLSM) and salesforce performance. Topics to be covered—*build the brand*; *support and build customer relationships*; and *set the conditions for building a competent, well-supported, highly motivated salesforce*—Figure 10.1.

Figure 10.1 Broad Leadership Responsibilities

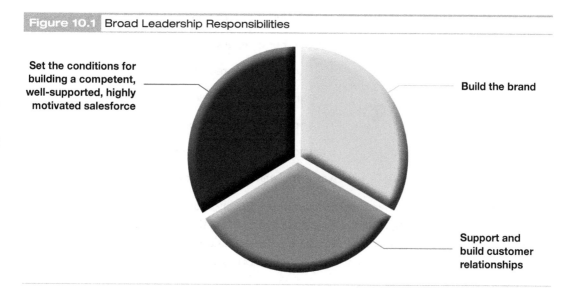

Set the conditions for building a competent, well-supported, highly motivated salesforce

Build the brand

Support and build customer relationships

 Build the Brand

In recent decades, the value of a firm's brands—corporate, business, product—has become recognized as a major contributor to shareholder value. Branding has evolved from a lower-level tactical concern to a matter of considerable strategic importance in many firms, mainly because of its relationship to *customer lifetime value*.[1] The firm's critical brand-building activity can be found at multiple levels of the firm, business, or product. As a practical matter, branding has two major related benefits for FLSMs and their sellers: It opens doors at customer organizations, and it enhances the firm's credibility.

Open Doors

For many years, McGraw-Hill ran various versions of an advertisement targeting B2B firms. Each version featured a different stern-looking purchasing executive, but identical copy:

I don't know who you are.

I don't know your company's customers.

I don't know your company.

I don't know your company's record.

I don't know your company's product.

I don't know your company's reputation.

I don't know what your company stands for.

Now, what was it you wanted to sell me?

McGraw-Hill was selling advertising space for its print publications. Certainly, advertising may be an effective means of creating customer awareness and building the firm's brand. But an important senior management responsibility is to use whatever brand-building means are available to pave the way for sellers/FLSMs. A stronger brand raises the chances of securing entry into customer organizations and scheduling appointments with key decision makers and influencers.

For many years, television advertising was largely the province of B2C firms. In recent years, many B2B firms have also entered this medium as a way of building brand (firm) awareness. After all, customer executives that sellers want to reach are also people who, when not at their jobs, watch television.

One sales leader lauded the behavior of his firm's senior managers and marketing organization in providing branding support for the salesforce:

> "We're not Coca-Cola, but we have a great brand, and we're great at marketing. Our CEO and the marketing group do a very good job of brand building. Marketing gets our name out there for anything and everything—CEO meetings with the president, or being on CNN about gay rights; and *Fortune* loves us. Customers know who we are, so we can get meetings that other firms cannot. Then it's our job to drive value in those meetings."

Enhance Credibility

The value proposition lies at the heart of the product/market-segment strategy, but a value proposition is nothing more than a promise. By offering value propositions, sellers/FLSMs make promises to customers. When customer personnel influence/make purchase decisions, they certainly take those promises into account. But, they must also assess the probabilities that the seller's firm will, in fact, honor those promises. **Brand equity** represents the *stock of credibility the firm commands* to raise those probabilities in customers' minds.

Building brand equity is, typically, a long-term challenge. Continually keeping promises to customers is probably the best approach, but a host of communications options are available to gain awareness—like appearing on CNN—along with other conventional methods. In addition, the Internet has spawned many digital advertising and social media options for the firm to raise awareness, enhance receptivity for its sellers, and build credibility. Social media strategies and easily navigable websites are critical elements in modern approaches to brand building. Amazon is the poster child for doing these things well, and has been highly successful in building a strong brand.

One sales leader described his firm's efforts:

> "We have a Facebook page but we scarcely post on it—just new technology, new products, new upgrades. But if you look at the page, most of it is customers giving their success stories. That's just great for our brand."

To be successful in brand building, senior management must invest the appropriate financial and human resources to develop and implement creative messaging. The goal: to construct the *right* messages, and use the *right* communication channels, at the *right* time, to break through the clutter and reach desired customer targets.

Senior managers can build credibility in their day-to-day activities, as they interact with individuals outside the firm. The sales leader at a fast-growing telecommunications firm made a comment that especially applies to this aspect of senior management responsibilities:

> "From a sales perspective, one of my themes is that *everybody is in sales*. You may not be necessarily selling the product, but you are always trying to sell your company."

Senior leaders can also help build the brand by developing a positive culture and providing sufficient resources to give excellent customer service. One FLSM told us:

> "Top management has developed a very supportive culture, going back over many years. The founder stated, 'If you take care of your employees, they will take care of the customers.' We run a very tight ship—no fat—but employees are very supportive of each other, and of our customers. Our service levels are the best in the industry; we are known for that. Our brand is our differential advantage."

Question for FLSM readers: Are your senior managers doing enough to build your brands—firm, business, product?

Questions for senior sales managers, sales leaders, and senior managers: Are you doing enough to build your brands—firm, business, product? What more can you do to support your sellers/FLSMs?

Support and Build Customer Relationships

Many people from different functions and at different organizational levels are involved in brand building, Senior management's role is to set clear objectives, clarify what is required, provide resources, then make sure plans are made and executed correctly. From a day-to-day perspective, when it comes to brand building, senior managers are *hands off*.

Support and build customer relationships requires more *hands-on* activity. This task may even start at the board of directors level, when sales leaders tap into the web of contacts that outside board members possess. Regardless, senior managers are typically much more involved in the selling process than board members are. Of course, senior management's direct involvement with customers helps build the brand, but potential positive effects go much deeper.

Opportunities for senior managers to interact with and build relationships with customers include events organized by the firm or by third parties. Perhaps the most common types of third-party events are trade shows and related conferences. One sales leader described his firm's experiences with trade shows:

> **"The big international trade show is coming up shortly. We will be meeting with customers for three days nonstop. All my sellers and FLSMs will be there, plus several of our senior managers. There will be a lot of meetings, so this is a great opportunity to nurture and build relationships."**

Sales leaders have many opportunities to build relationships at such third-party-organized events, but investing in firm-organized events may deliver better returns. We consider two broad types of formal events: large scale and small scale.

Large-Scale Formal Events

In large-scale formal events, senior management develops and implements concepts for bringing together executives from customer firms, along with sales leaders, FLSMs, sellers. Typically, the firm organizes these events on a periodic basis; firm executives provide some intellectual content and discuss future company plans. Customer executives offer feedback on firm performance. These events have beneficial effects for customer executives: They can discuss problems with peers, share best practice, test ideas. After all, life can be quite lonely for senior executives within a business organization. These events are a great opportunity to socialize, and a welcome change of pace for a couple of days. And, of course, along with work, the host firm may build in social events, sometimes including spouses/significant others.

Salesforce.com conducts large-scale formal events for current and potential customers, believing that the creativity and significant resources it invests puts the firm ahead of competitors. One Salesforce.com FLSM described the events, known as *Dreamforce*:

> **"We hold a dozen *Dreamforce* events at major cities around the world, but our main event is every fall in San Francisco. We started this user conference more than ten years ago with 1,300 attendees; now we host around 130,000 for four days of high-energy sessions. The 1,500 individual events include keynotes by thought leaders and industry pioneers. We analyze industry trends, and show current and potential customer teams**

our latest solutions. Attendees also get inspiration by networking with peers who are already Salesforce.com customers. We also provide *hands-on* training and certification, and even hold preconference training sessions. *Dreamforce* tailors content specific to many industries, roles, and company size—whether you're a company of five or a *Fortune 500* enterprise.

"We encourage FLSMs to have their salespeople invite current and potential customer personnel to *Dreamforce. Dreamforce* creates a very positive customer experience; attendees become part of the Salesforce.com *cult*. It's really pretty amazing. One time I sat at a lunch table with someone who'd attended an event in Amsterdam. He looked at me and goes: 'I'm not even sure why I'm here.' By the end of the event he turned around and goes: 'I get it; who do I need to talk to?'"

Several things stand out from this FLSM's report:

- Salesforce.com provides significant content to attendees—products, industry issues/trends—to improve attendees' *intellectual capital*.

- FLSMs and sellers are encouraged to attend with current/potential customers.

- Current customers help make sales to potential customers.

- Salesforce.com is doing something right: growth in attendees from 1,300 to 130,000 in ten years!

Another firm operates a similar large-scale event in higher-education software. One FLSM described a recent annual conference:

"We have a four/five-day national conference every year. We get close to 10,000 attendees. It's the largest higher-education conference in the world. We bring out the VPs from many different departments—they give us terrific support. The great thing is the ability to meet with so many customers. Our local user groups are really great, but this meeting gives us the ability to spend more time with each of our customers in a relaxed setting where they really open up."

Small-Scale Formal Events

FLSMs/sellers have the responsibility for building on the firm's brand image, educating customers about the firm and its products/services, and making sales. Senior managers can aid FLSMs by design-ing specific approaches to achieve these goals, and periodically be directly involved. One device used by several FLSMs we interviewed (discussed earlier) was *lunch-and-learn* sessions with current and potential customers.

Salesforce.com puts significant effort into these small-scale events as well as multithousand *Dreamforce* spectaculars. Recall from Chapter 5 what one Salesforce.com sales leader told us:

"The thing I cannot emphasize enough is that we sell a *branded experience*. That's pretty unique. The FLSMs who do really well here know how to leverage all the branded things we do, from *Dreamforce* to customer-on-customer dinner events—they are like nothing I've ever seen in the industry.

"At these dinners [sometimes lunch-and-learn sessions], we may have around 30 CIOs [chief information officers] or other C-Suite members, from current and potential customers. A couple of Salesforce.com execs get the session off, and then our guests just sell to each other—it's really unique. The core outcome is educational, but we also personalize our relationships. Our success is derivative of those FLSMs who can pull off those events.

"Successful FLSMs must know how to leverage company resources. The guys who do really, really well here do it year in and year out. And you see the rising stars coming through and learning how to do it. But I see guys fail, and fail miserably, when they try to do it on their own. They try to bring a very traditional sales model to their districts, and they just get blown up."

Customer Boards

Many firms put on various events for major customers. During these events, the firm receives feedback on performance, but executives also engage in conversations about future plans—for both firm and customers. Cisco follows a *listening-post* philosophy of keeping the firm's *ear to the ground*. Cisco is one of the leaders in these efforts.

Cisco operates several boards—*Global Customer Advisory Board, Partner Board, Top 400 Seller Board*. Senior Cisco leaders already spend significant amounts of time in the field in front of customers; these boards are, in effect, an extension of the firm's extensive customer focus. The former head of Cisco's *Global Customer Advisory Board* spoke with us:

"These are our largest, most complex enterprise and service-provider customers, plus a few public-sector customers. We get the CIOs/CTOs [chief technology officers]; these guys have accountability to their functions and businesses, and they hold the purse strings. We put them in front of our CEO, the operating committee, and the guys who build our products/services/solution sets—we can really test out our assumptions, and scope out opportunities and challenges. We assess how our strategy and investments might align to achieving the business outcomes customers are seeking—that's not always easy to do. The advisory board has given us a real sense of clarity around where we need to move faster, and what we need to do differently. We know this is going to be a journey but, to the extent we do a better job, that also benefits our customers.

"In the short run, customers can learn our *point of view* on industry direction. These meetings are customers' opportunity to test their assumptions about Cisco and its products/services/solution sets, and figure out what capabilities they need going forward. From the customer perspective, these meetings are very high touch with our developers. We operate a similar program with our channel partners."

Cisco is not the only high-tech firm that believes in customer advisory boards; Oracle similarly places heavy emphasis on working with customers in an advisory-board format. Said Oracle's sales leader:

"In this company, we have recruited customers to over 400 advisory boards covering products, functions, and specific industry needs. These boards give participants a voice

and a vote on what's really important to their company and their industry, and what they want to see baked into the software."

In the most advanced customer-centric firms, senior managers spend considerable time in the field with sellers/FLSMs, interfacing with customers. Customer boards are, in effect, a means of upping that commitment. These boards are a powerful way of presenting the firm to customers, and hearing about customer expectations and firm performance firsthand. When appropriately designed and managed, customer boards offer significant value to the firm and customers alike.

Time Commitment

FLSMs are responsible for the major managerial tasks concerning sellers. But there is no reason why more senior sales managers/sales leaders should not also spend time in the field with customers. Sometimes this sort of intervention is required—a big deal is in the works, or an issue must be resolved at a level more senior than the FLSM. On these occasions, sales leaders should not hesitate to be involved, using the authority of their position to move the firm's agenda forward.

But these occasions should not be the only time sales leaders get involved with sellers and FLSMs. Consider what a sales expert with a national reputation told one of the authors (NC) recently:

> "Early in my career, I was a rookie salesperson for a major chemical company; I suppose I had been with the firm for two or three years. I got a call from the national sales manager; he was four or five managerial levels above me. I wondered what I had done wrong. He said, 'I'm going to be in your territory next Thursday for a morning meeting, but I have the afternoon free. Why don't you set up a couple of customer meetings, then you can drop me off at the airport, so I can catch an evening flight.'
>
> "That's what happened. I took him to two of my major customers; they were delighted. It was great for my relationships with them. But what I remember most was the time we spent together in the car after those customer meetings. We had real conversations about selling, and I gained some real insight that's stayed with me all these years."

This anecdote is not meant as an argument for sales leaders to spend a lot of time traveling with sellers, although we have no problem with sales leaders gaining firsthand knowledge of field activities. But it is a reminder of the value sales leaders can offer individual sellers. If the opportunity arises, sales leaders should seriously consider spending some time in the field. Not only will they add value at customers, and impart some wisdom to sellers, they may also learn something by spending time in the trenches!

But sales leaders should be aware of potential downsides to such activities, and work to avoid them. As one sales leader shared with us:

> "We, that is the sales leaders, want to be available to all our sellers to visit with customers, especially when they're trying to persuade them to choose us versus someone else. In some cases, that is intimidating to sellers. Some may resist. They say: 'If the senior guy comes, sees me make a pitch, and concludes I didn't do that right, it could be threatening.' That's not what we want; we want to be a resource, not get in their way. We just want to win the deal."

Frankly, we don't have a lot of sympathy for sellers who take this position, and neither should sales leaders, nor these sellers' FLSMs. To be coached is part of the deal, but sales leaders should also foster a culture where mistakes are tolerated, at least once.

Executive-Sponsor Programs

A more formal time commitment for both sales leaders and the entire senior management cadre (including C-Suite executives), concerns *executive sponsorship*. These programs enable the firm to broaden customer relationships. Generally, executive sponsorship concerns the firm's major customers, but may also encompass fast-growing smaller customers with high potential. In executive-sponsor programs, senior executives take on a level of responsibility for individual customers, in addition to their regular day jobs. Because of their stature and position in the managerial hierarchy, executive sponsors can make commitments on the firm's behalf that neither individual sellers nor FLSMs can make.

The growth of executive-sponsor programs is testimony to the recognition, by senior management, of the importance, for the firm, of securing revenues from customers. Mostly designed for key/strategic/global account programs, executive sponsorship can be a valuable resource for sellers in building customer relationships. Executive sponsors may also serve as escalation points when FLSMs experience organizational blockages in securing company resources.

We should be clear: Executive sponsorship should not interfere with the regular sales managerial hierarchy but, rather, be an additional resource to support sellers/FLSMs. Indeed, in the best-run executive-sponsor programs, it is clearly understood that despite their high position, senior managers *work for* sellers/FLSMs when occupying the executive-sponsor role.

As discussed in Chapters 4 and 6, it should come as no surprise to readers that executive involvement with customers can vary markedly from one senior executive to another. Some senior executives believe interaction with customers is *not my problem*. Managers holding this perspective believe the salesforce should just do its job; senior management involvement is unnecessary. If there's a salesforce problem, the answer is straightforward—replace personnel. Furthermore, actual involvement with customers can be decidedly negative when senior executives act as *loose cannons* (seagulls). We strongly favor senior executives acting as *growth champions*, but recognize value in the *deal maker* and *social visitor* roles. (Chapter 6, pp. 149–153, has an extensive discussion.)

Former Cisco CEO John Chambers exemplifies the growth champion role; reputedly Chambers made 200 CEO calls in just a few weeks using Cisco's *Telepresence* video-conferencing system. Salesforce.com CEO Marc Benihoff seems to act as both growth champion and deal maker. One FLSM described his experience with Benihoff:

> "Our CEO often steps in to support strategic deals. For example, he structured a couple of deals with Coke; he is quite involved with that account. He definitely helps you think through things very differently. I've been in more than a half-dozen meetings with him; he always challenges your thinking. That is good."[2]

There are, of course, other ways for senior executives to assist in the sales process, without going so far as formal assignment of senior executives to customers. One alternative is assignment of senior executives by opportunity size. Firms with a solid pipeline process identify opportunities early. Over and above the FLSM's assistance to the seller, they may assign senior executives to opportunities that reach a certain *deal potential* revenue threshold. Said one sales leader:

> "One of our biggest weaknesses is that sometimes our sellers are afraid to put opportunities into the pipeline where everyone can see them. Big potential deals are like honey to bees; all sorts of our people want to get in on the action. The seller and FLSM lose control, and possibly quota attainment. But we hold sellers and front-line managers very accountable to bring the *right* resources, for the *right* deals, at the *right* time. We actually assign senior executives as sponsors on specific opportunities."

Innovative Processes

Alcoa goes one stage further in building customer relationships: seeding current and potential customers with believers in its products. Consider what a senior Alcoa manager told us:

> "In our aerospace system, senior Alcoa executives spend extensive time creating an environment to make customers open to innovation. We interact with the top universities that train aerospace and aeronautical engineers. We help design curricula, teach classes, have design contests, and offer internships and jobs. We show students and faculty the latest and greatest in metals. These kids are going to be designing airplanes over the next 20 years—they know Alcoa, they know metals, and they feel pretty good about it. We also do opinion work with other influential groups—airline executives, pilots, mechanics, and frequent travelers. We are creating a very favorable climate for demanding metallics in airplanes, particularly Alcoa metallics."

Relatedly, world-leading management consulting firm McKinsey expects newly hired consultants to stay about six to ten years with the firm. McKinsey is quite willing to lose consultants to high-level jobs at its customers, but works hard to maintain contact, in part via an alumni magazine and alumni events. When the former employee's new employer wants advice, which consulting firm will it likely call?

For both sellers and FLSMs, building customer relationships is a crucial part of their jobs, as they strive to improve sales performance. Senior management can play a major role by constructing and funding events that enhance the relationship-building process. They can also raise success probabilities by personal involvement and developing relationships with high-placed customer executives.

Set the Conditions for Building a Competent, Well-Supported, Highly Motivated Salesforce

Building a competent, well-supported, highly motivated salesforce is a critical challenge for sales leaders. Populating the salesforce with a cadre of high-quality FLSMs (the topic of this book) is part of the answer. The other part is putting in place the conditions to allow those FLSMs to be successful. This task is a continuing challenge for sales leaders, as the selling job continually evolves. The firm must correspondingly evolve its sales strategy and sales organization structure—Chapter 9—

in response to changing markets, and customer needs, priorities, problems, pain points. Consider what an FLSM told us regarding new decision-making units (DMUs) and decision-making processes (DMPs) in the telecommunications industry:

> "Sellers of the past were formerly engineers; they knew a lot about our *boxes*—speeds-and-feeds. Some were very good at building relationships—the key to success. Today, the industry has evolved; customers are looking for solutions. So, we have to go beyond speeds-and-feeds; we have to understand what's driving customer decisions—service velocity, cost savings, revenue generation, or transforming the network? We must learn about their problems, then figure out how we can help create an overall solution. We can't just sell the box—it's just a commodity. Now we sell services, wireless solutions, and software. We create solutions that improve all of those areas. Our sellers used to figure out deals on a napkin at a bar. Today, it's very different: different value propositions, different decision makers and influencers, different decision processes."

The selling job may be especially challenging when major shocks occur, like corporate mergers and acquisitions. One FLSM recounted such a situation:

> "The salesforce we merged with was a dud. They had managers that were not motivated, and individual sellers that didn't really know how to sell as their customers evolved. The organization was tired and lacked motivation. Sellers spent a lot of time just trying to solve customer problems, but not trying to sell them anything.
>
> "Our current sales leader came in with a new sales model, and he got rid of people. Almost all the sales managers left, mostly on their own. They saw the *writing on the wall*, that the bar was being raised big time. And he started getting the right people. He introduced a classic seven-step sales process to which we all must adhere, and shaped up our use of data so we have better visibility to what's going on. He transformed the entire sales organization from one that didn't know how to qualify, didn't really know how to sell, and lacked motivation, into an organization that believed there was hope, and opportunity to be successful."

Each salesforce requires an *effective system* for building and maintaining a highly competent, well-supported, and motivated salesforce. Critical elements are *recruiting, selecting, developing, supporting, rewarding, recognizing, motivating,* and *retaining high-quality sales talent.* Developing, leading, directing, and managing such a system is a core sales leadership responsibility. Of course, sales leaders should keep the pulse of their sellers via regular managerial processes, including 360 feedback and skip-level reviews. In this section, we touch on each of these core elements.

Recruit and Select Sales Talent

Recruitment options range across a spectrum from decentralized to centralized (detailed in Chapter 2). The extremes are:

■ *Decentralized.* The FLSM is more or less totally responsible for recruiting and selecting sellers. Recruiting is an ongoing task. Recruitment is part of the FLSM's job description. The FLSM continually interviews potential candidates—internal and external—building a *bench* (inventorying sellers) on which to call when a vacancy opens up. In this model, the sales leader plays a hands-off role, merely giving final approval and ensuring the appropriate HR boxes have been checked. But, on an ongoing basis, size and quality of the bench may be built into MBOs (management by objectives) for individual FLSMs.

- **Centralized.** Sales leadership, working with HR, takes full responsibility for recruiting and selecting sellers. The rationale is that FLSMs should implement the sales strategy; the firm will provide FLSMs with the tools—including sellers—so they can do that job. In centralized systems, FLSMs are typically presented with *approved* candidates they may accept or reject. The sales leader at a global package-delivery firm talked about his firm's new centralized system:

  > "We've taken our FLSMs out of the hiring process. They have the final yea or nay decision, but we outsourced all the interviewing, testing, and screening. That's simplified their lives, one less thing to worry about."

Most firms operate somewhere between these decentralization and centralization extremes.

Develop Sales Talent

Superior recruiting and selecting sales talent are important responsibilities for sales leaders, but ongoing development is equally crucial. As we note frequently in this book (and earlier in this section), the selling job continues to evolve along with requirements for enhanced intellectual capital—*stocks* and *flows*. Hence, sales leaders should ensure they pay continuous attention to developing sales talent. There are several specific reasons:

- Great sales talent can address increased customer demands and customer evolution in DMUs and DMPs.

- Great sales talent drives the firm to meet and exceed customer expectations; it's an important source of hard-to-replicate differential advantage.

- Investment in developing sales talent is a powerful means of retaining high-performing sellers; hence, more consistent value delivery to customers.

- Improved sales talent enhances firm options for future FLSM and senior management positions, and helps drive a firm-wide external orientation.

The financial return that firms may earn from investing in training sales talent can be impressive. According to one expert:

> "Our studies show we secure a 3.9 percent return for our investment in capital items versus an 8.5 percent return for human capital investment. Essentially, we have more knowledgeable sellers. What drives this finding? They command higher prices and deeper customer loyalty,"

And from another sales leader:

> "Quite simply, we won't get our target return on investment if the money we put into new product development is not complemented by investment in the resources needed to sell them."

Developing sales talent commences with a good *onboarding* process. Most firms have sales training programs for newly hired sellers; often these programs are quite extensive. One FLSM shared his firm's process:

> "We have invested in an excellent training team. Our onboarding process takes several months. We are teaching skills, but also inculcating our company culture—how we approach the market. So, we have product training, sales-skill training, online training. Then they do buddy/mentor training. They'll be working with their FLSMs, and they potentially come back to the classroom for more training. And this is all part of the onboarding process."

Generally, sales-talent development follows a hierarchical model—onboarding/entry-level training for new hires, then additional training as the nature of the sales job evolves. Entry-level positions are varied—telesales, web-enabled, combination web-enabled/telesales, field sales. There has been a substantial recent uptick in digital-enabled positions, not only for targeting small and medium-size businesses, but increasingly for decision makers/influencers in large corporate customers. Of course, each of these sales jobs requires a different type of training.

Successful sellers frequently progress through different types of selling jobs—with a focus on attributes/features versus benefits/values versus customer solutions; selling to individuals at customers versus selling to multiple-person DMUs; individual selling efforts versus managing a sales team with solid-line and/or dotted-line relationships. Different types of selling jobs require different intellectual capital stocks and flows. Hence, the firm should ensure training is available for sellers as their sales jobs evolve, and as they change jobs. Training may be internal or provided by external experts, and may be offered at the firm or at off-site conference centers—in part to avoid day-to-day distractions. Increasingly, self-study online options are attractive.

Firms that are really serious about developing sales talent not only provide extensive training for sellers, they examine sellers on retention of learning, via examinations. Some firms are even moving toward certifications. Training is not just an interesting, even enjoyable, break from the regular day-to-day work experience. Learning to be a better seller (and better person) is a serious business; sales leaders should ensure they get a decent return on their training dollars.

Consider the perspective of the sales leader for a global package-delivery firm:

> "We want to make sure our sellers are well-educated on all our products, services, and solution designs (especially considering safety and security). We take them through diversity and inclusion training, so they are better citizens and better human beings. Then they interface better with the many people they work with, inside and outside the firm. We are looking at certification—tests and grading—to elevate seller status."

The best sales-talent-development programs operate in the context of a career-path framework that provides career options for sellers. Sales leaders should offer sellers the ability to acquire real skill and experience, and provide opportunities for upward mobility, both as potential FLSMs/senior sales managers/sales leaders and as sellers. The firm should make clear what options are available, and what it takes to get there.

Although promotion into management ranks is a goal for many entry-level hires, sales leaders should be clear that status and take-home pay are not inexorably linked to position in the management hierarchy. Rather, a career as a professional seller is highly valued and can be highly compensated. Indeed, sales leaders should create a professional sales-career track, in part to retain high-quality sales talent. As noted, the professional sales ladder requires regular learning and skill acquisition to enhance the seller's intellectual capital.

In the context of building a competent, well-supported, highly motivated salesforce, corporate management should demonstrate respect for the sales function, and communicate that respect throughout the firm. Great companies love their sales organizations. Top managers should speak of sales as *critical to a customer-focused strategy*, not as a *necessary evil*. Enlightened executives understand sellers' importance in serving customers, growing revenues, and creating sustainable differential advantage.

Notwithstanding the effort and resources sales leaders put into recruiting, selecting, and developing sellers, at the end of the day, those sellers must be successful. They must perform at high levels, and be accountable for their results. One FLSM summarized his experience and perspective:

> **"The people I have seen fail do not feel accountable if something is going sideways, if something is not going well with the customer. They are sort of laissez-faire about it. This firm has a no-lose attitude; someone who buys into that attitude is successful."**

Support Sales Talent

Sales leaders can do many things to support the selling effort. Simple things like ensuring sellers' commission checks are correct and arrive on time can be very important. Introducing more complex, yet more effective, systems and processes also has an important role to play. As one software sales leader told us:

> **"During the past 24 months, we've totally redone the plumbing; we have been advancing all the tools we could, like sales enablement. If a prospect or customer has a question the salesperson can't answer, the seller can just go into our knowledge system and post the question. There is someone assigned to that product/service/technology who will get back to them with the appropriate response. We also implemented a new system for contracts and proposals. This system empowers the reps through corporate-margin-related-discounting guidelines and other processes; they work quicker and smarter, and don't have to check so much with their FLSMs."**

Another sales leader focused on what he called *evidence-based selling*. He told us:

> **"It's one thing for our sellers to present customers with a solid value proposition that works for them in their business. But it's quite another to back that up with examples of successful implementations at other customers. So, we moved to *evidence-based selling*. We *collect* stories from satisfied customers; we *distribute* those stories on our website— easily searchable by sellers; and we continually *refresh*—to keep things current, and to encourage our sellers to keep checking the website and staying up-to-date."**

Whereas some firms have made these sorts of investments, other firms have held back, causing significant unhappiness for some sales leaders. The view one sales leader expressed was typical of these frustrations:

> "We do not have enough tools for our FLSMs and sellers. We are missing out today, and are a ways from where we ought to be. When we're with a customer, we can be in a reactive mode within minutes or seconds. For example, rather than give a price, we have to take it to a pricing specialist; it just takes too long."

Market Information. By virtue of spending long periods of time with customers, sellers pick up all sorts of information about marketplace activities—customers, customers' customers, competitors, environmental factors. Individual sellers see only data concerned with their territories. Effective FLSMs develop systems and processes for sharing information (collected by sellers) in district-wide meetings, to enhance seller perspectives beyond their specific territories.

Even more powerful are firm-wide systems and processes that focus on these and related types of data. Such systems and processes source, filter, select, sort, combine, and distribute information submitted by individual sellers across the salesforce. These information digests, prepared regularly, can be highly valuable to individual sellers and their FLSMs. When combined with independently secured market and competitive intelligence, sellers and FLSMs have powerful weapons to wield in their territories and districts.

Many firms use audio- and video-conferencing approaches to allow geographically dispersed individuals to access information content and selling tools, and to hold meetings at a distance. Tablet computers also provide access to both the latest sales tools and deep expertise, and the ability to deploy these at the point of customer contact.

Corporate can also develop support organizations to free up time for selling. Two FLSMs provided their perspectives:

> "We are very fortunate. Our sellers only have to sell. We have a sales support organization that does all the RFPs, all proposals, all contracts, all product presentations, all everything."

> "We have very aggressive customers who were continually calling our sellers to find out the status of their orders. My guys were spending a lot of time calling the plant to check. It really took away from their selling effort. So, we put in a web-based system, so customers could check status themselves. That is really great, and has made my guys much more efficient. This system has also improved customer satisfaction."

Competitive Information. One area where many firms, and hence sellers and FLSMs, are deficient is competitive intelligence. It was clear from our interviews that many firms could do better. One sales leader expressed a common view when he lamented:

> "We do not do a good job of competitive intelligence; our marketing guys are doing other things. If a competitor comes out with a new product, we do not usually know about it. We only find out when salespeople hear about it, if a salesperson attends some presentation or other. We really do not have any marketing/industry people that stay on top of the competition. We don't have a budget for that."

The sales leader's narrative clearly represents a problem. The seller's job is to offer customers superior benefits/values to those offered by competitors, and hence secure differential advantage. That task is rather difficult if the seller does not know what the competitor is offering! Reasons for this failure are captured by the sales leader's "our marketing guys are doing other things," and "we don't have a budget for that." But perhaps we should not lay all of the blame for this state of affairs at senior management's door.

Questions for our FLSM readers:

- Do you know the names and backgrounds of competitor FLSMs in your districts?

- How many of your sellers can answer a similar question about competitor sellers in their territories?

- Can you or your sellers articulate the sales strategies those competitor FLSMs and their sellers are executing?

Fortunately, there is a way to address the competitive-intelligence problem. Marketing can be involved, but sales leaders can design and operate a process solely within the sales organization. One sales leader explained her firm's approach, introduced in Chapter 4:

> "We operate a *shadow system* for securing competitor intelligence. We have four or five competitors that are worth worrying about. I have assigned each of these competitors to one of my regional sales managers [RSMs]. In addition to their regular day jobs, they *shadow* these competitors. Essentially, they build information networks throughout the salesforce—other RSMs, some FLSMs—and some folks in marketing. They also receive web alerts when *their* competitor takes some action, posts financials, and so forth. The shadows provide reports quarterly, as well as *flash* reports if anything critical has occurred. All reports go to the RSMs, and to FLSMs to share with their sellers. It's extra work for the RSMs, but we get a lot of value."

Two of the more recent developments in supporting sales talent are sales enablement—Appendix 9, and sales playbooks—Appendix 10.

Provide Worthwhile Sales Leads

How many times have you heard marketing executives complain: "We provide the sales force with scores of leads, but they don't follow up on them"? How many times have you heard sellers and FLSMs say: "We get all of these leads from marketing, but they're never any good"? These statements are all too frequent.

Sales leaders and marketing executives must solve this problem. Presumably, marketing wants to do a good job and deliver valuable leads; the salesforce wants good leads also. There are likely three causes for the salesforce receiving insufficient valuable leads:

- ***Insufficient numbers of leads.*** Marketing's job is to provide leads. Marketing has many tools—advertising, promotional events, trade shows are traditional methods. And, increasingly, digital methods are coming into play. Good website design and tracking website visitor behavior are newer methods that offer considerable promise.

■ *Ill-developed good leads.* Marketing and sales must develop an agreed-upon set of criteria that potential opportunities must satisfy before being passed to the salesforce. Marketing must both secure leads, then validate via the agreed-upon criteria. When marketing sends leads to the salesforce, frequently *less is more.*

■ *Inappropriately delivered leads.* Sounds pretty obvious, but many firms have several sales-forces, each with different objectives and responsibilities. Marketing must ensure that the *right* leads reach the *right* FLSMs/sellers in the *right* salesforces.

Summing up the problem, one sales leader we talked to offered his perspective:

> "Receiving high-quality sales leads is highly motivating for sellers; receiving lousy leads is not! It's just a timewaster. Sales leadership and marketing must work together to make the lead generation and delivery process positive for sellers."

Build a Firm-Wide External Orientation. More than any other functional head, sales leaders understand the importance of a *corporate-wide external orientation.* Sales leaders know viscerally that the salesforce must earn revenues for the firm to make profits, survive and grow, and enhance share-holder value. Sales leaders know that the core requirement for the firm is to satisfy evolving customer needs, in the face of competitors trying to do the same thing. Sales leaders also know their authority is limited: Sellers make promises to customers, but delivering on those promises requires commitment from many individuals in a variety of functional positions within the firm. Support from other func-tions is important throughout the selling process, but particularly in the *design* and *implementation* stages of the selling process:

■ *Design*—to explore the possibilities of satisfying customer needs.

■ *Implementation*—to make sure the firm follows through on promises sellers make to customers.

To ensure the salesforce receives necessary support from across the firm, each organizational member must internalize the importance of satisfying customer needs, *no matter what their partic-ular job happens to be.* How to achieve this state of affairs? Senior sales leaders cannot do this alone; they require the support of other functional heads. But most of all, the external-orientation message that customers are the source of all revenues, and that without revenues *no one gets a paycheck,* must come from the top of the organization—CEO, chief operating officer, and the entire executive suite.

Hopefully, these top executives feel the same way about customers as sales leaders do. Regardless, a major sales-leader task is to ensure that information coming from the top of the organization—speeches, written communications, leadership actions, monitor-and-control systems—emphasize this core message: "Sales revenues are critical; for our firm to be successful, all organizational members must support our sellers as they strive to do their jobs and provide all organization members with their livelihood."

Not only should organizational members understand the importance of satisfying customer needs, they should also realize some customers—key/strategic/global accounts—are more import-ant to the firm than others. The firm should treat these customers accordingly. The sales leader of a major scientific instrument firm reported on a lesson his firm learned about communicating and clarifying information about its most important customers throughout the firm. He told us:

> "At this very important customer, we believed we were the sole-source supplier for an expensive hand-carried analyzer. Engineers would just point the machine at a physical object and press a button—the readout would report the constituent elements. But once in a while, a machine would be dropped or fall off a desk; then the customer sent it back to our shop for reconditioning—that was standard practice.
>
> "One day, we had a high-level customer meeting that involved a tour of the customer's plant. As we were coming back through their offices, we were surprised to see several of our main competitor's products. When we questioned our customer, they essentially said to us: 'Your products are the best, but we often have problems with reconditioning. Sometimes the machines come back right away; other times we have to wait several weeks. So, we decided to diversify our risk by getting a second supplier.'
>
> "Right away, I got in touch with our reconditioning department. It turned out, they operated a FIFO [first in, first out] system. That was the reason for the variable response times. I spear-headed an agreement to prioritize damaged machines from our most important customers. That took care of the problem."

Reward and Recognize Sales Performance

Sales leader for a manufacturing firm:

> "What's really important around here is that we get the R&R right—recognition and reward."

Recruiting high-quality sales talent, and securing high performance from that talent—well recruited, well selected, well developed, well supported—is a critical sales-leader responsibility. Two of the primary tools in the sales leader's arsenal are to *reward and recognize*.

Reward. Clearly, financial rewards are a big issue for attracting competent sellers, motivating them, and securing high levels of sales performance. Financial rewards also play a major role in seller retention (below). According to our interviewees, seller take-home pay is shifting toward greater pay at risk (incentive compensation). For sellers, risk pay is typically in the form of commission and/or bonus, based on quota attainment. Of course, sales compensation is generally a hot-button issue, for the sales organization and for HR departments. Regardless, managing the sales compensation system is a key responsibility of sales leaders. If they believe modifications are required, they should push strongly for those changes.

One sales leader expressed his frustration; he also clarified that sales leaders and HR departments do not necessarily see eye to eye:

> "This is a good company to work for, so we have very low attrition throughout, not least with FLSMs, so it's tough to get promoted. Right now, our pay structure is 80:20—salary:

bonus—with a four-times component on the 20 percent. So, a seller who has a good year and handily beats quota can do really well. I want to get more leverage—60:40—but that is a big change and will take a lot of work internally. Also, we pay quarterly, so if a seller maxes out before the end of the quarter, s/he doesn't have a lot of incentive to keep working hard. I want to shift that to pay annually, but I'm getting pushback from HR. But I shall win, and we'll probably do a transition."

Quarterly pay cycles are common, but other firms are far more commission- and bonus-based than this firm. One FLSM assessed the salary portion of seller compensation:

"Our salespeople could not live on their salaries, but we pay a great commission. Our *hunters* work with the same compensation structure as our *farmers*, but they also have a monthly recoverable draw. That keeps them in pizzas and hamburgers."

In most salesforces, the key driver of take-home pay is *output* performance, typically based on sales revenues versus quota. In some cases, FLSMs received their quotas from sales leaders, then allocated that quota among sellers, based on available opportunities—territory characteristics like number of potential customers and customer penetration. But in most cases, sales leaders developed quotas for individual seller territories; FLSMs had no (or minor) ability to affect individual seller quotas.

Also, in some firms, sellers impact the salary portion of their compensation by selling the entire product portfolio, and/or by performance against other key performance indicators, typically assessed by FLSMs. One FLSM told us:

"This is part of our Performance Enhancement System. Sellers increase their base salary by making good use of marketing materials, number of opportunities they identify, sales funnel management, and things like that. I make those assessments."

Seller compensation systems are critical for implementing sales strategy. Absent a compensation plan that, at least directionally, spurs the kinds of behaviors consistent with the strategy, even the most talented and committed FLSMs will be hard-pressed to deliver desired results. Key considerations for compensation-system design are:

- **Total compensation:** Base salary plus target incentive pay from commissions/bonuses. Not included: cash awards from recognition programs (below), benefits. Sales leaders must establish, via public/private survey data, median pay and relevant pay ranges for each specific sales job in their industries. Generally:
  - Higher-skilled sellers have higher total compensation targets. Policies that pay sellers *less* than established market medians tend to attract less-skilled sales talent, and have inferior talent-retention performance.
  - Policies that target above median total compensation—for example, 75th percentile—typically attract premium sales talent, and have better retention. Firm compensation costs are higher, but more talented sellers *should* deliver higher sales revenues. Sales leaders would be wise to test this assumption for their firms and markets.

- **Compensation mix:** The ratio of base salary to incentive at target total compensation. Example: Target total pay = $100,000; base pay = $70,000; target incentive pay = $30,000; thus compensation mix = 70:30. In fact, the most common U.S. mix is 70:30. Generally:

  - More transactional-type sales jobs have compensation mixes with higher proportions of pay at risk, to motivate greater selling effort—60:40 or 50:50.

  - More technically focused sales jobs, with long sales cycles, tend to have compensation mixes with lower proportions of pay at risk—80:20 or 90:10.

  - In situations with exceptionally long lead times—years—and difficult-to-forecast sales revenues, salary-only plans may be appropriate.

- **Upside leverage:** The ratio of potential pay above target compensation to percentage pay at risk. Example: Suppose *compensation mix* = 80:20—pay at risk = 20 percent. Also, suppose sellers can earn 40 percent of target pay for excellent performance. Then, *upside leverage* = 40:20 = 2:1. Generally:

  - *Aggressive* leverage—3:1 and higher—is associated with more transactional-type sales jobs, where the firm seeks to motivate high selling effort. Classic situation: high-growth/high-market-share objectives.

  - *Regressive* leverage—less than 1:1—used when sales are *spikey*; sales performance is unpredictable. Regressive plans protect the firm from overshooting its incentive-compensation budget. In the most extreme cases, incentive compensation is *capped*—no additional incentive compensation regardless of sales performance. As a general rule, the authors are opposed to incentive-compensation caps!

Designing sales compensation plans is not simple, nor for the faint-hearted. As the foregoing discussion demonstrates, sales leaders have many variables to consider. But a crucial first step, before contemplating sales compensation design, is identifying sales jobs. Sales leaders must tailor each compensation plan to a specific sales job. We are not talking about *sales titles*; in many firms, people with different sales titles actually do more or less the same job. Our focus is on the actual selling job—*digital hunter* is different from *account manager*, is different from *solution specialist*. Each sales job requires a different skill set and a different compensation plan. Well-formulated compensation plans are an important tool for skilled FLSMs to leverage in seeking best efforts and high performance from their sellers. Conversely, poorly designed sales compensation plans are—regrettably and all too frequently—barriers that FLSMs must clear to appropriately direct, lead, and manage their sellers.[3]

Recognize. Without doubt, financial compensation is a powerful motivator for sellers, but it is by no means the only approach, nor necessarily the most effective. Sales leaders have an important role to play in formulating recognition programs that provide seller motivation. These programs may operate independently of FLSMs, or they may enable FLSMs to provide recognition for members of their sales teams.

Recognition is important for virtually all people in many walks of life. Recognition is especially important for sellers; after all, they spend much of their work lives alone—traveling to, and waiting for, meetings. And they get lots of rejection. *The importance of seller recognition cannot be overstated.* One sales leader shared the following example:

> "We had this one seller (let's call him Jack) who was the most successful seller we have, probably ever had. Our compensation system is pretty heavily commission-oriented, so each year Jack earned in the high six figures. So even after taxes, he took home a very nice chunk of change. In addition, we have a company-wide, seller-recognition system. Jack received the top award for several years running; he was clearly top dog. Then we changed the recognition criteria; I think someone in HR decided we should spread the recognition around. So, this one year, Jack was still earning high six figures, but he did not receive the number-one award. So, he just quit—walked away from that huge compensation package. I always knew recognition was important for sellers, but never to that extent."

Sellers are by nature competitive and want to be recognized for doing a good job. Well-designed recognition programs can make FLSMs much more effective. Sales leaders may provide tools that help FLSMs fine-tune seller behaviors. Recognition can be both monetary and nonmonetary, and can be provided privately, in small groups, or in large public forums. Each approach has its place.

Options and illustrative situations for recognition programs directed by sales leaders:

- *Monetary, large group*—for achieving specific important strategic results. Awardee(s) selected by sales leaders, widely advertised.

- *Nonmonetary, large group*—classically, announcement of annual selection to President's Club, including trip (plus significant other) to attractive destinations.

Options for FLSMs to provide recognition, with support from sales leaders:

- *Monetary, sales team or individual*—for achieving important tactical results specified by sales leaders. Sales leaders provide budget for small individual rewards to specific sellers.

- *Nonmonetary, sales team or individual*—sales leaders develop a culture in which FLSMs provide *shout-outs* for a seller acting positively or performing well, but otherwise these rewards are at FLSMs' discretion.

Some sales leaders make a point of recognizing sellers (and FLSMs), as and when appropriate. Returning to the sales leader we noted in Chapter 7:

> "I think everybody wants to be recognized, so I send notes throughout the salesforce. Sometimes these are personal: 'Congratulations on your anniversary.' Or, I'll send a plant to someone who's moving house, or a bottle of wine to someone who's on vacation. Sometimes my notes are performance-related: 'I noticed your territory was up 5 percent.' Or: 'I see your district was down Y percent; what can I do to help?' It doesn't have to be big stuff. I write a lot of notes, just as a personal form of recognition."

Many firms operate annual firm-wide evaluation systems for employees. They may, for example, be graded on a three-point system—needs improvement, meets expectations, exceeds expectations.

Typically, firms impose strongly enforced guidelines on the percentage of employees in any department or team that must fall into each category.

There are good reasons for strong guidelines, but sales leaders should be prepared to relax such strictures if circumstances demand, or they risk blowback. Let's hear the perspectives of a sales leader and FLSM respectively:

> "You should make sure you're using your recognition and awards appropriately. I was going to say *sparingly*, but that's not necessarily true. If you're seeing a lot of good stuff, call it. Call it like you see it."

> "I have five guys. This year, I pushed very hard in our ratings, and got three of them rated *exceeds expectations*. We have an internal quota; we cannot rate too many people too high. Thankfully, senior management was flexible, as they should have been. After all, we were the only group in the firm to exceed expectations in quota achievement."

Additional Motivation for High Sales Performance[4]

Rewarding and recognizing sales performance are age-old ways of motivating sellers to perform at a high level, but more subtle ways can also be highly effective. Several top-performing sales organizations recruit sales reps to serve on advisory councils and committees. An office-products company rotates people from throughout its sales representative and sales management ranks for one-year assignments on a *compensation advisory board* and a *marketing-advisory team*—in addition to their normal duties. Serving on such boards is a powerful form of recognition that also builds teamwork across the entire sales organization. The sales leader at this firm explained:

> "It's not just some guy in the home office giving the salesforce a comp plan or a marketing plan. We now have folks in the field who advocate to their peers. So, things are embraced a lot easier by the sales reps, as opposed to Moses coming down from the mountain and saying: 'I'm from the home office. Here's your marketing plan. Here's your compensation plan.'
>
> "Another thing it does is break down the civil war between different functions, especially between the field salesforce and marketing. Everybody is forced to look at the world from each other's viewpoint. So, the sales guy who thinks the zero-percent financing deal would be great on every product gets to understand why you really can't stay in business that way, and have to restrict that to slow-moving products in inventory."

Other sales organizations place salespeople on advisory and planning groups. When a high-tech firm found that its sales reps were spending too much time on administrative tasks, the sales organization asked a committee of sales reps how to improve the situation. Recruiting sales reps to join in the sales organization's decision making is a form of finding and fostering leadership in the field. The sales leader commented:

> "In sales, you keep your field strong because they're closest to the customer. They understand more of what's going on, and you have to empower them to make the calls and take the decisions. When people say about the best sales talent, 'Oh, those guys

are great, they should move to headquarters,' actually they shouldn't. They should stay in the field, closest to the customer. That's where they serve us best. You get the real deal of what's going on in a shorter period of time, the closer your best people are to the customer."

At a bio-tech firm, sales reps are empowered to help make decisions in an area usually thought of as management's exclusive domain: hiring. The sales leader told us:

"We have a number of sales reps interview a prospective hire, so they have buy-in and mentorship responsibility from the beginning. We pass a little of the front-line management a step down, so the existing sales reps have a vested interest in helping the new sales reps succeed. It's like they say: 'It takes a village to raise a child.' It's the same thing with sales."

Two sales leaders from other firms were quite agreed on the empowerment issue:

"Our sales organization is empowered to make decisions on the fly. We set a vision and overall objective, and we propose possible plans of action. But we allow the field to develop the steps of execution."

"We don't dictate how people do things in the field."

Involvement in managerial decisions can be a powerful motivator for sellers and enhance teamwork across the entire sales organization. More generally, empowering sellers fosters leadership and ups the salesforce's game.

Retain High-Performing Sales Talent

In the section on FLSM attrition earlier in this chapter, we noted that the implicit contract between employer and employee has been shattered. Gone are the days when young people in their 20s would join a business organization and expect to retire with a company pension, 30-plus years later. Quite simply, the human-resource market is increasingly efficient. Although greater market efficiency may help firms attract and recruit talent, by the same token, *retention* has become more difficult.

Many of the topics discussed in this section not only help improve sales performance, they also help in sales-talent retention. Some options:

- *Well-designed financial compensation systems*—drive sales performance; lead to high compensation for successful sellers.

- *Well-designed recognition programs*—make successful sellers feel appreciated. Appreciation makes sellers feel more positive about the firm.

- *Development programs*—periodically allow sellers to build their intellectual capital and be more successful.

- *Well-designed career paths*—provide good direction to individual seller careers.

- *Support systems and processes*—enable sellers to be more effective, more efficient, and hence to perform at higher levels.

Of course, sellers may not always appreciate benefits the firm supplies. Senior leaders have a responsibility to invest in the appropriate systems and processes to deliver these benefits/values. They must also develop a recognition of that value among the firm's sellers.

Regardless, some talented sellers will leave; that sends sales leaders back to the drawing board for attracting, recruiting, and selecting sales talent. However, it is not unusual that some of those departed sellers may become candidates for hiring (rehiring). We share an example from a successful seller:

> "Selling is my profession and my passion. I worked for this firm for several years. They treated me very well and I earned good money. I grew in the job, received excellent training, and had increasing responsibility with more important customers. Then I got hired away. The compensation package was just that much more attractive; I decided I couldn't turn it down. But after a year or so, I decided the extra compensation just wasn't worth it. It wasn't one thing, but overall I just didn't receive the support I was used to getting. So, I applied to come back, and here I am. My comp is down a little, but I'll get up there in a couple of years. What I guess I learned is that *the grass isn't always greener…*"

Maintaining a high-performing salesforce may be difficult when the firm makes a major strategic change that seriously affects the salesforce. One sales leader explained what happened at his firm, and how corporate management stepped up to the plate:

> "We made a major strategic change regarding our product portfolio—we withdrew many products as we rationalized. This was the right thing to do long-term, but it caused significant trauma for our sellers. We pay 100 percent commission, and they were looking at an immediate drop in pay. No one seemed to know the potential short-term impact of this rationalization, so corporate stepped in. For the next year, corporate guaranteed sellers' take-home pay. Essentially, we switched from 100 percent commission to 100 percent salary, while the new strategy took hold."

One important factor in retaining sales talent is reinforcing morale in the salesforce. Certainly, the FLSM has a major role to play in this regard, but FLSMs operate under an umbrella constructed by senior firm leaders. Bad behavior by company leaders, lawsuits, and negative press may take a severe toll. We interviewed one sales leader whose organization suffered considerably while operating under a consent decree:

> "That really hurt us for several years, but we kept plugging away. I think that's more or less behind us now. Our customers understand that *stuff happens*. It was a real wake-up call, but we're now a better company, and I think our customers recognize that."

Somewhat closer to home for most salespeople is the nature of what they are selling. Is product quality high? Do firm products outperform competitor products? Does the firm continually refresh its product line? We heard from one FLSM:

> "Over the years, our new-product-introduction record has been quite unimpressive. But in the past two years, we've had two major introductions. These were very exciting for

our sellers; they are reenergized to show new products and solution sets to clients. The entire salesforce culture has changed dramatically."

In this book, we focus on FLSMs for securing high levels of sales performance from their seller teams. But FLSMs/sellers cannot achieve desired performance levels unless corporate management and sales leaders make appropriate decisions for building a competent, well-supported, motivated salesforce. Many factors are involved. Without doubt, sales leaders face critical challenges, but they must create the conditions for staffing the salesforce with the best possible sales talent, then investing in their success.

Summary

Chapter 10 is the last of three chapters in Part II of *The Front-Line Sales Manager – Field General*. This chapter comprises three important topic areas where appropriate resource allocation and effective decision making can have an important positive impact on sales performance. *Build the brand* focuses on creating a positive backdrop for sellers meeting with customers. A positive brand image gives sellers credibility when they seek appointments with important customer contacts. A positive brand also heightens sellers' believability when they present the attributes/features/benefits/values of the products/services they are selling.

Notwithstanding sellers' abilities to build solid relationships with important members of customer purchasing DMUs, sometimes it's necessary to bring in the big guns to *support and build customer relationships*. Certainly, FLSMs play this role to a certain extent, but more senior managers, even the C-Suite, may be necessary. After all, the higher up the managerial hierarchy, the greater the ability to commit the firm. The FLSM's resource acumen plays an important role here, but this ability must be matched by a recognition and desire by senior managers to support the selling effort.

Arguably, we have left the most important senior management/sales-leader responsibility to last—*set the conditions for building a competent, well-supported, highly motivated salesforce*. Part I of this book focused on the six acumen dimensions—*strategic, organizational, business, team building, resource, personal*—that FLSMs must possess to be successful. But for FLSMs to be successful, senior managers/sales leaders must provide the appropriate raw material by making good decisions regarding *recruiting, selecting, developing, supporting, rewarding, recognizing, motivating,* and *retaining high-quality sales talent*.

Endnotes

1. The forecast discounted stream of profits from a customer, during the lifetime of its relationship with the firm. For more information, N. Capon, *Managing Marketing in the 21st Century* (4th ed.), New York: Wessex, 2017, Chapter 2.

2. Not only does Benihoff play an important role with customers, he also provides an implicit coaching value for FLSMs.

3. For in-depth information on sales compensation plans: D. Cichelli, *Compensating The Sales Force: A Practical Guide to Designing Winning Sales Reward Programs* (3rd ed.), McGraw-Hill, 2018.

4. Material in this section taken from N. Capon and G. Tubridy, *Sales Eats First*, Bronxville, NY: Wessex, 2011.

A Glimpse of the Future?

Janet Wilson, sales vice president for Midwest Manufacturing, reflected on the decisions she had made in the previous year:

"The CEO appointed me to shape up the salesforce. Previous performance was not poor; in fact, it was more than adequate. But the CEO and board of directors believed it could be much improved. I was given a free hand to make whatever changes I saw fit, and the CEO promised to back me up.

"The salesforce I inherited was geographically organized and comprised around 600 sellers. These sellers were directed and managed by 80 FLSMs [front-line sales managers]. Sitting above the FLSMs were 15 regional managers, and four zone managers above them—my direct reports. This organization structure, with minor modifications, had been in place for many years. There was also a strategic/key account organization that reported to me; that did not require any immediate attention.

"I firmly believe the key to exceptional sales performance is exceptional FLSMs, so I started there. We used the sixfold *acumen* model—*strategic*, *organizational*, *business*, *team building*, *resource*, *personal*—to design an FLSM assessment protocol and an FLSM training program. We assessed all 80 FLSMs. We decided that about two-thirds were (or had the potential to be) superior FLSMs. The remaining third were reassigned to other positions—some returned to be sellers; others left the firm.

"Among those that made the cut, there was wide competence variation. Regardless, we put them all through extensive training, with tests and examinations. The successful managers received FLSM certification. Some washed out of the program; others had to repeat segments. FLSM certification is very serious business for us.

"To replace the FLSMs we lost, we scoured our 600 sellers. We beefed up the career-planning process and identified several candidates that had serious FLSM potential. We also hired in several FLSMs from the outside. These two groups went through a similar training program as the in-place FLSMs, but with additional training, since they had not previously been FLSMs, at least not with our firm.

"We looked very hard at sales-district design but, for the most part, I did not mess with district boundaries. We did make some changes, but only at the margin—fairly minor. We wanted FLSMs to act as though the district was *their business*; as though they had equity ownership. So, we erred on the side of keeping existing boundaries, unless there was a compelling reason to change. Also, we were making major changes, so I preferred to put serious district-boundary decisions off for a while.

"My basic view regarding the sales organization was the following. Within the previous several years, many technical advances had affected the sales function, but none had had much effect on the sales organization structure. The relevant changes I saw were:

- significantly greater availability of data

- superior analytic tools

- more communications options—Internet, Skype, video-conferencing

"Overall, my ability to know what was going on in the field and to communicate with organizational members was so much greater than that of my predecessors who designed the current organization. For them, geographic proximity throughout the salesforce was paramount. I believe proximity is critical for FLSMs and their sellers, but not so much for relationships between/among other levels in the sales management hierarchy.

"So, I took the following steps:

- Enhanced my analytics group to do a better job of setting annual sales revenue quotas by *sales district*; they calendarized those quotas by month and quarter. What I did do was halt the practice of setting quotas by sales territory. I took the view that we were developing/had developed exceptional FLSMs. We gave FLSMs hard targets, but they should have the ability to distribute their district quotas among their sellers—after all, they know their districts better than anyone.

- Shaped up the sales revenue measurement system so we know, on a day-to-day basis, what revenues we earn. We scarcely use data at such a granular level, but we now have very good *output* measures that we can use to track performance by month and quarter. So, we can see, by district and territory, where we're on track versus quota, and where we have problems.

- Implemented a serious pipeline system. We now have a well-defined six-stage selling model from opportunity identification to sales revenues earned. At my level, we have target numbers of opportunities at each pipeline stage, and standards for funnel velocity. FLSMs use the identical structure for their district pipelines. As with quota setting, they decide how to parcel out the numbers, in various pipeline stages, among their sellers. We take a very firm line on populating the pipeline—it's mandatory for all sellers to keep pipeline information up-to-date. We are almost as serious about these FLSM *intermediate-macro* pipeline measures as we are about sales quota achievement.

- Clarified *micro-intermediate* measures. These are the sorts of things customers do that head toward making sales. We identified an entire set of these variables. We make sure FLSMs report progress on a periodic basis.

- Created a way to measure FLSM behavior—how they spend their time—*input* variables. We developed a robust category system for what FLSMs do. FLSMs must provide this information daily, so we now have a very good baseline of what FLSMs are actually doing.

- Blew up the hierarchical sales organization structure—no regional managers; no zone managers.

"I took the view that our regional and zone managers were, in effect, generalists, and that we'd be better off with specialists at that hierarchical level to manage our FLSMs. First, I divided the FLSMs into three groups:

■ *High performers.* These FLSMs are quota beaters. Year after year their districts exceed quota. Frankly, they don't require a lot of directing or managing. They are real leaders. At senior salesforce management levels, our job is essentially to keep out of their way, support them as necessary, and let them do their jobs.

■ *Moderate performers.* Generally, these FLSMs are close to meeting quota but we cannot rely on them to hit their numbers every year. They are good, but not great, FLSMs. There's something missing—could be a lot of different things. They require some attention so we can get them into the top group.

■ *Marginal performers.* These FLSMs are a long way from making quota. They're a mixed bag. Some may be long-tenured FLSMs who just haven't kept up with the changing environment; others may be rookie FLSMs who are finding their feet. With good direction, management, coaching, training, and more experience, some members of this group will make it. Others we shall have to move out.

"Then, in place of regional and zone managers, I appointed three types of *performance managers*—A, B, C—to address these different types of FLSM. Each of these senior managers reports directly to me:

■ *Performance manager A.* These managers have responsibility for high-performing FLSMs. Of the three types of performance manager, they have the largest span of control. We do not expect that they will need to get deeply into the details of district performance very often.

■ *Performance manager B.* These managers are responsible for moderate-performing FLSMs. Their job is to diagnose district performance and figure how to get these FLSMs to raise their games and perform at a higher level. Each performance manager B has fewer direct reports than performance managers A.

■ *Performance manager C.* At some level, these managers have the toughest job. Their direct reports are not performing well at all. They have to get deep into the district weeds to figure out turnaround plans, and they have to make the tough calls on whom to place their bets, and whom to move out—then they have to replace. Each performance manager C has relatively few direct reports.

"The broad idea is that each of these performance manager types will develop expertise in the particular challenges their group of FLSMs face, and so shift our overall performance upwards. There is also a fourth type of senior sales manager—customer focused:

■ *Customer-expert managers.* From time to time, our customers want to talk to a senior sales manager. Sometimes our sellers/FLSMs need this sort of help to gain access at high levels in customer organizations. So I have appointed customer-expert managers to fulfill this role. They react to requests from the field, but also monitor attractive opportunities so they can offer support as needed.

"Overall, this new organization is a major change from the traditional geographically focused RSMs and zone managers. I'm not certain our system of A, B, C performance managers and customer-expert managers is the last word on salesforce reorganization, but I certainly believe we are headed in the right direction.

"One issue we had to deal with is that a specific district may place in different performance categories from quarter to quarter. We address this issue by tracking FLSM category membership directionally. When the change is negative, we may bring in another pair of senior-sales-manager eyes to look at the situation. That's also especially useful if FLSM replacement is on the table. All these senior folks are located right here, so I can have good face-to-face conversations.

"So, the bottom line organizationally is that I no longer have any zone managers (previously four), nor any regional managers (previously 15). Rather, I have experts in specific areas related to FLSM performance, and market opportunities. I didn't do this to save money, although I have done that. I think the managerial money we spend is just much more effective in this new system. But the core foundation is the strength of our FLSM cadre, and the investment we have made in that position.

"When you spend that sort of money on FLSMs, you expect them to step up to the plate, make tough decisions, and secure high performance. We train them to be able to do just that. When you have that concentration of strength at that managerial level, you can decentralize decision making, push it down and empower FLSMs. The key is having an effective monitor-and-control system that cues my senior sales managers to critical issues.

"From my perspective, the tough issue in this job is deciding what decisions should remain at corporate and what I can delegate. What is on the table right now is seller compensation. In virtually every salesforce I know, and certainly here, it's centralized—we make all compensation-structure decisions at corporate.

"But conditions vary from district to district. We are contemplating letting FLSMs choose compensation plans for their districts, from a vetted set of alternatives, based on the level and type of growth we expect. Of course, we shall set parameters, so things don't get out of whack, and stay within our total compensation budget. But we want FLSMs to behave as though their districts are their own businesses—like franchises to sell the firm's products/services. It seems to me, therefore, that providing discretion over financial compensation is a logical extension of our focus on empowerment.

"Notwithstanding the major changes we have made, and those we are contemplating, what I see as the major learning here is quite simply this: We could not even have contemplated, what I believe are significant salesforce management innovations, without our strong conviction in the critical nature of the FLSM role, and the investment we have made."

Appendices

Participating Companies*

Abbott Diagnostics

Align Technology

Allscripts

CareFusion

CenturyLink

Cisco

Dexcom

Ellucian

Essendant

FedEx

Fujitsu Network Communications

Genzyme Sanofi

Halyard Health

Intralinks

Jack Henry & Associates

Johnson Controls

LinkedIn

Philips Healthcare

Qiagen

Research Now

Salesforce.com

Sonoco

Symantec/Veritas

---

* Company names at interview time. Some companies are divisions or subsidiaries of larger organizations.

Interviewees

Sales Leaders and Front-Line Sales Managers*

Abbott Diagnostics
Gregory Ahlberg — Vice President, Sales — USA
Sharon ("Shar") Batley — Enterprise Sales Manager
Rob Bravo — Enterprise Acquisition Sales Manager

Align Technology
William Pretto — Senior Director, Sales Effectiveness
Kent Braud — Regional Manager
Tony Stemerick — Regional Business Manager

Allscripts
John Pigott — Vice President Sales, Payer and Life Sciences
Robert Maluso — Vice President, Payer Market Sales
Dan Pucci — Vice President, Life Sciences

CareFusion
Todd Garland — Group Vice President
Mark Branday — Vice President, Strategic Accounts

CenturyLink
Bill Cheek — President, Wholesale
Don Horton — Director, Strategic Sales Management
Lynn Smullen-Volz — Segment Vice President, International

Cisco
Gordon Galzerano — Director, Global Enterprise Business
Todd Eby — Regional Sales Manager
Jaclyn Lanasa — Regional Sales Manager

---

* Organizational positions at interview time—2015.
Names in **bold** indicate senior sales leader.

Dexcom
Laura Endres — National Sales Director
Don Plotts — Regional Sales Director, East Region
Beth Sweeny — District Business Manager, Rocky Mountain District

Ellucian
Bruce Mann — Vice President, Global Field Operations
David Denig — Area Sales Director
Pete Masterson — Director, Strategic Accounts

Essendant
Tom Sixta — Group Vice President
Chris Kelley — Regional Sales Manager
John Watson — District Sales Manager

FedEx
Dave Edmonds — Senior Vice President, Worldwide Services

Fujitsu Network Communications
Paul Fagan — Senior Vice President, Sales and Marketing
Peter D. Halverson — Director, North American Carrier Sales
Phil Herrington — Sales Director

Genzyme Sanofi
Stephanie S. Okey — Senior Vice President, Head of North America, Rare Diseases;
　　U.S. General Manager, Rare Diseases
Lily Flood — Regional Director, Rare Diseases

Halyard Health
Chris Lowery — Vice President, Global Healthcare Sales and Marketing
Tim Habegger — Regional Manager — South East
Maurice Monserez — Regional Manager — Pacific Coast

Intralinks
Leif O'Leary — Senior Vice President, Sales — Americas
Peter Frintzilas — Vice President, Enterprise Sales — North America
Shaun Per — Director of Enterprise Sales — North America

Jack Henry & Associates
Stan Viner — General Manager, Sales
Rick Keith — Regional Sales Manager
Leo Mallamaci — Director of Sales, Eastern U.S.

Johnson Controls

Dave Clark — Vice President, Sales, Marketing and Strategy
Abigail Butkus — Market Sales Manager

LinkedIn

Prakash Venkataraman — Senior Consultant, Executive Development
Kathleen Else — Large Enterprise Manager, Talent Solutions — Central U.S. and Canada

Philips Healthcare

Greg Nesbitt — Vice President, National Accounts — USA
Dan Nacey — Vice President, Healthcare Alliances
Steve Weiss — Region Sales Manager

Qiagen

Jonathan Mensch — Senior Director, Global Commercial Excellence
John Alexandrou — Director, Inside Sales Molecular Diagnostics and Life Sciences

Research Now

Carter Cathey — Vice President, Sales Operations — Americas; Sales Technology — Global

Salesforce.com

Dan Smoot — Senior Vice President, Market Readiness
Beth Kaplan — Senior Director, Sales Leader Enablement
Ryan Radding — Regional Vice President, Sales — Financial Services Vertical
Bart Seidner — Regional Vice President

Sonoco

Philippe Erhart — Division Vice President and General Manager — Sonoco Display & Packaging
Megan Bekker — Director, Sales and Marketing U.S. — Global Display & Packaging

Symantec/Veritas

Marianne Horan — Vice President, North America Sales and Marketing Operations — Symantec
Patti Cameron — Senior Director, Global Sales Enablement — Veritas

Discussion Guide for Sales Leaders

Role and Characteristics of Outstanding Front-Line Sales Managers

1. How has the role of your salesforce changed in the past few years?

2. What are the core external challenges you face in directing and managing the salesforce? (e.g., greater competition, globalization)

3. What are the core internal challenges you face in directing and managing the salesforce? (e.g., relationship with other functions, salesforce enablement)

4. Describe your sales organization (e.g., inside/outside; hunters/farmers; key account managers/ regular sellers; number of sellers; hierarchy—VP, regional sales manager, district sales manager, sellers; product/market specialists).

5. Describe how customer demands have changed since the great recession. What problems do they have to face, and how do your sellers help them get solved?

6. Describe how you have changed/improved the salesforce to meet these challenges. What enablement tools have you leveraged?

7. What are the key metrics by which you judge the performance of your sales organization? (e.g., sales, margins, relationships, new customers)

8. Describe the role of front-line sales managers (FLSMs) on a spectrum ranging from inspecting to enabling.

9. If sellers solve problems for customers, how do FLSMs get them positioned to do so successfully?

10. Where do your FLSMs come from? (e.g., outside/inside; salesforce/other)

11. How do you measure the effectiveness of your FLSMs? (e.g., training/coaching, specialist/ technological support, senior sales management, KPIs)

12. How would you characterize the behavior of your best FLSMs?

13. How does this characterization differ from that of most of your FLSMs—what makes your best FLSMs unique? Tenure, wisdom/experience, personality, education, etc.?

14. What jobs are available for FLSMs to be promoted into?

15. Please indicate one or two names of your best FLSMs that we could interview. Why did you select them?

Discussion Guide for FLSMs

Role and Characteristics of Outstanding Front-Line Sales Managers

1. How long have you been a manager? What job(s) and experiences did you have before?

2. Describe your unit; how many sellers serving what types of market?

3. Tell me about your company and what you sell.

4. What kinds of customers do you serve—which industries, who does the buying?

5. What problems do you solve for these customers?

6. Tell me how the role of the seller has changed over the years.

7. Has this also changed the role of the manager? In what ways?

8. What are the most important things you do to help your sellers succeed?

9. Which functions/positions do you interact with internally to get the job done? Which are most crucial? Most helpful? Most disappointing? Why?

10. Describe your role as a manager; discuss where you are in the range between inspection and enablement.

11. How would you describe your salespeople? (e.g., hard worker, challenger, relationship builder, lone-wolf, reactive problem solver). Do you manage different sellers in different ways? How?

12. How is your performance measured? What goals do you have?

13. How do you set goals for your sellers?

14. Let's talk about time allocation. Provide hours per week that you spend:
    - How much time in the field? Doing what?
    - How much time doing admin work?
    - Time devoted to planning?
    - Meeting with the management hierarchy?
    - Travel?
    - Other big blocks of time

15. Describe your interactions with your manager. What kind of support does he/she provide you?

16. Is there any training available to front-line managers when they are promoted into the job? After promotion, for more experienced managers?

17. What tools do you use that are critical? How could these tools be improved? What tools are missing?

18. If you could change one thing about your job, what would that be? What impact would this have?

19. What is it that makes you a high-performing manager?

20. Suppose a colleague was promoted to a role like yours. How would you advise them to help them be successful?

21. Where do you go after the front-line manager job? What are your career ambitions?

Competitive and Environmental Pressures on the Firm

We conceptualize pressures on the firm as comprising two types—competitor and environmental.

Competitor Pressures

The firm faces a competitive structure comprising several different types of competitor[1]:

- *Current direct competitors*—traditional competitors offering customers products/services similar to firm offerings.
- *New direct entrants*—recent market entrants from some other geography/industry.
- *Indirect competitors*—offering similar customer value as direct competitors, but with different technologies/business models.
- *Supply-chain competition*—competition from customers integrating backward; or from suppliers integrating forward.

At any individual customer, the firm may face different types of competitor, and different individual competitors.

Environmental Pressures

These pressures are more general in nature than the competitor pressures; these pressures affect all players in an industry—firm, customers, competitors. We use the **PESTLE** acronym to identify these pressures:

- Political—related to actions by governments
- Economic—health of the economy—GNP, inflation, interest rates, capital markets
- Sociocultural—cultural norms and their evolution
- Technological—innovation and development of new ways of doing things
- Legal/regulatory—legal system, regulations, degree of enforcement
- Environmental (physical)—*mother nature*—natural forces

---

1. Adapted from M.E. Porter, *Competitor Strategy: Techniques for Analyzing Industries and Competitors*, New York: Free Press, 1980.

A Growth-Strategy Framework for FLSMs and Their Sellers[*]

This strategic framework comprises five elements: vision, mission, growth path, timing of entry, market/market-segment strategy.

Vision

Vision is a description of the firm's ideal future state—not too broad, nor too specific, nor easily achieved. Corporate vision concerns the entire firm; business vision focuses on an individual business. Examples: Amazon—*To be the world's most customer-centric company*; Disney—*To make people happy*; Ford (early 20th century)—*A car in every garage*; Google—*To organize the world's information and make it universally accessible and useful*; Salesforce.com—*The end of software*. Well-developed visions are outward-looking; aspirational yet realistic; but do not raise customer expectations beyond the firm's ability to deliver.

Mission

Mission is more specific than vision. Mission guides the search for opportunities.[1] A well-developed mission keeps the firm focused in a limited arena where success is likely. Mission avoids dispersing firm energy and resources in multiple directions. Mission states what the firm/business will do—and, by omission, what it will not do! The most useful missions articulate specific markets/market segments the firm/business will address, and the sorts of products/services it will offer. Typically, firms evolve their missions—sometimes broadening, sometimes narrowing.[2]

---

[*] Adapted from N. Capon, *Managing Marketing in the 21st Century* (4th ed.), New York, Wessex, 2017, Chapter 7.

1. These *vision* and *mission* definitions are not universally accepted. What we note as a *vision*, some firms call a *mission*.

2. Frequently, growing firms expand their missions as new opportunities become available. Conversely, some publicly traded established firms, believing their broad scope leads to a *conglomerate discount*, narrow their missions.

Growth Path

Growth path is more focused than mission. Growth path is specifically concerned with trade-offs between expected financial return and risk, as the firm applies competencies/resources against potential opportunities.

Figure A6.1 shows the growth-path matrix's two dimensions—market, product/technology. We trisect each dimension—existing, related, new—to form nine matrix cells—A through I. Each cell represents a different type of opportunity. We can usefully combine individual cells to develop four broad approaches to growth:

- Market penetration (cell A)
- Product growth (cells B, C)
- Market growth (cells D, G)
- Product/market diversification (cells E, F, H, I)

The further away from cell A the firm operates, the greater uncertainty regarding product performance and market conditions. The firm must trade off risk with potential financial returns from new opportunities.

Figure A6.1 Growth Path

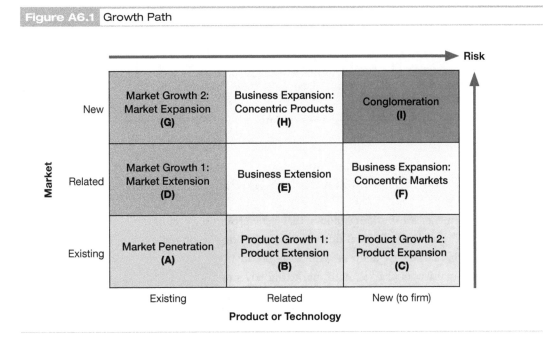

Timing of Entry

Along with identifying the right growth path, when to seize an opportunity—**timing of entry**—is also crucial. We identify five product life-cycle stages—introduction, early growth, late growth, maturity, decline. Early stages have high uncertainty in both products and markets, but uncertainty decreases as the life cycle evolves. Correspondingly, competitive pressures typically increase. Figure A6.2 explores links between the first four life-cycle stages and specific strategic options for timing of market entry:

- **Pioneer**—blazes trails, creates new markets via consistent and extensive R&D.
- **Follow-the-leader**—enters rapidly growing markets on the heels of pioneers.
- **Segmenter**—enters established markets in late growth by adding benefits/values for specific market segments.
- **Me-too-er**—enters mature markets with limited product lines.

Figure A6.2 Timing of Entry

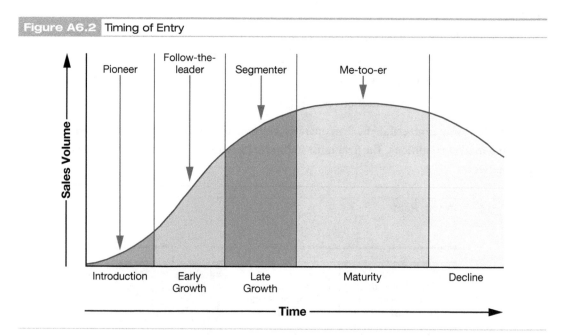

Market/Market-Segment Strategy

The foregoing elements are building blocks that generate a set of market opportunities for the firm to consider. Typically, individual businesses comprising a firm address separate markets. The decision of which markets to address with firm products/services—where to play—is typically made at a high organizational level, with marketing advising corporate/business leaders. For each chosen market, marketing conducts segmentation studies and selects one or more product/market segments to address—typically no firm has sufficient resources to address all identified segments. Both segmentation approaches and choice of segments to address are crucial.

Customers in any market have broadly similar needs, but finer-grained needs differ from market segment to market segment. Because of these differences, the basic unit for developing product/market strategy is the **product/market-segment strategy**. The firm targets one or more market segments. For firms addressing multiple market segments, the product/market strategy combines two or more product/market-segment strategies. We focus on the market-segment strategy.

Objectives

The starting point for product/market-segment strategy is decisions about *objectives*. We consider two related types of objectives:

■ *Strategic objectives*—typically stated as growth/market share, profit, cash flow.

■ *Operational objectives*—tightly linked to strategic objectives but focus on results: How much? By when?

Positioning

The heart of the product/market-segment strategy, *positioning* comprises four core elements:

■ *Customer targets*—specific organizations, decision makers/influencers where the firm will expend effort to convince about the benefits/values it offers.

■ *Competitor targets*—organizations offering related benefits/values to similar customer targets.

■ *Value proposition*—the basic reason(s) customer targets will purchase/recommend firm products/services rather than alternatives.

■ *Reasons to believe*—why customer targets should believe the firm will fulfill promises made in the value proposition.

Implementation

Implementation of a product/market-segment strategy comprises two parts—*market facing* and *firm facing*:

■ *Market facing*—these elements are the tools marketing possesses for executing the market-segment strategy. These tools are broadly known as the marketing mix or the 4Ps:

– *Product*—all aspects of the firm's product and/or service.

– *Promotion*—communication options including mass and digital communications, and personal communications like selling and service efforts.

– *Price*—concerned with what the customer actually pays—includes list price, discounts, credit terms.

– *Distribution* (or *Place*, to conform to the 4Ps framework)—how the customer secures possession of the product/gains access to the service.

■ *Firm facing*—actions the firm must take to execute on market-facing actions. These actions embrace the daily work activities of many functional departments, including R&D, operations, contracts, customer service, technical service, logistics, procurement. Marketing has a responsibility to ensure firm functions do what is required to implement market-facing requirements.

Sales Operations*

A common feature of modern-day sales organizations is sales operations (also called sales ops or SO). Historically, SO was a low-level function charged mainly with producing sales reports and ensuring salespeople were paid appropriately. Today, SO enhances the science of sales. SO also makes sales processes more fact-based, reliable, and predictable. Activities vary across firms, but mature SO departments form a flexible interface among marketing, field sales, in-house sales, and customer support processes. SO strives for both continuous improvement and transformational change.

Consider what two sales leaders had to say about their SO departments:

> **"Our sales ops team has identified the ten major levers of sales performance. They help us determine which levers to pull to maximize performance at any given time."**

> **"Sales ops is the glue that brings sales and marketing together in a way that produces more value for the company and more value for the customer."**

A useful conceptualization of what sales-operations departments actually do is as a *front office* and a *back office*.

Front Office

SO drives top-line sales growth by improving sales productivity—sales enablement—Appendix 9. SO works with marketing to ensure programs and events are effective. SO enhances the sales experience by developing and continually updating a central database of firm-wide sales knowledge. SO draws data from corporate marketing and R&D, product divisions, local competitive intelligence, salesforce best practice, success stories. SO shapes and segments these data for specific sales roles and steps in the sales process. SO produces playbooks—specific customer solutions for individual salespeople—Appendix 10. SO innovates with new sales tools, and becomes deeply involved when sales roles change, like developing strategic/key account managers.

Back Office

SO focuses on efficiency by handling repetitive, scalable tasks like:

- **Approval processes**—develops processes and guidelines to help salespeople navigate their own organizations.
- **Bids and contracts**—provides price information; drafts bid proposals and contracts.

---

* Reference to The Alexander Group sales-time study (Chapter 8).

- *Complaint management*—ensures the firm expeditiously addresses customer issues.
- *Executive-sponsor program*—manages the executive-sponsor program for high-value customers—recruits, selects, assesses, replaces.
- *Experiments*—conducts experimental pilots to push the envelope on selling effectiveness.
- *Lead generation and qualification*—interfaces with marketing to ensure sales leads have value to salespeople.
- *Low-value activities*—develops alternative processes to minimize salesperson time.
- *Monitor-and-control*—develops metrics, creates standards, and designs dashboards to assess sales-pipeline performance. Designs and manages customer and sales employee-satisfaction surveys.
- *Pipeline management*—constructs a system and ensures consistent/complete data entry.
- *Reward and recognition*—designs salespeople's and sales management compensation and recognition programs.
- *Role clarity*—constructs position descriptions for different selling roles; sets sales quotas; structures career paths.
- *Sales planning*—provides frameworks and templates for salespeople to prepare sales territory, account, and pre-call plans.
- *Sales-time management*—defines optimal sales-time profiles for various roles. Balances time among sales, service, administration; measures actual sales time against standards.
- *Training*—designs and implements training programs for salespeople and sales managers.

The firm must allocate resources between front-office and back-office activities. One major high-tech firm operates 20:80 in mature markets, but increases front-office allocation in uncertain developing markets.

Sales-Pipeline Velocity

Sales-pipeline velocity is a useful way to measure the *intermediate* performance that leads directly to future *output* performance. Essentially, sales-pipeline velocity measures the firm's success in converting sales opportunities into sales revenues, during a particular time period—month, quarter, year. Sales-pipeline velocity is especially useful as a diagnostic—comparing current velocity (and its components) with some historic standard. Such comparison provides options for velocity improvement. Sales-pipeline velocity can be measured at the firm level or at various control units—regional, district, individual seller. The basic formula for sales-pipeline velocity is:

$$\text{Pipeline Velocity} = \frac{\text{Number of Qualified Opportunities} \times \text{Success Ratio (\%)} \times \text{Opportunity Size (\$)}}{\text{Sales-Cycle Time (days, weeks)}}$$

The firm can improve velocity by securing more qualified opportunities, improving the success rate, increasing opportunity size, and/or shortening the time between qualifying opportunities and securing sales revenues.

We can measure sales-pipeline velocity overall, or for specific stages in the sales-pipeline process. We provide two worked examples, for the same salesforce:

New qualified opportunities

Suppose: New qualified opportunities = 100

Success rate = 30 percent

Average opportunity size = $50,000

Sales cycle = 100 days

Then:

$$\text{Pipeline Velocity} = \frac{100 \times 30\% \times \$50,000}{100} = \textbf{\$15,000} \text{ per day}$$

Bids submitted

Suppose: Bid opportunities = 30

Success rate = 50 percent

Bid size = $75,000

Sales cycle = 30 days

Then:

$$\text{Pipeline Velocity} = \frac{30 \times 50\% \times \$75,000}{30} = \textbf{\$37,500} \text{ per day}$$

Note:

- Bids submitted are fewer than number of qualified opportunities.
- Success rate is higher for bids submitted than for qualified opportunities.
- Bid-opportunity size is greater for bids submitted. (Perhaps the firm only submitted bids for higher-value opportunities.)
- Cycle time is much shorter for bids submitted than for qualified opportunities.

As a practical matter:

- Bid opportunities/bids submitted and bid size are measured for the time period under consideration.
- Success rate and sales cycle are measured for an earlier comparable period.

Sales Enablement

Sales enablement is an increasingly important function within the salesforce, typically as part of a sales-operations department, but sometimes as an independent unit. At best, sales enablement pulls together and leverages multiple functions—information technology (IT), marketing, sales operations, training—to help FLSMs prepare and coach sellers. First-rate sales-enablement functions assume three key responsibilities:

- **Grouping**—accumulate, sort, and consolidate sales content/tools in ways that make sense to sellers. Provide sellers intuitive ways to access the firm's intellectual property (IP), and save seller time—no more searching for *needles in haystacks*. Options for grouping include customer solution, industry vertical, product, sales-process stage.

- **Curation**—thoughtfully choose specific IP needed to compete successfully in target market segments and/or sales-based customer groups. Specific considerations for inclusion:
  - Most up-to-date content/solutions to solve customer problems.
  - Training modules for building required skills to credibly present solutions to customer executives who *own* the problems.
  - Latest tools—cases, return on investment (ROI) calculators, references—to enhance attractiveness/credibility of firm offers.

  To do a good job, the curator must keep the firm's IP up-to-date; rate materials so sellers can find *best-in-class*; eliminate dated/demonstrably inferior content. Good sales-enablement functions know *less is more*.

- **Development**—good sales enablement spots *content holes*; it teams with other functions—IT, marketing, sales operations, training—to create materials and programs where needed. Sales enablement stays close to sellers, listens to feedback, and tracks outcomes—sales initiatives, product launches—to ensure closed-loop learning and improvement cycles. Sales enablement wants to know if the seller:
  - Gained access to customer decision makers/influencers.
  - Presented firm offers credibly.
  - Enhanced relationships with customer decision makers/influencers.
  - Secured improved sales results.

Put simply, sales enablement connects sales programs/content with results. FLSMs work closely with enablement teams to help make their sellers successful. One sales leader shared her experience:

> "A few years ago, we had an aha moment; we recognized we had no consistency in the way we addressed customers, and no clear expectations. So, we developed a consistent approach to engaging customers, and a consistent sales process for exploring opportunities. Then we went further to pull together the various solutions we offer, to produce a set of solutions that all sellers have access to."

We can probably all agree that inconsistency in addressing customers, at least at a broad level, is not a positive state of affairs. Sales-enablement programs may be the answer for many firms.

Sales Playbooks

A *playbook* is a content-based sales tool, usually created and distributed from a shared technology platform. The playbook comprises a single, current version of all materials relevant to a specific issue.

A playbook provides FLSMs and sellers with on-demand access to advice, resources, tools to guide actions and enhance performance in common, yet complex, situations. In addition to the FLSM play-book (Chapter 8, p. 206), firms generally use three different playbook types:

- ■ *Sales-process playbooks*—identify important selling situations; lay out sales-process steps, collateral, required time investment.

  The medical-device firm sales leader explained using a playbook to shift from transactional selling to a very different enterprise sales-solution approach:

  > "We didn't just have to increase the amount of FLSM-seller coaching time, we had to overhaul our entire sales process. We did this with help from a *sales-process playbook*. Initially, the rules of engagement for the new sales model were unclear. We had to optimize collaboration among numerous roles in the enterprise account selling cycle. A critical element was documenting the sales motions required to network above the traditional end-user call points. This element was central to the playbook.
  >
  > "We rolled out the playbooks in 10 countries as we deployed the new enterprise coverage model. The playbooks had a vital role in guiding sellers in new behaviors. In the first 18 months, enterprise contract wins beat expectations by more than 20 percent. The playbook was not the only reason for success, but it certainly set us up for success."

- ■ *Onboarding playbooks*—contains guidelines for FLSMs and new hires, to get new hires up to speed and be productive as quickly as possible. One FLSM pointed out:

  > "When I lose a productive seller, for whatever reason, I want my new seller to be productive from the get-go. I can't afford an unproductive territory. I plan for vacancies—expected and unexpected—by maintaining a bench of potential hires, inside and outside the firm, so the time delay is minimal. When the new person shows up, I go right into the onboarding playbook. I have hired many sales reps so what is in the playbook is not really new to me. But it's very thorough, and is a useful resource to effect getting new people productive ASAP."

■ *Coaching playbooks*—designed for FLSMs when assessing sellers and designing individual development plans. The playbook comprises experiences, insights, tools required for performance improvement, and guidelines on time investment.

The sales leader at a leading medical-device firm explained how a coaching playbook had played a major role in significantly modifying seller behavior by redefining the FLSM job:

> "We were facing reduced access to physicians and clinical stakeholders. But our sellers also had to increase face time with administrative decision makers—under immense cost pressure navigating the impact of healthcare reform. We also had to deal with huge consolidations, shifts toward integrated-delivery networks, and group purchasing organizations. We had to rethink both seller and FLSM roles to focus time on the right tasks at the right buyers. We established best practices for FLSMs, so they could ensure sellers received the necessary coaching to adopt our new approach. We redefined the FLSM role to reduce super-selling and administrative tasks, and increase seller-coaching time.
>
> "We translated the redefined FLSM role into a *coaching playbook*. The playbook provided recommended actions and time allocations for coaching; it also offered tips and tools to find more time for high-value activities. The playbook offered scripts and guidelines for different engagements with sales-team members, including team conference calls, field visits, in-person meetings, one-on-one telephone calls. Working with the playbook, FLSMs increased productivity so they could focus more effectively on increasing seller time with the new decision makers. Enhanced coaching on the new relationship model significantly increased seller productivity."

CPSIA information can be obtained
at www.ICGtesting.com
Printed in the USA
FFHW011501241219
56785381-62519FF

9 781732 546943